The Presidential Election of 2020

The Presidential Election of 2020

Donald Trump and the Crisis of Democracy

Edited by
William Crotty

LEXINGTON BOOKS
Lanham • Boulder • New York • London

Published by Lexington Books
An imprint of The Rowman & Littlefield Publishing Group, Inc.
4501 Forbes Boulevard, Suite 200, Lanham, Maryland 20706
www.rowman.com

6 Tinworth Street, London SE11 5AL, United Kingdom

Figure 3.1: *Source*: Candidate delegate totals collected by author from CNN 2020 election webpages.

Figure 6.1: *Source*: National Election Pool exit poll conducted nationally by Edison Research, as reported by CNN.

British Library Cataloguing in Publication Information Available

Library of Congress Cataloging-in-Publication Data

Names: Crotty, William J., editor.
Title: The presidential election of 2020 : Donald Trump and the crisis of democracy /
    Edited by William Crotty.
Description: Lanham : Lexington Books, [2021] | Includes bibliographical
    references and index.
Identifiers: LCCN 2021018548 (print) | LCCN 2021018549 (ebook) |
    ISBN 9781793625571 (cloth) | ISBN 9781793625564 (ebook)
Subjects: LCSH: Presidents—United States—Election—History—21st century. |
    Democracy—United States—History—21st century. | United States—
    Politics and government—History—21st century. | Trump, Donald, 1946-.
Classification: LCC JK528 .P66 2021 (print) | LCC JK528 (ebook) |
    DDC 324.973/0933—dc23
LC record available at https://lccn.loc.gov/2021018548
LC ebook record available at https://lccn.loc.gov/2021018549

Contents

List of Figures and Tables

FIGURES

TABLES

Acknowledgments

A number of people contributed to the development of this book. To them, I am grateful.

Deborah Rooney, Colleen Wolfe, Diane Scherrer, and Karen Coughlin contributed invaluable insights and advice. Thank you to John A. Garcia, Scott L. McLean, Garrison Nelson, Walter J. Crotty, Rev. Edward J. Crotty, Thomas Ferguson, Bruce Caswell, and Daniel J. Sullivan, MD, MPH. Chris Doucette's expertise was most helpful. I appreciate the work by Joseph C. Parry, senior acquisitions editor at Lexington Books; Alison Keefner, assistant editor; and Carter Moran, acquisitions assistant, who guided the book through the publication process.

Mary Hauch Crotty's contribution to this project was indispensable.

Introduction

William Crotty

The presidential election of 2020 represented a crisis point in American history. Nothing less than the future of America's democracy was at stake.

The analyses in this book evaluate what happened in the culture created by Donald Trump's presidency that led to concerns over the viability and resiliency of the nation's democracy. The January 6, 2021, violent assault on the Capitol in the effort to overturn the vote and establish an authoritarian system of government evidenced the severity of the challenge facing the nation.

The first two chapters are by William Crotty. The first reviews and assesses the actions, political chaos, and threat to the country represented by the Trump presidency. In the second chapter, Trump's mental status, his health in general, and the intensity of his relationship with a cult-like following, all political issues of concern throughout his time in office, are analyzed in relation to how they impacted the 2020 election.

The forces let loose during the Trump years are likely to continue as fundamental concerns in American politics.

The potential threat of a coup could become an issue of lasting concern. A comprehensive, in-depth investigation of what happened in the Capitol assault by a commission along the lines of the one that took place after the 9/11 attacks has been proposed.

The two introductory chapters are followed by three additional analyses of the elections: a review of the presidential selection process in Chapter 3 by Barbara Norrander in a year in which the COVID-19 pandemic's impact necessitated a flexible and shortened primary season; an analysis of the principal forces influencing the national vote by Arthur C. Paulson leading to the Biden victory in Chapter 4; and an assessment in Chapter 5 by John J. McGlennon of the tides of change taking place in state politics in transition that led to Biden's Electoral College win and, after the Georgia runoff victory by the Democratic Senate candidates, narrow control of the Senate in addition to the House.

In Chapter 6, Susan A. MacManus and Amy N. Benner look at the 100th anniversary of women receiving the vote and its impact on American politics. The gender vote was polarized and the women's vote made a sizeable contribution to the Biden victory. Shayla C. Nunnally in Chapter 7 analyzes racism and its consequences for American politics. It is, and has been throughout the life of the Republic, the most divisive issue in politics and in society. Her question in the chapter title sums up the problem: "Democracy, When?" In Chapter 8, John C. Berg reviews the nation's reaction to the existential threat of climate change and environmental protections meant to help meet the crises. There is a time limit at play in this, denied by Trump who did not believe in science or climate change. It was to be a priority of the Biden administration in approaching the crisis with the urgency it demanded. Thomas R. Marshall in Chapter 9 introduces the three competing visions for health care, continually divisive issues in politics. These are Medicare for All; an expansion and improvement of the Affordable Care Act, including the addition of a public option, Biden's position; and the Trump proposals to lessen the federal government's role in health care. One thing became clear: the Trump option was rejected. Marshall also assesses concerns over the pandemic and its impact, the single most important concern of voters in the election.

Concluding the book in Chapter 10, John Kenneth White compares contemporary conditions to historical precedents in times of crises that challenged the nation and its leadership. The results to date have led to periods of renewal. White also reviews the politics and infighting that transformed the Republican Party into Donald Trump's cult of personality.

The future of course has yet to be written. In the short term, it looks much like the immediate past. At a minimum, it promises to be a critically important period in the evolution of America's identity as a democratic nation.

Chapter 1

Donald Trump and His Presidency

William Crotty

INTRODUCTION

Donald Trump's presidency was a tense and dangerous time for Americans. The following explains what took place and why it happened. It analyzes the significant events and crises that tested a president's leadership ability and fitness for office and the resilience of the country's institutions and its commitment to democracy.

There had been nothing to compare with Trump and his presidency in American history.

The Mind of a President

"I have the right to do whatever I want as president" (Brice-Sadler 2020). This was Donald Trump's conception of his powers as president. As for how to get what he wanted: "Real power is—I don't even want to use the word—fear."

His approach to business and politics: "If somebody hits you, you've got to hit 'em back five times harder than they ever thought possible" (*New York Times* Editorial Board 2020a).

"They can't stop me." This was Trump's response to impeachment (Bennett 2019). "I could stand in the middle of Fifth Avenue and shoot someone and wouldn't lose any voters, okay," Trump said, mimicking firing a gun with his fingers. "It's, like, incredible" (Bump 2019).

And finally, for this or any other acts, he could not be indicted. Trump and his lawyers argued that a sitting president could not be indicted for crimes committed while he was in office or for anything else he might do. Total power, no accountability. This was Trump's conception of the presidency.

As for democracy in general, democratic theorist and historian Timothy Snyder wrote: "[Trump] never took democracy seriously nor accepted the legitimacy of its American version" (Snyder 2017, Snyder 2021). He had other things in mind.

WHY TRUMP WAS WHAT HE WAS

Donald Trump inhabited a strange personal world, one cut off from normal feelings and associations. It was built on fear, division, and conspiracy theories, bizarre and disturbing as to the evil that existed in the world and against which he had to fight. It had little relationship to the space most inhabited. His family, and specifically an overly dominant and demanding father, Fred Sr., had been the formative influence in his childhood. The imprint lasted throughout his life. His niece, Mary Trump, a trained clinical psychologist, explains:

> First, he needed to convince his father he was a better and more confident son than his brother Freddy was; then because Fred [Sr.] required it of him, he came to believe his own public relations. "By the time of the election [2016] Donald met any challenges to his sense of superiority with anger, his fear and vulnerabilities so effectively buried that he didn't even have to acknowledge that they existed. And he never would." (Mary Trump 2020, 11)

Trump's father offered a path to survival within an extraordinarily dysfunctional family, serving as the model to be imitated. Donald Trump, unlike Fred Jr., his older brother and Mary Trump's father, who had not managed to live up to his father's expectations and committed suicide, became his father's favorite. As it turned out, this ensured his father's guidance and financial support throughout his career.

Trump largely ignored his mother, a woman who was often ill and who Trump saw as weak and most often physically and emotionally distant. His father was the decisive force in his life. Fred Sr. was an unusually demanding and threatening figure. Trump's position in the family, such as it was, depended on winning his father's favor. This he did. Within the family, he was the chosen one.

The cost was high. Mary Trump says he never emotionally developed in any way that approached a normal process of maturation. It was the armor he took with him into the world at large.

Trump went to the exclusive Kew-Forest preparatory school where his father had served on the board of directors for close to 30 years. There he developed a reputation for bullying and fighting younger and smaller children and arguing with teachers in class. The situation was bad enough that the school with the father's permission decided he should attend the New York Military Academy. At 13, he did.

He graduated from the military school and led its marching contingent down Fifth Avenue in an annual parade, a particular honor. His father had donated a building to the academy.

He went from there to Fordham University for several years and then transferred to the Wharton School for Finance at the University of Pennsylvania. When he graduated he prohibited both universities from ever making his grades public. His sister Maryanne Trump Barry did his homework for him in both high school and college.

THE BUSINESS CAREER OF DONALD TRUMP

When Trump graduated from college, he started at the top. His father gave him a million dollars to begin his business which he was not required to repay. His father also appointed him to a position in the Trump Organization where he had responsibility for supervising a series of building and other real estate holdings and properties. Fred Sr. surrounded Trump with able people who understood real estate and how the corporation operated.

At this time also, Fred Sr. created the image of Trump as a decisive, ruthless, and successful billionaire. This he sold to tabloids such as the *New York Post* and other media. The image stayed with Trump despite his bankruptcies. It established his reputation in real estate and then in New York's social circles and the business world and was a major part of his campaign for, and tenure during, his presidency.

Mary Trump was taken back by its durability given the number of business failures Trump had experienced.

As far as Trump was concerned, he had done everything on his own. He had said his father had lent him one million dollars to get started but he had paid it back, which was not true.

"Donald today is much as he was at three years old: incapable of growing, learning, or evolving, unable to regulate his emotions, moderate his responses, or take in and synthesize information" (Mary Trump 2020, 197).

In Mary Trump's words, Trump was "delusional about his 'greatness'" (Mary Trump 2020, 196).

Nevertheless, in 1987, a manual that offered business advice, *The Art of The Deal*, by Donald Trump and ghostwriter Tony Schwartz, helped to make Trump a household name. He used it to present himself as a spectacularly successful and tough-minded businessperson (Trump with Schwartz 1987). It stayed on the *New York Times* best seller list for almost a year, including in the number one position for 13 weeks. Trump cited it as his second favorite book after the Bible. He was not religious.

His reputation as a financial genius was about to undergo an intense and unexpected reassessment. The *New York Times* ran a lengthy series on his financial dealings. Rather than being a world-class billionaire and real estate tycoon, Trump had experienced five bankruptcies and had been involved in a number of shady to illegal business activities. His record of success was built on illusion.

Maryanne Trump, his sister, kept his personal, business, and financial records once Trump entered real estate and she paid his taxes. Mary Trump managed to have Maryanne discuss with her at length Trump's financial transactions. She taped the conversations, unknown to Maryanne, and made 19 boxes of Trump's records available to the *New York Times* for its extensive exposé of Trump's five bankruptcies, tax abatements, and financial dealings in the mid-1990s (BBC 2020). The exposé came to 13,000 words, one of the most extensive in the newspaper's history. It was updated periodically (Barstow et al., 2018; Enrich 2020; Enrich et al. 2020).

The *New York Times* investigation showed that Trump had been given $413 million in today's dollars by his father. Trump's parents gave their children over $1 billion. This should have resulted in a tax bill of $550 million or more. The Trumps paid a tax one-fifth of that ($52.2 million) (Buettner et al. 2018). A good deal of Trump's funding came from questionable to fraudulent tax schemes.

Trump had lost over $1.17 billion in core business deals—mostly casinos, hotels, and apartment buildings—over the decade 1985–1994. These included such individual investments as the airline, the Trump Shuttle, the casinos in Atlantic City, and the Plaza Hotel in New York. His losses during this period were believed to be greater than those of any other U.S. taxpayer (Buettner and Craig 2019; Barstow et al. 2018).

There is more. For example, Trump attempted, while Fred Sr. was still alive, to change his father's will to make himself the sole executor of his estate. The father believed Trump might use the estate's wealth to pay off his debts and refused to go along with the plan. Fred Sr. died at age 93 in 1999 after suffering from Alzheimer's disease for a number of years (Kranish 2020). This set off a bitter family dispute over the inheritance that ended in the courts (Kranish 2020).

The tax and financial records showed a number of things. Most obviously, they documented in detail and over a decade Trump's financial incompetence. They also showed his boldness, his willingness to engage in any scheme as egregious as it may be to add to his personal wealth. Third, they showed his and his family's intention to pay the minimum they could get away with in taxes regardless of the amount owed. And finally and more indirectly (Mary

Trump was clearer on this point), they indicated how little such dealings and the burden of the financial failures affected him or his self-perception of his abilities (Mary Trump 2020, 197).

Trump's response to the revelations was to attack, and have his lawyers attack, the Internal Revenue Service (IRS) and the *New York Times* for what they claimed was the use of faulty information. Trump believed he had accomplished more than anyone and he did it all by himself. It was a position he never changed (Mary Trump 2020, 16–17).

Deutsche Bank, victimized by Trump, came to his rescue. The bank had a history of illegal, corrupt, and unethical dealings. It had lent money to the Nazis to build Auschwitz, to dictators in Eastern Europe, laundered money for Putin and Russia, and engaged in unlawful transactions on Wall Street (Schmid 1999). Over a 20-year period it had loaned billions to Trump and his family (Don Jr., Eric, Ivanka) and to his son-in-law Jared Kushner and his family.

Various internal bank investigations of these dealings had been conducted over the years but the claim was made that they never reached the highest levels of the bank's leadership.

The Trump–Kushner association may have turned out handsomely for the bank. Barack Obama's administration had conducted an investigation of the bank's operations in the United States. No charges had been filed by the time Obama left office. Trump appointed former Deutsche Bank lawyers and staff to key regulatory and prosecutorial positions in his administration. The Deutsche Bank abuses and fraud that the Obama administration report had uncovered were not heard about again nor were the multiple federal criminal investigations underway under Obama once Trump took office (Drucker and Enrich 2020).

The willingness of Deutsche Bank to overlook Trump's financial irresponsibility, continue to fund his activities and to use him to market and oversee some of the hotels, golf courses, resorts, businesses, buildings, and other properties most of which he no longer owned is an example of his unusual ability to survive the consequences of his actions.

Trump's reaction to the revelations of his bank dealings was familiar. Trump called Susanne Craig, one of the *New York Times* reporters who wrote the exposé of his financial dealings. Craig was in the process of preparing a report with others on her team on Trump's isolation from Wall Street among other issues. He took exception to her account of his relations to Deutsche Bank. The bank he said was "totally happy with me." He told her she should check with the head of the bank. Then he gave her the name of an official at the bank, Rosemary Vrablic. She, on behalf of the bank, had handled large loans to marginal corporations and individuals at times. She had a business association with both Jared Kushner and his family and Donald Trump and his family. She was not the president of the bank.

Trump also told Craig "I can do business with the biggest banks in the world" and "I just don't need any money." Neither claim was true (Enrich 2020, 306).

Trump came out of the disclosures of the 1990s with his financial transactions in a precarious economic position (Buettner et al. 2020). His reputation as a financial giant and successful billionaire was gone among those who followed such things. Financially, and despite he and his siblings' selling the father's estate for which he received $170 million, his debts remained and his source of income was limited.

Trump, through a series of court actions, managed to keep the IRS from making his tax returns available to the press and public as candidates for the president had done in previous campaigns and that his opponents had done. In early July 2020, the Supreme Court delivered a split decision on subpoenas for Trump's tax returns, rejecting his broadest claim of absolute immunity. The Court also ruled that lower courts had not done enough to show that Congressional subpoenas from Democratic committees considering impeachment requests for such records were justified. Effectively the Supreme Court passed the issue back to lower courts. Trump continued to fight the ruling, ensuring he would not be forced to release tax and financial records to prosecutors and Congressional committees before the November 3, 2020 election. Under the ruling, the House of Representatives had to show the Appeals Court that their request for records was narrow and legitimate (*New York Times* Editorial Board 2020b). The decision at the time was hailed as a victory for the rule of law. Trump never made his tax records public while he was president. Once out of office, the Supreme Court issued a brief unsigned order which meant Trump could no longer shield his tax returns.

Manhattan district attorney Cyrus Vance Jr. led a New York state case in which justices unanimously rejected Trump's argument that he was immune from criminal subpoenas while in office, and second, that Trump was not entitled to learn more about the scope of its grand jury findings in their criminal investigation into his business dealings. Grand jury proceedings are by law conducted in secret (Hong and Rashbaum 2020). The district attorney's investigation into Trump's financial dealings continued past the election and represented the most serious of the inquiries facing Trump in or out of office. Following the Supreme Court ruling allowing prosecutors access to his tax records, Trump's accountants, Mazars USA, immediately turned over eight years of personal and corporate tax returns to the Manhattan District Attorney's office.

Trump took to selling "branding" rights, that is, relying on his image as a hardened, no-nonsense and successful billionaire to endorse products. The image had remained intact with the public at large (if not with his peers on Wall Street). He allowed various products to use his name for a fee. These included the Trump Shuttle Airline; Trump Wine (he had bought a vineyard in Virginia in 2011, later owned and operated by his son Eric as the Trump Winery); and Trump University, which offered real estate workshops and business seminars from 2005 to 2010. It eventually was labeled a fraud by New York's attorney general and closed by the courts. In a settlement Trump was to pay $25 million to defrauded students. Trump also owned or branded resorts, golf courses, residential towers and office buildings, and hundreds of products to bring in money.

Unexpectedly at this point, his luck would change. An offer from TV producer Mark Burnett revived Trump's career and put him on the road to the presidency. Burnett proposed a reality television show, building on Trump's reputation as a no-holds-barred, successful billionaire as host. The show was "The Apprentice." In it various would-be business people would as a team take on a project or task, with Trump judging their merits. The ultimate goal for contestants was to be a job working for Trump. At the end of each program, Trump would have participants inform on their team members, accusing them of poor work. Trump would listen and then pick who he thought was the biggest loser, declaring what would become the show's tag line, "You're fired!" It became part of the country's lexicon. Trump was famous and had become a national celebrity once again (McIntire et al. 2020).

The *New York Times* ran an exposé of Trump's operations on September 27, 2020 (the election was November 3). Periodically the *Times* published more information on Trump's finances (Buettner et al. 2020).

The record of Trump's financial dealings is one of failure. Surprisingly perhaps given what has been referred to as the "Trump Show" and the image he fostered, he was a failure at real estate.

Trump and his lawyers claimed in response to the revelations that Trump has paid tens of millions of dollars in personal taxes to the federal government and that "most, if not all, of the facts appear to be inaccurate" (Buettner et al. 2020).

Perhaps not surprisingly, the revelations as expected had little impact on the election. Most had heard these or related accusations before. His opponents believed them. His supporters did not. They believed they were additional attacks without merit intended to hurt Trump's reelection chances.

TRUMP'S POLITICAL CAREER

While host of "The Apprentice," Trump began "the birther" movement, a racist and political attack on the legitimacy of Barack Obama's right to the presidency. Trump claimed Obama had not been born in the United States but in Kenya. His father was from Kenya and was a bigamist with a wife and family in Kenya. He had met and married Obama's mother, an American, while both were graduate students at the University of Hawaii (Maraniss 2012).

The birther movement lasted for five years. It did not end until President Obama reluctantly released his birth certificate from Hawaii to address Trump's persistent charges that Obama's presidency was not legitimate because of what Trump claimed was a foreign birth. The controversy faded after the release of the Hawaiian birth certificate.

Its significance for Trump was that kept him in the national news and the movement appealed to conservatives that came to form the basis for his campaign when he ran for president. It was the source of his support in the Electoral College and his actions and rallies in office played consistently to this group in the electorate.

Trump may have been a novice when his national celebrity status began with the reality show. It led to the creation of a conservative to Far Right core political following. The birther movement gave him the building blocs of his own political movement.

Trump took full advantage of it. The loyalty of his followers had a cult-like intensity that was impervious to attacks on Trump or his actions in office, however outrageous they might be.

In office, he rebuilt the Republican Party in his political image. Over 90 percent of Republican identifiers in the country supported him and his presidency as did virtually all Republicans in the Congress by the time of the 2020 presidential reelection race.

Over his four years in office Trump's base remained an intensely receptive, increasingly cult-like group of loyalists. It could be said to have won the Electoral College for him and therefore the presidency in the 2016 race and served as the solid nucleus of his support in the 2020 election.

Trump played to this political base throughout his first term. His administration proved to be an exercise in one-man rule and arbitrary and too frequently criminal behavior. His tweets, ad hoc statements, press conferences and his tirades, photo ops, and rallies were used to solidify the loyalty of his core voters. They were not intended to advance the interests of the nation. This was not one of Trump's concerns.

Trump was an ardent consumer of Fox News. Much of what he quoted came from Fox's Sean Hannity and his conspiracy theories of government. Without fact-checking, and given his strong dislike of experts or taking advice from government professionals, passing on such views to a public audience often got Trump enmeshed in controversies. Nonetheless given that these were aimed at his core followers they did little harm to his political standing. It is believed that they have actually reinforced a view of Trump as under constant attack by Democrats, liberals, and the "lying media" and helped Trump expand the number of his supporters. Many of his followers felt he was unduly vilified, a view he shared. In fact he believed the attacks against him, his ethics, and the questioning of his competence were the worst in history. The only competitor for such a recognition might have been Abraham Lincoln, according to Trump.

TAKING STOCK OF THE TRUMP PRESIDENCY

First, while many if not all presidents in the post–World War II period have been controversial to some degree, Trump has been the most controversial of any. The reason being he attempted with some success to move the United Sates in a completely different direction. He presented a fantasy world of his own making that he pushed hard for voters to accept. He made a sustained effort to introduce an authoritarian system of governing and moved the nation in that direction. His presidency was controversial and divisive. Trump was to rank as the worst president in American history.

Like much with his presidency, this was something radically different for the nation to deal with. It had no answers. The Constitution did not anticipate such situations. Though incompetent and unfit for office and psychologically unstable, the only resolution was to wait and watch until his four years in office were up and it was time for the next election. In the interim, much damage would be done to America's democratic institutions and to its relationships with its democratic allies.

Given his objectives, he enjoyed a great deal of success.

He was impeached twice but acquitted by a Republican-controlled Senate.

He appointed three right to extreme Far Right justices to an already unrepresentative Supreme Court. His last, Amy Coney Barrett, was confirmed immediately prior to the 2020 election, the fastest and least scrutinized in history.

Trump had appointed 227 conservative federal judges with lifetime appointments to the federal bench. This included three associate judges of the U.S. Supreme Court; 53 (approximately 30% of the total 179) U.S. Court of Appeals judges; 168 U.S. District Court judges (25% of the 677 judgeships across the district courts); and three judges for the U.S. Court of International Trade (Feeney 2020). Barack Obama appointed a total of 55 circuit judges to the U.S. Court of Appeals in his two terms. Trump's court appointments ensured him of a long-term influence in American politics.

Trump signed the biggest tax overhaul in three decades. It gave some minor, temporary tax relief to the middle and working class, but massive, permanent tax benefits to corporations and millionaires/billionaires. Trump believed it the most significant achievement of his presidency. It was defended as providing a massive spur to the economy. This never happened.

In line with his reputation was Trump's response to a neo-Nazi, white supremacist protest in Charlottesville, Virginia, which led to violence and the death of a counterprotester. Trump blamed both groups for the violence and said there were "very fine people on both sides." He refused to condemn violence or criticize white supremacists or members of hate groups when asked.

Trump opposed gun control and would not criticize police violence, as in the police death of George Floyd in Minnesota. Rather, he criticized the protesters and the Black Lives Matter movement and later, and repeatedly, the governor of Michigan, Gretchen Whitmer, for closing down the state to fight the spread of the virus. When the plot by 14 armed members of extremist hate groups, in training to kidnap, try, and execute the governor, and the armed militia that had taken over the state house was revealed (assault weapons but not protest signs could be carried into the Michigan state house), he again bitterly and verbally assaulted the governor.

Trump repeatedly insulted and opposed democratic allies and supported dictators.[1] He promoted an "America First" nationalist approach; withdrew from treaties on the environment and climate control such as the Paris Accord; cancelled the 2015 nuclear treaty with Iran and other Middle East countries; ordered an air strike that killed Iran's top general, Qasem Soleimani, in 2020, an act that led to talk of war; impulsively pulled American troops out of northern Syria in 2019 leaving the Kurds, who had fought with the Americans, at the mercy of invading Turkish forces with a long history of fighting them; took no action in the Russian bounty program when told of it; fought the Affordable Care Act in the courts, ending the tax penalty for those who did not enroll (the individual mandate) which had been assumed would undermine the program; never delivered on his health care plan, first promised in 2015 and repeatedly thereafter; and refused to lead in the fight against the coronavirus pandemic which contributed to over 9 million cases and over 230,000 deaths as of the 2020 election. More had died from the virus than the total of those killed in all wars combined since 1945.

Trump had given up on governing in the transition period and spent his time claiming he had won and the election was rigged and fraudulent. He mobilized the domestic terrorists that overran the Capitol and an overmatched skeleton police presence on January 6, the day of the final formal certification of the election outcome by Congress. The demonstrators sacked the Capitol and Congressional members' offices before being allowed to leave with no effort at arrests. Five people died including one police officer in the course of the takeover and two other officers by suicide in the following days. Others were seriously injured and hospitalized.

This was not Trump's concern. Rather, in place of governing he spent hours watching Fox News each day. Trump had gone golfing over 300 times by the beginning of the postelection transition and on a regular basis thereafter. He was reportedly extremely upset that following the assault on the Capitol, the Professional Golfers Association (PGA) cancelled its contract to hold their 2022 PGA Championship Golf Tournament at the Trump National Golf Club in Bedminster, New Jersey. The PGA feared that an association with Trump would be detrimental to their brand after the insurrectionist assault by domestic terrorists with Trump's encouragement. The cancellation reportedly bothered Trump more than the intense public reaction to the assault on the Capitol.

Numerous corporations began to disavow their previous support for Trump and for the 147 Republicans (8 senators and 139 representatives) who voted in the Joint Session of Congress to challenge the Electoral College certification that led to the January 6 riot. These included Disney, Coca-Cola, Walmart, Home Depot, Marriott, and JPMorgan Chase. A number of companies and sites that process financial transactions vowed to cut off campaign contributions to those legislators. The city of New York moved to terminate its contracts with the Trump Organization to operate various recreational facilities in the city. Deutsche Bank, a previous major source of business loans used to fund Trump's hotels and golf courses, announced it would no longer do business with him. After flagging many of his "tweets" as questionable in the days following the election, the social media platform Twitter which Trump credited with helping him win office permanently suspended his account. Facebook and Parler, a rightwing site, followed. Apple and Google announced they would no longer host the social networks that had provided Trump and his followers direct access to the public, severely limiting their group communication options.

Trump had a dreadful record as president. Yet 74,216,154 Americans voted for him in the 2020 presidential election, 46.9 percent of the votes cast. Eighty-five to over ninety percent of Republicans believed his claims that the election was stolen. Over 200 Republicans in the House and most in the Senate said nothing or supported his views on election fraud, implicitly and explicitly, agreeing with Trump's charge that he had won the election.

He and they could continue to be a problem in American politics that would need special attention. Trump personally as well as his associates (Lindsay Graham (R/SC) for example) called elected Republicans—governors, election officials, state legislative leaders, and local election boards—arguing that they should throw out millions of votes and declare Trump the winner of the Electoral College. An hour-long telephone call to the official in charge of elections in Georgia gave a clear idea of a not normal president's thinking.

In Georgia, the state vote was not changed. Two Democrats campaigning for the Senate in a separate runoff election defeated two incumbent Republican senators. On January 5 the outcome gave control of the Senate to

Democrats. Biden would have Democratic majorities, tenuous as they were, in both houses of the Congress when he entered office.

Following the seditionist takeover of the Capitol on January 6, there was fear of more violence on Inauguration Day and at state capitals in an attempt at a coup.

Things had changed. The National Guard (reportedly 25,000 in number) had taken over the District of Columbia and other police and National Guard were active in the states. The Inauguration went off peacefully and the states had not experienced the disruptions feared. Meanwhile the FBI and prosecutors had been engaged in an aggressive effort to identify and arrest those most prominently involved in the domestic terrorist assault of January 6 at the Capitol.

Trump had told acting department heads appointed by him during the transition to make any cooperation with Biden's people as difficult as possible and mobilized supporters to monitor the exchanges.

During his four years in office Trump never stopped campaigning. He began in 2016 and continued into his postpresidency days. He was a vigorous critic of mail-in ballots, claiming (falsely) that they were easily open to fraud. He directed his voters to go to the polls to ensure their ballots would be counted, police the voting and protect against abuse or the possible destruction of his votes, all intended to create confusion, disorder, and a grounds for overturning the results in the event the vote went against him.

Trump supporters at the federal and state levels followed his lead. His appointments of supporters and donors included Louis DeJoy as Postmaster General. DeJoy had donated $1.2 million to the Trump Victory Fund and served as finance chair of the Republican National Committee. He had been CEO of a logistics company which was intertwined with the U.S. Postal Office through contractual arrangements. It had been paid over $286 million in recent years for transportation and support services to the U.S.P.O. (Broadwater and Edmondson 2020). The postal service was key to the timely mailing of ballots to voters and their return to local election officials. Postal services were cut, leading to serious delays in the receipt and return of ballots to election officials and in the counting of those ballots. The states controlled by Trump governors as followers made their contributions. Texas cut the number of election ballot drop-off boxes to one per county. This most significantly affected Harris County (Houston), its largest county at approximately 2,000 square miles and a population of over 4.7 million, and Travis County, home to a reliably Democratic city, Austin, with a population of over 1.2 million.

Given the fear of COVID-19 transmission and anticipation of potential violence at polling places, Biden supporters voted more heavily by mail and through the drop-off ballot boxes. As a result, their votes were tallied late and the initial returns looked promising to Trump and his voters. Trump leveraged the early lead to claim that the election had been stolen when the final returns, four days after Election Day, favored Biden.

Given his record in office, a question came up as to why Trump was tolerated. Robert Jay Lifton, a psychohistorian, offers an explanation based on his research, particularly his investigation into the socialization of doctors in Nazi concentration camps during World War II (plus related research investigations he had engaged in) (Lifton 2017). The doctors were recruited to separate out those who would die in the gas chambers and those who would not. The work went against their ethical training and often personal values. Yet they ended up doing what they were brought in to do. He refers to the process of acceptance as "adaption to evil" and "the normalization of evil" and he applied it to Trump.

Lifton writes about Trump that "because he is president and operates within the broad contours and interactions of the presidency, there is a tendency to view what he does as simply part of our democratic process—that is, as politically and even ethically normal. In this way, a dangerous president becomes normalized, and malignant normality comes to dominate our governing (or, one could say, our antigoverning) dynamic" (Lifton 2017, xv–xix).

Along with the "normality" Lifton refers to, there is the public's "normality" of mental and emotional exhaustion in response to Trump's overwhelming media presence. Trump fatigue combined with emotional pandemic fatigue led to a public withdrawal into the normalization patterns discussed by Lifton.

In contrast to Trump, his opponent, Joe Biden, often appeared to be a media afterthought. The public consciousness was battered with Trump's views, theatrics, and reality TV showmanship. It was something Biden as a counterforce and reality check could not begin to compete with.

Much of what Trump did or said was bizarre. His most extraordinary conspiracy theories were not reported by the mainstream press. The symbolism implicit in his actions was not often spoken of nor its significance for the country's future discussed in the focus on the details and the sensationalism surrounding his behavior.

One incident took place when Trump returned from Walter Reed Medical Center after his hospitalization for COVID-19. Trump stood at attention on the balcony of the White House looking out at those assembled. At one point he saluted. It was an example of what Mussolini would do from a balcony in Rome and Hitler, ugly as this sounds, from a raised platform at their rallies, right down to the salute.

Trump may not have been a Hitler or a Mussolini. He did have a dictator-like approach and he did mimic, consciously or not, the actions and symbols common to those of dictators (Overy 2006; Bueno de Mesquita and Smith

2016; Laqueur 1976; Schedler 2006; and Dean and Altemeyer 2020). It was all part of the greater militarization of American government and the movement toward a more autocratic system of government.

As theorists in democratization have pointed out, most people do not know such transformative changes are in progress. Lifton does go a long way in helping to understand the American public's and, this should be mentioned, the media's, as the transmitting agency for such normalization processes, adaption to the eccentricities and existential threat of the Trump presidency.

POLICY AND POLITICS

The foundations of Trump's policy perspective were formed by his upbringing. His niece wrote that "Donald . . . understands nothing about history, constitutional principles, geopolitics, diplomacy (or anything else, really)" (Mary Trump 2020, 15–16).

Money-making was the standard, as his father and grandfather had taught him. The objective was to increase his personal wealth and his power. This is what drove his policy goals. When possible within this framework, opportunities to act out his anger or revenge against critics and opponents were welcomed.

It was all personal. It could provide a distraction from paying attention to more pressing national interests (COVID-19). What it was not was guided by professional expertise or a cumulative extension of what had gone before. His policy positions were erratic and highly personal in nature and often seemingly unrelated to much of anything else. The constant talk was that it did not advance any national interest, which was true enough.

IMMIGRATION POLICY AND THE SEPARATION OF ASYLUM-SEEKING FAMILIES

Immigration has always been a divisive issue in American politics.

It was the earliest, major issue to come to the Trump administration's attention. The controversy had begun in the Obama administration. Trump had inherited it and, with time, made it considerably worse.

Trump had pledged during the campaign to keep out robbers, criminals, and murderers from Mexico and Central America. He promised a wall, paid for by Mexico, would be built along the border to keep immigrants out. He vowed to deport illegal immigrants, estimated at 11 million people, from the country in his June 16, 2015, announcement speech. Closer to the election he lowered that number to 5–6.5 million after Latino advisors urged him to reconsider his threat (DelReal 2016).

The funding for the wall remained a problem. Trump redirected money appropriated by the Congress for the Department of Defense to build sections of the wall, an illegal action.

An early crisis emerged in relation to Trump's immigration policy. This led to the especially egregious practice of separating immigrant families and the jailing of their children in cages. As details began emerging and legislators and others began investigating, their accounts of the conditions faced as to the mistreatment of the children were moving. Reporters and human rights representatives "toured an old warehouse where hundreds of children were being kept in wire cages . . . the children had no books or toys, overhead lighting was kept on round the clock, and the children were sleeping under foil sheets. There was no adult supervision and the older children were changing the diapers of the toddlers" (Southern Poverty Law Center 2020; Soboroff 2020; and Thompson 2018).

It was the American Civil Liberties Union that took up the actual work of trying to reunite families. It set up offices in Central American countries and went to towns and villages to check the few official records that existed. They also questioned residents as to their knowledge of the families they were trying to reunite.

Trump's objective had been to discourage families of immigrants from attempting to enter the country. The policies chosen were inhumane but in the judgment of the Border Patrol and the president, they succeeded. "It was hard to argue that the shocking cruelty of the Trump administration's separation policy wasn't integral to achieving their objectives" (Soboroff 2020, 361).

The Biden administration began within its first days to work on the problems raised. In addition to the family separation policy, there was a backlog of people in Mexico waiting to get into the country and no clearly established rules to cover this or those in the country who had no desire to be deported.

Change in immigration policies would be far more difficult than Biden and his team anticipated. Groups of largely college students had tracked the Trump administration's changes made in the immigration process. "By the end of Trump's presidency . . . [they] had logged a thousand and fifty eight changes to the immigration system" (Stillman 2021). These included over 60 cases of "torture, sexual assault, and death" (Stillman 2021).

Trump had placed immigration policy under principal advisor Stephen Miller who held an animus toward immigrants. The objective was to constantly come up with more restrictive practices. Steve Bannon, a Far Right practitioner and Trump's first principal advisor, was a contributor to Miller's objectives. The regulations were then deposited in what was referred to as an area of "regulatory dark matter" where those adopted did not have to be announced or listed.

Further, Immigration and Naturalization had a gung-ho culture that welcomed Trump's tough approach. Republicans in Congress delayed the confirmation of the new director proposed by Biden, and Republican appointees by Trump to the courts took the opportunity to block Biden's policy approaches (Kanno-Youngs and Shear 2021).

Biden's immigration priorities were, first, to locate and void the changes the Trump administration had made. Second, Biden introduced an ambitious policy agenda to address the various dimensions of the problems raised. It was 180 degrees the opposite of Trump's.

COVID

The coronavirus pandemic had the greatest potential impact on the election of any of the crises. Those who had experienced COVID-19 (or who took the virus seriously) were more likely to vote for Biden and the Democrats.

Trump refused to recognize the virus or the severity of its impact. In a briefing on January 28, 2020, less than a month after word emerged from China of the new respiratory virus, Trump had been told by his National Security Advisor, Robert O'Brien, that the virus would represent the greatest national security threat of his presidency. A deputy advisor added that the anticipated worldwide health emergency would be on par with the flu pandemic of 1918 (which had killed an estimated 675,000 in the United States) (Costa and Rucker 2020). However, despite that dire warning, Trump claimed that the new virus was like the flu and would soon magically disappear. Journalist Bob Woodward revealed in his book, *Rage*, published in September 2020, that during a series of interviews with Trump earlier that year the president had told him of the severity of the pandemic potential, including that the virus was deadly and was airborne. Woodward did not release this information until the publication of his book in the early fall of 2020. Trump never did.

Trump himself developed a case of COVID-19 in October 2020. He said it was nothing to be afraid of or anything that would ruin a person's life (Weiland et al. 2021). He had recovered quickly by being treated with novel drug cocktails not available to the general public. Months later reports emerged that Trump's condition had been so serious there had been consideration of putting him on a ventilator (Collins and Acosta 2021; Reimann 2021).

He refused to supply any national leadership in organizing the fight against the pandemic or take any responsibility for his late recognition of its intensity, which led to the loss of over 340,000 lives by the end of the year, with a projection of 600,000 to die by the spring of 2021. Trump had campaigned to reopen schools, workplaces, churches, and other institutions he believed vital to the economy, despite the threat they posed for COVID-19 transmission. Regarding those exposed to the virus and those who died, his expressed attitude was "It is what it is!"

The United States led the world in the number of COVID-19 cases and in the number of deaths. The problem, especially the availability, distribution, and administration of the two COVID-19 vaccines which had become available in December 2020, became a major objective of the Biden presidency once in office. The goal was demanding. Biden immediately promised 100 million vaccinations to be administered in the first 100 days of the Biden presidency. A week later he said he envisioned an increase to 1.5 million shots a day. Impressive given what had gone before but still well short of the number of people that would need to be vaccinated on a daily basis given the magnitude of the population that had to be reached. Aware of this, in early February, Biden contracted for 200 million more doses of COVID-19 vaccine, bringing the total number of Pfizer and Moderna doses to be made available by summer to 600 million with the likelihood of other vaccines on hand by spring. It was expected this would supply the quantity necessary to vaccinate most of the U.S. population (Restuccia 2021).

Epidemiologists were generally predicting that it would be the end of 2021 before reasonable control of the virus might be achieved (referred to as "herd immunity," where enough people are immune to effectively limit viral spread). Moreover, the virus had begun mutating. New variant strains appeared to be significantly more transmissible, possibly more deadly, and potentially resistant to vaccines and monoclonal antibody treatments currently available (which Trump had been treated with). Moreover, it was also not clear the vaccines in use would prevent transmission, though they limited or prevented illness, at least for the current strains circulating. The opportunity for the virus to mutate increased as the virus spread so the urgency of efforts to halt transmission was clear.

It was found that the COVID-19 vaccination effort that Trump had claimed to be available did not exist. Vaccine supply and manufacturing capacity were limited. No practical plan for distribution to, or vaccination of, the population existed. The supply of vaccine for the second booster doses that Trump and his Health and Human Services Secretary, Alex Azar (a former pharmaceutical industry CEO), had said was stockpiled did not exist.

States had been left to their own devices as to how to prioritize and administer the limited vaccine supply. Public health funding had not been a priority of the Trump administration and the scarce resources limited the ability to respond to the challenges facing state and local health departments.

The problems were left to the Biden administration to deal with.

THE RUSSIAN PROBLEM: THE MUELLER REPORT AND
THE SENATE INTELLIGENCE COMMITTEE REPORT

The Mueller Report contained a wealth of information. It was well done, lengthy (448 pages), and eagerly anticipated. It also led to the prosecution and imprisonment of some of Trump's leading associates for lying about their association with Russian intelligence during the 2016 campaign. They would be pardoned or have their sentences commuted in the waning days of the Trump presidency.

Russia and its president Vladimir Putin were supporters of Trump's candidacy. Russian intelligence had hacked into social media and electronic data including the Democratic National Committee files, in spreading disinformation in 2016 that benefited Trump's campaign. The Ukraine, China, the Philippines, and others were asked by Trump also if they could provide him with information to use against Biden in the 2020 campaign. A telephone call to the Ukraine to solicit such support was the basis for Trump's first impeachment. As an incentive to do his bidding, Trump withheld $391 million in military aid needed by Ukraine to help resist the Russian invasion of the country. Inviting a foreign nation to become involved in domestic politics was a constitutional offense.

The Mueller Report did not draw any summary conclusions from its investigation. Mueller explained that the Department of Justice of which the FBI was a component part had a ruling that an in-office president could not be indicted or charged with criminal behavior and removed from office (Dellinger 2018; Macagnone 2019). Therefore, his report made no such judgments. He said it provided the information and left the ultimate decision to others.

This represented a major disappointment (Weissman 2020). The restrictions Mueller, once the director of the FBI, worked under were not made public until after the report was released.

Mueller did not force Trump to appear in person before the commission. He accepted written answers to questions which all agreed later were worthless.

Mueller proved less than cooperative in a number of ways. He refused to appear before Congressional committees to discuss the report unless subpoenaed. Once he was subpoenaed, he answered committee questions tersely, often saying that the information was in the report. He appeared frail and confused at times. On occasion he said something was in the report that was not. He rarely volunteered answers or information (although he did emphasize the Russian disinformation campaign of 2016 would be repeated in the 2020 election) and overall he appeared unhelpful, even unfriendly, apparently seeing the Congressional committees and the public as enemies. Given the level of anticipation that preceded the report's release, the outcome was less than satisfactory.

On Mueller's behalf, his report was thoroughly done within the limits set. It was convincing in the case it made against Trump. In these regards, and despite its weaknesses, it was one of the more effective investigations and attempts to assign culpability (to the extent it did) to come out of the Trump years.

Most significantly, the report did not do what the public expected, namely, decide if Trump should be impeached. The niceties of Justice Department procedures aside, it appeared to exonerate Trump (although it claimed not to). This is how Trump took it and declared victory. Given this, it faded quickly from public attention. However, it would later and unexpectedly again become a subject of public attention in the debate over the pardons the president was giving to those the Mueller Report had identified as working with the Russians. Many of them, including Paul Manafort, Trump's campaign chairman at one point; Roger Stone, a dirty trickster with ties that went back to the Nixon administration; Michael Flynn, former Trump National Security Advisor who twice, in written form and orally, admitted his guilt to the FBI and to Vice President Mike Pence; and Rick Gates, former Trump campaign aide and deputy inauguration committee chair, among others, received substantial prison time. Trump was to pardon or commute their sentences along with a considerable number of others in the closing days of his presidency.

The Mueller Report and the over 1,000-page, five-volume Senate Intelligence Committee report completed in August 2020 detailed the associations between the Trump campaign and Russian intelligence. The hacking and Russian disinformation campaign began again for the 2020 election but despite Trump's inaction on the matter, election officials were better prepared this time to keep the election process secure.

Trump himself refused to investigate the reports on 2016 and/or 2020 (Graham 2020). By the time of the reelection campaign, there was an active discussion of Trump serving as a Russian spy, as incredulous as this may sound. Both the Mueller investigation and the FBI had been charged with investigating this association. Both failed to do so.

After the January 6, 2021, sedition, the deadly invasion of the Capitol in which Trump had assembled, motivated, and sent domestic terrorists to the Capitol, he was impeached again. Found guilty by the House, the verdict to convict or not was left to the Senate. Majority Leader Mitch McConnell, who continued to exercise power in the Senate for a brief time after the election, rather than hold hearings immediately, delayed until after the Biden administration took office. The incoming Democratic Majority Leader Chuck Schumer agreed to also delay Trump's trial until February. Trump was the only president in American history to be impeached twice.

The House Impeachment Managers in the second impeachment of Donald Trump laid out the essence of a coup d'état in the making from Trump's efforts to have the states change their votes to the domestic terrorist assault on the Capitol. The postassault refusal of Republicans in or out of Congress to hold Trump accountable for his role in organizing the assault indicated that the foundations of an antidemocratic state existed and would continue to be active in American politics.

TRUMP'S IMPACT ON GOVERNMENT AGENCIES

Trump was determined to replace the leadership of government departments with supporters who shared his views as "acting directors" ("acting" since that allowed him to make appointments during Congressional recesses without going through the standard hearing and scrutiny of full-time appointments and because he could fire them at will and with little reaction if they did not do as directed). Health agencies and programs especially were targeted.

He had great success in turning professional government agencies into partisan outlets promoting his views and his reelection. As an example, the national Centers for Disease Control and Prevention (CDC) constantly changed its health advisories to adapt to Trump's goal of minimizing the virus's impact and reopening the economy. Trump diminished the threat and even at times the existence of the pandemic. CDC adapted its position and standards regarding communicability of the virus, testing, masks and other personal protective equipment, the reopening of schools, the economy, churches, and social life to match Trump's fluctuating assertions. All were intended to promote Trump's interests and his reelection.

The CDC liked to think of itself as the gold standard for public health concerns worldwide and in fact had received international recognition. Trump appointed as CDC director, Dr. Robert Redfield. He in turn appeared as a publicist for Trump and his attempts to minimize the threat the coronavirus posed to the country. "Redfield has enabled the fundamental scientific mission and processes of the CDC to be subverted by partisan political motives whose overall intent is to downplay the severity of COVID-19 and rush people back to work, and kids back to school, before it is safe to do so for the health of the overall population" (Cook 2020).

Redfield in the later days of the Trump presidency returned to the CDC to reporting virus developments accurately and to issuing recommendations on individual safety in line with the seriousness of the pandemic.

Other agencies that became agents to promote Trump included: the Food and Drug Administration, the Bureau of the Census, the IRS, programs dealing with election administration and requirements (including those at the state and local levels), the departments of Commerce, Defense and Homeland Security, Treasury, the Border Patrol, the Joint Chiefs of Staff and the American military, the CIA, the FBI, the U.S. Postal Service, and the Departments of Justice and State. These were independent agencies built up over the generations that were replaced with a leadership that did what it was told to do to advance Trump's interests. The quickness with which the government was turned into a public relations machine more familiar to dictatorships in third-world countries was one demonstration of a critical weakness in American government.

Overall, Trump showed considerable skills in the deflection of attention from more serious crises (COVID-19) to more superficial issues, in turning government agencies and programs into publicists for his reelection, and in creating and selling the existence of an alternative political universe to almost half of the American population.

TRUMP AND THE COURTS

Trump managed to reconstruct the Republican Party to promote his objectives. In the Republican-held Senate, led by Majority Leader Mitch McConnell in an authoritarian manner, the principal goal was to take control of the federal judiciary up through the Supreme Court. Trump, with McConnell as enabler, managed to get over 200 new federal judges confirmed for appointment to lifetime positions.

Trump had made two controversial appointments to the Supreme Court, Neil Gorsuch and Brett Kavanaugh. Both were Far Right conservatives whose temperament for the Court and intensity of their ideological beliefs were questioned. McConnell had blocked the appointment of Merrick Garland to the open seat that had been held by Justice Antonin Scalia. Garland, later Biden's choice to be attorney general, never received a confirmation vote in the Senate during the last year of the Obama administration. Garland was a member of the U.S. Court of Appeals for the District of Columbia Circuit. He was a respected, middle-of-the-road choice, known and supported by Republicans and Democrats.

Justice Ruth Bader Ginsburg's death six weeks before Election Day gave the president the opportunity to push for the quick addition of another Far Right nominee to the Supreme Court. This time the Republicans argued that short as the time period to act was, it would give Trump a 6–3 edge on the Court and ensure the integrity of the election (i.e., result in a Trump victory in November if he lost the Electoral Vote and challenged the results in the courts).

SUPREME COURT REPRESENTATION
AND AMY CONEY BARRETT

Trump nominated federal judge Amy Coney Barrett of the Seventh Circuit Court of Appeals to replace Ginsburg. He and the Republicans moved quickly to vote her onto the Supreme Court. She represented the sixth conservative to Far Right Supreme Court justice. He had been clear that if he did not win outright, he would appeal to the Supreme Court which he expected to decide for him.

Barrett had been appointed by Trump to the federal court in 2017. In that confirmation hearing before the Senate, questions were raised as to the nature of her odd to extreme religious practices and their potential consequences for decision-making by Senator Diane Feinstein. But they were not the priority. The same concerns were raised briefly in her confirmation hearing in 2020.

Barrett belonged to a small (1,800–2,000 members in the United States, Canada, and the Caribbean) civic offshoot of the Catholic Church which described itself as a charismatic covenant community, the "People of Praise" (Rousselle 2020). While emphasizing it was an ecumenical movement it remained heavily Catholic in membership and had a strong hierarchical leadership. Members professed to have a Pentecostal personal relationship with Jesus. The community expected women to observe obligations to their husband: they could not deny him sex and they were not to get pleasure from it. It was intended to produce as many babies as God allowed. Women were expected to be both obedient and subservient. They were not allowed to hold a position that exercised authority over men and all their actions had to be approved by a male authority figure. In families, corporal punishment of children was allowed.

The confirmation hearing was quick and led to a party-line vote in which the Democrats on the Senate Judiciary Committee refused to participate. The Democrats on the committee did make a case as to the importance of the nomination and, based on Barrett's record as a federal appeals judge, her writings while a member of the faculty at the University of Notre Dame Law School and the talks she gave, her likely votes on the Supreme Court on abortion, the Affordable Care Act, and other federal government programs and the impact of these on millions of lives.

Barrett and her "originalist" views (an exceedingly narrow interpretation of what the Constitution allowed) were confirmed by the Senate in a 52–48 mostly party line vote. Susan Collins (R/ME), up for reelection, was the only Republican to vote against her confirmation.

Some considered the movement to be a cult with rigidly controlled behavior, adherence to a series of beliefs well beyond the normal with a bias against freedom of thought or individual choice.[2]

The fear of those opposed to her nomination was that Barrett's religious beliefs would influence, or more directly, come to decide issues that came before the Supreme Court. Keeping an open and balanced mind and judging cases in terms of constitutional relevance critics feared would not be possible under such conditions.

What was clear and to which all would agree: Barrett, 48 years of age, was a political and religious conservative who, barring the unexpected, would be on the Supreme Court for decades to come.

If the Supreme Court was intended to dominate representation by one ideological point of view, the Court has met that standard. Or if it was intended as best it could to represent the mix of people and their views, and to interpret the Constitution impartially in their rulings, it does not come close.

A "LAW AND ORDER" PRESIDENT
AND LAFAYETTE SQUARE

The Border Patrol along with others from the Departments of Homeland Security, Treasury, and other federal agencies took on another responsibility in line with Trump's objectives of using force to make an example of cities seen as centers of out-of-control violence. This was in the aftermath of the George Floyd murder by police. Floyd was a Black man who died after a Minneapolis police officer knelt on his neck for 9:29 minutes. That incident was captured and widely circulated on social media and broader news channels. It led to nationwide protests.

To establish his credentials as a "law and order" president and advance his reelection objective as he saw it, Trump deployed combat-ready militia forces to cities run by Democrats where demonstrations were taking place. Trump drafted the border agents and the rest as part of his private army.

An incident that marked a turning point in the Trump presidency took place on June 1 (2020) at Lafayette Square across from the White House. A military force dressed in battle fatigues with AK-47s, tear gas and pepper spray (both banned for use in warfare under the Chemical Weapons Convention but allowed for law enforcement and riot control when warning is given), and other weapons, but with no identifying insignia on their uniforms, appeared along with the National Guard and with troops from the 82nd Airborne Division in reserve to forcibly clear peaceful demonstrators from the park. The demonstrators were protesting the killing of Floyd.

Trump had arranged for the nonviolent demonstrators to be cleared so he could stage a photo op of himself holding a Bible (upside-down) in front of a nearby shuttered Episcopal church once known as the "Church of Presidents." This allowed him to authoritatively march through the park, seemingly by himself, but with a group of officials following, his daughter Ivanka (with the prop bible in her purse), Cabinet members, Secret Service security, Mark Milley, head of the Joint Chiefs of Staff in military fatigues (who later expressed regret for creating a "perception of the military involved in domestic politics"), and staff officials among them, all following Trump.

Trump's posturing was a replication of scenes from World War II films and photographs of what Mussolini and Hitler would do as a reminder to people of their authority.[3] Other autocratic rulers—Juan and Eva Peron of Argentina—and those from lesser authoritarian systems would mimic such events as reminders of their power.

People were injured during the protests and counterprotests over Floyd's murder. The *Washington Post* found that eight people lost vision in one eye after being struck by police projectiles during one week of unrest (Kelly et al. 2020).

Combined with Trump's use of his paramilitary army in Portland, Kenosha, Detroit, and other cities, the militarization of American politics and the move toward a more authoritarian system had begun in earnest.

THE ASSAULT ON THE CAPITOL

Trump's mobilization of extremist hate groups known for their use of violence was a shock to most members of the Congress when thousands gathered to invade the Capitol on January 6, 2021. Many were outfitted in military gear including Kevlar (bulletproof vests), screaming threats and obscenities as they used battering rams and American flagpoles to break through windows and doors. Some used rock climbing techniques to ascend the steep concrete walls surrounding the building. They threatened the life of Mike Pence who had been presiding over the ceremony formally certifying Biden's Electoral College vote in his role as vice president. This infuriated Trump and the mob.

The domestic terrorist takeover was being televised. Viewers could watch a man swing off the Senate chamber balcony, land on the floor of the Senate, and sit in the chair Pence had been in moments earlier. Another waved to cameras as he strolled through the Capitol carrying Nancy Pelosi's speaker's lectern. A bare-chested man with face painted red, white, and blue, wearing a horned, coyote-tail fur headdress and brandishing a 6-foot spear was prominent in photographs taken of the dais of the Senate. In addition to Pence and Speaker Nancy Pelosi, the lives of others in Congress were threatened. A makeshift gallows was set up outside on the Capitol grounds. Two men clad in military-style clothing were seen in the Senate chamber holding plastic zip ties intended as restraints.

Any legislators they could find as the insurgents roamed the Capitol and the Congressional office buildings could have suffered the fate intended for Pence. Pence and Pelosi had been taken by Capitol Police to a safe area. They barely missed having contact with the terrorist insurgents. Members of Congress were evacuated to a crowded room where several Republicans refused to wear masks. A number announced they had tested positive for COVID-19 a few days later as a result. A Texas Republican Congressman died of COVID-19 a month later, the first sitting member of Congress to die of the virus.

Five people including a Capitol Police officer died in the attack. Nearly 150 officers were injured (Broadwater and Schmidt 2021). More deaths resulted when two police officers who had been on the scene committed suicide days later. An intensive investigation of what had happened and who was behind it was promised along with the prosecution of those who participated. Such a terrorist assault on the Capitol could, for those involved if found guilty, lead to 20 years in prison.

MILITARIZATION AND AUTHORITARIANISM

The militarization of politics, the introduction of violence, force, and Trump's private army in order to impose his will, and authoritarianism, the replacement of a democratic system of governing with an autocratic one, were major developments during the Trump presidency and may have established what will constitute a permanent threat to America's democratic government.

Most of the media persisted in reporting on his behavior as if he were a normal president operating within the accepted bounds of his office and, by implication, not much different from his predecessors.

Trump modeled how to transform a modern-age democracy into an autocracy. It took place in public view. Trump made little effort to hide his objectives or his road to achieving them.

Trump had the temperament of a dictator from the beginning. He had no respect for the rituals and rules of a democracy. He believed he was in charge, that he knew best what needed to be done, and that others should react quickly and unquestioningly to his decisions. Their role was to honor and celebrate his leadership. And although not necessarily a qualification for autocrat, he was a demagogue who would lead the movement to the realization of his vision. The consequence was that throughout his presidency, there was a steady and determined militarization of democratic practices in the move toward the authoritarian state he prized.

The outlines of this transition were made clear at different stages of his presidency. Certain events stand out as marking points: his early praise for dictators like Vladimir Putin in Russia, Kim Jong-un in North Korea, Recep

Tayyip Erdogan in Turkey, Xi Jinping in China; Lafayette Square and the use of force to clear away those peacefully demonstrating the police killing of George Floyd to allow Trump his photo op; the mobilization of a private army to subdue protests in urban Democratic-led cities; the public ignoring of constitutional safeguards and protections; the constant trashing of the electoral process culminating in the refusal to accept the results of the 2020 election; the effort Trump managed in the transition period to disrupt the orderly and peaceful transfer of power to the incoming administration; and the mobilization and directing of the deadly assaults on the Capitol in an attempted coup d'état.

There were a limited number of efforts to hold Trump accountable for his actions. There was the call to the president of the Ukraine seeking his help in the election that led to Trump's first impeachment. He was acquitted by a Senate that served as enablers or coconspirators throughout his presidency.

His second impeachment trial involved his organizing, motivating, and funding of the January 6 rally that led to the insurrection at the Capitol to instigate a coup (Trump's campaign provided individuals and organizations behind the rally with over $2.7 million in funding) (Greenwood 2021; Rosenberg and Rutenberg 2021). The Capitol assault was intended to negate the official Electoral Vote taking place that day and leave Trump indefinitely in charge of the nation. Trump was out of office at the time of the second Senate impeachment trial. He was again acquitted by the vote of the Republicans in the Senate.

Masha Gessen has written: "the Trump administration shared two key features with the Soviet government: utter disregard for human life and a monomaniacal focus on pleasing the leader, to make him appear unerring and all-powerful." She adds: "These are features of autocratic leadership" (Gessen 2020, xvi).

Trump employed many of the same broad techniques that Hitler and Mussolini did in their rise to power (Evans 2004). His contribution was considered to be adapting their approaches to a different age and the contemporary era's most powerful and successful democracy (Sanger 2020; Pilkington 2021). On this point Gessen has written: "Trump had come closer to achieving autocratic rule than most people would have thought possible" (Gessen 2020, xvi). Or, it could be added, most people recognized.

The Republican Party's embracing of authoritarianism began well before Donald Trump. His four years in office with its emphasis on the militarization of politics energized it and gave it a focus and discipline it did not have. In addition, it supplied a constant push toward establishing an autocracy.

It quickly became evident that the move toward authoritarianism would continue with Trump out of office (Applebaum 2000).[4] His goals would remain the same as would those of his supporters in and out of Congress.

Should, for whatever reason, he not be up to leading the movement, others had been willing, even eager, to take over Trump's leadership role.

A moderate center-right party that would exercise a reasonable voice in policy deliberations while supporting the nation's democratic commitments was needed in American politics. The Republican Party operated broadly along these lines before Barry Goldwater and Newt Gingrich in an extremist turn gained power, resulting in the period from Ronald Reagan to Donald Trump.[5]

Dealing with the contemporary threat to the democratic order was the single most important challenge facing the Biden presidency and the nation (Sanger 2020; Rosenberg and Rutenberg 2021).

IMPEACHMENT

The impeachment process is designed to make presidential removal hard to achieve (Gerhardt 2019).

That it does!

There have been only a handful of serious efforts to impeach presidents. Andrew Johnson, Lincoln's successor, was impeached by the House of Representatives in 1868. He survived conviction in the Senate by one vote.

There may have been a lesson here. If Johnson could not be removed from office, no one could (although the narrow grounds he was tried on played a major part in his acquittal). Richard M. Nixon resigned his office on August 8, 1974, on the eve of his impeachment and before the House of Representatives could vote on it.

Bill Clinton's impeachment in 1998 mixed the personal with the professional and constitutional. The argument could be made that he was impeached for his personal conduct (Independent Counsel 1998). This is not what impeachment was designed to do. He was acquitted by the Senate.

Donald Trump had the distinction of being impeached twice. He also had the distinction of being acquitted twice. The first impeachment came after the call to the president of the Ukraine asking for help in his 2020 reelection campaign and withholding $391 million authorized by the Congress to help the country fight the Russian invasion. Involving a foreign country in U.S. domestic politics is unconstitutional. Withholding the funds to the Ukraine pending an announcement by the country's president of an investigation into the business dealings of Biden's son, Hunter, established a quid pro quo arrangement. Hunter Biden had been paid a lucrative salary by one of the Ukraine's largest energy corporations, Burisma. The invitation to the Ukrainian president to be involved in a presidential election and the threat to withhold funds authorized by Congress made by Trump (which was done for a period of time) for his personal political benefit in the Ukrainian call was the basis for Trump's first impeachment (Nadler 2019).

Adam Schiff, the chair of the House Intelligence Committee that heard the witnesses in the first impeachment of Trump, was also head of the delegation that appeared before the Senate to present the case for the president's impeachment. Schiff made a vigorous statement that summarized the case against Trump, presented the evidence and challenged the Republican-dominated body with words from Robert Kennedy calling for "moral courage" (Schiff 2020).

The Senate's Republican majority was unmoved. It voted almost unanimously to acquit Trump. The exception was Mitt Romney (R/UT) who voted for conviction on one article, an abuse of power charge, on December 19, 2019. Romney was the first member of Congress ever to vote against his party on an impeachment vote.

Trump's second impeachment was based on his role in mobilizing, energizing, and dispatching domestic terrorists to invade the Capitol in a deadly confrontation with police. The House majority charged Trump with "high crimes and misdemeanors." He was impeached on one article of "Incitement of Insurrection" on January 13, 2021, a week before the Biden Inauguration. Ten House Republicans joined the Democrats in the impeachment vote (see table 1.1). Still and after the domestic terrorists' January 6 attack on the Capitol and the injury and deaths that resulted, the overwhelming majority of House, and more importantly Senate, Republicans voted not to impeach.

The evening before the impeachment vote, the House also passed a nonbinding resolution calling on Vice President Mike Pence to invoke the Twenty-fifth Amendment to remove Trump from office. In a nearly strict party-line vote (the one exception was Adam Kinzinger (R/IL), the resolution passed by a 223–205 vote (see table 1.2). Pence was not interested in leading such a movement.

Pence did assume the mostly ceremonial functions of a president after Trump gave up any pretense of governing in his final weeks in office (beyond

Table 1.1 House Vote on Trump's Second Impeachment, January 13, 2021 Article I. Incitement of Insurrection

Vote	Total	Dem.	Rep.
Yes	232	222	10
No	197	0	97
Not Voting	4	0	4
Outcome	Passed		

Source: Weiyi Cai et al. 2021. https://www.nytimes.com/interactive/2021/01/13/us/politics/trump-second-impeachment-vote.html.

Table 1.2 House Vote on Resolution Calling on Vice President Pence to Invoke Twenty-Fifth Amendment, January 12, 2021

Vote	Total	Dem.	Rep.
Yes	223	222	1
No	205	0	205
Not Voting	5	0	5
Outcome	Passed but not implemented; Pence refused to be involved in the process		

Source: Weiyi Cai et al. 2021. https://www.nytimes.com/interactive/2021/01/13/us/politics/trump-second-impeachment-vote.html.

pardoning associates and those who were reportedly told by Rudy Giuliani the going rate for a pardon was $2 million) (Levin 2021).

The second impeachment in broad terms resembled the first. The Democrats took it seriously and prepared their case in detail. The quality of the appeal to the Senate was praised by members of both political parties.

Trump's initial legal team for the impeachment quit shortly before the Senate trial. The lawyers brought in presented a confused defense that did not help his cause. It did not need to. Enough senators were already committed to support Trump regardless of the evidence or the House Impeachment Managers' presentation. The Senate acquitted Trump of all charges. The vote was guilty 57, for acquittal 43, with 67 (2/3 vote) by the Senate needed to convict.

Overall impeachment has not worked well in removing from office those unfit to be president or those with health issues or incapacitated in some manner.

Impeachment had come to impact how Trump would be perceived. As noted, he was the only president to be impeached twice, not the best way to be remembered in history (Glasser 2021).

Speaker Nancy Pelosi along with Representative Jamie Raskin (D/MD) proposed establishing a nonpartisan commission of psychological and medical experts to complete, as they saw it, the work of the authors of the Twenty-fifth Amendment. The Amendment provided for the removal and replacement of a president or vice president in the event of death, resignation, or incapacity.

Such an addition to the Constitution clarifying and expanding constitutional procedures was needed. The amendment in place, passed in 1967, had blind spots that required attention.

Such remedies however have implicit problems. If such a constitutional modification passed the Congress, which is unlikely given the supermajority needed, and if it received the necessary support from a supermajority of the states (again not likely), it would take years to become legislation. It would not apply to President Trump, which was the immediate problem. That concern remained. And then should the president in office decide to do what Trump had done as president and ignore the Constitution not much would have been achieved.

There may be other additional solutions that could be tried. What they are and how effective they might prove to be has yet to be decided.

TRUMP'S DEFENDERS

Most of Trump's defenders emphasized his public image as a successful billionaire businessman taking on the entrenched politicians of a corrupt and elitist Washington in the drive to "drain the swamp." In their view, he was opposed by the "Deep State" and the "lying media," and he was victimized and his efforts blocked to the extent possible. They saw Trump as fighting on in pursuing representation for average Americans.

It was an effective message and served to increase the numbers of his supporters and solidify their resolve. It was delivered by Trump in rallies, press conferences, and ad hoc briefings of reporters as well as executive actions that seemed to make little sense by themselves. His presidency played to his base in the electorate.

There are a number of books and articles defending Trump and his actions, praising his policies and approach, and attacking the hostility to his presidency. Historian and conservative political commentator, Victor David Hanson, can serve as an example of what were taken to be the more substantive defenses. Hanson makes the argument that Trump, a successful billionaire with no government experience, took office to fight the coastal elites who controlled national politics. He would represent previously unrepresented working people and Middle America and he would end corruption in politics. Trump as an amateur politician had a highly successful four-year term, in his eyes, and set the country on a much-needed alternative path. Trump performed a necessary service. Hanson considered the Trump presidency to be a major success and Trump to rank as among the most important presidents in history (Hanson 2020).

And if that is not enough, for the really committed, there is Nick Adams's *Trump and Churchill: Defenders of Western Civilization* (New York: Simon & Schuster, 2020).

Fox News, in reaching the most people and in the content of what it passes on, was the most effective and influential Trump promoter.

Defenders of Trump and his behavior accept his argument that his mission had been to reinvent America and that he did. Now the fight would be to keep America great.

Such defenses leave a few things out. They do not deal with Trump's mental health. Implicitly they accept his comeback to questions about his mental condition that he was a "very stable genius."

Most also leave out his personal attacks. John McCain spent five years in a Hanoi prison and when given the chance refused to leave until all prisoners were freed. For Trump, McCain was not a war hero. He said he liked people who were not captured (McCain was shot down over Hanoi during the Vietnam War and was severely injured). Trump mocked a *New York Times* reporter with a handicap and the Gold Star parents of a son killed in the Middle East war. He told onlookers to look at the face of Carly Fiorina and asked if anyone could vote for it (Fiorina was an opponent in the 2016 primaries). He compared another opponent, Dr. Ben Carson, to a child molester (before later appointing him to his Cabinet). And he criticized all women who opposed him, beginning with Speaker Nancy Pelosi, as "nasty" (this was a universal characterization followed by other insults).

This was the basis for a 2016 campaign that saw Trump in the primaries beat up to 17 opponents with a range of conservative issue appeals. Combined with an exceptionally active campaign style and a demagogic, substantively-other-worldly message, this won him the presidency. FBI director James Comey's timing in announcing the reopening of the agency's investigation of Trump's opponent Hillary Clinton's email use immediately prior to the election, a Trump campaign issue, and Clinton's strategic blunders helped also. In 2020, using much the same approach, Trump received over 74 million votes, the most ever except for Joe Biden.

SUMMARY

Donald Trump's "not-normal" behavior defined his presidency. It led to and demonstrated his failings as a leader who took no responsibility for his actions or failures to act, and how incompetent and unfit he was to serve as president.

Historian William E. Leuchtenburg, author of *The American President* (2015), wrote: "[T]he American presidency in the twentieth century became a much more powerful institution than it had ever been before and . . . that aggrandizement was brought about by the men who inhabited the White House . . . . I am persuaded that twentieth century America was significantly shaped by its presidents" (Leuchtenburg 2015, xiii–xiv).

The creation of the imperial president has carried over into the twenty-first century and has undergone an expansion of its powers.

Leuchtenburg was aware of the darker side of the presidency. "Too often, they have wasted the lives of our children in foreign ventures that should never have been undertaken . . . when they overreach, they need to be checked" (Leuchtenburg 2015, 812). Restraints on the use of their powers have seldom been effective.

Leuchtenburg concludes that the presidency is "what the President thinks it is" (Leuchtenburg 2015, xiv).

Donald Trump would agree.

CONCLUSION

The hope of course was that another Trump would not emerge and with him or her, "the media's acquiescence, confusion and exhaustion [that] have eroded the country's institutions, public life, and national spirit" that marked his four years in office (*New Yorker* 2020, 67).

As for lessons to be learned from Donald Trump's presidency, there were many. For one, not all presidents attempt to advance the welfare of the people. For another, a mentally unstable person can be elected to the presidency. At present, there is no effective way to deal with such a situation. The Twenty-fifth Amendment has proven ineffective. A constitutional remedy would be a first step. The damage to the country such presidents can cause is virtually limitless. Alternative options for dealing with such situations have been put forward by members of Congress and critics of the present system. Getting them through the Congress is another matter. In fact, realizing any long-range changes, given the attention placed on the immediate politics of the day, is unlikely.

The Trump presidency can serve as an example as to the extent to which corruption, self-aggrandizement, and abuse of office can be taken by a president. Priorities should be in developing standards for behavior and the means for effectively removing such a disabled president from office (Lee 2019). Holding presidents in or out of office legally accountable for crimes committed should be an accelerated extension of the rule of law. The practice of the Department of Justice and the FBI in that a sitting president cannot be indicted is nothing more than an opinion in 1973 in a memo written by an assistant attorney general in the Office of Legal Counsel (Maddow and Yarvitz 2020). The removal process needs to be codified in law. The American tradition of forgive-and-forget or issuing a pardon once a president leaves office encourages future abuses. Taking accountability seriously as an act against the state is a protective move long overdue.

Such changes might not prevent all future problems from developing but they should introduce into the system a level of responsibility now missing.

The introduction of needed reforms would make it more difficult for a Trump to win or to stay in office. The abolition of the Electoral College and the reliance on the popular vote in presidential elections would help. So would basic and balanced Congressional districts; effective public control of Big Money financing in elections; an enlarged and nationally representative

Supreme Court and one with term limits of five years;[6] the prosecution of criminal acts by a president in or out of office; an effective process for judging a president's inability, mental or physical, to meet the demands of office and an effective and quick means of removal from office; a multiparty system more closely representative of the variety of voters' views and one that provides alternatives to an authoritarian party in a two-party system that promotes autocracy and blocks legislative operations; and safeguards against politically appointed apparatchiks in the General Services Administration and other federal agencies from preventing the orderly postelection transitions of administrations.

Trump will likely play the role of president-in-waiting and critic-in-chief of the Biden administration, which in turn faces a massive job in reconstructing the nation. Biden would be attempting this with a House of Representatives with a reduced margin of Democrats and a divided Senate. Trump's four-year attack on the legitimacy and professionalism of the electoral process, uncalled for as it was, has been taken seriously by a large part of the population. It is one more hurdle Biden had to deal with.

The potential for a coup creates the nation's greatest problem. The previously unimaginable threat to attack the Capitol to void the election illustrated the magnitude of the problem. The full resources of the government would be needed to meet and suppress the challenge. This was the nation's number one existential threat. It is likely to continue well into the future. The effort to bring unity through a reasoned approach in meeting the policy needs of greatest concern may be illusionary under such conditions.

The consequences of the seditious assault on the Capitol were enormous. At a minimum, both the immediate and long-run future of the nation's democratic commitments became uncertain. The concept of a coup could become a permanent part of the American political landscape and the reality a continuing threat to the nation's democratic order.

Institutions by themselves are not adequate safeguards for limiting the behavior of elected authoritarians. Checks and balances and democratic norms do not deter a move to a more authoritarian political system. If this continues to be the case, the foundations of the Madisonian system of government may not be accepted as uncritically as they largely have been and may not lead to the complacency they once did. In fact, the institutions of democracy can be adapted, mobilized and weaponized to be used by would-be dictators in the transition to an authoritarian state. "The tragic paradox of the electoral route to authoritarianism is that democracy's assassins use the very institutions of democracy—gradually, subtly, and even legally—to kill it" (Levitsky and Ziblatt 2018).

Robert Dallek, author of studies of John F. Kennedy, Richard M. Nixon, and Lyndon B. Johnson, raises questions as to whether there was an unanticipated convergence of circumstances that produced a Donald Trump and thus the threat created to democracy will pass or if his presidency resulted from something more deeply embedded in American society.

"[A]ll of us [have] to wonder how we got here, and whether in the face of this unsettling moment in American history our democracy is reaching an untimely end, or [if] we are just passing through another of our episodic downturns that have unsettled our democratic Republic before" (Dallek 2020, 236).

The questions posed by Masha Gessen, who experienced growing up with the totalitarianism of the Soviet Union, are the right ones. After 9/11, restrictions on personal liberties and individual rights increased and after the Great Recession of 2007–2008 economic inequality increased. Gessen asks if we again will react by choosing "solutions that exacerbate the root problems" or "[W]ill we commit ourselves to reinvention?" (Gessen 2020, 233).[7]

As indicated, the demands a democracy makes on its citizenry are great. The rewards of the system are great also. The future, as far as can be seen, is likely to test the nation's resiliency and its commitment to a way of life, that while far from perfect has served it well.

NOTES

1. Carl Bernstein of CNN was known for his role with Bob Woodward, both with the *Washington Post*, in exposing President Nixon's role in planning the Watergate break-in. The revelations led to Nixon's resignation. Bernstein revealed Trump's lack of preparation, ignorance of substantive content, and promotion of his own interests in dealing with world leaders. He reported that those officials who most often were with Trump in his calls felt he was "delusional." They described how "he continued to believe that he could either charm, jawbone or bully almost any foreign leader into capitulating to his will, and often pursued goals more attuned to his family or his business agenda than what many of his senior advisors considered the national interest." Trump "took special delight in trashing former Presidents George W. Bush and Barack Obama" and in these calls to other countries' leaders suggested that "dealing with him . . . would be far more fruitful than during previous administrations." An official familiar with such calls with foreign leaders quoted Trump: "They didn't know BS." See Carl Bernstein, "From Pandering to Putin to Abusing Allies and Ignoring His Own Advisers, Trump's Phone Calls Alarm US Officials," *CNN*, June 30, 2020. https://www.cnn.com/2020/06/29/politics/trump-phone-calls-national-sec urity-concerns/index.html.

2. The religious and gender status practices of the People of Praise included their use of the term "Handmaiden." When Margaret Atwood wrote a novel presumably based on the sect in 1965, the title "woman leader" was adopted by the community to replace that of "Handmaiden."

3. On Hitler's rise to power see Richard J. Evans, *The Coming of the Third Reich* (New York: Penguin Books, 2004); and Richard Overy, *The Dictators* (New York: W.W. Norton, 2006).

4. Anne Applebaum develops the appeal of authoritarianism. The political system is based on a simple belief system that promises loyal supporters power and wealth. Conspiracy theories, a polarized politics and party system, enablers in government, and a compliant social media outlet all contribute to the transition to autocracy.

5. For a discussion of the erosion over time of institutions and public life leading to a devolution of democratic norms, see the *New Yorker*. 2020. Review of Eric Alterman, *Lying in State* (New York: Basic Books, 2020). September 7, P. 67. https://www.newyorker.com/magazine/2020/09/14/life-of-a-klansman-lying-in-state-little-scratch-and-the-queen-of-tuesday.

6. For further reading on possible reforms to the Supreme Court, see James MacGregor Burns, *Packing the Court: The Rise of Judicial Power and the Coming Crisis of the Supreme Court* (New York: Penguin Press, 2009); and Carl Hulse, *Confirmation Bias: Inside Washington's War Over the Supreme Court, From Scalia's Death to Justice Kavanagh* (New York: HarperCollins, 2019).

7. For further readings on democracy, see John Keane, *The Life and Death of Democracy* (New York: W.W. Norton, 2009); Arthur Paulson, *Donald Trump and the Prospect for Democracy: An Unprecedented President in an Age of Polarization* (Lanham: Lexington Books, 2018); and John W. Dean with Bob Altemeyer, *Authoritarian Nightmare: Trump and His Followers* (Brooklyn: Melville House, 2020).

REFERENCES

Applebaum, Anne. 2020. *Twilight of Democracy*. New York: Doubleday.

Barstow, David, Susanne Craig, Russ Buettner and Megan Twohey. 2016. "Donald Trump Tax Records Show He Could Have Avoided Taxes for Nearly Two Decades, The Times Found." *New York Times*. October 1. https://www.nytimes.com/2016/10/02/us/politics/donald-trump-taxes.html

Barstow, David, Susanne Craig, and Russ Buettner. 2018. "Trump Engaged in Suspect Tax Schemes as He Reaped Riches From His Father." *New York Times*. October 2. https://www.nytimes.com/interactive/2018/10/02/us/politics/donald-trump-tax-schemes-fred-trump.html

BBC. 2020. "Five Shocking Passages In Mary Trump's Tell-All Book." *BBC*.com July 14. https://www.bbc.com/news/world-us-canada-53328654

Bennett, John T. 2019. "Trump: House Dems Moving Toward Impeachment Because 'They Can't Stop Me.'" *RollCall.com*. September 24. https://www.rollcall.com/2019/09/24/trump- house-dems-moving-toward-impeachment-because-they-cant-stop-me/

Brice-Sadler, Michael. 2020. "While Bemoaning Mueller Probe, Trump Falsely Says The Constitution Gives Him the 'Right to Do Whatever I Want.'"

Washington Post. July 23. https://www.washingtonpost.com/politics/2019/07/23 /trump-falsely-tells-auditorium-full-teens-constitution-gives-him-right-do-whate ver-i-want/

Broadwater, Luke and Catie Edmondson. 2020. "Postal Service Has Paid DeJoy's Former Company $286 Million Since 2013." *New York Times.* September 2.

——— and Michael S. Schmidt. 2021. "Ex-Security Officials Spread Blame for Failures of Capitol Riot." *New York Times.* February 24.

Bueno de Mesquita, Bruce and Alastair Smith. 2012. *The Dictator's Handbook.* New York: PublicAffairs.

Buettner, Russ, Susanne Craig and David Barstow. 2018. "11 Takeaways From The Times's Investigation Into Trump's Wealth." *New York Times.* October 2. https:/ /www.nytimes.com/2018/10/02/us/politics/donald-trump-wealth-fred-trump.html

——— and Susanne Craig. 2019. "Decade in the Red: Trump Tax Figures Show Over $1 Billion in Business Losses." *New York Times.* May 8. https://www.nyt imes.com/interactive/2019/05/07/us/politics/donald-trump-taxes.html

———, Susanne Craig and Mike McIntire. 2020. "President's Taxes Chart Chronic Losses, Audit Battle and Income Tax Avoidance." *New York Times.* September 28. https://www.nytimes.com/interactive/2020/09/27/us/donald-trump-taxes .html

Bump, Philip. 2019. "If Trump Shoots Someone Dead on Fifth Avenue, Many Supporters Would Call His Murder Trial Biased." *Washington Post.* March 14. https://www.washingtonpost.com/politics/2019/03/14/if-trump-shot-someone-de ad-fifth-avenue-many-supporters-would-call-his-murder-trial-biased/

Cai, Weiyi, Annie Daniel, Lazaro Gamio and Alicia Parlapiano. 2021. "Impeachment Results: How Democrats and Republicans Voted." *New York Times.* January 13. https://www.nytimes.com/interactive/2021/01/13/us/politics/trump-second-imp eachment-vote.html

Collins, Kaitlan and Jim Acosta. 2021. "Trump's COVID-19 Condition Was So Concerning That Doctors Considered Putting Him On A Ventilator, Source Confirms." *CNN.com.* February 11.

Cook, Ken. 2020. "After COVID-19 Flip-Flops, CDC Director Must Resign." *CommonDreams.org.* September 21. https://www.commondreams.org/views/ 2020/09/21/after-covid-19-flip-flops-cdc-director-must-resign

Costa, Robert and Philip Rucker. 2020. "Woodward Book: Trump Says He Knew Coronavirus Was 'Deadly' And Worse Than The Flu While Intentionally Misleading Americans." *Washington Post.* September 9.

Dallek, Robert. 2020. *How Did We Get Here?* New York: HarperCollins.

Dean, John with Bob Altemeyer. 2020. *Authoritarian Nightmare: Trump and His Followers* Brooklyn: Melville House.

Dellinger, Walter. 2018. "Indicting A President Is Not Foreclosed: The Complex History." https://www.lawfareblog.com/indicting-president-not-foreclosed-co mplex-history

DelReal, Jose A. 2016. "Trump's Latest Plan Would Target At Least 5 Million Undocumented Immigrants for Deportation." *Washington Post.* September 1.

Drucker, Jesse and David Enrich, "Kushner Deal Draws Scrutiny." 2020. *New York Times* (appearing in the *Boston Globe*). August 4. D2. https://fcced.com/deutsche-probe-kushner-trump-personal-banker-38201426/

Enrich, David. 2020c. *Dark Towers: Deutsch Bank, Donald Trump, and an Epic Trail of Destruction*. New York: Custom House/HarperCollins Publishers.

———, Russ Buettner, Mike McIntire and Susanne Craig. 2020a. "The President's Taxes: How Trump Maneuvered His Way Out of Trouble in Chicago." *New York Times*. October 27. (Updated January 8, 2021). https://www.nytimes.com/2020/10/27/business/trump-chicago-taxes.html

———, Ben Protess, William K. Rashbaum and Benjamin Weiser. 2020b. "Trump's Bank Was Subpoenaed, Signaling Broader Criminal Case." *New York Times*. August 6. A1. https://www.nytimes.com/2020/08/05/nyregion/trump-taxes-vance-deutsche-bank.html

Evans, Richard J. 2004. *The Coming of the Third Reich*. New York: Penguin Books, 2004.

Feeney, Megan. 2020. "Trump Has Appointed Second-Most Federal Judges Through December 1st of a President's Fourth Year." *Ballotpedia News*. December 5. https://news.ballotpedia.org/2020/12/05/trump-has-appointed-second-most-federal-judges-through-december-1-of-a-presidents-fourth-year/

Gerhardt, Michael J. 2019. *The Federal Impeachment Process*, 3rd ed. Chicago: University of Chicago Press. x.

Gessen, Masha. 2020. *Surviving Autocracy*. New York: Riverhead Books/Penguin Books.

Glasser, Susan B. 2021. "Trump Impeachment II Was Just As Awful As the Original." January 14. https://www.newyorker.com/news/letter-from-trumps-washington/trump-impeachment-ii-was-just-as-awful-as-the-original

Graham, David A. 2020. "Trump Failed to Protect America." *The Atlantic*. December 18. https://www.theatlantic.com/ideas/archive/2020/12/trump-failed-protect-america/617429/

Greenwood, Max. 2021. "Trump Campaign Had Paid $2.7M To Organizers Of Rally Ahead Of Capitol Riot: Report." *The Hill.com*. January 22.

Hanson, Victor Davis. 2020. *The Case for Trump*. New York: Hachette Book Group/Basic Books.

Hong, Nicole and William K. Rashbaum. 2020. "Trump is Not Entitled to Details of Tax Returns Inquiry, D.A. Says." *New York Times*. August 14. https://www.nytimes.com/2020/08/14/nyregion/donald-trump-taxes-cyrus-vance.html

Independent Counsel. 1998. *The Starr Report*. Rocklin, CA: Prima Publishing.

Kanno-Youngs, Zolan and Michael D. Shear. 2021. "Trump Loyalists across Homeland Security Could Vex Biden's Immigration Policies. *New York Times*. February 3.

Kelly, Meg, Joyce Sohyun Lee and Jon Swaine. 2020. "Partially Blinded by Police." *Washington Post*. July 14.

Kranish, Michael. 2020. "Donald Trump, Facing Financial Ruin, Sought Control of His Elderly Father's Estate. The Family Fight Was Epic." *Washington Post*.

September 27. https://www.washingtonpost.com/graphics/2020/politics/donald-trump-father-will

Laqueur, Walter. 1976. *Fascism: A Reader's Guide*. Berkeley: University of California.

Lee, Bandy X. ed. 2017. 2019. *The Dangerous Case of Donald Trump*. New York: Thomas Dunne Books.

Leuchtenburg, William E. 2015. *The American President: From Teddy Roosevelt to Bill Clinton*. Oxford, UK: Oxford University Press.

Levin, Tim. 2021. "An Associate of Rudy Giuliani Told A Former CIA Officer That a Trump Pardon Would 'Cost $2 Million': Report." *Business Insider*. January 17. https://www.businessinsider.com/giuliani-associate-reportedly-trump-pardon-costs-2-million-nyt-2021-1

Levitsky, Steven and Daniel Ziblatt. 2018. *How Democracies Die*. New York: Crown Publishing Group. 8.

Lifton, Robert Jay. 2017. "Forward: Our Witness to Malignant Narcissism." In Bandy X. Lee, ed. *The Dangerous Case of Donald Trump*. New York: Thomas Dunne Books/St. Martin's Press. xv–xix.

Macagnone, Michael. 2019. "This Obscure 1973 Memo Kept Mueller from Considering A Trump Indictment." https://rollcall.com/2019/05/29/this-obscure-1973-memo-kept-mueller-from-considering-a-trump-indictment/

Maddow, Rachel and Michael Yarvitz. 2020. *Bag Man*. New York: Crown.

Maraniss, David. 2012. "Obama and Romney Both Come From a (sic) Ancestry of Polygamy." *Washington Post*. April 12. https://www.washingtonpost.com/opinions/obama-and-romney-both-come-from-a-ancestry-of-polygamy/2012/04/12/gIQA3TI8CT_story.html

McIntire, Mike, Russ Buettner and Susanne Craig. 2020. "How Reality-TV Fame Handed Trump A $427 Million Lifeline." *New York Times*. September 28. https://www.nytimes.com/interactive/2020/09/28/us/donald-trump-taxes-apprentice.html?action=click&module=RelatedLinks&pgtype=Article.

Nadler, Jerrold. 2019. "Impeachment of Donald J. Trump President of the United States." Report of the Committee on the Judiciary, House of Representatives. 116th Congress, 1st Session. December 13.

New York Times Editorial Board. 2020a. "Trump's Messy Divorce From New York." *New York Times*. September 26. https://www.nytimes.com/2020/09/26/opinion/sunday/trump-cuomo-new-york-revenge.html

New York Times Editorial Board. 2020b. "The Supreme Court Lets Trump Run Out the Clock." *New York Times*. July 9. https://www.nytimes.com/2020/07/09/opinion/supreme-court-trump-taxes.html

New Yorker. "Briefly Noted." *Newyorker.com*. September 14. 67. https://www.newyorker.com/magazine/2020/09/14/life-of-a-klansman-lying-in-state-little-scratch-and-the-queen-of-tuesday

Overy, Richard. 2006. *The Dictators*. New York: W.W. Norton & Company.

Pilkington, Ed. 2021. "Seditionaries: FBI Net Closes On Maga Mob That Stormed The Capitol." *TheGuardian.com*. February 6.

Reimann, Nicolas. 2021. "Report: Trump's COVID-19 Infection Was So Severe Officials Thought He Might Need A Ventilator." *Forbes.com*. February 11.

Restuccia, Andrew. 2021. "Biden Says U.S. Struck Deals For 200 Million More COVID-19 Vaccine Doses." *Wall Street Journal. wsj.com*. February 12.

Rosenberg, Matthew and Jim Rutenberg. 2021. "Key Takeaways from Trump's Attempt To Overthrow The Election." *NewYorkTimes.com*. February 1.

Rousselle, Christine. 2020. "Judge Amy Coney Barrett's Charismatic Catholicism – Who Are the People of Praise?" *CatholicNewsAgency.com*. September 19. https://www.catholicnewsagency.com/news/judge-amy-barrett-criticized-for-charismatic-affiliation--who-are-the-people-of-praise-17632

Sanger, David E. 2020. "Trump's Attempts To Overturn The Election Are Unparalleled In U.S. History." *NYTimes.com*. November 19.

Schedler, Andreas, ed. 2006. *Electoral Authoritarianism*. Boulder: Lynne Rienner.

Schiff, Adam. 2020. "Concluding Statement Transcript: Trump Impeachment Trial." January 24. https://www.rev.com/blog/transcripts/adam-schiff-friday-concluding-statement-transcript-trump-impeachment-trial

Schmid, John. 1999. "Deutsche Bank Linked to Auschwitz Funding." *New York Times*. February 5. https://www.nytimes.com/1999/02/05/news/deutsche-bank-linked-to-auschwitz-funding.html

Snyder, Timothy. 2021. "The American Abyss." *New York Times*. January 9. https://www.nytimes.com/2021/01/09/magazine/trump-coup.html.

———. 2017. *On Tyranny*. New York: Tim Duggan Books. 32.

Soboroff, Jacob. 2020. *Separated: Inside an American Tragedy*. New York: Custom House/HarperCollins Publishers.

Southern Poverty Law Center. 2020. "Family Separation Under the Trump Administration – A Timeline." Southern Poverty Law Center. June 17. https://www.splcenter.org/news/2020/06/17/family-separation-under-trump-administration-timeline

Stillman, Sarah. 2021. "The Race to Dismantle Trump's Immigration Policies." *New Yorker*. February 1. https://www.newyorker.com/magazine/2021/02/08/the-race-to-dismantle-trumps-immigration-policies

Thompson, Ginger. 2018. "Listen to Children Who've Just Been Separated From Their Parents at the Border." *ProPublica*. June 18. Retrieved June 19, 2018. https://www.propublica.org/article/children-separated-from-parents-border-patrol-cbp-trump-immigration-policy.

Trump, Mary L. 2020. *Too Much and Never Enough: How My Family Created the World's Most Dangerous Man*. New York: Simon & Schuster.

Trump, Donald J. with Tony Schwartz, 1987. *The Art of the Deal*. New York: Ballantine Books.

Weissman, Andrew. 2020. *Where Law Ends: Inside the Mueller Investigation*. New York: Random House.

Woodward, Bob. 2018. *Fear: Trump in the White House*. Front Matter (told to Bob Woodward and Bob Costa, March 31, 2016).

———. 2020. *Rage*. New York: Simon & Schuster.

Chapter 2

Donald Trump

A Personal and Political Profile and Impact on the Presidential Election of 2020

William Crotty

INTRODUCTION

Donald Trump's emotional stability and his physical health were issues from the beginning of his presidency to the end. His fitness for the job in this context was the most persistent of concerns throughout his years in office. The ideological blindness and loyalty of his supporters given his actions in office many found difficult to understand. These issues set the context for the 2020 election, easily one of the most critical in the country's history. The issue at stake, as many were to say, was the continuation of America's democracy.

THE PRESIDENT AS THE PROBLEM

Donald Trump dominated American politics. He had served for four years but it seemed like considerably more. His health, physical and more so mental, was constantly questioned and his erratic, even chaotic, presidency was often explained in these terms. He had fundamentally changed American politics, setting it in a direction no president in the history of the nation had ever contemplated. His reelection in the 2020 contest, as many from Barack Obama to Mary Trump had warned, could have resulted in an authoritarian country and a political system virtually no one wanted.

It made for a tense time, one with the country's fundamental direction the principal question underlying the election.

The following section looks at Trump's health and how it affected his stewardship of the presidential office. It assesses the 2020 election, indicated as one of the most important the nation has experienced, identifies the coalition of interests supporting Trump and his opponent, Democrat Joe Biden, and explains why Biden, with a message of unity, rebuilding the country and returning it to its ideological roots of liberty, justice, and the rule of law, won.

THE PHYSICAL HEALTH OF DONALD TRUMP

Donald Trump's physical health much like his mental health was questioned since he first entered the presidential race. When his health and physical fitness became a hotter topic than Trump found comfortable, he acted. He released a letter in December 2015 from his personal doctor attesting to his good condition. Excerpts from the letter drove the point home:

> December 4, 2015
>
> [H]is blood pressure, 110/65, and laboratory test results were astonishingly excellent . . . .
>
> His physical strength and stamina are extraordinary . . . .
>
> His cardiovascular status is excellent . . . .
>
> If elected, Mr. Trump, I can state unequivocally, will be the healthiest individual ever selected to the presidency . . .
>
> Signed:
>
> Harold N. Bornstein, M.D., F.A.C.G.
>
> Department of Medicine, Section of Gastroenterology
>
> Lenox Hill Hospital, New York, NY

Impressive! Except the doctor never wrote it. Trump dictated the contents of the letter to the doctor, had him sign it, and then Trump released it.

The stunt should have disqualified Trump from the presidency if there were any rules that applied. It should also have disqualified him in the eyes of voters. But it did not. It would be among the first of such incidents in a presidency full of them (Hamblin 2016).

Trump and Bornstein had a later falling out. Two months later, the physician told the *New York Times* that two Trump aides staged what he called "a raid" of his Manhattan office and removed all of Trump's medical files (Rogers and Altman 2018).

Trump burnished what he referred to as his "Superman" image by reporting that he slept only 4 hours a night, excelled at sports in his youth, had hidden reserves of energy, and enjoyed outstandingly good to excellent health.

His relentless campaigning lent credence to his energy claims. The rest was at best exaggerations of his true physical condition. His annual reports indicated an older man, considered medically overweight (243 pounds) who was known to enjoy fast food and who took pride in not exercising (Karni and Altman 2019). Nevertheless Trump's White House physician, Dr. Ronny Jackson, later to run into problems for his personal conduct, praised Trump's genes saying that if he had eaten healthier he might live to be 200.

Trump had made a sudden trip to the emergency room at Walter Reed Hospital in November 2019. Rumors circulated of a stroke or other serious condition such as a heart attack. The purpose of the visit was never made clear. Trump claimed it was a continuation of his annual physical assessment. The White House Medical Unit has the capability of performing routine medical procedures and tests, so the trip to Walter Reed was viewed as indicative of more serious medical issues. Vice President Pence was reported to have been put on "standby" should Trump lose consciousness, be sedated, or undergo surgery. The procedure was a normal precaution (Leblanc 2020). The Saturday trip to Walter Reed was his ninth visit there as president. It had not been listed on his schedule for the day and no details were released (Vigdor 2020). Trump later denied he had any medical conditions or illnesses. He told the White House physician to make public a statement supporting him and claimed the story about Pence on standby was not true (Choi 2020).

On a trip to West Point to deliver a commencement address, Trump had trouble walking down a short ramp and he needed both hands to hold a drink of water (Haberman 2020). Both incidents were commented on extensively and continued to raise fears as to his physical condition. There were other times when concerns about his physical health arose. During a December 2017 televised speech about the Middle East, Trump seemed to slur his words. He underwent an ultrasound on his carotid arteries in search of a clinical explanation. After all of these incidents, Trump or his staff either made no comment, indicated everything was fine or provided a questionable response (Dr. Jackson said that Sudafed taken for nasal congestion might have caused the word slurring).

Ultimately Trump was admitted to Walter Reed with COVID-19 and judging by what is known of the number and types of medications administered and the comments of his chief of staff, former Republican congressman Mark Meadows, the situation was serious. Still Trump's preoccupation with image continued. While still a patient, he left the hospital briefly to ride in a closed station wagon (the windows were sealed shut, exposing his Secret Service agents to the virus) so he could wave to the cameras, the press, and onlookers before returning to his bed.

He survived the virus. He had received an experimental drug treatment that the public had no access to. Trump took pride in his recovery and had considered wearing a "Superman" T-shirt that he would reveal after ripping open a button-down shirt upon his exit from the hospital (Folley 2020). He decided against it.

While Trump's health had always been a concern, the image he went to great lengths to present was the one to be found in the original letter he wrote for his doctor to sign.

He requested and took a cognitive screening assessment at Walter Reed Medical Center. Trump began to challenge Biden's health and mental acuity. He dared Biden to try to match what he believed to be his own outstanding standards of health and repeatedly said Biden should take the cognitive test he took. Trump, 74 years old, made an issue of Biden's age (77) and that he would be the oldest man to ever be elected president for a first term. (Ronald Reagan was elected to his second term at 73 and served until he was 77.) He repeatedly mocked Biden for wearing a mask, ridiculing its size (it was a standard size) and for staying "in his basement" rather than being on the campaign trail as he was. Biden emphasized that he was following CDC guidance, and his campaign events were much smaller given the social distancing requirements he followed. Conversely, Trump's events typically featured unmasked crowds of people standing shoulder to shoulder. Trump also mocked Biden as "Sleepy Joe" and claimed the former vice president and he should both take drug tests before the fall debates (Baker 2020). He had done the same thing in the race against Hillary Clinton in 2016 (Allen and Parnes 2017; Brazile 2017; and Crotty, ed., 2018).

It was projected that Donald Trump's behavior would get more unhinged as he came under increasing pressure. How far he would go and what he might do was unknown.

Trump had been seen by most mental health experts as having an extreme personality disorder that could lead to dangerous actions. It was questioned whether he had the ability to distinguish between reality and fantasy. His behavior after returning to the White House from his hospitalization for COVID-19 and the powerful steroid (Dexamethasone) he had received for the virus at Walter Reed raised questions anew as to potential changes in his mental condition and what it would mean for the nation.

Trump had received repeated dosages of strong drugs while hospitalized. One (Regeneron) was an experimental drug that required FDA approval. The unusual drug cocktail he took had had no experimental trial record as to potential side effects (Abel and Lazar 2020). In addition to the largely untested combination of three strong drugs, the steroid Dexamethasone alone can result in an unavoidable, altered mental state (a not uncommon side effect of powerful steroids) (Thomas and Rabin 2020). Euphoria, mood swings, personality changes, and aggravation of existing emotional instability or psychotic tendencies are listed as "warnings" for the drug (RxList 2020). It was thought to possibly account for Trump's increasingly out-of-control behavior, such as his briefly leaving Walter Reed for the car ride to wave to reporters and bystanders. This was at a time when best medical practice called for COVID-19 patients to be cared for in a "negative pressure room," constructed to contain the virus inside the patient's room to protect other patients and health care workers.

The day he was discharged, Trump stationed himself on a White House balcony overlooking the assembled crowd and dramatically saluted the flag, resembling photographs of the dictators of the 1920s and 1930s, Mussolini and Hitler.

The early discharge that Trump insisted on caused concern in the medical community as being premature (Baker and Haberman 2020a). His behavior became more oddly aggressive. He had begun repeatedly attacking Michigan governor Gretchen Whitmer. She was the intended victim of a plot by 14 members of extremist hate groups. They had been training for months to take over the Michigan State Capitol, take her prisoner, try her in a vigilante court, and then execute her for closing down the state in the pandemic. They were arrested by the FBI and state police.

Trump praised the domestic terrorists, stating that the governor should meet with the armed invaders and work out a deal. Rather than denounce those who had been arrested, he condemned the governor for shutting the state down. He had tweeted earlier "Liberate Michigan," taken as a spur to attacks such as the ones against Governor Whitmer (Bogel-Burroughs et al. 2020). He continued to support the white supremacist movement, as he had done in Charlottesville, Kenosha, and elsewhere. He continued to minimize the threat and deadliness of COVID-19 after leaving the hospital, saying he felt better than he had in years and people should not be fearful (Baker and Haberman 2020b).

"Don't be afraid of COVID-19. Don't let it dominate your life," Trump had tweeted as he left Walter Reed Medical Center on October 5, 2020 (there were 210,000 reported pandemic deaths in the United States at that time). He continued his large gatherings (2,000 were invited to the White House to celebrate his return, masks optional). His actions became more erratic and risky: he made on-again/off-again statements regarding his intentions to participate in the second debate (the debate ultimately was cancelled when Trump refused to do it remotely); he returned early to the campaign trail and the mass rallies he loved while his health remained in question; he exposed his staff to the virus; he returned to normal activities 10 days after becoming symptomatic (the CDC guidelines were to wait 20 days); he called the Democratic vice presidential candidate, Kamala Harris, a "monster" and a "communist"; he claimed that he contracted the virus from a meeting with Gold Star families in which he and others did not wear masks; and he and his doctors refused to clarify how long he had been diagnosed with the virus, important in establishing whether enough time had passed for him to no longer be a threat to spread the virus.

Dozens of staff in the White House with whom Trump and others inter-acted before and after his hospital stay came down with the virus. He continued to hold White House "superspreader" events and rallies of supporters exposing those in attendance to the virus. He abruptly cut off talks on government aid to individuals to help meet living costs while unemployed, an action the Federal Reserve chair warned would have "tragic" consequences. He later attempted to restart the talks but the indecision and lack of will shown ensured nothing would be done until the new administration took office (Edelman and Leung 2020).

Trump claimed after his discharge that catching the coronavirus was "a blessing from God." He portrayed the as-yet-unproven drug cocktail developed by the pharmaceutical company Regeneron he had been given as a miracle cure. He promised to make it free to anyone who needed it, although months later monoclonal antibodies such as those Trump received were very scarce with limited production underway (Haberman and Thomas). Shortly after Trump's promise, the Regeneron CEO commented to the media that any recovery Trump had would constitute a single "case report" and not be the definitive evidence that large randomized clinical trials could establish (Manfredi 2020).

The president appeared to be in the most unstable shape of his presidency to that point, the most enraged and impulsive in his decision-making and potentially of the greatest danger to the nation.

The coming of the virus had complicated Trump's reelection drive and his becoming a victim of COVID-19 himself made the situation more difficult.

Trump's personal doctor, Sean Conley, had managed his medical care at the White House and then assumed duties as press spokesman reporting on Trump's status after he was admitted to Walter Reed Hospital on October 2, a month before Election Day. Conley's media updates were brief, incomplete, and contained contradictory information. Trump's intensive, experimental treatment regimen did not match what medical experts expected from someone with the mild symptoms described by Conley. The medical updates were not well received and raised suspicions that Trump had been more ill than was reported (Baker and Haberman 2020c).

Conley continued to selectively report the results of tests and Trump's condition, leaving out information that would explain discrepancies in medications and lab results or could have given a clearer idea of Trump's prognosis. He refused to supply negative information. Conley held the rank of Commander in the Navy as well as serving as Trump's doctor. Given his Navy rank, he was under Trump's authority as commander-in-chief.

Trump himself later refused to say when he had last tested negative before his COVID-19 diagnosis or whether he had been tested the day of his first presidential debate with Joe Biden on September 29, as the Commission on

Presidential Debates had required. It was noted that Trump and his entourage had arrived at the debate venue late, raising suspicions of an intentional late arrival to avoid testing.

One of the major superspreader events was a ceremony held in the White House Rose Garden where Trump introduced his new Supreme Court pick, Amy Coney Barrett. It generated coronavirus cases among top officials who had been in attendance, largely unmasked. The White House made little to no effort to trace the contacts of guests and staff members at that event in order to minimize the spread of the virus (Mandavilli and Tulley 2020). Trump might have known he was positive at the time he debated Biden, raising the possibility of exposing Biden to the virus. He had not acknowledged having COVID-19 until Friday October 2, the day he was admitted to Walter Reed and three days after the debate.

Matters would get worse during the transition period and especially with the seditionists taking over the Capitol in the effort to institute a coup. But these were in the future at this point. It would prove to be the most substantial attempt during the Trump presidency to overturn the election results and guarantee his continuing in the presidency.

THE PRESIDENT AS THE PROBLEM: THE MENTAL HEALTH OF DONALD TRUMP

Was Donald Trump Mentally Ill?

Mary Trump, who should know, was clear on the subject. In her view, Trump was mentally and emotionally unstable and unfit for the office of president. He was a prisoner of his family upbringing. His continuing in office would be "the end of American Democracy" (Mary Trump 2020, 17).

"I have no problem calling Donald a narcissist" (Mary Trump 2020, 13). She also indicated it was likely Trump had other mental complications also.

Mary Trump made the point that for all the attention Donald Trump has received over the years, he had received little serious scrutiny. That was about to change.

Other psychologists have proposed that Trump had a "malignant personality disorder" or variations of such a condition.

It had been increasingly obvious that the president was the key to the problems the nation faced. He refused to take control of issues that demanded national attention. He spent his time and the powers of his office fomenting division, racial hatred, white supremacy, and street uprisings; defending or dismissing Russia's hacking of the 2016 and 2020 elections and its disinformation campaign promoting Trump's election; not notifying the joint chiefs of staff, Congress, or the American public of the bounties the Russians put on American soldiers in Afghanistan; serving as an advocate for Russian interests; establishing a personal paramilitary army to execute his wishes; engaging in criminal acts for which he was not held accountable; destroying government agencies and programs; and moving the nation ever closer to an authoritarian system in which he would serve as president-for-life. It was a dystopian, sick world to which only he could bring order.

The chaos, misleading statements and outright lies, and the refusal to take responsibility for anything that happened in his presidency presented problems. It showed a disregard for the Constitution, for the democratic norms, and the rule of law for which the country had no answer. Trump made, and governed, by his own rules.

One thing the criticism he received did do was to again raise questions as to Donald Trump's mental stability. Yet those most expert in diagnosing such conditions—the psychologists, psychiatrists, and relevant medical personnel—with the most to say in providing an understanding of Trump's mental status were prohibited by professional standards from doing so.

The prohibition in question was based on the 1973 Goldwater Rule which forbids mental health professionals from making assessments of a president's or presidential candidate's mental condition if the professional had not treated him/her in person and had their permission. The rule came out of the 1964 presidential race between Barry Goldwater (R/AZ) and incumbent president Lyndon B. Johnson. A concern shared by many during that campaign was a fear of potentially impulsive action by Goldwater, given his hatred of communism, if he had won the election in an upset and had control of nuclear weapons.

The American Psychiatric Association's (APA) directive known as the Goldwater Rule reads as follows: "[I]t is unethical for a psychiatrist to offer a professional opinion unless he or she has conducted an examination and has been granted proper authorization for such a statement" (APA 2010). The rule was adopted in 1973, nine years after the 1964 presidential race and at the height of the impeachment investigation by the House of Representatives of President Richard M. Nixon (Levin 2016; Maddow and Yarvitz 2020).[1]

The American Psychological Association's rule in relation to political figures reads: "When providing opinions of psychological characteristics, psychologists must conduct an examination 'adequate to support statements or conclusions . . . that psychologists should not offer a diagnosis in the media of a living figure they have not examined'" (McDaniel 2016).

The American Medical Association has also published guidelines stating that physicians should refrain "from making clinical diagnoses about individuals [e.g., public officials, celebrities, persons in the news] they have not had the opportunity to personally examine" (AMA 2016).

Trump's behavior however was clearly observable.

In addition to the symptoms of malignant narcissism as described by psychiatrists and psychologists, Trump appears to have met several of the criteria established for Narcissistic Personality Disorder (NPD) and possibly Antisocial Personality Disorder (APD) by the APA. These are described below.

A person needs to exhibit the presence of five of the nine criteria below to be clinically diagnosed as having a NPD:

1. A grandiose sense of self-importance
2. A preoccupation with fantasies of unlimited success, power, brilliance, beauty, or ideal love
3. A belief that he or she is special and unique and can only be understood by or should associate with, other special or high-station people or institutions
4. A need for excessive admiration
5. A sense of entitlement
6. Interpersonally exploitive behavior
7. A lack of empathy
8. Envy of others or a belief that others are envious of him or her
9. A demonstration of arrogant or haughty behaviors or attitudes (APA 2013, *Diagnostic and Statistical Manual of Mental Disorders (DSM)*; Ambardar 2018).

The DSM-5 diagnostic criteria for APD are based on the presence of three of nine behavioral characteristics:

1. A pervasive pattern of disregard for and violation of the rights of others, since age 15 years, as indicated by three or more of the following:
   a) failure to conform to social norms concerning lawful behaviors, such as performing acts that are grounds for arrest
   b) deceitfulness, repeated lying, use of aliases, or conning others for pleasure or personal profit
   c) impulsivity or failure to plan
   d) irritability and aggressiveness, often with physical fights or assaults
   e) reckless disregard for the safety of self or others
   f) consistent irresponsibility, failure to sustain consistent work behavior, or honor monetary obligations
   g) lack of remorse, being indifferent to or rationalizing having hurt, mistreated, or stolen from another person
2. The individual is at least 18 years old.
3. Evidence of conduct disorder typically with onset before age 15 years. (APA 2013, *Diagnostic and Statistical Manual of Mental Disorders*; Fisher and Hany 2020).

The criteria would appear to offer a good description of Donald Trump's behavior.

John D. Gartner was a clinical psychologist and former professor in the Department of Psychiatry at Johns Hopkins University School of Medicine. He circulated a petition on Facebook in early 2017, "Mental Health Professionals Declare Trump Is Mentally Ill And Must Be Removed." In it he called for the removal of Trump from office because he had "a serious mental illness that renders him psychologically incapable of competently discharging the duties of President of the United States." Despite the Goldwater Rule, the petition was signed by some 25,000 psychiatrists, psychologists, and therapists. Gartner contended that Trump "manifestly" met the DSM-published criteria for at least three personality disorders: NPD, APD, and Paranoid Personality Disorder. He described this as a "toxic brew" that equates with "malignant narcissism," which is not a formal Diagnostic and Statistical Manual category but a condition originally developed by psychoanalyst Eric Fromm (*Psychology Today* 2017).[2]

Gartner contended that because the APA's diagnostic criteria described problematic behaviors which were observable, motivations (which might be determinable by a psychiatrist actually treating a patient) were irrelevant. Moreover, he argued that the mental health community had an obligation to protect the public from what was a "clear and present danger." He felt that the Goldwater Rule no longer governed since it predated (1973) the DSM making behaviorally-based diagnoses acceptable.

The petition by Gartner was controversial given the standards set by the national professional associations (Willingham 2017). The issue would surface again in the very last days of the Trump presidency.

A "normalization" of Trump's record in office and such events as that of Lafayette Square illustrated a basic Trump approach, that is, the use of democratic rights and institutions (freedom of press, electoral processes) as weapons employed to realize quite different objectives from those they were intended for (Dean and Altemeyer 2020).

Clinical psychologist Elizabeth Mika explains the strategy that a demagogue and would-be autocrat such as Trump would use in his messaging to the masses: "No tyrant comes to power on the platform of genocidal tyranny, even though such ideas may be brewing already in the recesses of his mind. Each and every one of them promises to bring back law and order, create better economic conditions for the people, and restore the nation's glory" (Mika 2017, 312).[3]

The message is one thing, the ultimate goal another. The constant fear was that as Trump came under more pressure his actions would become more extreme. The deadly insurrectionist assault on the Capitol, endorsed and motivated by Trump in the attempt to engineer a coup, bears witness to the reality of such fears. Mika adds that the "narcissistically psychotic character of the tyrant himself: solipsistic, withdrawn from reality, and full of grandiose and paranoid beliefs [was] impervious to the corrective influences of objective facts" (Mika 2017, 315). The concern as to what Trump might do was increased by the knowledge that in four years in the office of the presidency, nobody had been able to stop him from doing what he wanted to do. The fear was justified as the postelection attempts at a coup showed.

Democratic theorist and historian Timothy Snyder adds another dimension. Totalitarianism and authoritarianism are not the same. But they do share a number of similarities. Snyder writes that totalitarianism [and authoritarianism] remove the distinction between private and public and move the society away from normal politics. A world of conspiracy theories is created. It is seduction "by the notion of hidden realities and dark conspiracies that explain everything" (Snyder 2017, 90). And it could be added that is impenetrable to facts, logic, or by ongoing events. Snyder adds that Trump "never took electoral democracy seriously nor accepted the legitimacy of its American version" (Snyder 2021, 32).

Signs of Trump's malignant narcissism can be found in the strains of grandiosity and narcissism he exhibited (Mika 2017, 298–318). He bragged about being the world's greatest expert on 19 different subjects of which "No one knows more than me" (Blake 2016). In another context, he told advisor and friend, Roy Cohn, that he should become the nuclear peace negotiator for the United States in talks with Russia and other nations. He claimed it would take him only a few days to get up to speed and he believed that once in a room with someone he could talk him into taking his position on anything. It was a belief he had that applied to everything he did.

As for APD, Trump has been described as exhibiting the symptoms of a "sociopath." He violated the rights of others on a regular basis, did not and could not express empathy, was a serial liar, and never showed remorse or took responsibility for his actions. His record of sexual assault of women as he himself bragged about in the "Access Hollywood" tape is one example of his exploitation of others (Farenthold 2016).

Asked if he ever had even sought "forgiveness" from God, Trump said he did not think so and, as with other associations, he had "a great relationship with God."

In terms of paranoia, Trump made a number of claims as to bizarre happenings and promoted conspiracy theories such as his charge that thousands of Muslims in New Jersey celebrated the attacks of 9/11; FEMA established concentration camps; the Sandy Hook shooting of school students was a "hoax"; the truth had not been told about the attacks on the World Trade Center; Barack Obama had a Hawaiian official killed to hide his lack of an American birth certificate; Supreme Court Justice Antonin Scalia was murdered ("they found a pillow on his face"); former Republican congress-man and MSNBC cohost of its morning news show, Joe Scarborough, was involved in a murder; and Ted Cruz's father was associated with Lee Harvey Oswald in the assassination of John F. Kennedy, being among the more sensational (Gartner 2017, 88–103).

For an example of Trump's condition in full display, his telephone call to the Secretary of State in charge of Georgia's elections, Brad Raffensperger, could serve as one example.

Trump made a 1-hour call (it had been preceded by 18 unsuccessful attempts to call) to convince Georgia officials to find the votes to overthrow Biden's victory in the state and declare him the winner. It was part of his broader plan to overthrow the election results. In reality, it amounted to an attempted coup, a predecessor to the domestic terrorist assault on the Capitol.

Trump: "We have won this election in Georgia . . . . And there's nothing wrong with saying that . . . you've recalculated . . ."
Raffensperger: "Well Mr. President, the challenge that you have is the data you have is wrong." (Shear and Saul 2021)

Trump was persistent. The Secretary of State was clear: Trump had lost the election in Georgia.

"If Trump's words are taken 'literally,' you would have to conclude that he is psychotic" (Gartner 2017, 93–109). Trump's call to the Georgia Secretary of State might provide one example of what Gartner was referring to. Trump's role pre- and post- the domestic terrorists' assault on the Capitol would be another.

Trump's dystopian world vision was the basis for a 2016 campaign that saw Trump in the primaries beat opponents with a range of conservative issue appeals. Combined with an exceptionally active campaign style and a demagogic, substantively-other-worldly message, the approach won him the presidency.

DONALD TRUMP AND HIS SUPPORTERS: CULT-LIKE AND UNSHAKEABLE

Donald Trump presented an all-powerful father figure to people susceptible to such an appeal. In turn in a transactional exchange they gave him a sense of reaffirmation for his views and for his being. He gave them the image of an all-powerful figure to associate with. They in turn assumed such power for themselves as followers of Trump. Both sides, leader and supporters, benefited from the association. His supporters also gave him a core in the electorate and a loyalty of such intensity none of his actions, however disreputable, could shake. The negatives that related to Trump they believed were part of an elite assault on him, nothing more. In turn as president he spoke to their interests.

Trump put this appeal together. The irony was that of an alleged billionaire from New York speaking to a hardscrabble working class. He has not received the credit he might have as a political strategist and impressive campaigner (primarily for reasons of his dangerous and irrational actions as president). In this context, he showed an appreciation of the feelings of alienation, exclusion, and rage that affected the working class and the value of the approach in advancing his campaign. Trump was a danger to American democracy and a gross and unattractive personality. But he was also an able politician, a celebrity showman whose instincts served him well in his appeal to the working class. Whether the origins of his political instincts were in his emotional illness, specifically a carryover from childhood and indoctrination by his father, or some other force at work, the cultivation of an alienated working class was extremely effective.

Trump made his wealth work in his favor. He presented himself as an outsider and underdog while tapping into the working-class malaise by claiming he had beat the establishment. As his audience understood it, he shared their alienation and distrust of government and he played to such sentiments.

A number of groups in the electorate, once hardly known, supported Trump and his objectives. They included: the Christian Right, the New Apostolic Reformation, the members of the Republican Party as mentioned, QAnon, the NRA, the Jewish Right, white supremacist groups, and the Alt-Right and the working class.

Add to these the very wealthy and much of corporate America. Their loyalty was based on economic reward and they, unlike the hate groups mentioned, did not employ violence.

The extremist hate groups were among Trump's strongest supporters. Each had distinctive, even idiosyncratic, ways of involving themselves in politics on Trump's behalf and each had different levels of violence associated with achieving their ends. In action, they could be seen in the seditious, insurgent, and deadly attack on the Capitol, which they led.

From Trump they had gained a sense of empowerment and importance as well as a verbal representation of their interests (Hassan 2019; Ben-Ghiat 2020). To Trump, they provided a reaffirmation of views and self-worth as well as giving their loyalty. They could willingly engage in the violent acts that put others off. Both sides gained in a transactional arrangement that was of great benefit.

Steven Hassan, therapist, author, and former member of a cult (the Rev. Sun Myung Moon's Unification Church) argues in *The Cult of Trump* (2019) that Trump was a master in the use of "presidential propaganda." This, as adopted by Trump, was said to be based on Father Charles Coughlin's radio addresses in the 1930s. Coughlin opposed Franklin Delano Roosevelt's New Deal. He was an anti-Semite and an advocate for fascism and a proponent of the views of Hitler and Mussolini. His radio broadcasts on a national basis attracted large audiences.

Coughlin's techniques of persuasion should be familiar. They include: name-calling, labeling people or ideas so as to form an opinion without evidence ("crazy Hillary," the attacks on Kamala Harris); using glittering generalities—attaching words such as "terrific," "great," "smart," to people and ideas to foster acceptance; associating a respected person or institution or idea with another to generate a good or bad impression; endorsement by an admired public figure to achieve acceptance; card stacking—the relative use of facts, true statements or not; focusing on distractions to avoid discussing significant issues; lying outright or misstating an argument to create confusion; logical or illogical arguments to make a case; bandwagon—claiming everybody supports you and what you say; for Trump, if you're not with me to "Make America Great Again," you're part of the problem; and a plain folks approach—a politician's views are good because he/she is just like them, plain folk: "Trump is a brash billionaire who has nonetheless fostered a sense of identification with his targeted constituency by promoting an outsider, nonpolitician image by narrowing their issues and emotions [and] taking their struggle . . . as his own" (Hassan 2019, 124–26).

This point has been made before. It cannot be stressed enough. Trump excels at these skills and they are a key to his political success. Trump had the platform of the White House and a command of the news cycle that made his use of such techniques of persuasion unusually effective. He is not the first or only politician to use one or all of them but he took them to an unprecedented level.

Donald Trump was a master of an alternative-world propagandizing. Forty percent or better of American voters bought into it.

The dynamics and intensity of the leader–follower attraction is one that is most often beyond the understanding of outsiders. In attracting such followers, the leader "makes good-sounding—but openly unrealistic, bordering on delusional—promises to his supporters, and usually has no intention or ability to fulfill most of them (if any). He holds his supporters in contempt, as he does 'weaker' human beings in general, and uses them only as props in his domination-and adulation-oriented schemes (Mika 2019, 297).

Those who buy in to such a father-protector arrangement and the leader fulfilling his compulsions make a point of distinguishing themselves from nonbelievers and direct their aggressions and rage, by violence when useful, against what are seen as weaker members of the society. In effect, it is a subjugation technique directed at others and builds on their group's and leader's sense of vulnerability, emotional wounds, and inadequacy. In more extreme forms, it can lead to calls for purgings. The sense of aggression that evolves is encouraged by the leader as is the domestic terrorism that can follow.

Hassan writes: "He used all the influence techniques in his arsenal—inflaming resentments and anger, drumming up fear, exaggerating his accomplishments, insulting and demonizing the 'other'" (Hassan 2019, 184–85).

Trump did it all with flair. He promised he would fix their problems and the country's.

Telling his followers that they are brainwashed or that they are part of a cult or that they are weak is doomed to fail. It puts them on the defensive and establishes you as their enemy. In effect, it serves to close their minds (Hassan 2019, 196).

THE 2020 PRESIDENTIAL ELECTION AS A
CRISIS IN AMERICAN DEMOCRACY

Nothing less than America's democratic system of representation was on the ballot in the 2020 election. First, however, there is the question of how someone like Donald Trump was elected president. It took a perfect storm of events to bring Trump into the presidency.

The 2016 Presidential Race

James Comey, director of the FBI, announced in the summer of 2016 that the FBI was completing its extensive yearlong investigation into the Democratic nominee and former Secretary of State, Hillary Clinton's, use of a personal nonofficial server to send emails. He closed the case without finding evidence of classified information having been compromised. He referred the case to the Department of Justice for a prosecutorial decision, noting Clinton had been extremely careless in handling sensitive information. The FBI was also investigating the Trump campaign's extensive ties to the Russians during the election. This was not mentioned.

Comey reopened the investigation just days before the November vote, having come across a batch of new emails. He closed it again with only two days to go before the vote without having found any classified information leaks. By then the damage had been done. Trump had made it a major issue of the campaign. He had repeatedly encouraged his followers at rallies to chant "Lock Her Up" and the message took hold. Clinton lost the key Rust Belt states of Michigan, Wisconsin, and Pennsylvania by fewer than 80,000 total votes, and with them the Electoral College and the presidency. The shift of those votes, 0.06 percent of the 137 million cast, would have swung the election.

Comey's actions violated FBI protocol cautioning against becoming involved in elections. The FBI, for reasons unknown, had not reviewed the email records for leaks prior to announcing the reopening of the investigation. That alone probably cost Clinton the presidency.

Clinton also managed to run a disorganized campaign, as she had done in losing the nomination to Barack Obama in 2008. She had multiple senior advisors competing with each other and her campaign manager, while experienced in Virginia politics, was young and had no national experience. He depended on "analytics," that is, data analysis, to make decisions, did not know the state leaders of the party personally and did not return their telephone messages when they called, as for example, to warn of problems in the Rust Belt. Clinton did minimal campaigning in these states and the results showed. Joe Biden did not make the same mistake in 2020.

Clinton, much like the 17 or so serious candidates for the Republican Party's presidential nomination, did not know how to handle Trump's personal attacks or the stalking of her during one of the general election debates. Heavily favored again as in 2008, she lost the election in an upset.

The implications of the outcome of the 2016 election were enormous (Balz and Rucker 2016; Balz 2018; Schmidt 2020). Once the road to the White House had been established for such candidates, they will follow in Trump's wake. The threat to the nation's democratic system of representation can be counted on to reappear.

THE PRESIDENTIAL RACE IN 2020

The presidential election of 2020 was another matter. Trump had a dismal record in office to defend. He did so vigorously and disingenuously. He campaigned nonstop with up to five rallies or more a day. In these, he presented his version of his success.

Biden ran a more restrained campaign. He delivered his message effectively, especially in the weeks before the election, and he made a point in contrasting his character with that of Trump.

In some regards, Biden's campaign was unusual. He won the South Carolina Black vote and the state and a total of 10 of 14 states on Super Tuesday. These included states he had not campaigned in. He did well elsewhere in the Deep South, winning primaries in Alabama and Arkansas. He beat Senator Elizabeth Warren in her home state of Massachusetts, where Bernie Sanders had also campaigned heavily.

After Super Tuesday, about a third of Democratic primary delegates were allotted. Biden's success led the other candidates to withdraw from the race. Biden became the presumptive nominee.

Biden was not strongly disliked, as was Clinton (and even more so Trump) in 2016, and he ran as what he was: a centrist/moderate with an appeal to both Democrats and Republicans.

In reality, influenced by the Progressive candidates for the nomination, Senators Bernie Sanders and Elizabeth Warren, Biden had been moving his party's platform leftwards and he had begun comparing it to a Reconstructionist effort that would rival the New Deal. When he began to announce the specifics of his plans to fight the virus, revive the economy, reintroduce safeguards on the environment and confront climate change, deal with the immigration problem and work to strengthen democratic institutions, the dimensions of what he had been talking about took on a reality. They would become familiar in the press conferences and meetings held with reporters on a daily basis in the postelection period.

Biden picked Senator and former California attorney general Kamala Harris, a woman as he had promised, and a person of color as his running mate in the days immediately before the Democratic National Convention. After that both parties' national nominating conventions were pro forma, distance-based affairs. Biden emphasized his platform. Trump made his pitch; he had no platform nor did the Republican Party. The Democratic Convention heavily emphasized inclusion and diversity. The Republican Convention largely featured officeholders and family and friends of Trump as presenters and emphasized law and order and patriotism.

With that the campaign was in full swing: Trump campaigning furiously and Biden more selectively and discreetly. Trump resorted to a campaign style he was comfortable with, continued to insult Biden and Harris, and to present his record of success as he saw it. Biden in turn emphasized the need to follow science in dealing with the virus. He drew a distinction between how he would address the pandemic and Trump's approach to downplaying the virus, its severity, its prevalence, and epidemiologists' forecast of its impact on morbidity and mortality.

Biden led Trump by large margins in the polls, often by double-digits nationally with closer margins in the six to nine swing states up through Election Day.

Four days after the November 3 election, Biden was declared the winner by the Associated Press when returns from his native Pennsylvania were announced, pushing him over the 270 Electoral Vote threshold needed. Ultimately Biden won the Electoral College vote 306–232, and the popular vote by a margin of 51.3 percent (81,268,924 votes) to 46.9 percent (74,216,154) in an election with the largest turnout in history. Biden received the most votes ever, Trump the second most. This despite the pandemic and Biden's caution to voters to stay home and vote by mail. Ultimately, since the mail-in votes were counted more slowly, Trump's early vote margin fell over the course of the week, leading Trump and his supporters to claim vote fraud and that the election had been stolen. He would act on this belief in ways that could not be imagined: calling and demanding states change their count to make him the winner; the domestic terrorist assault on the Capitol; the refusal to acknowledge Biden's victory; the 90 or so cases he brought in the courts in the effort to change the vote; the decision to make the transition period as difficult as possible; his failure to congratulate Biden for his win, or to observe the tradition of receiving him and his wife at the White House or to attend the Inauguration.

VOTING IN THE 2020 ELECTION

The results of the vote emphasized the extent of the polarization in the nation and in the support for the political parties (see table 2.1). The divisions of the country were clearly represented in the competing parties' coalitions. Women, including suburban women, once Republican loyalists, favored Biden and the Democrats (but not by the numbers expected by analysts); males supported Trump and the Republicans; young people Biden, older voters Trump; white voters Trump, Black and Latino voters Biden; high school or less educated voted for Trump, college educated, Biden; both low income (under $50,000) and those making $100,00 or more, Biden (those in the millionaire/billionaire class were not polled separately but could be expected to be strong Trump supporters); urban voters Biden, small town and rural, Trump; and party identifiers supported the candidate of their party: Democrats Biden 95 to 4 percent and Republicans, Trump 91 to 8 percent. These last numbers establish the polarization in the party system and serve to indicate the level of its severity.

In relation to issues in the campaign, those who believe the economy and jobs to be the most important issue voted overwhelmingly for Trump; health care, 2–1 for Biden; immigration policy and the separation of children from their families, Trump (87 to 12%) but only 3 percent of voters considered this to be the most important issue facing the nation; abortion, Trump (90 to 9%) but only 3 percent again felt this the most important issue; law enforcement and police violence, among the 4 percent who thought this the most important, Trump was heavily favored; and on foreign policy, Trump again was a strong favorite.[4]

Issues given a low priority by voters favored Trump heavily. The best issue for Trump was the economy. Twenty-eight percent believed it the most important and 8 out of 10 of these voters supported Trump.

Table 2.1   Demographic Profile of Voters (*in Percent*)

Factor	Share of Vote	Biden	Trump	Other
Gender				
Men	47	46	52	2
Women	53	55	44	1
Age				
18–29	13	61	36	3
30–44	23	54	43	3
45–64	36	48	51	1
65+	28	48	51	1
Race or ethnic heritage				
White	74	43	55	2
Black	11	91	8	1
Latino	9	63	35	2
Education				
High school or less	27	46	53	1
Some college	34	48	50	2
College graduate	25	56	42	2
Postgraduate study	15	58	40	2
Income				
Under $50,000	38	53	45	2
$50,000–99,999	36	48	50	2
$100,000 or more	26	51	47	2
Living area				
Urban	20	65	33	2
Suburban	45	54	44	2
Small town	17	43	55	2
Rural	18	34	65	1
2016 Vote				
Hillary Clinton	38	96	4	0
Donald Trump	41	6	93	1
Other	6	57	28	15
Did not vote	15	56	42	2
Vote type				
Election Day	29	33	65	2
Early in-person	30	47	52	1
Mail	41	66	32	2

Source: Data compiled from Brian McGill, John West and Anthony DeBarros. 2020. Results compiled by the AP. "How We Voted in the 2020 Election." *Wall Street Journal*. November 17. https://www.wsj.com/graphics/votecast-2020/

The strongest issue for Biden was the coronavirus pandemic. Forty-one percent, the highest of any single issue, considered it the most important and 7 out of 10 of these voted (73 to 26%) for Biden. His second issue, well behind the virus but one that could be considered related to it, was health care, which 9 percent thought the most important and where Biden led two to one. With two issues in the campaign, climate change, which only 4 percent identified as their most important concern, and racism which only 7 percent thought most important, support for Biden was, respectively, 86 to 11 percent and 79 to 19 percent. In relation to racism and to the extent police violence was part of it, Trump commanded the vote division (81 to 17%) (see table 2.2).

Table 2.2   Most Important Issues Facing the Country (*in Percent*)

Issue	Share of Vote	Biden	Trump	Other
Economy and jobs	28	16	82	2
Health care	9	66	32	2
Immigration	3	12	87	1
Abortion	3	9	90	1
Law enforcement	4	17	81	2
Climate change	4	86	11	3
Foreign policy	1	23	72	5
Coronavirus pandemic	41	73	26	1
Racism	7	79	19	2
Do you think the condition of the economy is:				
Excellent/Good	43	17	81	2
Not so good/Poor	57	76	22	2
Do you think the coronavirus in the United States is:				
Completely/Mostly under control	19	7	91	2
Somewhat under control	30	25	73	2
Not at all under control	50	83	15	2
Which of the following comes closest to what you would like to see lawmakers do with the Affordable Care Act also known as Obamacare?				
Repeal the law entirely/ Repeal parts	49	13	85	2
Leave as is/Expand	51	87	12	1
In general how concerned are you about the effects of climate change?				
Very/Somewhat concerned	70	69	29	2
Not too/Not at all Concerned	30	8	91	1
In voting in this election, how important to you were Supreme Court nominations?	90	54	45	2

Source: Data compiled from Brian McGill, John West and Anthony DeBarros. 2020. Results compiled by the AP. "How We Voted in the 2020 Election." *Wall Street Journal*. November 17. https://www.wsj.com/graphics/votecast-2020/.

If the question were asked differently, the answer could be quite different. Voters were asked before the election if they thought police violence was a factor. Ninety-one percent said yes and they supported Biden 53 to 46 percent.

The voters were also asked if they thought Supreme Court nominations were a factor and of the 90 percent who said yes, 54 percent voted for Biden, 45 percent for Trump (McGill et al. 2020).

There were surprises. Trump's strong vote despite his incompetence and his showing in the presidential polls was one. The election also was considerably closer than realized at the time and closer than Hillary Clinton's much-publicized Rust Belt loss in 2016 (Bump 2016). Trump lost three swing states (Arizona, Wisconsin, and Georgia) by less than 1 percent margins, or just under 43,000 votes. Had he won those three states, the electoral count could have been tied (Swasey and Jin 2020). Under such conditions, a majority of the House of Representatives, with each state having one vote, would decide the winner.[5] Had Trump won those three states and also Nevada, another close swing state, he would have won the election with a smaller margin than the 2016 Rust Belt margin.

The outcome in Florida, where Latinos in the Miami area went heavily for Trump, was missed by early analysts. He had labeled the Democrats as socialists, evoking images of Fidel Castro and communism for the Cuban expatriate community. This was the only Latino bloc to vote for Trump. Some had lost their family homes or other properties as a privileged class in Cuba during Castro's Cuban revolution. This helped Republicans win Florida which otherwise was believed to be tightly competitive. Michael Bloomberg, the billionaire former mayor of New York City and a one-time contender for the Democratic Party's nomination, alone had spent $100 million in Florida on behalf of Biden's electoral bid. The Democrats still lost Florida by approximately 370,000 votes, 51.2 percent (5.66 million votes) to 47.9 percent (5.29 million).

Another state in which Democrats thought they might have a chance for an upset was Georgia. Biden did win the state. In addition, the two Senate races in the state went into a January 5 runoff. If the Democrats won both they would have a tie with the Republicans in the Senate. Vice President Kamala Harris as presiding officer would give them a one-vote majority. They did win the two races. The two party leaders, Chuck Schumer (D/NY) and Mitch McConnell (R/KT), were then put in the position of trying to agree on a mutually acceptable plan for conducting the Senate's day-to-day business.

In an unusual development, Republican Party leader Mitch McConnell continued the Republican control of the Senate and refused to allow Democrats to take over the chamber's committees. The Democrats needed a majority vote of the chamber under its arcane rules to do what a majority of voters elected them to do. As he did with virtually all the bills sent over by the House during Trump's four years, McConnell would not allow a vote to be scheduled. He relented in time and the Democratic Party took control of a divided Senate.

Trump refused to concede or initially to have his politically appointed heads of agencies cooperate with Biden's team in the transition (Rucker 2020; Donald Trump 2020). His General Services Administration head refused to sign a letter authorizing transition funding to the Biden team to allow them to begin the work of preparing to take over the government for three weeks after the election. This was normally a routine act that is done immediately after the winning candidate is announced in an election. This was, like much of the Trump presidency, a new experience for the country.

Trump's battle to overturn the election continued throughout the year and into 2021. The numerous lawsuits filed by Trump and Republicans in the states were gradually denied as being without merit and for lacking evidence. None of Trump's legal teams were disciplined for violating Rule 11 of the Federal Rules of Procedure, which bars frivolous lawsuits and baseless claims with potential sanctions for attorneys and law firms.

Trump sought recounts in a number of states, all of which reaffirmed Biden's victory. His intentions were clear. As he said to the Georgia official in charge of elections: "So look. All I want to do is this. I just want to find 11,780 votes, which is one more than we have. Because we won the state." Biden had won it by 11,779. The implicit threat of federal criminal action against the official in charge if he did not act was part of the effort at persuasion.

Texas tried to sue Pennsylvania, Georgia, Wisconsin, and Michigan to prevent them from casting their Electoral Votes for Biden, claiming election fraud, but without evidence. There were 126 House Republicans who attached their names to an amicus brief in support of the suit, joining 17 Republican Attorneys General from states overwhelmingly won by Trump. The four targeted states struck back in briefs filed with the Supreme Court.

On December 11, 2020, the U.S. Supreme Court issued a final rejection of the legal challenge engineered by the Texas Attorney General in a one-page order in which it said the complaint was denied for "lack of standing." The Court's ruling rested on the fact that Texas could not show it was injured by the way other states had conducted their elections and therefore it had no basis for its suit.

Christopher Krebs, director of the Cybersecurity and Infrastructure Security Agency, tasked with protecting elections from cyberattacks, announced the November 3, 2020, election was the safest in the nation's history. He was forced out (*Washington Post Live* 2020; Parks 2020). Attorney General

William Barr announced there had been no evidence of voter fraud and he would not be opening a Justice Department investigation. This constituted a break with Trump (Zapotosky et al. 2020; *New York Times Live* 2020).

As support for Trump's bid to overturn the election, by December widely described as an attempted coup, dwindled, members of Trump's staff and others including Attorney General William Barr announced they would be stepping down. Barr did so on December 23.

There were still those unwilling to give up a claim to the election (Moss and Shenkman 2021). Increasingly fringe personalities joined Trump in these efforts. They included Trump's personal attorney Rudy Giuliani, former U.S. National Security Advisor Michael Flynn, and Flynn's Texas attorney Sidney Powell. She was known to be a leading proponent of Far Right conspiracy theories, including one that Robert Mueller's Russia investigation was a ploy to force Trump from office and, with Giuliani, that there had been a Venezuelan plot that included its long-deceased president to rig voting machines in the United States. The voting machine corporation, Dominion, denied the charges and filed a $1.3 billion defamation lawsuit against Giuliani. He said he was not intimidated.

Flynn had twice pled guilty, orally and in writing, to lying under oath to FBI investigators and to Vice President Mike Pence about his communications with Russian intelligence during the 2016 campaign. Charges included Flynn's attempt to interfere with newly imposed U.S. sanctions on Russia by President Barack Obama for its role in the 2016 election and for Flynn's attempt to get Russia to scuttle an Obama administration effort to condemn Israel for a settlement in Palestine with a United Nations Security Council Resolution. He also misrepresented the extent of his work on behalf of the Turkish government. He had shown his allegiance to Trump in the past, among other things by leading "Lock Her Up" chants about Hillary Clinton during a Republican National Convention speech in 2016. Over his four years in office, Trump signed a total of 143 pardons or commutations of sentence. He issued a broad reprieve from any possible federal crimes in pardoning Flynn after the November election. More pardons were to come as the Inauguration drew closer.

Shortly after the election was certified by vote of the 50 state electors on December 14, reports emerged about an explosive White House meeting on December 18. Flynn had raised the idea of imposing martial law to overturn the 2020 election results. At the meeting, Flynn suggested to Trump appointing Sidney Powell as special counsel to probe election fraud claims. Giuliani wanted to order the Department of Homeland Security to seize voting machines. Most of those present opposed the suggestions, in particular White House Counsel Pat Cipollone and Chief of Staff Mark Meadows. There were accounts of "shouting matches" erupting among participants over the course of the meeting (Haberman and Kanno-Youngs 2020). That such extreme measures were at Trump's disposal again directed attention to the extent of the power Trump (or any president) had.

Trump went days without a public appearance after the election. It was in stark contrast to his previous constant media exposure. He paid no attention to the revelation of a 6–8 month hacking of federal agency files by the Russians. He spent his time golfing and continuing to insist that he had won the election and/or that it had been stolen. He continued to avoid any government work. Trump sought the appointment of a special counsel to investigate Biden's son Hunter Biden, claiming his Ukrainian and Chinese business dealings warranted a tax investigation. It did not happen.

One thing that did not change was Republican Party support for Trump after the deadly insurrectionist raid on the Capitol and revelation of the demonstrators' plans to find and physically punish (or worse) Vice President Mike Pence, Speaker Nancy Pelosi and, if present, incoming vice president Kamala Harris as well as any other members of the Congress that they came across. They found none. The level of support for Trump by Republicans remained much as it was before the Capitol takeover of the House and Senate.

Overall Trump's approval/disapproval rates nationally stayed close to that they had been: Forty-three percent gave the president a positive job approval rating, 55 percent disapproved. Sixty-one percent of voters said Biden won the election legitimately but only 21 percent of Republicans. Thirty-five percent of all voters but 74 percent of Republicans claimed Biden did not win legitimately (Dann 2021). Trump was the only president in the history of the Gallup Polls whose support never went above 50 percent during his term.

Ten Republicans in the House voted for Trump's second impeachment, a record number. But overwhelmingly Republicans in the House and Senate voted against impeachment. Eighty-seven percent (compared with 89% pre-election) of Republicans supported Trump. The assault on the Capitol and Trump's role in it did little to hurt Trump's standing among Republicans.

Trump issued a series of pardons for staff members, campaign officials, and friends during his final days in office. Although he used his clemency authority less than other U.S. presidents since 1900, with the exception of George H. W. and George W. Bush, his beneficiaries were granted relief largely for political reasons rather than as acts of mercy (Johnson et al. 2021; Gersen 2020). Trump had granted 237 acts of clemency during his term of office (143 pardons and 94 commutations of sentence) (Gramlich 2021).

Trump and his committed band of loyalists began eying January 6, 2021, the date Congress was due to vote to accept the election results, normally a ceremonial function, as an opportunity to achieve the ends they sought.

It turned out to be the most serious coup effort anyone had ever been aware of. Its planning largely took place on social media in the months preceding the attack on the Capitol (Rutenberg et al. 2021). Security officials had access to their plans. The organizers were doing it in public; there was no effort to hide what was about to happen. Yet when the insurrectionist assault on the Capitol occurred the police were badly overmatched. Five hundred from a force of 2,000 were on duty with backup only from the D.C. police. The National Guard was not involved. Both the D.C. National Guard and those from bordering states, Maryland and Virginia, needed Department of Defense authorization (since Washington was a district and not a state) to participate. Initially they did not receive it.

Larry Hogan (R/MD), the Maryland governor, said the Defense Department refused to let them go directly to the Capitol to help and for 3 hours or so put his state's National Guard, sent to help contain the violence, on traffic duty. The Virginia governor waited until the next day to contact the Department of Defense. By then the protocols were set and the state's National Guard were allowed to go directly to the Capitol but the immediate crisis was over.

A thorough investigation was promised to establish what happened and who was in charge and responsible (Barrett and Zapotosky 2021).

Once the police and their allies, several of whom were accused of being part of the conspiracy, took control and began moving demonstrators out of the Capitol and off the stairs and balconies outside they were moved along peacefully. The FBI had arrested 235 people relating to the invasion of the Capitol in an ongoing investigation with more to come. They had received more than 200,000 tips from the public about the siege, and were analyzing photos, videos, news coverage, and police officer testimony. Many "selfies" had been taken by the rioters themselves and shared on social media. A number of military veterans were charged in the attack. National Public Radio reported that nearly one in five of those arrested had or were serving in the military (Dreisbach 2021). Comparisons were made between the overwhelming police response during the summer to Black Lives Matter protests and to the peaceful demonstration in Lafayette Square where chemical agents and rubber bullets had been employed to the far more lenient response, beginning with a limited initial police presence, fewer arrests, and reluctance to use firepower on the largely white and violent crowd that conducted the assault on the Capitol (Chason and Schmidt 2021).

The main target of the domestic terrorists had been Vice President Mike Pence who presided over the Congressional certification of the vote. Pence did not have the power to overturn the vote. Trump, who knew little about the workings of government, and the protesters who assaulted the Capitol did not understand this and thus were threatening him as incited by Trump. They never did find the vice president, although coming close.

Congress determinedly returned in joint session later in the night to complete the task of certifying the vote. The final count was 377 in favor of certification (formal acceptance of the Electoral College vote) to 147 supporting at least one objection to counting Biden's Electoral Votes. This even after the chaos and violence of the Capitol attack. A few legislators did change their minds after the violence and voted for certification. Eight abstained. Vice President Mike Pence declared Biden formally certified as the winner at 3:40 a.m. on January 7.

The storming of the Capitol was a frightening, surreal event. It was hard to believe what was being shown on live television or to understand how or why it happened (Mogelson 2021).

An identification of those who assaulted the Capitol began almost immediately, with arrests and prosecutions planned. It turned out the FBI recognized most of the leaders of the more than a dozen extremist hate groups (QAnon, the Proud Boys, One-Percenters, No White Guilt, Boogaloo, Oath Keepers, etc.) who had led the insurrection (Freedman 2020, 21ff; Ferrara et al.).[6]

Donald Trump had organized the assault on the Capitol. He had used social media to urge his followers to come to Washington. He reportedly spent millions of the funds he had access to in support of the operation. He also sent the insurgents on their way with a rally outside the White House prior to the break-in. He emphasized that he had won the election but it was stolen from him and that this would be the last chance to save the country. He told the crowd in a 70-minute speech "You will never take back our country with weakness" and made it evident he was furious with Vice President Pence that he had not overturned the results. Joining Trump was Rudy Giuliani who ended by shouting to the protesters "Let's have trial by combat!" Representative Mo Brooks, a particularly energetic showman, and others participated in the send-off of the insurgent seditionists to the Capitol, leading to a resolution for his censure by two of his Congressional colleagues a week later.

Trump had promised to go with the insurgent seditionists to the Capitol ("we're going to walk down—and I'll be there with you . . . to the Capitol . . .") but did not (Blake 2021). In a message carried on social media later that afternoon, Trump did not condemn the mob action but told his supporters that they should go home in peace, they were very special and that "we love you." These events were the basis for his second impeachment (Sanger 2020).

Fears were expressed as to what might happen at the Inauguration and in the days leading up to it.

As for preparation for the January 20 Inauguration, coming two weeks after the assault on the Capitol, it was an entirely different situation. Washington had become an armed camp. The Capitol city was almost a ghost town with security forces everywhere, 7-foot fences with razor wire on top around major buildings, and no tourists, cars, or ordinary people in sight. The bridges over the Potomac were closed. Several Metro transportation stations were closed. Bus routes were redrawn. In all, 25,000 National Guard troops from 20 states had arrived to provide security in the city. The FBI urged all 50 states to also implement heightened security at their state capitals and many also stationed National Guard members around their state houses or governors' homes.

The Inauguration was to go off without incident and the states did not report any serious disruptions.

Trump was quiet. He stayed in the White House planning his pardons and organizing his departure ceremony from Washington to take place the morning of Biden's Inauguration.

The transfer of power from the outgoing to the incoming president at noon, January 20, 2021, was peaceful. Trump did not attend the ceremony. Vice President Pence did.

In his Inaugural Address, Biden pledged an active presidency and a fast start in the first 100 days. His agenda was ambitious, covering everything from a massive upgrade in the fight against the pandemic to rebuilding infrastructure and world alliances. The tone and substance were in direct contrast to that of the outgoing president.

Trump held a ceremony at Andrews Air Force Base, made brief remarks, and left on a flight to Mar-a-Lago, his Palm Beach resort. His future was uncertain. Although there was talk of Trump starting a cable news station to compete with Fox News and creating his own MAGA or Patriot political party, nothing was certain. Trump had collected millions of dollars from supporters to use as he saw fit after leaving office. Estimates were that Trump and the G.O.P. had received as much as $175 million from grassroots and online supporters after the November election, and Trump had a new PAC, "Save America." It had a war chest of $31 million at the end of 2020 with an estimated additional $40 million in a shared Republican Party account (Goldmacher and Shorey 2021). He had the financial resources to follow up on whatever he decided.

At the same time, Trump had personal financial challenges. His biggest creditor, Deutsche Bank, had announced they would limit his ability to refinance his debt. One analysis estimated he owed creditor at least $315 million, largely in mortgages on his hotels, resorts, and golf courses, several of which had not fared well during the pandemic (Lane 2021). A *Forbes* analysis put the figure at over a billion dollars in debt but with assets of $3.66 billion (Alexander 2020). On top of the financial stress, he was facing legal liability from New York state prosecutors over his taxes and business dealings in the state.

Biden had brought an openness not experienced for four years, a commitment to represent the interests of all Americans and a seriousness and level of experience and knowledge of government not seen during the Trump presidency to the office.

There was an almost palpable sense of relief. The country had survived. A new era had begun.

SUMMARY

The presidential election of 2020 was seen as a referendum on democracy. Barack Obama asked each American "to embrace your own responsibility as citizens to make sure that the basic tenets of our democracy endure. Because that's what is at stake now. Our democracy. . . . You can give our democracy new meaning. You can take it to a better place. You're the missing ingredient—the ones who decide whether or not America becomes the country that fully lives up to its creed" (Obama 2020).

Nothing less than America's democratic future had been on the agenda.

CONCLUSION

Democracies are fragile (Levin et al. 2021). They demand much of their citizenry in terms of interest, knowledge, and involvement. One of their major weaknesses is the structure of the democratic system in its reliance on collective decision-making through elections. This in turn directs attention to the levels of information and the willingness of people to be involved (i.e., to turn out and vote in particular).

American democracy has been extraordinarily successful and it has been resilient. Many believe it serves as a model for the rest of the world. With such success, and given the assumptions made as to the timeliness of the principles underlying its origins as found in the Declaration of Independence and the Constitution, many became complacent, feeling that it worked well enough. Rejection at the polls of efforts to institute an alternative system of government would be taken as verification of the strengths of America's democratic commitments. Trump and his assault on democratic norms and institutions could likely be seen as a passing phase in the nation's history. They may also make antidemocratic views acceptable in politics and even popular among a sizeable proportion of the electorate.

The country's success and longevity (which in reality does not compare to that of authoritarian systems) may work against its continuation as a democracy. Many have become potentially overconfident about the strength of its resilience (Gilligan 2019, 163–80). The result would be to take for granted as permanent the system in place, downplaying and dismissing threats to its future.

People may make the reasonable assumption that if most hold democratic values, the democracy is immune to efforts to change it into a more autocratic form. Unfortunately, this is not the case. Values and democratic cultures do not protect against any potential takeover of the system. Only 2 percent of the population ever joined the Nazi or Italian fascist parties and neither party ever won a majority of the popular vote in an election. Still they came to transform the German and Italian governing systems. They took power "with the support of political insiders blind to the dangers of their own ambitions" (Levitsky and Ziblatt 2018, 21). The members of Congress still claiming Trump won the election post-Capitol insurgency (as well as others in politics) may be of even greater danger than first realized in uncertain times.

A commitment to capitalism and a strong economy also do not prevent the descent into dictatorship. "The relationship between culture and other forms of democratic development to politics," Richard J. Evans, who analyzed the rise of Nazism, has written, "is not that direct or simple" (Evans 2005, xxiii).

Evans believed the intentions of German capitalists during the Great Depression to create a more receptive, profitable, and stable business climate led to their support for the Nazi Party which was the key to its success in taking control of the German government.

There is no one consensual solution as to what could stop such movements. Most of all, observers talk of broad voter support for the essentials that define a democracy—the rule of law, protections for civil rights, an institutional presence that reinforces the objectives of a democratic state, and so on.

Democratic theorists Steven Levitsky and Daniel Ziblatt go in a different direction. It is their contention that "Political parties are democracy's gatekeepers" (Levitsky and Ziblatt 2018, 26). To the extent this is the case, in the United States, as in many other countries, the state of the parties may be more of the problem for a democracy than its saviors.

The United States limits itself to a two-party system. In such a situation, the condition of the Republican Party in particular has to be of concern (Stevens 2020; Kabaservice 2012; Alberta 2019; and Wilentz 2019). The overwhelming majority of Republicans in the Congress and in the population at large, with rates of 90 percent and better, backed Trump, Trumpism ("America First") and the move toward authoritarianism.

It was a party led by a demagogue and would-be dictator. The choice for the voter then was between this and a divided Democratic Party (Progressive versus centrist, moderate) with a background of representation through tribal politics (identity politics) (Sides et al. 2018; Brazile 2017; Allen and Parnes 2017). Such a choice raises questions as to how representative and effective the party system can be, and the direction it is headed in, in serving the needs of the nation.

Timothy Snyder divides the Republican Party into two factions, the gamers and the breakers (Snyder 2021, 30ff). The gamers are composed mostly of politicians. They would game the system to stay in power. The breakers, composed mostly of party voters and Trump supporters, would break the system and start over. If so, an antidemocratic environment looks to be part of the future of the party system as far as can be projected. The election and the domestic terrorist assault on the Capitol appear then to be part of an ongoing story of a contentious time in American politics and the struggle to keep democracy alive in the nation.

As for Trump as an authoritarian, the signs were clear throughout his presidency. For those analytically inclined, the warnings and examples were a part of his message. For a president who made over 30,000 false or misleading claims or outright lies, as tracked by the *Washington Post*, there should have been little doubt (Kessler et al. 2021). Trump had also issued warnings of exactly what he was going to do. He often made startlingly bold predictions or threats: for example, that he was going to deport thousands of people; that he "could stand in the middle of Fifth Avenue and shoot someone and not lose voters"; that (in regard to sexual assaults on women) he didn't even wait to act because "when you're a star . . . you can do anything"; and that his mob of followers should march on the Capitol and fight. Many claims were so outrageous they were disregarded. Until they weren't.

Democratic theorist, Juan Linz, born in Germany, lived through Spain's antifascist civil war in the 1930s. He developed four keys for recognizing an authoritarian. These are that he or she ignored the democratic rules of the game, rejected the legitimacy of opponents or any type of opposition, advocated violence, and limited civil liberties (Linz 1978). These would appear to describe Trump and his actions.

In power, authoritarians immediately begin their assaults on individual liberties and democratic institutions and they can be relentless.

Such happened in the Trump years. There had been multiple attempts by Trump and his associates and Republicans in Congress and at the state level to overturn the presidential vote and have Trump declared president. This would establish Trump as the dictator he wanted to be in an authoritarian system in which he would exercise the unlimited power he dreamed of.[7]

He had made his objectives clear. In the second impeachment the House Democratic Managers who directed their party's effort had stated that Trump was "singularly responsible" for the seditious attack on the Capitol as part of a concerted campaign to reverse the election results (Fandos and Haberman 2021; Rutenberg et al. 2021).[8]

Most disturbingly he had convinced over 74 million voters, the second highest total in history, to support him, knowing what he stood for and what his objectives were. Trump received almost 10 million more votes in 2020 than in 2016. Trump's hold on the Republican Party was potent (Smith 2021). The threat to constitutional democratic government was real and it was immediate.

Biden did not see it in these terms. He decided to concentrate his efforts on the policy concerns facing the nation, which were substantial. The prosecution of insurgents and the domestic terrorists who participated in the assault on the Capitol and those who planned and incited the riots, Trump's impeachment, and the barriers placed in the way of relief reaching those under siege in the Capitol were to be left to the Congress, the FBI, and federal and state prosecutors to unravel and to hold those involved accountable.

To be clear, if not blunt, Biden as president refused, initially at least, to become involved in meeting the most serious issue confronting the nation and its survival, the effort to replace its democratic government with an autocratic one. It would appear to be hard to concentrate on economic inequality or immigration, as important as these issues were, knowing the democratic system itself was under sustained attack (Linskey 2021).

The previously unimaginable threat to attack the Capitol and void the election illustrated the magnitude of the problem. The full resources of the government would be needed to meet and suppress the challenge.[9]

This was the nation's number one existential threat. It would continue post-Trump. The effort to bring unity through a reasoned approach in meeting the policy needs of greatest concern could be illusionary under such conditions.

The consequences were enormous. At a minimum, both the immediate and long-run future were uncertain and the concept of a coup could become a permanent part of the American political landscape and the reality a continuing threat to the nation's democratic order.

The day after Trump's acquittal, an angry Speaker of the House, Nancy Pelosi, called the 43 voters who supported him "a cowardly group of Republicans." She also directed her attention to Republican Senator Mitch McConnell, who voted against impeaching Trump and then bitterly and intensely criticized him and his actions. As for proposals to censure Trump, she said this was intended to apply as an example to a member of Congress who used Congressional stationery for a personal business matter, not someone who directed a deadly and seditious assault on the Capitol.

Pelosi a few days later called for a commission similar to the 9/11 one to thoroughly investigate what happened on January 6, 2021, identify and hold responsible those who planned and directed the attack and recommend changes to ensure nothing like it would happen again.

Trump in turn announced to a Conservative Political Action Conference in late February 2021 of committed Republicans his intention to run for a second and implied third term as president ("I may even decide to beat them for a third time"). The movement away from democracy and toward autocracy was to continue and Trump was prepared to play an active role in bringing it about (Martin and Haberman 2021; Weigel and Scherer 2021).

Institutions by themselves are not adequate safeguards for limiting the behavior of elected authoritarians. Checks and balances and democratic norms do not deter a move to a more authoritarian political system. If this continues to prove to be the case, the foundations of the Madisonian system of government may not be accepted as uncritically as they largely have been and may not lead to the complacency they once did. In fact, the institutions of democracy in such cases can be adapted, mobilized, and weaponized to be used by would-be dictators in the transition to authoritarianism. "The tragic paradox of the electoral route to authoritarianism is that democracy's assassins use the very institutions of democracy—gradually, subtly, and even legally—to kill it" (Levitsky and Ziblatt 2018, 8).

As indicated, the demands a democracy makes on its citizenry are great. The rewards of the system are great also. The future, as far as can be seen, is likely to continue to test the nation's resiliency and its commitment to a way of life, while far from perfect, that has served it well.

NOTES

1. The timing of the 1973 Goldwater Rule adoption by the American Psychiatric Association was important. It is a complicated story. For an explanation, see Rachel Maddow and Michael Yarvitz, *Bag Man* (New York: Crown, 2020). The history of the Goldwater Rule is also described by Aaron Levin, "Goldwater Rule's Origins Based on Long-Ago Controversy." *Psychiatric News.* August 25, 2016. https://psychnews.psychiatryonline.org/doi/full/10.1176/appi.pn.2016.9a19.

2. John D. Gartner, as indicated, taught for just under three decades in the Department of Psychiatry at John Hopkins University Medical School. He used a term introduced by Eric Fromm, "Malignant Narcissist," to apply to Trump. Others have also. It has been described as "the most severe pathology" and "the root of the most vicious destructiveness and inhumanity" (quoted in Gartner 2017, 94). The concept has been defined as having four components: NPD, antisocial behavior, paranoid traits, and sadism. The condition has been applied to Hitler and Stalin. See the diagnoses in Bandy X. Lee, ed., *The Dangerous Case of Donald Trump* (New York: Thomas Dunne Books, 2019) in relation to Trump.

3. See Bandy X. Lee, ed. 2019. *The Dangerous Case of Donald Trump: 37 Psychiatrists and Mental Health Experts Assess a President.* New York: Thomas Dunne Books. It is not possible to review all of the 37 chapter diagnoses in this book.

Selected examples of the statements made in describing the assessments of Trump and the symptoms associated with his personality have been chosen to illustrate what are a diverse set of complex diagnoses.

4. A good source for detailed poll results on the 2020 presidential election can be found in Brian McGill, John West and Anthony DeBarros, "How We Voted in the 2020 Election," *Wall Street Journal* (results compiled by the AP), November 17, 2020. For demographic shifts from 2016 to 2020, see Chris Alcantara, Leslie Shapiro, Emily Guskin, Scott Clement and Brittany Renee Mayes, "How Independents, Latino Voters and Catholics Shifted From 2016 And Swung States For Biden and Trump," *WashingtonPost.com*, November 12, 2021. For a discussion of the relationship between increased voter turnout and election results, see Ted Mellnik and Adrian Blanco, "New Voters Gave Biden A Boost, But Not Everywhere," *WashingtonPost.com*, November 24, 2020.

5. In the event of a tie vote of the Electoral College, the House of Representatives by majority vote, with each state having one vote, selects the President and the Senate the vice president. The electors met on December 14, 2020, to cast their official vote. Only about half of states require their electors to vote for the popular vote winner. In 2016, seven "faithless" electors did not. https://www.270towin.com/content/electoral-college-ties/

6. David H. Freedman, "Can Science Stop QAnon?" *Newsweek*, October 23, 2020, 21–29; and Emilio Ferrara et al. "Characterizing Social Media Manipulation in the 2020 U.S. Presidential Election," *FirstMonday.org*, 2020, Annenberg School for Communication and Journalism, University of Southern California. A sign of the direction the Republican Party may be headed in was the election of Marjorie Taylor Greene to the House of Representatives from Georgia (Michael Kranish et al., "How Rep. Marjorie Taylor Greene, Promoter of QAnon's Baseless Theories, Rose With Support From Key Republicans," *Washington Post*, January 30, 2021). Green was a local member of QAnon and a major disseminator of conspiracy theories. She supported the execution of Democrats in 2019 and had written that the "Democratic Party [was] Involved With Child Sex, Satanism and The Occult" (Kranish story cited above). She claimed the mass shootings including the 2017 massacre in Las Vegas and the 2018 Parkland school shooting were frauds. She questioned whether 9/11 actually occurred and claimed laser beams from space may have started the California wildfires and other such conspiratorial thinking (Catie Edmondson et al., "G.O.P. Leader Criticizes Freshman for Remarks But Doesn't Punish Her." *New York Times*, February 4, 2021, A1; and Catie Edmonson, "Rep. Marjorie Taylor Greene Video: Obama Secretly a Muslim, Clinton Killed JFK, Jr., Pentagon Attack on 9/11 Is Questionable," *New York Times*, January 30, 2021). She was welcomed to the House of Representatives by the Republican Freedom Caucus and appointed to the prestigious House Education and Labor Committee and to the Budget Committee by Republicans. Some Congressional Republicans believed she represented the future of the Republican Party.

After the domestic terrorist attack on the Capitol, there was pressure on the Republicans to strip Greene of her committee assignments and expel her from the Congress. The Republicans refused. The Democratic majority then removed her from the committees.

7. There are many studies of the rise of authoritarianism to power in democratic states. They have much in common. See Richard J. Evans, *The Coming of the Third Reich* (New York: Penguin Books, 2005); Bruce Bueno de Mesquita and Alastair Smith, *The Dictator's Handbook: Why Bad Behavior Is Almost Always Good Politics* (New York: Public Affairs, 2016).

8. Tim Rutenberg et al. published an 8,000 word analysis in the *New York Times*, "77 Days: Trump Is Campaigning to Subvert the Election," February 12, 2001, A1. https://www.nytimes.com/2021/01/31/us/trump-election-lie.html. There are related accounts in the *Washington Post*, January 17, 2021 and by *CNN*, February 1, 2021. Officials reported on the low level of political participation among those who assaulted the Capitol. A surprising number did not even vote. They said they were part of the insurgency because President Trump asked them to be there.

9. A "Special Report" published by *Newsweek* on February 12, 2021, presents a comprehensive step-by-step account of the assault on the Capitol. It is its contention that officials' fear of Donald Trump paralyzed intelligence agencies and led to the takeover of the Capitol.

REFERENCES

Abel, David and Kay Lazar. 2020. "Trump's Twitter Storm Raises Some Concerns Among Doctors About Possible Risks of Powerful Steroid." *Boston Globe*. October 7.

Alberta, Tim. 2019. *American Carnage*. New York: HarperCollins Publishers.

Alexander, Dan. 2020. "Donald Trump Has At Least $1 Billion in Debt, More Than Twice The Amount He Suggested." *Forbes*. October 16.

Allen, Jonathan and Amie Parnes. 2017. *Shattered*. New York: Broadway Books.

AMA. 2016. "Ethical Physician Conduct in the Media." Reference Committee on Amendments to Constitution and Bylaws: Report of the Council on Ethical and Judicial Affairs. American Medical Association. CEJA Rep. 2-I-17. https://www .ama-assn.org/sites/ama-assn.org/files/corp/media-browser/public/hod/i17-refcom m-conby.pdf#page=41

Ambardar, Sheenie.MD. 2018. "What are the DSM-5 Diagnostic Criteria for Narcissistic Personality Disorder NPD?" *Medscape.com* May 16. https://www.med scape.com/answers/1519417-101764/what-are-the-dsm-5-diagnostic-criteria-for -narcissistic-personality-disorder-npd See also: Okoye, MD, Helen. "Narcissistic Personality Disorder DSM-5 301.81 (F60.81) *theravive.com*. Accessed February 8, 2021. https://www.theravive.com/therapedia/narcissistic-personality-disorder -dsm--5-301.81-(f60.81)

APA. 2010. "The Principles of Medical Ethics: With Annotations Especially Applicable to Psychiatry." American Psychiatric Association. Arlington, VA: American Psychiatric Association. Section 7.3. 9. https://www.psychiatry.org/File %20Library/Psychiatrists/Practice/Ethics/principles-medical-ethics.pdf

APA. 2013. *Diagnostic and Statistical Manual of Mental Disorders, 5th ed.* American Psychiatric Association. September 14 online. Washington, DC: American

Psychiatric Association. https://dsm.psychiatryonline.org/doi/book/10.1176/appi. books.9780890425596

Baker, Peter. 2020. "As He Questions His Opponent's Health, Trump Finds His Own Under Scrutiny." *New York Times*. September 17.

Baker, Peter and Maggie Haberman. 2020a. "Trump Leaves the Hospital, Minimizing the Virus and Urging Americans Not to 'Let It Dominate Your Lives.'" *New York Times*. October 6.

———. 2020b. "Leaving Hospital, Trump Minimizes Virus Risk: More Aides Get Sick as He Undermines Experts' Message." *New York Times*. October 6. A1.

———. 2020c. "President Lashes Out at His Aides With Calls to Indict Political Rivals." October 9.

Balz, Dan. 2018. "A Fresh Look Back at 2016 Finds America With An Identity Crisis." *Washington Post*. September 15.

——— and Philip Rucker. 2016. "How Donald Trump Won: The Insiders Tell Their Story." *Washington Post*. November 9.

Barrett, Devlin and Matt Zapotosky. 2021. "FBI Report Warned Of 'War' At Capitol, Contradicting Claims There Was No Indication Of Looming Violence." *Washington Post*. January 12.

Ben-Ghiat, Ruth. 2020. *Stongmen: How They Rise, Why They Succeed, How They Fail*. London: Profile Books

Blake, Aaron. 2016. "19 Things Donald Trump Knows Better Than Anyone Else, According to Trump." *Washington Post*. October 4.

Blake, Aaron. 2021. "What Trump Said before His Supporters Stormed the Capitol, Annotated." *Washington Post*. January 11.

Bogel-Burroughs, Nicholas, Shaila Dewan and Kathleen Gray. 2020. "F.B.I. Says Michigan Anti-Government Group Plotted to Kidnap Gov. Gretchen Whitmer." *Boston Globe*. October 8.

Brazile, Donna. 2017. *Hacks*. New York: Hachette Books.

Bump, Philip. 2016. "Donald Trump Will Be President Thanks To 80,000 People In Three States." *Washington Post*. December 1. https://www.washingtonpost .com/news/the-fix/wp/2016/12/01/donald-trump-will-be-president-thanks-to-8000 0-people-in-three-states/

Chason, Rachel and Samantha Schmidt. 2021. "Lafayette Square, Capitol Rallies, Met Starkly Different Policing Responses." *Washington Post*. January 14.

Choi, Matthew. 2020. "Trump Spins Rumors About His Own Health Into New Attack on Biden." *Politico*. September 3.

Crotty, William, ed. 2018. *Winning the Presidency 2016*. New York: Routledge.

Dann, Carrie. 2021. "Trump Approval Remains Stable in New NBC Poll, With Republicans Unmoved After Capitol Violence." *NBCNews*. January 17. https:// www.nbcnews.com/politics/meet-the-press/poll-trump-approval-remains-stable-re publicans-unmoved-after-capitol-violence-n1254457

Dean, John W. and Bob Altemeyer. 2020. *Authoritarian Nightmare*. Brooklyn: Melville House.

Dreisbach, Tom. 2021. "Nearly 1 in 5 Defendants In Capitol Riot Cases Served in The Military." *NPR*. January 21. https://www.npr.org/2021/01/21/958915267/near ly-one-in-five- defendants-in-capitol-riot-cases-served-in-the-military

Edelman, Larry and Shirley Leung. 2020. "Stimulus in Doubt as Trump Kills Talks." *Boston Globe*. October 7. 1.

Fandos, Nicholas and Maggie Haberman. 2021. "House Case Calls Trump 'Singularly Responsible' For Rampage at Capitol." *New York Times*. February 3. A1.

Farenthold, David A. 2016. "Trump Recorded Having Extremely Lewd Conversation About Women in 2005." *Washington Post*. October 8.

Ferrara, Emilio, Ho-Chun Herbert Chang, Emily Chen, Goran Murić and Jaimin Patel. 2020. "Characterizing Social Media Manipulation In The 2020 U.S. Presidential Election." *FirstMonday.org*. https://journals.uic.edu/ojs/index.php/fm/article/view/11431

Fisher, Kristy A. Fisher and Manassa Hany. 2020. "Antisocial Personality Disorder." Treasure Island, FL: StatPearls Publishing LLC. December 8. https://www.ncbi.nlm.nih.gov/books/NBK546673/

Folley, Aris. 2020. "Trump Wanted to Rip Open Shirt to Show Superman T-shirt When Leaving Walter Reed: Report." *The Hill*. October 11.

Freedman, David H. 2020. "Can Science Stop QAnon?" *Newsweek*. October 23. 21–29.

Gartner, John D. 2017. "Donald Trump is A) BAD, B) MAD, C) All of the Above." In Bandy X. Lee, ed. *The Dangerous Case of Donald Trump*. New York: Thomas Dunne Books/St. Martin's Press.

Gersen, Jeannie Suk. 2020. "The Dangerous Possibilities of Trump's Pardon Power." *New Yorker*. December 3.

Gilligan, James. 2019. "The Issue Is Dangerous, Not Mental Illness." In Bandy X. Lee, ed. 2019. *The Dangerous Case of Donald Trump*. New York: Thomas Dunne Books/St. Martin's Press.

Goldmacher, Shane and Rachel Shorey. 2021. "Trump's Sleight of Hand: Shouting Fraud, Pocketing Donors' Cash for Future." *New York Times*. February 1.

Gramlich, John. 2021. "Trump Used His Clemency Power Sparingly Despite A Raft of Late Pardons and Commutations." Pew Research Center. January 22. https://www.pewresearch.org/fact-tank/2021/01/22/trump-used-his-clemency-power-sparingly-despite-a-raft-of-late-pardons-and-commutations/

Haberman, Maggie. 2020. "Trump's Halting Walk Down Ramp Raises New Health Questions." *New York Times*. June 14.

——— and Katie Thomas. 2020. "Trump Calls His Illness 'A Blessing from God.'" October 7.

——— and Zolan Kanno-Youngs. 2020. "Trump Weighed Naming Election Conspiracy Theorist as Special Counsel." *New York Times*. December 19.

Hamblin, James. 2016. "The Bizarre Words of Donald Trump's Doctor." *The Atlantic*. August 31.

Hassan, Steven. 2019. *The Cult of Trump*. New York: Simon & Schuster.

Johnson, Kevin, David Jackson and Dennis Wagner. 2021. "Donald Trump Grants Clemency to 144 People (Not Himself or Family Members) in Final Hours." *USA Today*. January 20.

Kabaservice, Geoffrey. 2012. *Rule and Ruin*. Oxford: Oxford University Press.

Karni, Annie and Lawrence K. Altman, M.D. 2019. "At 243 Pounds, Trump Tips the Scale Into Obesity." *New York Times*. February 14.

Kessler, Glenn, Meg Kelly, Salvador Rizzo and Michelle Ye Hee Lee. 2021. "In Four Years, President Trump Made 30,573 False or Misleading Claims." *Washington Post*. January 20.

Lane, Sylvan. 2021. "Debt Cloud Hangs Over Trump Post-Presidency." *The Hill*. January 17.

Lee, Bandy X., ed. 2019, 2017. *The Dangerous Case of Donald Trump*. New York: Thomas Dunne Books/St. Martin's Press.

Leblanc, Paul. 2020. "Pence Was On Standby To 'Take Over' During Trump's Unannounced Walter Reed visit, New Book Reports." *CNN*. September 1. https://www.cnn.com/2020/08/31/politics/trump-walter-reed-visit-pence/index.html

Levin, Aaron. 2016. "Goldwater Rule's Origins Based on Long-Ago Controversy." *Psychiatric News*. August 25. https://psychnews.psychiatryonline.org/doi/full/10.1176/appi.pm.2016.9a19 See: Rachel Maddow and Michael Yarvitz. 2020. *Bag Man*. New York: Crown.

Levin, Sam et al. 2021. "Trump Acquittal: Biden Urges Vigilance To Defend 'Fragile' Democracy After Impeachment Trial." *The Guardian*. February 13.

Levitsky, Steven and Daniel Ziblatt. 2018. *How Democracies Die*. New York: Crown Publishing Group.

Linskey, Annie. 2021. "Biden Has Started Erasing Trump's Legacy. Now The Hard Part Starts." *Washington Post*. February 14.

Linz, Juan J. 1978. *The Breakdown of Democratic Regimes*. Baltimore: Johns Hopkins University Press.

Maddow, Rachel and Michael Yarvitz. 2020. *Bag Man*. New York: Crown.

Mandavilli, Apoorva and Tracey Tulley. 2020. "Leaving Hospital, Trump Minimizes Virus Risk: Limited Effort From the White House to Trace Contacts." *New York Times*. October 6. A1.

Manfredi, Lucas. 2020. "Regeneron CEO Says President Trump's Antibody Cocktail Treatment Is 'Case Report.'" *Foxbusiness.com*. October 11.

Martin, Jonathan and Maggie Haberman. 2021. "Trump's Republican Hit List at CPAC Is A Warning Shot To His Party." *New York Times*. February 28.

McDaniel, Susan H. 2016. "On the Couch, or Off: Candidates and Therapists." *New York Times*. March 11.

McGill, Brian, John West and Anthony DeBarros. 2020. "How We Voted in the 2020 Election." *Wall Street Journal*. Results compiled by the AP. November 17.

Mika Elizabeth. 2017. "Who Goes Trump? Tyranny as a Triumph of Narcissism." In Bandy X. Lee, ed. 2017. *The Dangerous Case of Donald Trump*. New York: Thomas Dunne Books/St. Martin's Press. 298–318.

———. 2019. In Bandy X. Lee, ed. *The Dangerous Case of Donald Trump (Enlarged Edition)*. New York: Thomas Dunne Books/St. Martin's Press. 297.

Mogelson, Luke. 2021. "Among the Insurrectionists." *New Yorker*. January 25.

Moss, Walter G. and Rick Shenkman. 2021. "How and Why Trump Was Almost Re-Elected. *LAProgressive.com* February 23.

New York Times Live. 2020. "Presidential Transition Highlights: Justice Dept. Has No Evidence of Fraud That Would Undo Biden's Win, Barr Says;" *NYTimes.com /live*. December 2.

Obama, Barack. 2020. "Address to the Democratic National Convention." August 19.

Parks, Miles. 2020. "Fired Official Says Correcting Trump's Fraud Claims The 'Right Thing To Do.'" *NPR.org*. December 1.

Psychology Today Editorial Staff/Hara Estroff Marano. 2017. "Shrinks Battle Over Diagnosing Donald Trump." *Psychology Today*. January 17. https://www.psy chologytoday.com/us/blog/brainstorm/201701/shrinks-battle-over-diagnosing-d onald-trump?page=1

Rogers, Katie and Lawrence K. Altman, M.D. 2018. "Trump's Former Doctor Says Office Was Raided and Files Seized." *New York Times*. May 1.

Rucker, Philip. 2020. "Trump Escalates Baseless Attacks On Election With 46-Minute Video Rant." *Washington Post*. December 2.

Rutenberg, Jim, Jo Becker, Eric Lipton, Maggie Haberman, Jonathan Martin, Matthew.

Rosenberg and Michael S. Schmidt. 2021. "77 Days: Trump's Campaign to Subvert the Election." *New York Times*. February 3.

RxList. 2020. "Dexamethasone: Uses, Dosage, Side Effects, Interactions, Warning." *RxList.com*. Accessed October 19, 2020. https://www.rxmist.com/dexamethasone -drug.htm#warnings

Sanger, David E. 2020. "Trump's Attempts To Overturn The Election Are Unparalleled In U.S. History." *NYTimes.com*. November 19.

Schmidt, Michael S. 2020. *Donald Trump v. The United States*. New York: Random House.

Shear, Michael D. and Stephanie Saul. 2021. "Trump, in Taped Call, Pressured Georgia Official to 'Find' Votes to Overturn Election." *New York Times*. January 3.

Sides, John, Michael Tesler and Lynn Vavreck. 2018. *Identity Crisis*. Princeton: Princeton University Press.

Smith, David. 2021. "Trump's Acquittal Seals His Grasp On The Republican Party." *The Guardian*. February 13.

Snyder, Timothy. 2017. *On Tyranny*. New York: Tim Duggan Books. 90.

———. 2021. "The American Abyss: Trump, the Mob and What Comes Next." *New York Times Magazine*. January 17.

Stevens, Stuart. 2020. *It was All a Lie*. New York: Alfred A. Knopf.

Swasey, Benjamin and Connie Hanzhang Jin. 2020. "Narrow Wins In These Key States Powered Biden To The Presidency." *NPR*. December 2. https://www.npr .org/2020/12/02/940689086/narrow-wins-in-these-key-states-powered-biden-to- the-presidency

Thomas, Katie and Roni Caryn Rabin. 2020. "Troubling Facts From Physicians Undercut Trump." *New York Times*. A1.

Trump, Donald. 2020. "Donald Trump's Speech On Election Fraud Claims Transcript." December 2. https://www.rev.com/blog/transcripts/donald-trump- speech-on-election-fraud-claims-transcript-december-2

Trump, Mary. 2020. *Too Much and Never Enough*. New York: Simon & Schuster.

Vigdor, Neil. 2020. "Trump Went for a Medical Checkup That Was Not on His Public Schedule." *New York Times*. November 17.

Washington Post Live. 2020. "A Conversation With Former CISA Director Christopher Krebs." *WashingtonPost.com/live*. December 2.

Weigel, David and Michael Scherer. 2021."Trump Rules Out Third Party As He Moves To Firm Up Control of GOP." *Washington Post*. February 28.

Wilentz, Sean. 2019. "The Culmination of Republican Decay." *The New York Review of Books*. October 10. 9–12.

Willingham. 2017. "The Trump Psych Debate: Is It Wrong to Say He's Mentally Ill?" *Forbe*s. February 19. https://www.forbes.com/sites/emilywillingham/2017/02/19/psychologist-calls-on-colleagues-to-sign-petition-for-trumps-removal/?sh=3 34980b364f3

Zapotosky, Matt et al. 2020. "Barr Says He Hasn't Seen Fraud That Could Affect The Election Outcome. *Washington Post*. December 1.

Chapter 3

The 2020 Presidential Nominations

Barbara Norrander

The 2020 presidential nominations presented both new and typical patterns. The Democratic field stood out as the largest and most diverse group of candidates. By mid-March a once-in-a-century pandemic interrupted the schedule of the primaries, causing states to scramble to select new, later dates and adopt new voting methods. The two national conventions also were forced to change their formats due to COVID-19. Still, the overall dynamics of the 2020 Democratic nomination mirrored that of recent decades. Most Democratic candidates dropped out of the contest early, some in 2019 and more in early 2020. Long before the last primary vote was cast, Joe Biden had, for all practical purposes, sewn up the Democratic nomination as he had a substantial lead in delegates and all of the other candidates withdrew from the race. An early end to the nomination race is the most typical outcome in recent presidential nominations. On the Republican side, President Donald Trump was easily renominated, just as was true for Barack Obama in 2012 and George W. Bush in 2004. This chapter will highlight the new and traditional elements of the 2020 presidential nominations. As President Trump was easily renominated, most of the discussion will be of the Democratic nomination.

THE RULES

Ultimately, the purpose of Democratic presidential primaries and caucuses is to select delegates to attend the party's summer national convention, where the presidential candidate is officially nominated through a roll call of state delegations. A candidate needs the support of 50 percent of convention delegates to become the party's nominee. Since the late twentieth century, the selection of these delegates is tied to the support candidates receive from primary voters or caucus participants. Delegate slots are first allocated to each state and Washington, DC, by the national Democratic Party using a formula that accounts for the state's population and support for Democratic candidates in past elections. Delegates are also allocated to capture preferences of residents in five U.S. territories and Americans living abroad. One-fourth of each state's delegates are awarded to candidates based on their statewide vote totals, while three-fourths are awarded based on votes in each Congressional districts. A candidate needs at least 15 percent of the vote to be awarded any delegates, and delegates are distributed among the remaining candidates proportionally to their vote totals.

Several new rules were in place for the 2020 Democratic nomination. One set aimed to broaden participation in the caucuses used by a handful of states in recent years. Caucuses are local party meetings open to registered voters. Caucuses are held on a specific date and time, typically a weeknight. In prior years, this meant that those with work or family obligations could not participate. Turnout in caucuses is considerably lower than in presidential primaries. In 2016, participation rates in Democratic caucuses averaged 8 percent compared to 30 percent in presidential primaries (Norrander 2020). However, despite these low turnout numbers, an increasing number of Democrats were participating in caucuses, but how many would attend and in which locations made it more difficult for local parties, which conduct the caucuses, to adequately prepare. For 2020, caucus states were encouraged to find other ways for voters to participate. The Iowa Democratic Party attempted to create a method for virtual participation in its caucuses, but security issues were too daunting. Instead, Iowa Democrats held satellite caucuses in 87 locations both within and outside of Iowa. Alternatively, other caucus states accepted absentee ballots from those who could not attend. Caucuses are just the first step in delegate selection for these states. Participants from the caucuses are selected to represent their candidate at later county, Congressional district, and state conventions. Delegates who attend the party's national convention are selected at the Congressional district and state conventions.

Caucus participants have one advantage over primary voters. Participants in Democratic caucuses have a second round of voting, which allows supporters of candidates who fail to meet the 15 percent threshold to reallocate their support to another candidate in the second round. Still, in prior years this process of initial and second-round support was not transparent, as caucus states such as Iowa only reported an estimate of the number of state convention delegates awarded to candidates based on second-round totals. Thus, Iowa and other caucus states reported state delegate equivalents, or SDEs, to indicate the potential support for each candidate at the party's state convention. In 2020, caucus states would report candidate support in the initial round, the second round, and the SDEs.

Only three states (Iowa, Nevada, Wyoming) and three territories (American Samoa, Guam, and Virgin Islands) retained the traditional caucus format in 2020. Four previous caucus states switched to holding party-run primaries. More limited state and local party budgets mean that fewer polling places are available with party-run primaries than there are in states where the government pays the cost of running the primary. However, innovations could be more easily introduced in party-run primaries. In 2020, three of the states with party-run primaries (Alaska, Hawaii, and Kansas) adopted rank-choice voting. Primary voters would rank between three and five presidential candidates. If a voter's first-choice candidate did not meet the 15 percent threshold, this voter's support would be transferred to their second-choice candidate. The Wyoming caucuses also used rank-choice voting, and Wyoming Democrats switched to all-mail ballots with the advent of COVID-19.

Another change in 2020 Democratic rules involved superdelegates. Primary and caucus results determine how many pledged delegates are distributed to each candidate. Pledged delegates are obligated to vote for a specific candidate at the national convention. Since the 1980s, the Democratic Party has a second type of delegate, a delegate who is a Democratic elected official, such as a senator, or a top party official, such as a state party chair. These are "superdelegates," who historically have been free to support any candidate, without regards to the primary or caucus vote in their state. Superdelegates were established to provide a voice at the convention from party members in government offices who would be working with any future president. However, superdelegates have been controversial. In 2016, the vast majority of superdelegates endorsed Hillary Clinton prior to the start of primary voting. Supporters of Bernie Sanders felt this provided Clinton with an unfair advantage. In 2020, there would be 770 superdelegates versus 3,979 pledged delegates.

Democratic Party rules in 2020 provided a more limited role for superdelegates. If one candidate had the support of half of the pledged delegates (e.g., 1,991 delegates) then that candidate would be nominated on the first, and only, convention vote, and superdelegates would not vote. If no candidate had the support of half of the pledged delegates on the first round of voting, the convention would move to a second round of voting in which superdelegates could vote for any candidate they prefer. Superdelegates could only vote on the first round of convention voting if one candidate had the support of 50 percent of both pledged and superdelegates (e.g., 2,376 delegates). Biden gained the support of 50 percent of pledged delegates by June 6 and 50 percent of all delegates by July 7, allowing both pledged and superdelegates to vote on the first, and only, presidential roll call at the Democratic National Convention.

While new national party rules in 2020 altered the structure of caucuses and changed the roles of superdelegates, many decisions about primaries and caucuses are made by state governments and state parties. States decide whether to hold a primary or a caucus. National Democratic Party rules since 2008 designate a front-four schedule: Iowa caucus, New Hampshire primary, Nevada caucus, and South Carolina primary. After those events, states may choose any date between the beginning of March and the beginning of June. Some states hoping to have more influence on the presidential nomination choose dates in early March. Other states hold later presidential primaries to combine them with their primaries for Congressional and state-level offices, saving the state the expense of holding two primaries.

The presidential nomination process is complex because it was never rationally planned. Many elements happened by chance. New Hampshire traditionally had an early primary during an era when only a handful of states held primaries and a win in a late primary could be just as important at convincing convention delegates that a candidate could win the fall general election. Iowa's path to the front also happened by accident because in 1972 it needed 30 days between all of the events tied to a caucus: caucus night, followed by a county convention, a Congressional district convention, and finally a state convention. Other elements are determined by the national government. Campaign finance laws from the 1970s limit the amount of money that can be directly contributed to candidates. In 2020, that limit was $2,800 which could only come from U.S. citizens and green card holders. However, Supreme Court rulings interpreting campaign spending as a form of free speech allowed for the development of outside groups, such as Super PACs, that can spend freely in support of any candidate. However, Super PAC money had only a small role in the 2020 Democratic contests. Finally, candidates make many of the important decisions. They decide whether to run at all. They decide where and how to campaign, how to raise funds, and what issues to stress. No one entity is in charge of presidential nomination rules, producing a complex process. However, patterns often reoccur across election years.

THE LARGE, DIVERSE FIELD OF
DEMOCRATIC CANDIDATES

In total, 29 individuals entered the race for the 2020 Democratic Party's presidential nomination. On July 28, 2017, John Delaney, a former U.S. House representative from Maryland, was the first to jump into the race. The last candidate to enter would be Michael Bloomberg, former mayor of New York City, who entered the race on November 14, 2019. Not all of the candidates were in competition at the same time. Richard Ojeda, a West Virginia state senator, was the first to withdraw from the contest on January 25, 2019. By the time Bloomberg entered the race, nine candidates besides Ojeda had dropped their bid for the Democratic nomination.

In recent decades the most typical presidential nominees are senators or governors. Senators and governors have the advantage of greater name recognition, established fundraising networks, and successfully winning statewide electoral contests. Competing for the 2020 Democratic presidential nomination were eight current or past senators: Michael Bennet (CO), Cory Booker (NJ), Kirsten Gillibrand (NY), Mike Gravel (Alaska), Kamala Harris (CA), Amy Klobuchar (MN), Bernie Sanders (VT), and Elizabeth Warren (MA). Only Klobuchar, Sanders, and Warren would remain in the race to compete in the Iowa caucus. Four current or past governors entered the race: Steve Bullock (MT), Deval Patrick (MA), John Hickenlooper (CO), and Jay Inslee (WA). All but Bullock exited the Democratic race in 2019.

Members of the U.S. House of Representatives are less likely to run for the presidency and less likely to win the nomination. House members are disadvantaged by typically lower profiles, having won in a Congressional district which is often more homogeneous than a state, and facing reelection if they are currently serving in the House. Nevertheless, seven current or former members of the U.S. House became candidates for the 2020 nomination: John Delaney (MD), Tulsi Gabbard (HI), Seth Moulton (MA), Beto O'Rourke (TX), Tim Ryan (OH), Joe Sestak (PA), and Eric Swalwell (CA). All except Gabbard dropped out of the race prior to the Iowa caucuses.

Candidates from other political offices included four current or former mayors. Two New York City mayors were in the fray: former mayor Michael Bloomberg and current mayor Bill de Blasio. Two small-city mayors became candidates: Pete Buttigieg (South Bend, IN) and Wayne Messam (Miramar, FL). Julian Castro formerly served as Secretary of Housing and Urban Development in President Barack Obama's Cabinet, while Richard Ojeda served in the West Virginia state senate. Among this group of six candidates only Buttigieg and Bloomberg would still be in the contest at the onset of 2020.

Three candidates had not previously been elected to a political office. Marianne Williamson was a spiritual leader, political activist, and author. Tom Steyer was a wealthy hedge-fund manager active in Democratic Party circles especially on environmental issues. Andrew Yang was a business entrepreneur and focused his campaign on economic issues. Yang attracted a number of young supporters, who became known as the Yang Gang. Williamson dropped out in 2019, while Yang and Steyer struggled during the early caucuses and primaries.

The final candidate in 2020 was a member of an elite group of candidates that are few in number but often the most successful candidates. That is former vice presidents. Joe Biden served as Barack Obama's vice president. He previously had a long political career as a senator representing Delaware. Vice presidents are well known by the public and connected to party activists and donors. Two recent vice presidents who became their party's nominee were George H. W. Bush in 1988 and Al Gore in 2000.

While many of the 2020 Democratic candidates shared backgrounds in political office similar to prior nominees, the 2020 Democratic pool of candidates was the most diverse in other aspects. Six women made the bid for the 2020 presidential nominations: Gabbard, Gillibrand, Harris, Klobuchar, Warren, and Williamson. In recent nomination races, only one woman entered the race: Hillary Clinton in 2008 and 2016 Democratic contests, Michele Bachmann in the 2012 Republican race, and Carly Fiorina in the 2016 Republican quest. Hillary Clinton in 2016 was the first woman selected by a major American party as their presidential nominee, while two previously had been named as vice presidential nominees (Geraldine Ferraro on the Democratic ticket with Walter Mondale in 1984 and Sarah Palin on the Republican ticket with John McCain in 2008). Joe Biden in the March 15 debate with Bernie Sanders promised to select a woman as his vice presidential running mate. On August 11, one week before the national convention, Biden announced he had selected Kamala Harris. Thus, Harris became the nation's first female vice president when Biden won the presidential election.

The 2020 Democratic field also was the most diverse in terms of ethnic backgrounds. Booker and Patrick were African Americans. Yang's family hailed from Taiwan, while Gabbard's family originated from the Pacific island of Samoa. Kamala Harris was biracial with her father immigrating from Jamaica and her mother from India. Castro and Ojeda were Latino. In terms of age, four of the candidates were in their 70s (Biden, Bloomberg, Sanders, and Warren) while Buttigieg at 38 was only three years over the constitutional requirement that a president be at least 35 years old. Buttigieg also was the first openly gay candidate for president.

Such a large and diverse field of candidates brought forth a number of questions. One was whether there was a preelection year frontrunner who would have an advantage as the primary voting began. Second, without a frontrunner would any candidate win enough votes in the primaries to accumulate the 50 percent of convention delegates needed to win the nomination on the first ballot? If not, the Democratic Party would have a contested convention, where multiple rounds of balloting would be necessary to select a presidential nominee. The last multiballot convention occurred in 1952 when Adlai Stevenson obtained the Democratic nomination on the third round of balloting. Finally, large fields of candidates can produce unpredictable results, such as the unexpected nomination of Donald Trump in 2016.

THE INVISIBLE PRIMARY

The "invisible primary" is the year or two before the presidential election year. During this time period, candidates decide whether to run, raise campaign funds, hold initial campaign events, make media appearances, and hope to attract endorsements from elected officials or high-ranking party officials. Candidates through these activities strive to make gains among the public as measured in public opinion polls. Prior to the late twentieth century, many of these preelection year activities were less public, thus the invisible primary name. However, preelection year events now play a role in shaping the fates of candidates. One candidate may emerge as the frontrunner—leading in fundraising, elite endorsements, and the public opinion polls. Other candidates fail to make progress and leave the contest before the first vote is cast.

With so many 2020 Democratic candidates the question was would any one become the preelection year frontrunner. Joe Biden as a former vice president was well known. Bernie Sanders, who finished second in the 2016, also had high voter recognition. Yet each had disadvantages as well. Biden failed twice before in trying to obtain the Democratic presidential nomination (1988, 2007), he was prone to gaffes, and if elected would be one of the oldest presidents. Sanders appealed to the progressive wing of the party but many questioned whether he could expand his support across a broader base of voters. In addition, in 2020 he would have challengers, such as Elizabeth Warren, also vying for the support of the party's progressive wing. Indicators of frontrunner status such as money raised, elite endorsements, and opinion poll standings were split between Sanders and Biden, and other candidates did not trail behind by much.

Money is an important resource for candidates. Money pays for candidate travel, advertisements, social media, and staffs. Candidates' ability to garner donations from American citizens also indicates their strength among potential voters. By the close of 2019, Sanders led in funds raised with $107 million, followed by Warren at $81 million and Buttigieg at $75 million.[1] Biden placed fourth in the amount raised at $59 million. Sanders's advantage in fundraising was due to his bid for the 2016 nomination. He already had a group of Americans willing to contribute to his campaign. Biden's totals appeared as a weakness given his stature as a former vice president, although he also declared later than other candidates and thus began fundraising later as well.

Two 2016 Democratic candidates had little need to court donors. Billionaires Tom Steyer and Michael Bloomberg relied on their own personal wealth to fund their campaigns. In 2015, both contributed $200 million to their presidential bids. Eventually Bloomberg would commit $900 million to his campaign (Goldmacher 2020, March 20). Wealthy candidates in prior years also contributed substantial sums of their own money to their presidential nomination bids. Trump in 2020 and Mitt Romney in 2008 each spent $40 million of their own money in their bids for the Republican presidential nomination (Norrander 2020).

Elite endorsements are another sign of candidate support. The website *FiveThirtyEight* tracks endorsements from leading political figures, weighting the importance of an endorsement by the office held by that person. For example, an endorsement by a former president is worth 10 points, one from a governor is worth 8 points, and one from a member of the U.S. House is worth 3 points.[2] With this formula, Biden led at the start of 2020 with endorsements worth 175 points, Warren was second at 66 points, Klobuchar third at 50 points, and Sanders fourth at 48 points. Klobuchar, as many other candidates in 2019, received most of her endorsements from political figures in her home state of Minnesota. Sanders continued to have weak support from Democratic governors, senators, and House members as he did in 2016. Biden was the first choice of Democratic leaders in 2020, but fewer elites were endorsing candidate in 2020 than in 2016. In 2016, most of the Democratic Party elite made endorsements, and three-fourths of these went to Hillary Clinton (Cohen 2018).

In recent decades, debates played a prominent role during the invisible primary. In an attempt to limit and set the boundaries for these debates, the Republican Party in 2016 created party-sanctioned debates. In 2020, the Democratic Party followed suit. Six debates would be held in 2019, and candidate qualifications would be increasingly stringent as time went by. To qualify for the first debate, a candidate needed to attract the support of 1 percent in three national or early state polls or obtain campaign donations from 65,000 individuals across at least 20 states. Twenty candidates met the criteria for the first debate, and ten faced off against one another on either June 26 or 27, 2019. With each subsequent debate, the criteria for qualification became more stringent. Poll standing numbers and contribution requirements increased and candidates needed to meet both conditions. By the time of the last preelection debate on December 19, only seven candidates made the cut. To qualify for this debate, a candidate needed support from 4 percent in four early state or national polls (or 6% in two early state polls) and have donations from 200,000 people with at least 800 in 20 different states. The 11th and last Democratic primary debate was held on March 15, 2020, between Bernie Sanders and Joe Biden. That debate was held at CNN's Washington studios without an audience, due to the coronavirus.

Primary debate performances can influence voters' candidate choices. One reason is that voters tend to know less about these candidates, especially during the invisible primary stage. A second reason is that all candidates are from the same party. Thus, party identification does not lock voters into favoring only their party's candidate. Primary debates provide lesser known candidates with the opportunity to introduce themselves to a national audience. Yet, a stage crowded with numerous candidates limits the amount of time most candidates receive. Still, candidates hope that they will score points with voters by taking a particular issue stand or contrasting their traits with other candidates on the stage.

Just as important as the actual debate is how the media interpret the outcome. The media like to declare winners and losers (Azari 2019). When a lesser-known candidate is declared as being among the winners of a debate, her or his fortunes may rise in terms of additional media coverage and campaign donations. For example, Kamala Harris was viewed as one of the winners in the first Democratic debate. She had criticized Joe Biden's opposition to school busing, a policy that allowed Harris herself to attend an integrated school. Harris's poll standings rose from 6 to 12 percent, and her debate performance also increased campaign contributions (Cadelago 2019). However, the debate "bump" did not last, and Harris withdrew in December due to a shortage of campaign funds.

Candidate attrition is a major trait of the presidential nomination contests (Norrander 2006). Candidates who fail to do well in fundraising, name recognition, or garnering primary votes drop out of the race. Some candidates leave the race during the invisible primary stage. Fourteen Democratic candidates withdrew before December 31, 2019: Bullock, de Blasio, Gillibrand, Gravel, Harris, Hickenlooper, Inslee, Messam, Moulton, Ojeda, O'Rourke, Ryan, Sestak, and Swalwell. Four more would exit in January 2020, before the Iowa caucuses: Booker, Castro, Delaney, and Williamson. Many of these candidates began and ended their bids as relative unknowns. Yet a few of these candidates appeared to have greater potential, such as Harris and O'Rourke, but they failed to raise sufficient funds or to stand out consistently on a crowded debate stage. This left 11 candidates in the running for the 2020 Democratic nomination.

The public remained divided in their support for the candidates at the end of the invisible primary. On December 31, 2019, Biden led in the public opinion polls as averaged by the website *FiveThirtyEight*. Biden had the support of 27.7 percent of Democratic voters. Sanders was favored by 17.7 percent and Warren by 15 percent. Public support for all other candidates fell below 10 percent.[3] Democratic voters were more unified in 2016, with Hillary Clinton in December 2015 leading Sanders 55 to 30.3 percent.[4] However, the leader in the national public opinion polls does not always win the nomination. Clinton also led in the public opinion polls in 2007, but ultimately lost the nomination to Barack Obama. With no clear frontrunner at the close of 2019, the 2020 primaries would decide which candidates survived, which would quickly leave the field and ultimately, which candidate would become the Democratic Party's presidential nominee.

THE FRONT-FOUR CONTESTS

New Hampshire has held an early presidential primary since the early decades of the twentieth century. The early date for the Iowa caucuses began in the 1970s. As more states in the late twentieth century switched to primaries, holding an event at the front of the primary and caucus calendar came to be viewed as more important. In 2008, the national Democratic Party decided to expand the front of the calendar to include more ethnically diverse states, and thus added the Nevada caucuses and South Carolina's primary to create a front four. The Republican Party signed onto this calendar in 2012. Today's presidential nominations unfold first in the front-four states, followed by a multistate Super Tuesday with the remaining primaries scheduled throughout the spring months.

Because Iowa and New Hampshire are at the front of the calendar, residents of these states have ample opportunities to view the candidates. Throughout the invisible primary phase, candidates spend considerable time in these two states holding rallies and other face-to-face events. Combined, the 2020 candidates spent 928 days campaigning in Iowa and 666 days in New Hampshire. Among the major candidates, Klobuchar spent the most days in Iowa at 71, while Yang topped the list in New Hampshire at 50 days.[5] Elizabeth Warren included in her rallies a "pinkie line" to encourage young girls to pursue their dreams and concluded her events with a selfie line for those wanting a photograph with the candidate. Some candidates, such as Bernie Sanders, held large rallies with live music, while other candidate events were smaller meet and greet opportunities. The other two early states also receive some of this "retail" politics but still not as much as do Iowa and New Hampshire.

In 2020, the Iowa caucuses again led off the calendar with voting in 1,678 precincts across the state. In addition, Iowa set up 87 satellite caucuses: 60 in Iowa, 24 in other states, and 3 in foreign countries. Participants in the caucuses would have two rounds of voting. An initial first round was to determine the "viability" of the candidates, meaning having the support of at least 15 percent of the participants. Supporters of candidates who did not meet the viability criteria could switch their support to another candidate in the second round. New in 2020, participants filled out forms indicating their first-round preference and any change of support in the second round. Prior to 2020, the initial and second-round support for candidates were not reported from the local caucuses. Instead, only the SDEs were reported. In 2020, new caucus rules required each local caucus leader to report totals from the first and second round of voting and the SDE totals.

On caucus night, these new requirements led to confusion at caucus sites, and the mobile application ("app") local caucus leaders were to use to send results to the state party malfunctioned. As a result, the Iowa state party was unable to produce an accurate count on caucus night. A final, official tally was not available for three days. By that time, the media and public focus had turned to New Hampshire. Nevertheless, Buttigieg and Sanders both claimed victory. Sanders bested Buttigieg in the second-round vote at 26.8 to 25.3 percent. Yet Buttigieg edged out Sanders in SDEs at 26.2 to 26.1 percent. Warren finished third, Biden a disappointing fourth, and Klobuchar placed fifth. None of the other candidates had more than 1 percent of the vote in the second tally.

New Hampshire came second and Sanders would win, as he did in 2016. One reason is that New Hampshire is in Sanders's backyard, as Sanders hails from next-door Vermont. As in Iowa, Sanders and Buttigieg finished in the top two with Sanders overtaking Buttigieg 25.6 to 21.2 percent in vote totals. Klobuchar finished in third place at 19.7 percent, briefly bringing her into the top tier candidates. Warren placed a disappointing fourth, as she too was from the region, as a senator representing Massachusetts. Biden's fifth-place finish greatly diminished his position as the frontrunner. Sanders's 2020 New Hampshire vote total, however, was not as impressive as his 2016 victory over Clinton of 60 to 38 percent. Still, in 2020, Sanders could lay some claim to winning the first two events, and no candidate had won the Democratic Party's presidential nomination without winning in either Iowa or New Hampshire since 1992. Due to dismal showings in Iowa and New Hampshire, Bennett, Patrick, and Yang dropped out. The Democratic field shrank to eight candidates.

In contrast to the first two states where the Democratic electorate is overwhelming white, the next two events brought in more diverse Democratic electorates. The Nevada Democratic electorate is approximately 20 percent Hispanic and 15 percent Black, while the South Carolina Democratic electorate is 57 percent Black (Bacon 2020). This would not bode well for candidates whose appeal so far had been mostly among white voters, such as Buttigieg and Klobuchar. The Nevada Democratic electorate also has a large number of union voters, but in 2020 the influential Culinary Union failed to endorse any candidate. Sanders would add to his 2020 totals with a win in the Nevada caucuses. Sanders garnered 41 percent of the final round vote which translated into 47 percent of the SDEs. Biden did slightly better in Nevada than the previous two contests, placing second, with half as much support as Sanders. Still, Biden's campaign was struggling. Buttigieg and Warren rounded out the top four in Nevada's vote.

In hindsight, South Carolina became the pivotal event for the 2020 Democratic nominations. Biden won big in South Carolina with strong support from African American voters. His victory was aided by a crucial endorsement from Jim Clyburn, the long-term South Carolina representative who had worked with Biden in the past. Biden's promise to appoint a

Black woman to the Supreme Court allowed Clyburn, who was Black, to give an enthusiastic endorsement to Biden (Allen and Parnes 2021). Biden won nearly half of the primary vote, coming in at 48.6 percent of the vote. Sanders placed a distant second at 19.8 percent. Steyer finished third, which was disappointing as he had committed more resources to the South Carolina primary than did the other candidates. Biden's win in South Carolina was not only a crucial victory in that state, but his strong support among African American voters was a signal to Black voters in the upcoming southern state primaries held on Super Tuesday. South Carolina proved as important in 2016, when Hillary Clinton's large winning margin among Black voters in South Carolina foretold her lopsided victories in the southern Super Tuesday primaries. The same would happen for Biden.

After South Carolina in 2020 three more candidates suspended their campaigns. When Steyer saw that his heavy advertising campaign in South Carolina did not pay off, he left the race. Buttigieg was not able to replicate his strong showings in Iowa and New Hampshire in either Nevada or South Carolina. Klobuchar's momentum strategy required her to have placed better in the first three contests and also relied on Biden's campaign continuing to falter. Buttigieg and Klobuchar left the race after South Carolina. Both endorsed Biden and appeared with Biden in campaign events. Thus, after South Carolina only four candidates who contested the first four events remained in the race: Biden, Sanders, Warren, and Gabbard. Added to this total was a new candidate, Michael Bloomberg, who had not entered the first four events, instead relying on his nearly unlimited campaign funds to be competitive in the numerous Super Tuesday primaries.

SUPER TUESDAY

Super Tuesdays are a common occurrence in presidential nominations since the late twentieth century. In 1988, southern states joined together on an early March date to create a regional primary, and many southern states retained their Super Tuesday dates in subsequent years. Other states across the nation pick and choose whether they want to hold their primary on Super Tuesday, with some states entering and leaving in each election cycle. Thus, the size of Super Tuesday in each election year varies. The largest Super Tuesday was in 2008 when 47 percent of convention delegates were chosen. Super Tuesday in 2020 would select a more typical 34 percent of the convention delegates. Still, with the large number of delegates at stake on Super Tuesday, candidate strategies turn to delegate accumulation as their goal. In contrast, the first four events select only 4 percent of the delegates, but the prize from these events is the momentum candidates can claim from a crucial early victory.

With Biden's decisive win in South Carolina and strong support among African American voters in southern states, Biden dominated on Super Tuesday. As shown in table 3.1, Biden won 10 events on Super Tuesday, with seven of those victories coming in southern or border states. Sanders won in five states, including his home state of Vermont. The slow count of ballots in California, where many people vote by mail and those ballots only needed to be postmarked by Election Day, hampered Sanders's ability to claim a crucial victory on election night. Bloomberg scored his only victory of the nomination season with a win in the caucuses held in the territory of American Samoa where only 351 votes were tallied. Immediately after Super Tuesday, Warren and Bloomberg dropped out of the race. Gabbard dropped out after the March 10 primaries, leaving only Biden and Sanders remaining in the contest.

Super Tuesday is crucial to the overall dynamics of a nomination contest. Sometimes, the nomination race is over after Super Tuesday, such as in 2000 when George W. Bush's main competitor John McCain dropped out and on the Democratic side, New Jersey senator Bill Bradley dropped out leaving Al Gore as the sole candidate. Most frequently, Super Tuesday establishes a leader who eventually wins the nomination, usually prior to the end of the last primaries. Thus, in 2016, Donald Trump established a lead after Super Tuesday, and a split field between Marco Rubio, Ted Cruz, and John Kasich prevented any of the other candidates being able to overcome Trump's lead. Infrequently, a "tied" vote on Super Tuesday leads to a long, drawn-out battle between two candidates that endures to the last primaries, as happened in the 2008 and 2016 Democratic nominations.

After Super Tuesday in 2020, the Democratic field essentially narrowed to two candidates: Biden and Sanders. Yet, this did not lead to a prolonged two-candidate race. One reason is that Biden won twice as many victories on Super Tuesday as did Sanders. Second, the exit of Buttigieg, Klobuchar, and Bloomberg eliminated Biden's rival for the moderate segment of the Democratic Party. Third, in the subsequent multistate March 10 series of primaries, Biden again dominated, winning five primaries to Sanders's sole victory in a party-run primary in South Dakota. Fourth, many Democratic voters simply wanted a candidate who could beat President Trump. With his string of victories and more moderate stances, Biden looked as the more electable candidate to many Democratic voters. Finally, the onset of COVID-19 disrupted the remaining schedule of primaries and refocused the public's attention away from the nomination battle.

Table 3.1   Percent of Votes for Candidates in 2020 Democratic Primaries and Caucuses

State	Date	Format	Biden	Sanders	Warren	Bloomberg
Iowa	February 3	Caucus	15.9	26.2	18.1	0.0
New Hampshire	February 11	Primary	8.5	26.1	9.4	0.0
Nevada	February 25	Caucus	20.2	46.9	9.7	0.0
South Carolina	February 29	Primary	48.6	19.8	7.1	0.0
Alabama	March 3	Primary	63.8	16.7	5.8	11.8
American Samoa	March 3	Caucus	8.8	10.5	1.4	49.9
Arkansas	March 3	Primary	40.6	22.4	10.0	16.7
California	March 3	Primary	27.9	36.0	13.2	12.1
Colorado	March 3	Primary	24.6	37.0	17.6	18.5
Maine	March 3	Primary	33.9	33.0	15.8	12.0
Massachusetts	March 3	Primary	33.6	26.8	21.6	11.8
Minnesota	March 3	Primary	38.8	30.0	15.5	8.3
North Carolina	March 3	Primary	43.7	24.6	10.7	13.2
Oklahoma	March 3	Primary	38.7	25.4	13.4	13.9
Tennessee	March 3	Primary	41.8	25.1	10.4	15.5
Texas	March 3	Primary	34.6	29.9	11.4	14.4
Utah	March 3	Primary	18.4	36.1	16.2	15.4
Vermont	March 3	Primary	22.1	50.9	12.6	9.4
Virginia	March 3	Primary	53.3	23.1	10.8	9.7
Democrats Abroad	March 3	Primary	22.7	57.9	14.3	2.2
Idaho	March 10	Primary	48.9	42.4	2.6	2.4
Michigan	March 10	Primary	53.6	36.8	1.7	4.7
Mississippi	March 10	Primary	81.0	14.8	0.6	2.5
Missouri	March 10	Primary	60.4	34.7	1.2	1.5
North Dakota	March 10	P. Prim.	39.8	53.3	2.5	0.8
Washington	March 10	Primary	38.1	36.8	9.2	7.9
Northern Marianas	March 14	Convention	36.4	63.6	0.0	0.0
Arizona	March 17	Primary	50.2	37.6	6.7	0.0
Florida	March 17	Primary	61.9	22.8	1.9	8.4
Illinois	March 17	Primary	58.9	36.2	1.5	1.5
Wisconsin	April 7	Primary	63.1	31.8	1.5	1.0
Alaska	April 10	P. Prim.	55.3	44.7	0.0	0.0
Wyoming	April 17	Caucus	72.2	27.8	0.0	0.0
Ohio	April 28	Primary	72.4	16.7	3.5	3.2
Kansas	May 2	P. Prim.	76.9	23.1	0.0	0.0
Nebraska	May 12	Primary	76.8	14.1	6.3	0.0
Oregon	May 19	Primary	67.4	21.0	9.8	0.0
Hawaii	May 22	P. Prim.	63.2	36.8	0.0	0.0
Maryland	June 2	Primary	85.7	8.0	2.6	0.7
Pennsylvania	June 2	Primary	79.3	18.0	0.0	0.0
Rhode Island	June 2	Primary	78.8	15.3	4.4	0.0
Indiana	June 2	Primary	78.8	14.0	3.7	1.0
Montana	June 2	Primary	76.7	15.1	8.2	0.0
New Mexico	June 2	Primary	75.3	15.5	6.0	0.0
South Dakota	June 2	Primary	77.5	22.5	0.0	0.0
Washington, DC	June 2	Primary	76.5	10.1	12.9	0.0
Guam	June 6	Caucus	69.6	30.4	0.0	0.0

(Continued)

Table 3.1   Percent of Votes for Candidates in 2020 Democratic Primaries and Caucuses (*Continued*)

State	Date	Format	Biden	Sanders	Warren	Bloomberg
Virgin Islands	June 6	Caucus	94.7	5.3	0.0	0.0
Georgia	June 9	Primary	84.9	9.4	2.0	0.7
West Virginia	June 9	Primary	71.2	13.3	3.3	2.2
New York	June 23	Primary	70.2	17.7	5.1	2.4
Kentucky	June 23	Primary	76.2	13.6	3.2	0.0
New Jersey	July 7	Primary	85.3	14.7	0.0	0.0
Delaware	July 7	Primary	89.4	7.5	3.1	0.0
Louisiana	July 11	Primary	79.8	7.5	2.4	1.6
Puerto Rico	July 12	Primary	62.4	14.8	1.6	14.2
Connecticut	August 11	Primary	86.9	11.8	0.0	0.0

Source: Candidates' vote percentages based on vote totals from official state election sites accessed by the author. Results of caucuses and party-run primaries accessed from the state parties or media websites. Iowa and Nevada percentages are based on the SDE results.
Note: P. prim. = party-run primary. Bloomberg dropped out of race on March 4, Warren on March 5, and Sanders on April 8.

COVID-19 AND THE CHANGING PRIMARY CALENDAR

COVID-19 changed Americans' lives in 2020. In early March, music concerts, sports events, and Broadway shows started to be cancelled. Flights into the United States were being restricted. By mid-March, a COVID-19 case had been confirmed in all 50 states. Trump declared a national emergency on March 13, and Congress passed the Coronavirus Aid, Relief, and Economic Security Act on March 27. COVID-19 also began to disrupt the Democratic nomination contest. The March 17 primaries were the first to be impacted by COVID-19. Ohio rescheduled its primary to April 28. In the remaining three primaries, voters began to use alternatives to Election Day voting. Illinois saw an increase in mail-in ballots and early in-person voting but still had an overall drop in turnout. Voting in Arizona and Florida was less disrupted due to a history of high numbers of mail-in ballots in these states (Garrison 2020). Biden won each of these states by 50 percent or more of the vote.

More and more states began to delay their primaries. In total, 16 states and two territories rescheduled their primaries or caucuses. Many moved their contests to June or July, often to coincide with their primaries for Congressional and state offices. Connecticut moved its presidential primary to August 11, just a few days before the national convention. Three states kept their early May primaries. Three other states plus Washington, DC and Virgin Islands maintained their early June dates. Keeping its April 7 date, Wisconsin demonstrated the problems that could arise in holding an election during widespread concern over the virus.

Wisconsin would be an important event for Bernie Sanders. It was his last hope of stemming Biden's march to the nomination. Sanders had won Wisconsin in 2016 with 57 percent of the vote. But after losing 8 of the 10 events since Super Tuesday, even a lopsided Wisconsin win might not have been enough to salvage Sanders's campaign. The 2020 Wisconsin primary revealed the problems of conducting elections during the pandemic. Polling locations are staffed by temporary workers who are often retirees working more out of patriotism than for the small pay. Yet these elderly citizens were those most likely to fear COVID-19. As a result, many locations in Wisconsin were not able to open the regular number of polling sites. In Milwaukee only 5 sites out of 180 were open, in Green Bay only 2 out of 31 opened, and in Waukesha, a suburb of Milwaukee, only 1 voting site was open. As a result, many potential voters had to decide whether to endure long lines in order to vote. Absentee balloting was complicated by a Wisconsin requirement that a ballot not only needed the signature of the voter but also that of a witness to the voter's signature. A legal battle over when absentee ballots needed to be received led to further confusion over using absentee ballots, perhaps sending more voters to the polls (Herndon et al. 2020). In the end, Biden bested Sanders 63.1 to 31.8 percent. Sanders withdrew from the contest, leaving Biden as the sole remaining candidate and as the Democratic Party's presumptive presidential nominee.

The presidential nomination is all about winning convention delegates by winning votes. Figure 3.1 illustrates how Biden accumulated delegates through his primary victories. The first four events in February chose few delegates, with Sanders leading Biden 60 to 54 delegates. With the March 3 Super Tuesday contests, Biden began to pull ahead of Sanders by approximately 70 delegates, and by his win in Wisconsin in early April, Biden's lead grew to 300 delegates. As Sanders dropped out of the contest after Wisconsin, Biden's delegate totals continued to grow. Biden had a sufficient number of delegates to win on the first convention ballot on June 6 when he had 1,992 pledged delegates. When all the pledged delegates were assigned after Connecticut's primary, Biden was supported by 2,727 delegates. Sanders's total stood at 1,118 delegates, while the numbers for the other candidates were Warren at 60, Bloomberg at 44, Buttigieg at 21, Klobuchar at 7, and Gabbard at 2.[6]

THE RENOMINATION OF DONALD TRUMP

Sitting presidents running for renomination almost always have an easy path. Such was the case for President Donald Trump. A handful of states cancelled their Republican primaries, a pattern that also occurred with the

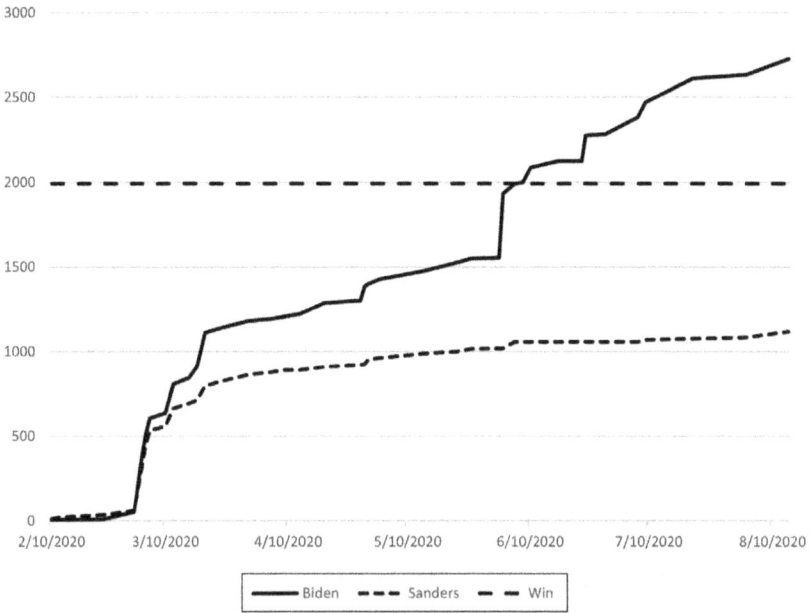

Figure 3.1 Accumulation of Convention Delegates by Biden and Sanders. Note: Win is the number of pledged delegates (1,991) necessary to secure the nomination at the convention. Sanders dropped out of the race on April 8, 2020.

renominations of President George W. Bush in 2004 and President Barack Obama in 2012. Other Republican state parties adopted winner-take-all rules to distribute all of their convention delegates to the primary winner to consolidate support behind Trump. Such tactics were not necessary. Trump faced only nominal challenges from three former Republican officeholders: Bill Weld (MA), Joe Walsh (IL), and Mark Sanford (SC). Sanford left the race in November 2019, Joe Walsh left after the Iowa caucuses, and Weld exited the race in mid-March when Trump secured the support of the 50 percent of Republican delegates needed for the nomination. Weld was the only one of the three to win any delegates, and he only won one delegate.

As sitting presidents do not have to worry about their renomination, they use the spring months to prepare for the fall general election. Sitting presidents raise money for their primary campaign and spend it hiring staff, planning strategy, holding rallies, running commercials, and raising more money. Trump's reelection campaign spent $22.7 million on advertising by mid-June. As Biden claimed the mantle of the Democratic Party's presumptive nominee by April, he too began to strategize for the general election. Biden began his "fall" advertising in June with a $15 million buy for television, radio, and digital platforms (Goldmacher 2020, June 8).

THE UNUSUAL NATIONAL CONVENTIONS

Normally, the Democratic and Republican national conventions are four-day events of speeches, group meetings, and networking among delegates. A large convention hall is packed with delegates from 50 states, Washington, DC, and the territories. Network and cable television set up booths inside the convention hall to broadcast the events to the nation. The main stage of the convention hall is the site for speeches by party stalwarts, up-and-coming politicians, and representatives of various constituency groups. A prewritten party platform is ratified. The president and vice president are formally nominated as their delegate totals accumulate through a roll call of the states. The party's presidential nominee ends the convention with his or her speech, which is followed by a balloon drop to round out the festivities.

The goal of past convention extravaganzas was to uplift the fortunes of the party's nominee by showing the qualities and policies of the nominee and the strong, unified support of the party behind the nominee. In prior decades, a successful convention could give the presidential candidate a "convention bounce" in the public opinion polls. However, research by political scientist Thomas Holbrook shows that in recent years convention bounces are typically smaller due to publicity during the primary process and the tightening of presidential candidate support based on partisanship (Hampson 2016).

COVID-19 upended plans for the 2020 national conventions. The Democratic Party originally scheduled its convention for July 13–16 to be held in Milwaukee, Wisconsin. On April 2, Democratic officials announced that the convention would be delayed until August 17–20. As illnesses and deaths from COVID-19 continued to grow in numbers and as social distancing recommendations could not be accommodated in a convention hall filled with thousands of delegates, the Democratic Party began planning for a virtual convention. Their August convention featured recorded and live speeches streamed from settings across the country. The roll call of states for Biden's official nomination took place across the country as select delegates announced their states' tallies. Following tradition, Biden gave his acceptance speech on the last night of the convention, but not before a packed convention hall. Rather, Biden gave his speech in a nearly empty room populated by state signs rather than convention delegates. The traditional indoor balloon drop was replaced by outdoor fireworks.

President Trump wanted to retain as much of a conventional convention as possible. Two years before, Charlotte, North Carolina, was selected as the site for the Republican convention. Planning a convention is a long and expensive process. Yet, as the COVID-19 pandemic worsened, North Carolina officials announced that a large-scale convention in Charlotte would not be possible. Trump and Republican Party officials looked for an alternative site. Jacksonville, Florida, was chosen, but on July 23, Florida officials also indicated that a large-scale convention would not be possible. Eventually, the Republicans returned to a small, one-day gathering of around 300 delegates in Charlotte to conduct the party's business, such as casting the roll call vote for president. Breaking from tradition, the Republican Party in 2020 did not develop a platform of issue positions but issued a one-page statement in support of Trump and opposition to the positions of former President Obama and Joe Biden. Across the other three days of the convention, Republican officials and individuals close to President Trump gave speeches from various locations across the country. On the last day of the convention, Trump gave his acceptance speech from the South Lawn of the White House. The Republican convention too ended with outdoor fireworks.

THIRD-PARTY NOMINATIONS

Third parties, or minor parties, nominate candidates for president not with the belief that these candidates will win the election but to garner more attention for their parties with hopes of gradually increasing their number of supporters. Thus, third parties often face a choice between nominating someone from their ranks who is a true believer in the party's issues, or alternatively, nominating a candidate with a national reputation who could draw in more voters, even if these candidates may not agree with all the party's issues. Running the same presidential candidate over multiple years is another strategy to increase the public's awareness of the party and its presidential nominee. In recent years, both the Libertarian and Green parties have adopted these later strategies, such as in 2000 when the Green Party selected longtime consumer advocate Ralph Nader as their party's nominee and the Libertarian Party picking former New Mexico governor Gary Johnson as their nominee in 2012 and 2016.

In 2020, both the Libertarian Party and the Green Party adopted the strategy of nominating individuals from within their ranks who agreed with the party's issue positions. At the May 22–24 Libertarian Party virtual convention, the party nominated Jo Jorgenson, a Clemson University lecturer, as their presidential nominee, and as their vice presidential candidate selected Spike Cohen, a podcaster. Jorgenson won the nomination in the fourth round of balloting, and Cohen on the third round. The Green Party nominated Howie Hawkins, an original founder of the party, as its presidential nominee through a virtual convention held from July 9 to 12. Hawkins had the support of 59 percent of the delegates. Activist Angela Nicole Walker was selected as the vice presidential candidate.

CONCLUSION

The 2020 presidential nominations had elements that were both typical and atypical of past years. In typical fashion, Joe Biden won the presidential nomination as most of the other candidates faltered and left the nomination race. After a slow start, Biden won a crucial victory in South Carolina and followed that up by winning the most delegates on Super Tuesday. Biden continued to add to his delegate totals with subsequent primary victories. The 2020 Democratic race was over on April 8 when Bernie Sanders left the race. Yet, such an early close to a nomination race is the most typical pattern for presidential nominations since the late twentieth century. President Donald Trump, just like past presidents, easily won his party's renomination. Yet 2020 had unique elements as well. The Democratic Party instituted new rules for caucuses and superdelegates. The initial Democratic field of candidates was the largest and most demographically diverse set of candidates. And foremost, a once-in-a-century pandemic upended the schedule of the final months of primaries and led both parties to modify their national conventions to a virtual format.

NOTES

1. Fundraising totals as published by The Center for Responsible Politics, https://www.opensecrets.org/2020-presidential-race.
2. FiveThirtyEight. "The 2020 Endorsement Primary." https://projects.fivethirtyeight.com/2020-endorsements/democratic-primary/.
3. FiveThirtyEight. "Latest Polls." https://projects.fivethirtyeight.com/polls/president-primary-d/national/.
4. FiveThirtyEight. "2016 National Primary Polls." https://projects.fivethirtyeight.com/election-2016/national-primary-polls/democratic/.
5. These figures are from *Fox News* Candidate Tracker. The full numbers include both the major candidates and candidates who withdrew during the invisible primary. While Yang spent 50 days campaigning in New Hampshire, he spent 54 days campaigning in Iowa. https://www.foxnews.com/elections/2020/primary-results/candidate-tracker.
6. Delegate totals as listed on CNN webpages throughout the nomination events. https://www.cnn.com/election/2020/primaries-and-caucuses.

REFERENCES

Allen, Jonathan, and Amie Parnes. 2021. "Inside Jim Clyburn's Biden Election Endorsement—And How Biden Almost Blew It." *NBC News*. January 25. Accessed January 25, 2021. https://www.nbcnews.com/think/opinion/inside-jim-c lyburn-s-biden-election-endorsement-how-biden-almost-ncna1255414.

Azari, Julia. 2019. "What We Know about the Impact of Primary Debates." *FiveThirtyEight*. Accessed June 5, 2020. June 24. https://fivethirtyeight.com/fe atures/what-we-know-about-the-impact-of-primary-debates/.

Bacon, Perry Jr. 2020. "How Will the Democratic Primary Change Now That It's Moving to More Diverse States?" *FiveThirtyEight*. Access June 15, 2020. February 14. https://fivethirtyeight.com/features/how-will-the-democratic-primary-change -now-that-its-moving-to-more-diverse-states/.

Cadelago, Christopher. 2019. "Harris Surges to Third Place in National Poll After Debate." *Politico*. June 30. Accessed June 5, 2020. https://www.politico.com/story /2019/06/30/kamala-harris-democratic-debates-1390740.

Cohen, Marty. 2018. "2016: One Party Decided." In Robert G. Boatright, ed. *Routledge Handbook of Primary Elections*. New York: Routledge. 255–272.

Garrison, Joey. 2020. "The Coronavirus Effect: How Much Did it Hurt Democratic Primary Turnout?" *USA Today*. March 19. Accessed January 25, 2021. https://ww w.usatoday.com/story/news/politics/elections/2020/03/19/coronavirus-effect-how -much-did-democratic-primary-turnout-hurt/2864013001/.

Goldmacher, Shane. 2020. "Michael Bloomberg Spent More Than $900 Million on His Failed Presidential Run." *New York Times*. March 20. Accessed June 8, 2020. https://www.nytimes.com/2020/03/20/us/politics/bloomberg-campaign-900-milli on.html.

———. 2020. "Joe Biden Begins First General Election TV Ad Blitz." *New York Times*. June 18. Accessed June 18, 2020. https://www.nytimes.com/2020/06/18/us /politics/joe-biden-ads-trump.html.

Hampson, Rick. 2016. "Convention 'Bounce' Ain't What it Used to Be." *USA Today*. August 4. Accessed February 1, 2021. https://www.usatoday.com/story/news/poli tics/elections/2016/08/04/post-convention-bounce-trump-clinton-polls/88001488/.

Herndon, Astead W., Nick Corasaniti, Stephanie Saul, and Reid J. Epstein. 2020. "Wisconsin Primary Recap: Voters Forced to Choose Between Their Health and Their Civic Duty." *New York Times*. April 7. Accessed January 27, 2021. https:// www.nytimes.com/2020/04/07/us/politics/wisconsin-primary-election.html.

Norrander, Barbara. 2006. "The Attrition Game: Initial Resources, Initial Contests and the Exit of Candidates During the US Presidential Primary Season." *British Journal of Political Science* 36: 487–507.

———. 2020. *The Imperfect Primary: Oddities, Biases and Strengths in U.S. Presidential Nomination Politics, 3rd edition*. New York: Routledge.

Chapter 4

Stability and Change in the 2020 Election

An Election Like No Other

Arthur C. Paulson

It was an election year like no other.

As the election year opened, we were entering the final year of the first term of the 45th president of the United States, Donald Trump. He already had been a president like no other. Trump, the Republican, had been elected president in 2016 by winning the Electoral College while narrowly losing the popular vote to Democrat Hillary Clinton. His term began with investigations into suspected Russian interference, in his favor, in the 2016 election, then featured his controversial immigration policies, distressingly ambiguous or supportive attitudes toward white supremacy, his unilateral withdrawal from international economic, environmental, and security agreements, his politicization of the Justice Department, his distrust of the U.S. intelligence community, and finally, his impeachment (first impeachment as it turns out) by the House of Representatives and his acquittal after a trial in the Senate. All this was taking place in a polarized political environment that the president was polarizing all the more.

At least the economy seemed to be humming along well, with the president claiming that his tax cuts and deregulation had been the decisive factor in promoting economic growth and reducing unemployment.

Then, as the calendar was turning to 2020, the COVID-19 global pandemic struck. The response of the president of the United States was at first to deny it, then to proclaim that it would all be over soon, then to announce that we were turning the corner, ignoring the science and the scientists, all while the number of cases and deaths in the United States and around the world mounted. When scientists and public health officials recommended safety protocols such as wearing masks, social distancing, and avoiding crowds, the president responded by turning the protocols into polarizing issues, rather than a unifying strategy for the country to survive the virus. Indeed, he offered no national strategy to combat the virus. Meanwhile, the economy faded and unemployment jumped while the virus spread.

Then came the killing of George Floyd by the police in Minneapolis, one more in a series of police-involved killings of African Americans, and the demonstrations that followed across the country, serving to dramatize the racial divide that has always been a factor in American life.

Finally, during the heat of the 2020 campaign, came President Trump's nomination of Judge Amy Coney Barrett to the U.S. Supreme Court, and her confirmation by the Senate, despite the refusal of majority Republicans to even consider the court nominee presented by President Obama during the campaign year four years before. The dispute over the confirmation process and the deep ideological divide about the court only illustrated another point of polarizing conflict among Americans.

All of the turmoil and chaos had left the political attitudes, party loyalties, and voting behavior of most Americans undisturbed. After an election year like no other, the election itself was not so unique. Democrat Joe Biden won an election that was about as close as most of the presidential elections since 2000, with a very stable alignment of voters, apparently as polarized as ever.

Of course, it came as no surprise when President Trump, unlike every previous incumbent president who lost an election, declined to concede and challenged the results, despite the clarity of the outcome. In a less polarized time, perhaps even Donald Trump might not have tried his closing gambit. The refusal of the president to accept the results gracefully, and his perpetuation of the lie that the election was stolen turned into mobilization of a mob to mount a violent attack on the Capitol, and the impeachment of President Trump by the House of Representatives. What we know at this writing about the attack on Congress and the Constitution is probably quite limited compared with what we have yet to learn, and we can only guess at how much danger to the Republic it represents.

As president, Donald Trump may have exacerbated polarization to the point of undermining the constitutional order. However, he is not the cause of polarization so much as he is the product more than a half century of polarizing change in the American politics.

We should not allow this episode to let us forget that there was an election in 2020, and that the American people spoke through a process that remains central to the life of the Republic.

THE 2020 PRESIDENTIAL ELECTION IN
THE AGE OF POLARIZATION

Democrat Joseph Biden was elected president in an election that showed a record turnout with significant increases everywhere. But in terms of the partisan share of the vote and where that vote came from, the 2020 election resembled much more than it differed from 2016 or other elections in the twenty-first century. Along with the coalitions of voters supporting the Democrats and Republicans, the coalition of states reflected more stability than change. In the familiar reference to "blue" states and "red" states, 47 states and the District of Columbia voted in 2020 as they have in most presidential elections of the twenty-first century. Only three states differed: Georgia and Arizona, which Joe Biden took from the Republican column, and Iowa, which has voted Democratic and Republican three times each since 2000 (see figure 4.1).

As close as the 2020 election was, it was not as close as the election of 2000, when the results in Florida were challenged for 36 days, and as in 2016, the Republican was elected without winning the popular vote. But Joe Biden won by a popular vote margin, four percentage points, that surpassed

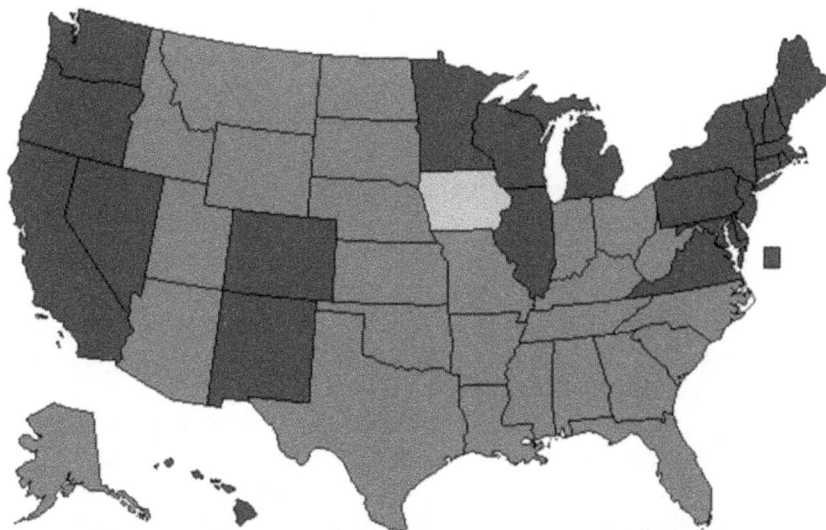

Figure 4.1   States in Presidential Elections, 2000–2020. Note: States shaded according to the party that won the most elections in the since 2000. Blue=Democrats. Red=Republicans. Green=Voted Democratic and Republican three times each.Maps constructed with permission, Dave Leip, www.uselectionsatlas.org.

either president reelected over the past two decades, Republican George W. Bush in 2004 and Democrat Barack Obama in 2012. The only winner whose margin in this century surpassed Biden's was Obama, first elected in 2008 by 5 points.

But the election was close enough to persuade President Trump, even though lacking in evidence, that he could challenge the results in several states, and perhaps, by hook or by crook, reverse enough Electoral Votes to retain his office. He had no valid reason to expect that outcome, but the presence of some close states (even if not close enough) and the fact of the Electoral College gave him hope, however misguided.

Much is made of the unique and counter-constitutional presidency of Donald Trump, and it ought to be. In this chapter, I will join my colleagues in that chorus. But Donald Trump may not have resisted the results of the 2020 election with the determination he did, and he certainly would not have gained the support he did from fellow Republicans in that closing gambit, had it not been for the era of polarization in which we find ourselves.

POLARIZATION AND REALIGNMENT

Party polarization in the twenty-first century is widely recognized by scholars, journalists, and the general public. But the process of ideological polarization in American politics is not of that recent origin. Rather, it is traced to a party and electoral realignment that began at about the middle of the twentieth century. In 1948, the Democrats adopted a national position in favor of civil rights at their national convention, generating a rebellion by the "Dixiecrats," the most hard-line segregationist southern Democrats. President Harry Truman was elected anyway, but Democratic presidents John F. Kennedy and Lyndon B. Johnson were still dealing with the opposition of southern Democrats when they fought for the Civil Rights Bill, which passed in 1964. President Johnson, a Texan, speculated that the Democrats would lose the south for a generation. If anything, that speculation has turned out to be an understatement.

In 1964, Senator Barry Goldwater of Arizona won the Republican presidential nomination. That year, Goldwater, the nominee for president of the "party of Lincoln," voted against the Civil Rights Bill, joined by scattered Republicans in the House and Senate. Eight years later, Senator George McGovern of South Dakota won the Democratic presidential nomination.

Both Goldwater, a conservative Republican, and McGovern, an antiwar liberal Democrat, were defeated in landslides by the incumbent presidents they were challenging. In between those two landslides, in 1968, Republican Richard M. Nixon was elected president over Democrat Hubert H. Humphrey by a very narrow plurality, each polling 43 percent of the popular vote.

George C. Wallace, the segregationist conservative Democrat running as a third-party candidate, polled most of the rest. The issue of race remained fundamentally divisive in American politics, as it always had been and remains today. But by 1968, the Vietnam War was dividing the country and a number of issues, most prominently abortion, would be bundled within a few years into confrontations between political subcultures in American life.

The 1964–1972 period was one of critical realignment in presidential elections, as the Republicans were becoming the conservative party in American politics, and the Democrats the liberal or progressive party. Realignment was not immediately apparent because Watergate interrupted the electoral change. But between 1968 and 1988, the Republicans won five out of six presidential elections. The only exception was 1976, right after Watergate, when both parties nominated moderates, President Gerald Ford, the Republican, and Jimmy Carter of Georgia, the Democrat. Carter was narrowly elected (by about the same margin as Joe Biden in 2020), and he carried 10 out of 11 states of the south, the only Democrat to win the south since 1964. But even Carter, the southern Democrat, could not have won the south without the Black vote, made possible by the Twenty-fourth Amendment to the Constitution (outlawing the poll tax) and the Voting Rights Act of 1965. Ford won the white vote in the south in 1976. Even after Watergate, President Ford probably would have been elected had he not pardoned Richard Nixon.

Starting in 1964, the Republicans generally ran strongest in the south in presidential elections, which had for so long been the "solid south" for the Democrats. The Democrats ran strongest in the northeast, long the geographic base for the Republicans. While 1976 broke the pattern for one election, it was restored in 1980 and has been in place ever since. Meanwhile, the Democrats increased the majorities they had in Congress after Watergate, in 1974. Between 1968 and 1988, presidential and Congressional elections almost always produced divided government, usually a Republican President and a Democratic Congress. But by 1994, a long secular realignment produced Republican majorities in both houses of Congress, including Republican majorities in House and Senate seats from the south.

The above discussion reaffirms a remarkable consistency to the political geography of the United States (Archer et al. 1988; Archer et al. 1996; Burnham 1970; Paulson 2007, 2018; Rabinowitz and MacDonald 1986; Reiter and Stonecash 2010; Schantz 1996; Speel 1998; Sundquist 1983). The same states tend to vote together over long periods of time, and when states realigned, they tended to flip together. This is illustrated by figure 4.2, which presents electoral maps comparing coalitions of states during two periods. The first runs from the presidential election of 1880, after the end of reconstruction, to 1944, the last reelection of Franklin D. Roosevelt, and the last election before the Dixiecrat revolt of 1948. The second period covers presidential elections since 1964. With very few exceptions, today's blue states,

1880-1944

1964-2020

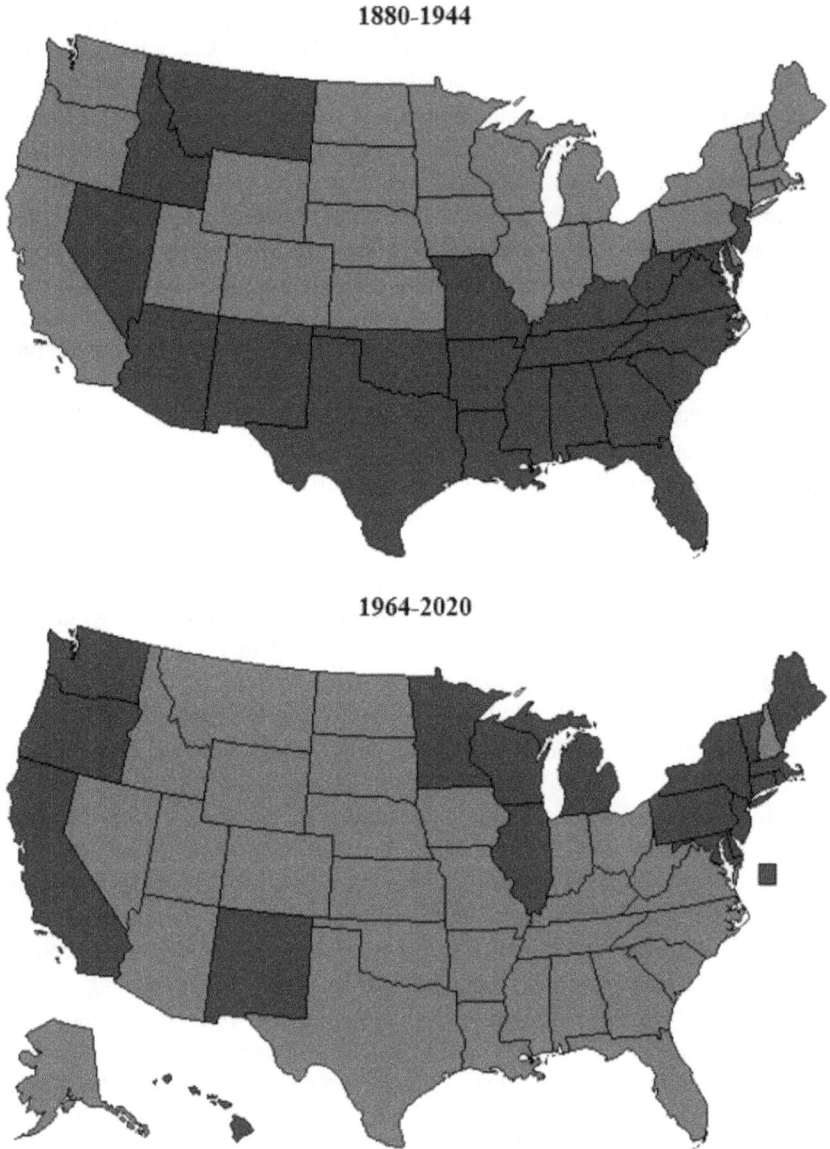

Figure 4.2   Realigning Coalitions of States in Presidential Elections, 1880–2020. Note: There are 17 elections between 1880 and 1944, nine won by the Republicans, eight won by the Democrats. There are 13 elections between 1964 and 2012, seven won by the Republicans, six won by the Democrats. States shaded according to the party that won the most elections in each era. Blue=Democrats. Red=Republicans. Maps constructed with permission, Dave Leip, www.uselectionsatlas.org.

for the Democrats, were once Republican states, and today's red states, for the Republicans, were once Democratic, including the solid south. Each map is virtually a mirror image of the other.

Table 4.1 shows state-level correlations among presidential elections since 1880. Every election is correlated with the realigning elections of 1896 and 1932, 1964 for the Republicans, 1972 for the Democrats, and 2020. The

Table 4.1   Correlations of Vote by States in Presidential Elections 1880–2020

Democrats					Republicans			
1896	1932	1972	2020	Election	1896	1932	1964	2020
.62	.73	−.58	−.30	1880	.67	.74	−.55	−.47
.63	.78	−.61	−.45	1884	.56	.74	−.48	−.31
.64	.84	−.60	−.38	1888	.68	.86	−.65	−.45
.37	.56	−.47	−.26	1892	.78	.88	−.77	−.32
1.00	.67	−.66	−.49	1896	1.00	.70	−.69	−.45
.82	.86	−.68	−.34	1900	.83	.84	−.72	−.30
.52	.80	−.60	−.18	1904	.61	.82	−.67	−.22
.66	.86	−.66	−.32	1908	.74	.88	−.75	−.33
.53	.86	−.60	−.20	1912	.55	.70	−.62	−.09
.73	.88	−.68	−.31	1916	.78	.90	−.75	−.34
.58	.79	−.70	−.26	1920	.67	.82	−.68	−.28
.47	.79	−.64	−.22	1924	.72	.95	−.73	−.39
.47	.77	−.36	−.16	1928	.49	.76	−.56	−.18
.68	1.00	−.60	−.38	1932	.70	1.00	−.72	−.38
.76	.93	−.63	−.30	1936	.75	.94	−.70	−.31
.60	.86	−.60	−.17	1940	.64	.85	−.67	−.20
.57	.84	−.56	−.14	1944	.61	.84	−.65	−.16
−.21	−.29	.30	.06	1948	.47	.62	−.69	−.15
.29	.58	−.32	−.05	1952	.29	.57	−.37	−.06
.41	.64	−.31	−.24	1956	.55	.79	−.66	−.26
−.18	.08	.33	.37	1960	.26	.49	−.30	.11
−.60	−.71	.68	.50	1964	−.69	−.72	1.00	.55
−.66	−.70	.89	.69	1968	.26	.56	−.23	.20
−.66	−.60	1.00	.69	1972	−.56	−.53	.70	.66
−.06	.44	.43	.36	1976	.01	.41	.17	.39
−.15	.30	.40	.43	1980	−.40	−.02	.40	.66
−.57	−.20	.82	.69	1984	−.49	−.18	.49	.69
−.53	−.37	.87	.66	1988	−.52	−.33	.62	.67
−.35	−.03	.69	.67	1992	−.54	−.61	.75	.73
−.56	−.24	.76	.77	1996	−.62	−.45	.67	.77
−.58	−.31	.72	.84	2000	−.58	−.40	.62	.88
−.62	−.42	.81	.90	2004	−.59	−.43	.62	.90
−.62	−.51	.78	.94	2008	−.60	−.52	.63	.93
−.58	−.41	.74	.95	2012	−.56	−.42	.59	.95
−.47	−.32	.69	.99	2016	−.39	−.38	.55	.98
−.49	−.38	.69	1.00	2020	−.45	−.38	.55	1.00

Correlations are Pearson's calculated by the author. Data drawn or derived from Dave Leip, www.uselec-tionatlas.org (accessed December 24, 2020).

correlations indicate positive and mostly strong correlations, among elections from 1880 to 1944, and among elections since 1964. But almost all elections between 1880 and 1944 are negatively correlated with elections starting in 1964. The shift is sufficiently sudden to suggest the distinct change in the partisan electoral environment at the middle of the twentieth century.

The literature on the theory of realignment is rich with the original conceptualizations of realignment (Burnham 1970; Key 1955, 1959; Sundquist 1983), applications of realignment theory (Andersen 1976, 1979; Bartels 1998, 2000; Clubb, Flanigan and Zingale 1990; Reiter and Stonecash 2010; Speel 1996; Wilson 1985), offers of the dealignment alternative (Burnham 1978; Ladd 1978, 1981; Ladd with Hadley 1978; Silbey 1991), critiques of the fundamental assumptions and usefulness of realignment theory (Mayhew 2002), and efforts to revive or defend the concept of realignment (Burnham 1991; Campbell 2006; Paulson 2007; Stonecash 2006).

Regardless of one's view of the usefulness of realignment theory, there has been at least one compelling realignment in our history. The realignment in the electorate took almost a half century to complete, starting slowly in 1948, reaching critical proportions in presidential elections between 1964 and 1972, and extending decisively to Congressional elections by 1994. Today's polarized party system is the result.

THE PRESIDENTIAL ELECTION OF 2020

All the turmoil of 2020 started with the pandemic which kept Americans on edge and added a fever pitch to the issues that followed throughout the year. The presidential campaign was as vicious as it was polarized. But in the end, even with the defeat of an incumbent president, there was more stability than change in the results of the presidential election. The country remained both polarized and closely divided between the major parties, as it has been since the turn of the twenty-first century, and the electoral coalitions of the two parties remained largely intact.

Demographic patterns of support for the two parties generally persisted. The racial divide and gender gap remained definitive factors in electoral behavior, as did the split between urban and rural voters. Trump won among white voters, particularly white men, and rural voters, while Biden won among nonwhites, particularly African Americans, women, and urban voters.

The most significant change in the 2020 election was not in who people voted for, as much as that the people voted. The turnout, 67 percent of the eligible voters, was the highest in more than a century (McDonald, 2020). However, increased turnout by itself appeared not to significantly change electoral outcomes in most states.

Otherwise, the pockets of electoral change were enough to elect Democrat Joe Biden President.

STATES IN THE 2020 PRESIDENTIAL ELECTION

Democrat Joseph Biden defeated President Donald Trump, the incumbent Republican, by 51 to 47 percent of the total popular vote, by 52 to 48 percent of the two-party vote.[1] Biden's share of the two-party vote represented a gain of one point over the performance of Democrat Hillary Clinton in 2016. This time, unlike 2016, the Democrats carried the popular vote by enough to carry states that delivered a majority in the Electoral College. In fact, Biden defeated Trump by an Electoral Vote of 306–232, exactly the reverse of the result of 2016.

The popular vote for both parties remained highly correlated at the state level with recent elections. The state-level correlations between 2020 and 2016 were .99 for the Democrats and .98 for the Republicans (refer to table 4.1). Indeed, had all of the states shifted uniformly along with the one percentage point gain nationally for the Democrats, Biden would have won the Electoral Vote by 307 to 231. He would have taken Pennsylvania, Michigan, and Wisconsin from Trump (as he did), along with Florida (which Trump retained, actually gaining a percentage point himself). But if the shift in the vote of the states was not exactly uniform, it was actually quite close to that.

In 2020, as in 2016, narrow partisan pluralities and the presidency itself were reversed by the movement of a few states in one electoral direction. In 2016, Trump was elected president even without winning the popular vote by taking Pennsylvania, Michigan, Wisconsin, Ohio, Iowa, and Florida from the Democrats. In 2020, Joe Biden was elected president by regaining Pennsylvania, Michigan, and Wisconsin, while taking Georgia and Arizona from the Republicans. Thus, in two consecutive close elections with very little electoral change, there were eight states that flipped once or twice.

Winning Pennsylvania, Michigan, and Wisconsin was the central focus of the Biden campaign, and he won all three, narrowly. In 2016, Trump carried all three by virtue of a small shift across each state toward the Republicans. Biden regained all three with an even smaller shift back. There was almost no change in the regional strengths and weaknesses of the parties in any of the three states.

Biden carried Pennsylvania with 51 percent of the two-party vote. He swept Philadelphia by a 4–1 margin and carried the Philadelphia suburbs with about 58 percent of the vote. He carried Allegheny County around Pittsburgh by a 3–2 margin. Trump carried the rest of the state with almost 60 percent of the vote and the broad swath of rural counties between Philadelphia and Pittsburgh with over 60 percent.

Biden also carried Michigan with just over 51 percent of the two-party vote. He carried Wayne County around Detroit by over 2–1, and nearby Washtenaw County around Ann Arbor and the University of Michigan by almost 3–1. In the Detroit suburbs, as usual, Democrat Biden won Oakland County, while Republican Trump won the more working-class Macomb County next door. However, Biden ran up a larger margin in Oakland County than Trump did in Macomb, reversing the same comparison from 2016. Trump carried most of the rest of the state to the west and north with 56 percent of the vote, slipping two percentage points from his 2016 performance there.

In Wisconsin, the shifts were even smaller, with a statewide shift toward the Democrats of less than a percentage point. In 2016, Trump carried the state by 23,000 votes. In 2020, Biden won Wisconsin by 20,000. With margins similar to four years before, Biden carried Milwaukee County by better than 2–1, Dane County around Madison by better than 3–1, while Trump prevailed in most of the rest of the state with about 57 percent of the vote.

It is tempting to conclude that Biden, by winning these three states, was elected president by rebuilding a "blue wall" across the upper Midwest. After all he was regaining three states that had consistently voted Democratic, and more Democratic than the country for a quarter century of more prior to Trump's upset in 2016. But there is no "blue wall." The shift back to the Democrats in Pennsylvania, Michigan, and Wisconsin was very small indeed, and even as Biden was elected, all three states voted slightly more Republican than the country as a whole. In 2016 and 2020, all three states were not returning to the Democratic fold so much as behaving like swing states. Moreover, had Biden polled one percentage point less in these states and across the country, he would have been lost the election, even while winning the popular vote, like Hillary Clinton in 2016.

Ohio and Iowa were swing states that Trump carried in 2016. He carried both again in 2020 by similar margins. As with the above three states, there was little regional change in patterns of support in Ohio or Iowa, Biden winning most of the larger cities, Trump winning the rural areas. There was one important exception. In Ohio, in both 2016 and 2020, Trump carried most of the string of suburbs and exurbs along Lake Erie between Cleveland and Toledo.

While the upper Midwest seems increasingly competitive, the Democrats have encountered more favorable trending in parts of the Sunbelt, as demonstrated in Georgia and Arizona. In both states, as in the states above, the regional patterns of support have remained consistent, but the Democrats have been making net gains, enough for Joe Biden to carry both states in

2020. In both states, and in others across the south and west, Democratic gains can be traced to two structural factors: racial diversity and urbanization.

In Georgia, Biden made a gain in the two-party vote of about three percentage points from 2016, to carry the state by only 11,000 votes, 49.5 to 49.3 percent. He carried Fulton County around Atlanta with 73 percent of the vote, and neighboring DeKalb County with 84 percent. Biden also carried areas around the smaller cities, such as Athens (around the University of Georgia), Augusta, Savannah, Macon, and Columbus. Trump carried the more rural areas to the north, south, and east of Atlanta, with over 60 percent of the vote. On balance, it was enough for Biden to become the first Democrat to carry Georgia in a presidential election since Jimmy Carter in 1980.

In Arizona, Biden gained two percentage points in the two-party vote to win the state by slightly more than 10,000 votes, 49.4 to 49.1 percent. All of the counties in the state but one repeated their partisan leanings except for the largest and most hotly contested county in the state, Maricopa. Biden carried Maricopa County by 45,000 votes, exactly the margin Trump enjoyed four years before. It was more than enough to flip the state.

Georgia and Arizona are the best examples of previously Republican Sun Belt states trending Democratic. In the south, Georgia is following the trend set in Virginia, which has now voted Democratic in four consecutive presidential elections. In Virginia, urban and metropolitan areas are central to what has become Democratic majorities in the state, with much of the Tidewater region following Richmond into the Democratic column, while the Washington, DC, suburbs in the north are even more Democratic, coming to resemble the northeast of the United States more than the south. Similarly, North Carolina, which voted for Obama in 2008 and then returned to the Republican column in the last three presidential elections, is behaving in recent times more like a swing state than a solidly Republican state. Texas is another potential example of the trend, although it remains behind the curve, in the Republican column by a solid margin in 2020.

Arizona seems to be following the trend set in New Mexico and Colorado, both of which were recently swing states but are now leaning more heavily Democratic. It would appear that in the west, both the Hispanic vote and urbanization explain increasing support for Democrats.

However, in both Georgia and Arizona, a critical turning point has not yet been reached. Even while Biden was carrying both states, both remain swing states, still voting slightly more Republican than the country in 2020.

Finally, Florida is the classic swing state going back three decades, as best dramatized by the controversy in 2000, when George W. Bush carried the state by 537 votes. Bush carried Florida twice for the Republicans, while Barack Obama carried Florida twice for the Democrats. Now, Republican Donald Trump has carried Florida twice. The state was still close, to be sure, but Trump's margin actually increased in 2020. The geographic distribution of the vote in Florida in 2020 followed the pattern of recent elections. Biden carried Miami, Broward County and Palm Beach County, on the southern tip of the peninsula, the Orlando area, and the area around Tallahassee. Biden also added Jacksonville to his support. Tampa Bay was closely contested. Trump carried most of the panhandle and the exurbs to the south. Indeed, Trump padded his margin in 2020, probably for two reasons. First, while Hillary Clinton carried Miami-Dade by a 2–1 margin in 2016, Biden won with barely 53 percent of the vote. It is probably no coincidence that while Biden enjoyed a 2–1 margin among Hispanics across the country, in Florida his support among Hispanics was also only 53 percent, reflecting reduced support among Cuban Americans. Cuban Americans were apparently driven away by the opening of relations with the Castro regime by the Obama administration, and by the charges of "socialism" hurled at Biden and the Democrats by the Trump campaign. Second, Trump probably enjoyed some advantage at the polls after claiming Florida as his home state before the 2020 campaign began in earnest.

While the eight states that have flipped once or twice in the Trump elections did not show very significant statistical change in their voting behavior in 2020, such small shifts as could be found were enough to be decisive in the election of Joe Biden to the presidency, and indicate that more electoral change may be on the horizon in the near term. That electoral change may yet see demographic change within the states, breaking up the long stable coalition of states discussed at the outset of this chapter. The time may come, perhaps sooner rather than later, when convenient references to "blue" states and "red" states may lose its usefulness.

VOTER TURNOUT AND ITS ENHANCEMENTS

There was a significant increase in voter turnout in 2020, from 60 percent of eligible voters in 2016 to 67 percent. This increase certainly contributed to the Democratic victory, although marginally.

The political battle over voter access was influenced by the pandemic, as most states made voting easier in response to public safety concerns. There was a relationship between "red" states and "blue" states on the one hand and voter access policies on the other, although cause-and-effect can hardly be assumed. Ten states had almost universal vote-by-mail policies, five of them, all in the west, predating the pandemic.[2] Of the ten, nine voted Democratic in 2020. Twenty-six states allowed voting by mail, but required voters to request ballots. The Democrats and Republicans each carried 13 of those states. Nine states required an excuse to vote by mail, and all included COVID-19 among the valid excuses. Five of those nine voted Republican. Finally, six states required excuses to vote by mail, but did not include fear of COVID-19 as a valid reason. All six voted Republican.

However, the impact of voter access policies on the result of the election should not be overstated. Only five states changed partisan columns in the 2020, and almost all states followed their historic patterns of voting, undisturbed by increased turnout. Moreover, the uniformly high correlations between state-level voting in 2020 and recent elections are evidence that new voter access policies in general and voting by mail in particular had a limited impact on electoral outcomes.

This is not to discount the impact of voter turnout on election outcomes, regardless of voter access policies. Arizona and Georgia both saw significant expansions of voter turnout in 2020, which almost certainly proved decisive for the Democrats in those states. Arizona's turnout increased from 56 to 66 percent, and Biden carried the state by only 10,000 votes. But Arizona has employed vote by mail for some time. In Georgia, turnout increased from 60 to 68 percent, and Biden won the state by 10,000. In Georgia, this outcome has been traced to the very effective turnout drive by the Democrats. But Trump had an excellent ground game across the country too. Turnout was increased measurably everywhere, in a few states by more than Arizona and Georgia, and most states still saw very little change from recent years in electoral outcomes.

EXIT POLLS: THE PEOPLE

The exit polls, conducted by Edison Research for the National Election Pool, were a methodological challenge in 2020, due to the large number of voters who voted early or by mail. Altogether, the sample size was 15,590, weighted to the actual results of the election (see tables 4.2 and 4.3).

Like the electoral map, the exit polls reveal more stability than change in the presidential election of 2020. There was continuing evidence of almost universal partisanship, ideological polarization, and a culture gap voting behavior. However, if most of the patterns of 2016 continued in 2020, there were nevertheless pockets of change that led to the election of Joe Biden.

The racial divide, so central to electoral politics as it is in American life, remained pronounced. Democrat Joe Biden polled 87 percent of the African American vote while he lost the white vote to President Trump by 58 to 41 percent. However, while there was virtually no change in the white vote, Trump made small gains among "nonwhite" voters, which might be considered surprising given his stated positions and behavior in response to issues of public violence against Blacks and related protests.[3] Nevertheless, Biden

Table 4.2   Exit Polls in 2020 Presidential Election (By Population Characteristics)

	2020		Trump (R) Change
	D	R	2016–2020
White (65)	41	58	0
African American/Black (12)	87	12	+4
Hispanic/Latino (13)	65	32	+3
Asian (3)	61	34	+5
Female (52)	57	42	0
Male (48)	45	53	0
LGBT=Yes (7)	64	27	+13
LGBT=No (93)	51	48	0
Married (56)	46	53	0
Single (44)	58	40	+2
Urban (29)	60	38	+3
Suburban (51)	50	48	−2
Rural (19)	42	57	−5
Age 18–29 (17)	60	36	−1
Age 30–44 (24)	52	45	+3
Age 45–64 (38)	49	50	−3
Age 65 + (22)	47	52	−1
Protestant (43)	39	60	+2
Catholic (25)	52	47	−5
White Evangelical, born again (28)	23	76	−5
None (22)	65	31	+5
No college (19)	46	54	+3
Some college (39)	51	47	−5
Bachelor's degree (27)	51	47	+2
Advanced degree (15)	62	37	0
Under $30,000 (15)	54	46	+5
$30,000–$50,000 (20)	56	43	+1
$50,000–$100,000 (39)	57	42	−8
$100,000–$200,000 (20)	41	58	+10
Over $200,000 (7)	44	44	−5

Source: NBC News (Live exit polls 2020: Election Day exit polls for Trump vs. Biden (nbcnews.com) and
   The New York Times (Election Exit Polls 2020—*The New York Times* (nytimes.com) publication of data
   from Edison Research for the National Election Pool.

won the Hispanic vote by nearly 2–1, and won among Asian Americans by better than 3–2.

The gender gap, a cornerstone reality to electoral outcomes for four decades, remained in place. Biden won among women with 57 percent of the vote, while Trump won among men with 53 percent. As usual, there was also the gap between married couples (more Republican) and singles, and between those who identified themselves as LGBT (more Democratic) and those who did not.

The gap between urban and rural voters, so important to the outcome in 2016, remained in 2020. Joe Biden polled 60 percent of the urban vote, while President Trump polled 57 percent of the rural vote. However, only about one voter in five lives in a rural area, and in four of the five states that flipped

Table 4.3   Exit Polls of 2020 Presidential Election (By Party, Ideology, and Issues)

	2020		*Trump (R) Change*
	D	R	*2016–2020*
Democrats (37)	94	5	−4
Republicans (35)	6	94	+4
Independents, other (26)	54	41	−7
Liberals (24)	89	10	0
Moderates (38)	64	34	−7
Conservatives (38)	14	85	+4
Union (20)	56	40	−2
Nonunion (80)	50	49	+1
Approve Trump (50)	8	91	
Disapprove Trump (49)	96	3	
Most important issue:			
Economy (35)	17	83	
Racial inequality (20)	92	7	
Coronavirus (17)	81	15	
Health care (11)	62	37	
Crime/Safety (11)	27	71	
Economy good or excellent (49)	22	78	
Economy fair or poor (50)	80	17	
Pro-Choice (51)	74	24	
Pro-Life (42)	23	76	
Keep Obamacare (51)	80	18	
Overturn Obamacare (44)	21	78	
COVID-19 policy going well (51)	18	81	
COVID-19 policy going badly (48)	87	11	
Court appointments important (60)	52	46	
. . . not so much (37)	50	48	
Climate change serious (67)	69	29	
. . . not so much (30)	15	84	
Racism=problem (69)	68	30	
. . . not so much (28)	14	84	
Voted for candidate (71)	46	53	−10
Voted against opponent (24)	68	30	+21

Source: NBC News (Live exit polls 2020: Election Day exit polls for Trump vs. Biden (nbcnews.com) and *The New York Times* (Election Exit Polls 2020—*The New York Times* (nytimes.com), publication of data from Edison Research for the National Election Pool. As the incumbent party and the issues changed between 2016 and 2020, not all issues are subject to valid comparison between the two elections.

from Trump to Biden, large Democratic majorities of the urban vote proved decisive. Moreover, more than half of the voters across the country live in suburbs, and their small shift from Trump to Biden proved decisive in the national popular vote. While Trump won a small plurality in the suburbs in 2016, Biden won a small plurality in 2020.

Age was unchanged as a factor in voting behavior. As in 2016 and other recent elections, the youngest voters gave the Democrats their strongest support (60% of voters between age 18 and 29), while the strongest support for Trump came from voters over 65 (52%).

Religion remained a factor, with Trump winning among Protestants by about 3–2, the same margin he gained among them in 2016. But while Trump won among Catholics in 2016 with 53 percent of the vote, Biden won in 2020 among Catholics, with 52 percent. Religiosity was even more important as Trump won among white Born-Again voters with 76 percent of the vote. But Trump's support among Born-Again voters was reduced from 81 percent in 2016. Biden won among voters who identified with no religion by about 2–1.[4]

Education remained the strong indicator in voting that it was in 2016, providing continuing evidence of economic frustration and a cultural divide. Trump carried the vote of those who had never been to college with 54 percent. Biden polled 51 percent of the vote among those who had been to college, whether they graduated or not. Among those with an advanced degree, Biden won with 62 percent of the vote.

When Donald Trump was elected in 2016, one of the most noted elements of his coalition was his showing among working-class voters, stronger than usual for a Republican. Actually, there was little new in that showing. In our polarized era, the working class itself has been more polarized than united. On the left, you have economic progressives who support the welfare state in general, the Affordable Care Act in particular, and tend to vote Democratic. On the right, you have social conservatives who fear not only the decline of manufacturing and mining employment, but also their way of life, and tend to vote Republican. David Apter (1964) once predicted the growth of a technological class system, composed of the "technologically competent" on the top, and the "technologically superfluous" on the bottom, while the class growing in numbers would be the "technologically obsolete" in the middle.

What Everett Carll Ladd (1978, 1980) referred to as the "inversion of the New Deal order" had appeared as the "silent majority" for Nixon and the "Reagan Democrats," and reappeared for Trump in 2016. That inversion was slightly reinverted in 2020, to the benefit of Joe Biden.

Actually, there never was a mass exodus of working-class voters from the Democrats. But in 2016, there was a difference of only six percentage points between voters with the lowest incomes and those with the highest incomes, reflecting some increase in Republican support among working-class voters. In 2020, there was a mild increase in the partisan differences in the vote by income. Biden won with 54 percent of the vote among those with the lowest incomes, and polled about 56 percent among middle-income voters. Trump won upper-middle-income voters with 58 percent of the vote. There was almost no change among the lowest income voters, while Biden gained about 10 points among middle-income voters, and Trump gained about 10 points among upper-middle-income voters. With increased working-class support, Biden was able to regain decisive ground, particularly in Pennsylvania, Michigan, and Wisconsin.

EXIT POLLS: PARTY, IDEOLOGY, AND ISSUES

In 2020, voters continued, and if anything increased, their pattern of voting the party line. According to the exit polls, 94 percent of Republicans and Democrats alike voted for the candidate of their party for president. The same proportion of voters who voted for their party's candidate for president voted for their party's candidate for the House of Representatives. Ideological polarization was almost as strong as, and the rough equivalent to, partisan loyalty. While 89 percent of liberals voted for Democrat Joe Biden, 85 percent of conservatives voted for Republican Donald Trump. The election was decided by the 54 percent of independents and 64 percent of moderates who voted for Biden for president.

As usual, retrospective voting played an important role, but the voters were responding not only to competing sets of priorities and values, but to competing senses of reality.

Perhaps the best general example of retrospective voting is the comparison of the votes of those who approved of Donald Trump with those who did not. Reflecting continued polarization, according to the exit polls, about half of the voters approved of Trump, and about half did not. Of those who approved of President Trump, 91 percent voted for him; among those who did not, 96 percent voted for Joe Biden.

President Trump was hoping that the economy would be the leading ingredient for retrospective voting in his favor. He had done what supporters would expect of a Republican President, providing tax cuts and deregulation, along with enhanced economic growth. As with other issues, the electorate was polarized on the economy. About half of the voters thought of the economy as "good" or "excellent" and among those, Trump prevailed by almost 4–1. Among the half who thought the economy was only "fair" or "poor," Joe Biden won by better than 4–1. But among those who thought the economy was the most important issue, Trump won by 6–1. Unfortunately for Trump, only 35 percent of the electorate thought the economy was the most important issue, down from 52 percent in 2016. Biden won the other two-thirds of the voters by almost 3–1.

A major reason for the reduction in people who considered the economy the most important issue was the presence of the coronavirus, which dominated national attention for most of the year. The polarization of the electorate applied to the virus, not only in terms of the politicization of the belief in science and wearing masks, but also in the evaluation of President Trump's handling of the virus. Overall, 51 percent of the voters thought the handling of the virus had gone well, and those voters supported Trump by over 4–1. Meanwhile, 48 percent of the voters thought that virus policy had gone poorly, and Biden won their votes by 8–1. Despite the overwhelming attention given to COVID-19, only one voter in six thought that the virus was the most salient issue. Among them, 81 percent voted for Joe Biden.

The coronavirus enhanced attention to health care, identified by 11 percent of the voters as the most important issue. Among them, 62 percent voted for Joe Biden. But as with so many issues, the electorate was polarized on health care, and close to evenly divided on the Affordable Care Act, also referred to as Obamacare. Among the 51 percent that favored retaining Obamacare, Biden ran up a margin of better than 4–1. Among the 44 percent who prefer ending Obamacare, Trump won by a little less than 4–1.

In a year in which the country was already on edge, it is not surprising that the issue of race, historically always with us, would be ever present. After the deaths of George Floyd, Briana Taylor, and other African Americans at the hands of police, demonstrations brewed across the country and nearly matched the virus for public attention. The result was that 20 percent of the voters identified racial inequality as the most important issue facing the country. Of those voters, 92 percent voted for Joe Biden. But the issue of race was as polarized as usual. Altogether, 69 percent of the voters considered racism to be a problem in America. Among them, Joe Biden won by 2–1. Among the 28 percent of voters who denied that racism is a problem, Trump won by 6–1. Apparently in response to the demonstrations, most of which were peaceful, but many of which were accompanied by violence, 11 percent of the voters identified crime and public safety as the most important issue. Donald Trump received 71 percent of their votes.

Similar polarization prevailed on the environmental issue of climate change, even if the public was not that evenly divided. About two-thirds of the electorate recognized climate change as a serious issue. They voted for Biden by a 2–1 margin. The one-third of the electorate who denied climate change as a problem voted for Trump by 6–1.

Abortion remained the polarizing issue it has been for nearly half a century. On an issue that was much more closely divided, voters who identified themselves as closer to the pro-choice position voted for Biden by 3–1, while those closer to the pro-life position voted for Trump by the same 3–1 margin.

The exit polling on these issues provided more evidence of continuing polarization in American politics. But even more compelling evidence of severe polarization came from a president who would not concede, who openly devalued the legitimacy of American elections before the world, and whose speech and conduct contributed to assault by a violent mob on the Capitol building of the Republic.

THE AFTERMATH

In 2020, there was more stability than change in the presidential election itself. But we cannot say the same for the Trump presidency. Moreover, what the outgoing president of the United States did to create turmoil in the aftermath of the election leaves questions that cannot yet be answered about the future of the American polity. What we do know is that even if order has been restored, the election of 2020 was not followed by a peaceful transfer of power.

It was no surprise when after the election, President Trump refused to concede. Beforehand, he had said that any election that he lost and that included voting by mail would have been "rigged." Afterward, he confirmed his position that the election had been stolen from him and urged his supporters to mobilize to "stop the steal." His lie that the election was stolen led to his inspiration of politics by mob, the attack on the Capitol, and ultimately, his impeachment by the House of Representatives.

Trump's campaign and supporters first attempted numerous strategies to reverse the result, particularly in six close states: Pennsylvania, Michigan, Wisconsin, Georgia, Arizona, and Nevada. The Trump campaign, along with Republicans in several states, filed lawsuits publicly claiming fraud but providing the courts with no evidence to support those claims. He prevailed on occasional procedural issues, such as putting aside ballots in Pennsylvania for later adjudication, but there was no evidence of any fraud or any errors in the count anywhere that would have changed the election outcome, or even produced any significant differences in the share of the vote won by the candidates. Trump attempted to prevail on Republicans in state legislatures to cancel the presidential election after the fact and appoint Republican electors. And he attempted unsuccessfully to persuade Secretary of State Brad Raffensperger of Georgia, a Republican, to "find" him 11,780 votes to reverse the result in that state.

As the day for counting the Electoral Vote in Congress approached, Trump urged supporters to gather in Washington, DC, and he said publicly that he was counting on Vice President Mike Pence to decline to accept state certificates of electors, which Pence informed him he was constitutionally unable to do. Nevertheless, on January 6, 2021, a majority of Republicans in the House and a minority of Republicans in the Senate were ready to support motions not to certify electors from the six states.

It is now apparent that extensive planning produced a turnout of Trump supporters for the day of the count (Baker 2021; Ballhaus et al. 2021), and the president showed up to provide the rhetoric they wanted to hear. His long speech urged them to march on Congress, or as the *Wall Street Journal* editorial page put it, "the leader of the executive branch incited a crowd to march on the legislative branch."[5] Apparently, the president had encouraged mass sedition, and the crowd, becoming a mob, had responded with a violent invasion of the Capitol building, in an attempt at least to stop the count of the Electoral Vote, or perhaps more, to do bodily harm to the vice president and members of Congress.

In Congress, when order was restored and business had resumed, Republican challenges to the Electoral Votes of Arizona and Pennsylvania proceeded. Neither house approved either challenge, although a reduced minority of Republican senators and a majority of Republican Representatives voted in favor of both. The election of Joe Biden was confirmed.

Thereafter, there were calls for the resignation of Senators Ted Cruz of Texas and Josh Hawley of Missouri, the leaders of the challenge in the Senate, and even a call that the Republicans who voted for the challenges in the House be expelled. Further, there were calls from many Democrats and some Republicans that the president resign, or be removed by the process provided for by the Twenty-fifth Amendment, and House Speaker Nancy Pelosi announced that bills of impeachment were being prepared. Within a week, the House voted to impeach President Trump by 232–197, including 10 Republicans in favor.

At this writing, we still do not know most of what happened at the Capitol, and we are almost certain to learn more through investigations by law enforcement and by Congress. Facts yet to emerge are not likely to serve the interests of Donald Trump, his supporters who stormed the Capitol, or any Republican members of Congress who may have facilitated the attack.

What happened on January 6 goes well beyond polarization. It was, for all practical purposes, an attempted coup promoted by the president of the United States. It was conducted by people, including the president, who have no understanding of the Constitution, or of the concept of ordered liberty so central to the Constitution. The beliefs of those who attacked the Capitol are not so much an ideology as a dogma, informed by lies, and shaped by what and who they are against, rather than what they are for. It is distressing, although not surprising, that the invaders of the Capitol were carrying symbols that expressed their racism and their sense of white supremacy. The attack may not have occurred in less polarized times and would not have happened even now without Donald Trump. But the people who invaded the Capitol, extremists for sure, did not represent a small fringe that is going to go away. Whatever happens to Donald Trump, his most extreme supporters will still be with us. Indeed, extremists of both left and right, perhaps more numerous on the right, have always had their corners in American culture.

After the attack, political leaders of both parties offered rhetoric about the need to work together in an atmosphere of political unity. But polarization in American politics is not likely to be reduced significantly any time soon.

Two reasons for that have been discussed in detail above. First, as discussed above, while ideological polarization has always been a factor in American life, it has become tied to partisan polarization over the past half century or so. The result is that many voters choose whose team they are on before they begin to think about the issues (if they think about the issues at all) or the candidates.

Second, the issues themselves are becoming more polarizing. In addition to the "culture wars" issues, we have the increasing salience of the environment, particularly the urgency of climate change. Finally, economic issues have become more polarizing. During periods of strong and shared economic growth, economic issues can be compromised with much more ease than cultural issues. But postindustrial modernization has yielded a new economy over the past half century (Gordon 2016; Levinson 2016). Even when the business cycle is high, economic growth is about half of what it was a half century ago, environmental limits threaten economic growth, and technological change threatens jobs and ways of life, particularly in declining industrial sectors. Increasing economic inequality has rendered economic issues as polarizing as cultural issues have been (Bonica et al. 2015; Hare and Poole 2014; McCarty, Poole and Rosenthal 2016; Poole and Rosenthal 1984). Polarization on economic issues, however, has not rebuilt New Deal-like class coalitions in voting behavior. According to the exit polls, there is polarization within people with both the highest incomes and lowest incomes in their party loyalties.

In the wake of Trump's refusal to accept the election results, support of his refusal by many Republicans, the attack on the Capitol, and the refusal of most Republicans to support impeachment after that attack, we are lacking in the knowledge we need about the future of the two-party system. We know the Democrats have shifted toward the left, with a small socialist faction. We also know that as president, Joe Biden expects to follow a more moderate-to-liberal policy agenda. But what about the Republicans? Many Republicans apparently continue to support Trump, even after the attack on the Capitol. How many Republicans will oppose Trump and his allies? Has much of the Republican Party shifted so far right that they no longer support the Constitution of the United States? The Republicans who continue to support Trump and other ultraconservatives have become more like a cult than a political party, intolerant of any competing opinion. The Republican primaries for House and Senate seats, as well as for governorships, will offer some evidence about the future of the party.

Finally, there has always been a streak of ideological intolerance in American political culture. As Alexis de Tocqueville (2000, 244) put it in his classic observation of American democracy: "I know of no country where, in general, less independence of mind and true freedom of discussion reign than in America."

More than a century later, Louis Hartz (1955, 58–59) put it this way:

This then is the mood of America's absolutism: the somber faith that its norms
are self-evident . . . .

> It was so sure of itself that it hardly needed to become articulate . . . it has rested on miles of submerged conviction, and the confirmation ethos which that conviction generates has always been infuriating because it has refused to pay its critics the compliment of an argument.

Hartz was writing in a time in which he was responding to McCarthyism. The intolerance of "un-American" ideologies was taken by many at the time of being directed at foreign powers. But McCarthy and his allies used much of their energies attacking Americans whose beliefs were "un-American." Today, it seems that it has become more systemic for many Americans to regard Americans who disagree on the issues as "un-American" because they disagree. Today, increasing numbers of Americans do not trust our institutions of government, and do not trust each other, at least when it comes to national politics.

If polarization is likely to remain a reality in American political life, can the Republic survive, or even thrive, in such a system?

A committee sponsored by the American Political Science Association once released a report that concluded that American democracy would benefit from "responsible" parties offering distinct programmatic choices to the voters (APSA 1950). The model for responsible parties, of course, was taken from parliamentary governments that already had responsible party systems. Ironically, the authors were imagining more polarized parties in America. Today, in the United States, we have what amounts to parliamentary parties without parliamentary government.

So, the question becomes, can polarized parties work in our separation of powers system? That question needs to be answered, because a polarized party system is what we will have for the foreseeable future. The separation of powers requires conflict to be tempered by compromise and consensus, a condition we cannot rely upon in today's polarized environment. Navigating a separation of powers system with polarized parties will require consensus among elites that the Republic itself is more important than who wins an election or a policy debate, and indeed, that the Republic is more important than anyone's political career. It will require leaders with character willing to tell people the truth about the challenges we face. It will take informed citizens willing to hear the truth, and willing to hear what they do not want to hear.

The current crisis will not be solved with Donald Trump out of office. We are simply being presented with another opportunity to keep the Republic.

NOTES

1. Data for results of the 2020 election drawn or derived from 2020 Presidential Election Results: Joe Biden Wins—*The New York Times* (nytimes.com) and Dave Leip, www.uselectionatlas.org.

2. My original source for the voter access policies comes from UNDERSTANDING THE U.S. ELECTION: Voting by mail | Reuters News Agency (reutersagency.com). Accessed January 9, 2021.

3. I am using the polling language in my reference to the 33 percent of the population sorted as "nonwhite." This includes "Hispanics and Latinos," who are more racially diverse than that categorization would suggest.

4. I find it interesting that the exit polls report "not enough data" to yield significant evidence of about the Jewish vote.

5. "Donald Trump's Final Days." *The Wall Street Journal.* January 8, 2021. A16.

REFERENCES

Apter, David. 1964. "Ideology and Discontent." In David Apter, ed., *Ideology and Discontent.* New York: The Free Press.

APSA. 1950. *Toward a More Responsible Two Party System.* New York: Rinehart.

Andersen, Kristi. 1976. "Generation, Partisan Shift, and Realignment: A Glance Back at the New Deal." In Sidney Verba, John R. Petrocik and Norman H. Nie, ed., *The Changing American Voter.* Cambridge, MA: Harvard University Press.

———. 1979. *The Creation of the Democratic Majority: 1928–1936.* Chicago: University of Chicago Press.

Archer, J. Clark, Fred M. Shelly, Fiona M. Davidson, and Stanley D. Brunn. 1996. *The Political Geography of the United States.* New York: Guilford.

———, Fred M. Shelly, Peter J. Taylor, and Ellen R. White. 1988. "The Geography of U.S. Presidential Elections." *Scientific American* 259: 44–51.

Baker, Peter. 2021. "America On Edge as House Weighs 2nd Impeachment: Polarizing Action vs. Needed Guardrail." *The New York Times.* January 10. 1, 14.

Ballhaus, Rebecca, Joe Palazzolo and Andrew Restuccia. 2021. "Course for Capitol Riot Set Early." *The Wall Street Journal.* January 9. A6.

Bartels, Larry. 1998. "Electoral Continuity and Change, 1868–1996." *Electoral Studies* 17: 301–326.

———. 2000. "Partisanship and Voting Behavior, 1952–1996." *American Journal of Political Science* 44: 35–50.

Bonica, Adam, Nolan McCarty, Keith T. Poole, and Howard Rosenthal. 2015. "Congressional Polarization and its Connection to Income Inequality." In James A. Thurber and Antoine Yoshinaka, eds. *The Sources, Character and Impact of Congressional Polarization.* 357–377. New York: Cambridge University Press.

Burnham, Walter Dean. 1970. *Critical Elections and the Mainsprings of American Politics.* New York: Norton.

———. 1978. "American Politics in the 1970s: Beyond Party?" In Jeff Fishel, ed. *Parties and Elections in an Anti-Party Age.* Bloomington: Indiana University Press.

———. 1991. "Critical Realignment: Dead or Alive?" In Byron E. Shafer. *The End of Realignment? Interpreting American Electoral Eras.* Madison: University of Wisconsin Press.

Campbell, James E. 2006. "Party Systems and Realignments in the United States." *Social Science History* 30: 359–386.

Clubb, Jerome M., William H. Flanigan, and Nancy H. Zingale. 1990. *Partisan Realignment: Voters, Parties and Government in American History.* Boulder: Westview Press.

"Donald Trump's Final Days." 2021. *The Wall Street Journal.* January 8. A16.

Gordon, Robert J. 2016. *The Rise and Fall of Economic Growth: The U.S. Standard of Living Since the Civil War.* Princeton, NJ: Princeton University Press.

Hare, Christopher and Keith T. Poole. 2014. "The Polarization of Contemporary American Politics." *Polity* 46: 411–429.

Hartz, Louis. 1955. *The Liberal Tradition in America.* New York: Harcourt, Brace and World.

Key, V. O. 1955. "A Theory of Critical Elections." *Journal of Politics* 17: 3–18.

———. 1959. "Secular Realignment and the Party System." *Journal of Politics* 23: 198–210.

Ladd, Everett Carll. 1978. "Shifting Party Coalitions – 1932–1976." In Seymour Martin Lipset. *Emerging Coalitions in American Politics.* San Francisco: Institute for Contemporary Studies.

———. 1980. "Liberalism Upside Down: The Inversion of the New Deal Order." In William Crotty, ed. *The Party Symbol: Readings on Political Parties.* San Francisco: W.H. Freeman and Company.

———. 1981. "The Brittle Mandate: Electoral Dealignment and the Presidential Election of 1980." *Political Science Quarterly* 96: 1–25.

——— with Charles Hadley. 1978. *Transformations in the American Party System: Political Coalitions from the New Deal to the 1970s.* New York: Norton.

Leip, Dave. 2020. www.uselectionatlas.org.

Levinson, Marc. 2016. *An Extraordinary Time: The End of the Postwar Boom and the Return of the Ordinary Economy.* New York: Basic Books.

Mayhew, David. 2002. *Electoral Realignments: A Critique of an American Genre.* New Haven: Yale University Press.

McCarty, Nolan M., Keith T. Poole and Howard Rosenthal. 2016. *Polarized America: The Dance of Ideology and Unequal Riches.* Cambridge, MA: MIT Press.

McDonald, Michael P. 2020. Voter Turnout Data - United States Elections Project (electproject.org)

NBC News. 2021. Live exit polls 2020: Election Day exit polls for Trump vs. Biden (nbcnews.com)

The New York Times. 2021. (Election Exit Polls 2020 - The New York Times (nytimes.com)

Paulson, Arthur. 2007. *Electoral Realignment and the Outlook for American Democracy.* Boston: Northeastern University Press.

———. 2018. *Donald Trump and the Prospect for American Democracy: An Unprecedented President in an Age of Polarization.* Lanham, MD: Lexington Books.

Poole, Keith T. and Howard Rosenthal. 1984. "The Polarization of American Politics." *Journal of Politics* 46: 1061–1079.

Rabinowitz, George and Stuart Elaine MacDonald. 1986. "The Power of the States in U.S. Presidential Elections." *American Political Science Review* 80: 65–87.

Reiter, Howard L. and Jeffrey M. Stonecash. 2010. *Counter-Realignment: Political Change in the Northeast*. Cambridge: Cambridge University Press.

Reuters News Agency. 2021. Accessed January 9, 2021. UNDERSTANDING THE U.S. ELECTION: Voting by mail | Reuters News Agency (reutersagency.com)

Schantz, Harvey L. 1996. "Sectionalism in Presidential Elections." In Harvey L. Schantz. *American Presidential Elections: Process, Policy and Political Change*. Albany: State University Press of New York.

Silbey, Joel H. 1991. "Beyond Realignment and Realignment Theory." In Byron E. Shafer. *The End of Realignment? Interpreting American Electoral Eras*. Madison: University of Wisconsin Press.

Speel, Robert W. 1998. *Changing Patterns of Voting in the Northern United States: Electoral Realignment, 1952–1996*. University Park: Pennsylvania State University Press.

Stonecash, Jeffrey. 2006. *Political Parties Matter: Realignment and the Return of Partisan Voting*. Boulder: Lynne Reiner.

Sundquist, James L. 1983. *The Dynamics of the American Party System: Alignment and Realignment of Political Parties in the United States*. Washington, DC: Brookings.

Tocqueville, Alexis de. 2000. Harvey C. Mansfield and Delba Winthrop, ed. *Democracy in America*. Chicago: University of Chicago Press.

Wilson, James Q. 1985. "Realignment at the Top, Dealignment at the Bottom." In Austin Ranney. *The American Elections of 1984*. Durham, NC: American Enterprise Institute/Duke University Press.

Chapter 5

The 2020 Election and the States

Federalism Takes the Stage

John J. McGlennon

States play a critical role in the national election of the president and vice president. States shape the presidential nominating process of both parties and constrain the parties in terms of ballot access, deadlines, voting conditions, and certification processes (Whitesides and Renshaw 2020). The 2020 election placed enormous stress on the states to retain their right to have their elections recognized by the incumbent president and Congress (Fandos 2021), and to adapt to a pandemic that threatened the health and safety of voters and election workers (Whitesides and Renshaw 2020). This chapter explores the role of parties, explains the stability of state electoral preferences in the twenty-first century, and analyzes the few states that were most competitive (and decisive) in the presidential vote. Based on this analysis, it provides an explanation of how these state elections were decided and to what extent this was due to the unique character of Donald Trump or Joe Biden versus more permanent realignment of the electoral coalitions of the parties. Finally, it addresses the structural bias of the Electoral College as a challenge to popular control of the presidency.

THE ASSAULT ON THE STATES AND THE CAPITOL

To call the 2020 presidential election unprecedented ranks among the great understatements of American politics. Extreme partisan polarization amid a highly engaged and largely angry electorate lent a volatile atmosphere to the contest. Add a completely self-interested president willing to ignore any norm or law, repeat debunked conspiracy theories, and lie with impunity, usually with the assistance of a compliant Republican Party (Montgomery 2020). Layer on a pandemic that caused some states to be caught flat-footed and others to rush to adapt election laws to accommodate voters who feared the long lines in small spaces that typified Election Day voting. Bring it to a near conclusion with the outgoing president inciting an insurrection at the Capitol, attempting to halt the reporting of the election of Joseph R. Biden Jr. as 46th president (Dozier and Bergengruen 2021).

The legislative effort was widely criticized by all Democrats and some Republicans as a violation of the constitutional provisions for the presidential election, a process that recognizes that states are responsible for conducting the election within their boundaries under their laws, and that their certification of a single slate of electors should be considered final. Even before this insurrection, Trump had lobbied, cajoled, threatened, flattered, and/or berated state election officials, state and federal legislators, even the vice president, to overturn state certifications. In the absence of credible (or any tangible) evidence of election irregularities, Trump's campaign and its allies lost more than 60 legal challenges in the states all the way to the U.S. Supreme Court (versus no wins in court). Challenges by Trump's ever-changing and increasingly preposterous "legal team" resulted in blistering rulings from judges and incessant mocking from late-night comedians.

On January 6, in the midst of the counting of Electoral Votes and challenges to states by a majority of the Republican caucus of the U.S. House of Representatives, an insurrectionist mob of Trump supporters forcibly invaded the Capitol to disrupt the reporting of the vote. Incited by Trump and his closest allies, domestic terrorists led bands of "Make America Great Again" zealots forcing their ways into the House and Senate Chambers, attacked Capitol and District of Columbia Police officers, contributing to the death of one and seriously injuring others, and temporarily halting the counting of the Electoral Votes. Even after this assault on the Congress, the Republicans who challenged the acceptance of properly certified state election results persisted in their quest, supported by the majority of the Republicans in the House and a handful of GOP senators.

Ultimately, of course, Trump's efforts at subverting the election failed. But the centrality of states in the presidential election process was in stark relief throughout the election year. This chapter examines the 2020 election through this lens of federalism. The nomination process for Democrats, and to a much smaller degree for Republicans, did reflect variations from state to state that had significance. But the larger stories of states in this election were contests over participation, a common theme in American politics. The battles over rules which can inhibit or encourage voting have raged throughout history, but took on a kind of blunt force in this election. The COVID-19 pandemic caused states to consider means to allow voters to cast ballots outside of the Norman Rockwell-styled, flag-festooned precinct with a line of civic-minded citizens waiting patiently, not distanced, in a school gymnasium.

The remainder of this analysis will focus on the results of the November election in the states: How did the states vote compare to the recent and slightly more distant past? Does this reflect a distinctly Trumpian impact, and if so, how will that impact be felt in elections to come?

The nation moved through the twentieth century from alternating stable party dominance to a realigning period that pulled people from their party moorings to more candidate-centered, split-ticket dynamics. By the start of the twenty-first century, the polarization of the electorate transformed parties into two stable and internally cohesive camps. Election outcomes have become less temporary swings of power between modestly divergent parties than door-to-door combat between sworn enemies. Views on issues are filtered through assumptions that the other party represented evils or dangers to the survival of the nation. In the end, this "fight to the death" became literal for Trump supporters.

STATES AND THE PARTY NOMINATIONS

The functions of the national political parties are largely centered on the election contest for president of the United States. The Democratic and Republican National Committees write the rules for nomination, organize the quadrennial conventions which adopt platforms and nominate the candidates, and provide a shell to be occupied by the successful nominee for the course of the election campaign.

The actual power of the national parties is significantly constrained by American federalism. Elections are the province of the states (Hetherington and Larson 2010). There is no federal agency that actually conducts elections, and only limited (though increasing) federal rules for the elections. Though the national parties have the right to establish the process for nomination, they do so with recognition of the preferences and requirements of the states. New Hampshire has long held the parties hostage to their demand that they have the first in the nation primary. State leaders know that the potential sanction they face for violating national rules that might prefer to allow a more representative state be the first primary is loss of their state's convention delegates. The attention the Granite State receives from its primacy on the calendar far outweighs the tiny delegation sent by the state to the national conventions. Thus, New Hampshire, by law, sets its primary date as one week earlier than any other state. For the 2012 nominating contest, that briefly led to a game of chicken in which New Hampshire tentatively set its primary for December of 2011 (Reynolds 2011).

So the primary calendar emerges out of a process of demand and threat, of efforts to balance and persuade. Democrats wound up with a four-state first act, with Iowa's caucuses (allowed by New Hampshire, because it was not a primary), followed by New Hampshire's open primary, Nevada caucuses, and the South Carolina party-run primary. For Democrats in 2020, the process proved troublesome. Iowa's caucuses, while ending in a tie between former South Bend, Indiana mayor Pete Buttigieg and Vermont senator Bernie Sanders, generated a large turnout but was a public relations disaster. The software program designed to produce quick and accurate results instead created mass confusion and finger-pointing between the national and state parties (Pfannenstiel 2020). With two "winners" and a fourth-place finish for Joe Biden, the campaign moved on to New Hampshire. In the Granite State, Sanders barely held off Buttigieg, Minnesota senator Amy Klobuchar surged as a moderate favorite, Massachusetts senator Elizabeth Warren dramatically underperformed in her neighboring state, and Biden limped in at fifth place.

Nevada emerged as a first test in a state with a large minority population (primarily Hispanic voters, many unionized Las Vegas workers) and Bernie Sanders prevailed in caucuses over Biden's relatively distant second place. The ordering of South Carolina's primary as fourth in the contest became perhaps one of the most consequential presidential primaries in history. The state, with a large African American Democratic constituency, was galvanized by an overwhelming desire to defeat President Trump and concerned that Sanders's more left-wing stance could not attract the moderates needed to win the election. House Majority Whip James Clyburn, the state's longtime Black Democratic congressman, rallied support for Biden (Collins et al. 2020).

Biden swept South Carolina's primary and was immediately recognized by all his competitors but Sanders as the consensus candidate. Three days later, Biden swept through 10 of 14 states on March 3 (Bradner 2020). Sanders won four primaries, but would not win another state primary and only one caucus state (North Dakota) on the way to the national convention.

What the Democratic contests demonstrated once again was the impact that state election law has on this national party contest. Open versus closed primaries, caucuses versus primaries, ballot access requirements and availability of polling places, early voting, absentee mail ballots, and the like produce the possibility of varied electorates and sometimes caused the national or state party to opt in or out of state-run contests, where they have that choice.

Among Republicans, though there were initially some challengers to Trump, the state and national parties reflected their subservience to the incumbent by ignoring requests for debates and even cancelling nomination primaries and caucuses in four states (Isenstadt 2019). In several others, the lack of competition resulted in either no choice on the GOP ballot or no election at all. The ability to shut down competition could not be complete, however, as most states with presidential primaries provide for an election, whether contested or not. Even in those cases, adjusting proportional representation rules could increase the threshold for a share of the state delegation to the national convention.

THE COVID-19 PANDEMIC AND THE PRESIDENTIAL ELECTION IN THE STATES

The expectations of a highly polarized, controversial, and unpredictable presidential election in 2020 were well established before the start of the election year. But a crucial factor in the election was only a faint whisper as the election year began. Rumors of an outbreak of a new infectious virus sweeping through the city of Wuhan, China, were attracting the attention of public health professionals around the world. By the end of January, Trump had been briefed on the potentially devastating impact of the disease as it threatened to spread well beyond China. As he disclosed to *Washington Post* journalist Bob Woodward, Trump was well aware of the ominous threat posed by the virus, which would soon overwhelm nations around the world, including the United States (Costa and Rucker 2020).

The responses to the pandemic extended to nearly every aspect of life, both domestically and internationally. In the very early stages of the presidential election year, states and localities scrambled to find ways to conduct elections concurrently with being overwhelmed by illness and death. As the impact of the virus extended from its coastal American origins in the states of Washington, California, and then New York and into the Midwest, the implications for spring primaries and local elections began to emerge.

In Wisconsin, a fierce contest over a seat on the state's Supreme Court produced demands for some kind of accommodation for voters. The demands, primarily from urban area Democrats, were rejected by Republican state legislative leaders, who insisted on conducting a "normal," predominantly in-person Election Day, in an effort to protect the incumbent conservative justice who was facing a serious challenge from a Democratic-supported liberal. Primary day produced viral photos and videos of long lines of voters, standing at a distance on cold, snowy sidewalks, intent on voting in reaction to a perception that urban and minority voters were being discouraged from casting ballots. A high turnout produced a decisive win for the liberal challenger, narrowing the conservative margin on the high court to 4–3 (Cole 2020).

With growing concern over the virus spread and loss of life, states began to respond, often with some sharp partisan divides. States like Ohio, New York, and Pennsylvania undertook election changes like easing absentee ballot requirements, expanding early voting options, and even delaying primary elections. Some of these decisions would become flashpoints in closely contested states in the general election, even where the changes were adopted by the same party that would then contest the revisions in court (Sprunt 2020).

Extraordinary times led to extraordinary adaptation in election administration: drive-through voting, with poll workers distributing and collecting ballots in Personal Protective Equipment, drop boxes for mail ballot return, and provision of mail ballot applications to all registered voters in some states. Virtually all of these efforts became flashpoints for conflict between the parties, with President Trump launching a direct assault against the encouragement of mail ballots, as he complained that this was improper and unfair, despite his own reliance of absentee ballots in most of the recent elections in which he had voted. His argument boiled down to the idea that mail ballots were fine when they had been used primarily by Republicans who applied for them, but that offering applications to all voters made the process too easy and too open to fraud. Throughout the election, Trump persisted in his assault on the mail ballots as an effort to steal the election, even as his allies in state and national GOP circles recognized that Trump's discouraging the use of this voting technique was irrational, given past GOP success in mail ballot programs.

Conflict quickly arose over other voter accommodations, as the Ohio secretary of state and the Texas governor both ordered county election officials to provide only one drop box location each, regardless of the population of the county. In Ohio, urban counties like Cuyahoga (Cleveland), Franklin (Columbus), and Hamilton (Cincinnati) were allowed only the same option as counties with only a few thousands of residents. In Texas, Harris County (Houston) has 4.7 million residents and was authorized to establish the same one drop box as Loving County (estimated population of 169 in 2020).

The history of the United States is replete with contention over the expansion or contraction of the electorate. Though our history ultimately shows a significant progression in voting rights over the centuries, no era is free from countermovements to limit, constrain, or eliminate participation by some, usually those who have the least resources, and are most easily silenced. What we can see in the heated battles and court fights from Texas to Michigan to Pennsylvania to Georgia and beyond is the impact of a chasm that has opened between the two major parties in American politics.

No issue of policy or process arises in the political system without being seen primarily through the lens of partisanship, a lens that some have suggested is equally evident on both sides of the political divide but which others have assigned more directly to a hardening of attitudes much more completely evident among Republicans, as they have first encouraged their voters to perceive their opponents in the most threatening light, and who have now become prisoners to a radicalized electorate who view the democratic process as corrupted because it produces results that they do not accept.

Add to this the efforts of President Trump's choice to lead the U.S. Postal Service, Louis DeJoy. A major Trump donor with a background in supply-chain logistics, DeJoy undertook efforts which Democrats asserted were designed to prevent the timely delivery of absentee ballot applications and the return of completed ballots (Durkee 2020).

Given that the president had made clear that he would view any election which he lost as fraudulent, Trump's focus seemed much less on the practical implications of voting changes, but on a way to lay grounds for challenging the election.

COMPARING TWO ERAS AS REFLECTED IN THE ALIGNMENT OF THE STATES

Polarization has certainly driven Americans increasingly into two distinct camps with little common ground. Today's political landscape is a stark contrast to the more centrist experience of the second half of the twentieth century (Abramowitz 2018). Then, voters were unmoored from partisan affiliations and open to persuasion, and elections were contests for the middle. Policies emerged from compromise that crossed party lines, a concept that now seems quaint. Today, legislating is a zero-sum game in many instances, and as a result, Congress has become remarkably unproductive (Deane and Gramlich 2020).

We now turn to examine the patterns of state electorates in the first two decades of the twenty-first century in comparison to the previous 40 years of state alignment in presidential contests. We will see how different the state-by-state outcomes were in the earlier period and how predictable the results are today, how what were national election contests now devolve to battles costing hundreds of millions of dollars to move a handful of states 2 or 3 percent from their previous results (Hecht and Schultz 2015). This highly stable and predictable electoral map preceded Donald Trump's ascendance in some ways but may have been altered by him. His defeat in 2020 raises the question of whether the configuration of the presidential map will retain its basic form or not.

REALIGNING AND DEVIATING ELECTIONS

American political parties are comprised of coalitions of voters whose attachment to each party relates to social, economic, and demographic factors.

These coalitions are not static, but often see voters move to varying degrees in and out of parties from election to election. Sometimes these changes produce long-term movements, such as the conversion of white Southerners to the Republican Party throughout the latter half of the twentieth century (Hershey, 2017, pp. 159–73). The national transition of Black Americans to the Democrats began with the New Deal of Franklin Roosevelt, but accelerated in the 1960s, concurrent with passage of the Civil Rights and Voting Rights Acts and the emergence of a "Southern Strategy" by the Richard Nixon-era GOP.

These large-scale and durable shifts have characterized realignment of the parties. Other, more temporary shifts have had important impacts on presidential and other elections, but have been marked by a return of the deviating partisans. The "Reagan Democrats" of the 1980s and the rural and Southern regional support for Jimmy Carter in his 1976 campaign did not transform the electorate in a fundamental way.

The concepts of "critical," "realigning," and "deviating" presidential elections have a long history, stretching to the mid-twentieth century, with the groundbreaking works of V. O. Key (1955), and Campbell, Converse, Miller, and Stokes in *The American Voter* (1960). Realigning elections usually reflect fundamental shifts in the electorate and can include unidirectional shifts, bidirectional shifts with a partisan advantage, or bidirectional shifts with offsetting impacts. These shifts, because they tend to be longer lasting, also may be less related to an individual candidate or election. Deviating elections are more likely to result from temporary disruptions in the party coalitions, often tied to particular candidates or issues that are temporary. Examples include Dwight Eisenhower's nonpartisan image (he was recruited by some in both parties as a presidential contender) or the 1912 GOP schism, which produced Woodrow Wilson's victory.

Movement of Demographic Groups within the Party Coalitional Structure in the Twenty-first Century

The dynamic process of party realignment has been evident throughout the first fifth of the twenty-first century. These changes have included some deviating shifts as well as more permanent realignments. Overall, the national electorate has moved toward the Democrats as a result of what has been called the "Rising American Electorate" by Stan Greenberg and James Carville (2015). The fact that Republicans have won the popular vote only once in the six national contests between 2000 and 2020 lends credence to the "demography is destiny" theory. As the white share of the electorate declines, as metropolitan areas continue to grow, and younger voters express more liberal values, Democrats gain.

The disaffection of the college educated (especially women) over conservative social values and antiscientific ideology contributes substantially to Democratic attractiveness (Pew, 2020). However, Republicans have been able to win half of those elections due to the structural advantage enjoyed by rural states in the Electoral College and the GOP's ability to maximize their advantages (Skelley 2021). Massive Democratic majorities in California and New York did not help Al Gore and Hillary Clinton claim the White House as they failed to win knife's-edge outcomes in Florida in 2000 and Michigan, Pennsylvania, and Wisconsin in 2016. These elections saw a significant movement among the electorate, with both parties experiencing losses and gains. Though it might be expected that the Democratic gains would outstrip Republican advances, in fact the GOP managed to mobilize their voters effectively to overperform expectations.

In 2000, George W. Bush mobilized white Evangelicals in rural areas, while Democratic nominee Al Gore managed to run competitively in growing metropolitan areas. By 2004, as Bush sought his second term, he was consolidating support from religiously conservative voters but experiencing some weakening among the more libertarian Republicans, especially in the Western United States. Despite Bush's vaunted appeal to the "soccer moms" of suburbia, who had been rechristened "security moms" following the September 11 attacks, in fact the election saw the first clear movement of suburbs toward the Democrats. Disillusioned with the war in Iraq and Afghanistan, dismayed by Bush's social conservatism and apparent antiscience agenda, suburban bedrocks of Republicanism went Democratic for the first time in decades.

This was also a time of increasing partisan division, fueled by the Gingrich revolution in Congress, the bitterly contested 2000 election decided by the Supreme Court, and the increasing ideological differences between Republicans and Democrats. As Bush focused on juicing rural white turnout, John Kerry's campaign also focused on generating higher levels of participation among reliably Democratic areas, with support from minority voters and blue-collar communities attracting particular attention. Persuasion of independent swing voters became secondary to activation of low-propensity base voters as partisan polarization intensified. In a time when voter turnout was generally flat, there seemed ample opportunity to attract new voters on both sides of the aisle.

The GOP seemed to have the superior Get Out The Vote program, despite surges in both parties' support that lifted turnout by nearly 17 million votes. The combination of growing suburban support and base mobilization, along with the increasingly unpopular military actions in the Middle East intensified with midterm elections that delivered Congress to the Democrats in 2006.

With the nomination of the first Black presidential candidate by the Democrats in 2008, turnout increased again, primarily among minority and younger voters, as Barack Obama won the largest popular and Electoral Vote margin in the six contests. Obama's two elections solidified the Democratic hold on more affluent suburbs and generated lopsided wins in college towns and central cities. But even in the midst of his powerful win, Obama lost Democratic votes in rural areas to the Republicans, a trend which has continued to this day.

By the middle of the second decade of the century, suburban voters were moving sharply toward the Democrats, especially those with more affluent and college-educated citizens as well as those suburbs becoming increasingly diverse in race and ethnicity. Republicans were gaining increasing shares of the vote in rural areas regardless of region, as political, cultural, religious, and educational differences reinforced the sense among each party's voters of distance from their opposite party numbers. Complicating matters for the understanding of the scale of partisan movement, Republicans benefited massively from a structural point of view when Obama's first midterm election delivered both houses of Congress and many state governments to the GOP. Control over redistricting in states as diverse as Alabama and Wisconsin, Pennsylvania and Missouri cemented Republican advantages in these states over political competition. Dismantling labor union influence, restricting voter access, maximizing Republican advantages in drawing legislative and Congressional lines were some of the initiatives undertaken by Republican state leaders.

At the presidential level, as rural states fell off the list of partisan battlegrounds, Republican candidates won marginal advantage in the Electoral College. Obama's reelection in 2012 produced a more narrow victory than his initial win. With the historic significance of 2008 accomplished, Obama was less able to excite a base that may have expected a more robust set of legislative accomplishments and a speedier recovery from the Great Recession of 2008. Turnout declined and the president's margin was reduced to half the 2008 number.

The 2016 victory of Donald Trump over Hillary Clinton came with a surprising twist. A number of counties across the nation which had voted twice for Barack Obama shifted to Trump. These so-called pivot counties were often home to blue-collar workers who found Trump's "stick it to the establishment" themes energizing. These localities overwhelmingly stuck with Trump in 2020, but were offset by larger Democratic margins in the suburbs. Joe Biden prevailed in a record low percentage of counties, but these counties contained a substantial majority of the nation's population and more than 70 percent of the nation's Gross Domestic Product (Muro et al. 2020).

ALIGNMENT OF STATES COMPARED
TO EARLIER ERAS

The full flowering of partisan polarization became evident in the new century's presidential elections, with high predictability of state outcomes and the narrowing margins in the Electoral College. In the six elections from 2000 to 2020, none were won with as much as 70 percent of the Electoral College vote, and in four of the cases, the winning candidate failed to reach even 57 percent. In comparison, of the 10 elections between 1960 and 1996, no winner received less than 55 percent of the Electors, and in four cases, the winner captured more than 90 percent (see table 5.1).

Landslides of this magnitude meant that not a single state remained committed to any one party throughout the 40-year period (though the District of Columbia never deviated from Democratic support once they began to participate in 1964). In contrast, since 2000, 35 states and the District have voted for the GOP or Democrats every time, and another 9 have deviated only once. Five states split their results 4–2, with Florida and Ohio going Red more often, while Colorado, Nevada, and Virginia have voted Blue in the last

Table 5.1   Presidential Elections in the States: 1960–1996 vs. 2000–2020

Year	Dem % Vote	GOP % Vote	Dem % Electors	GOP % Electors	Other Electoral Votes
1960	49.72	49.55	56.4	40.8	2.8
1964	61.05	38.47	90.3	9.7	
1968	42.72	43.42	35.5	55.9	8.6
1972	37.52	60.67	3.2	96.7	.2
1976	50.08	48.01	55.2	44.6	
1980	41.01	50.75	9.1	90.9	
1984	40.56	58.77	2.4	97.6	
1988	45.65	53.37	20.6	79.2	
1992	43.01	37.45	68.8	31.2	
1996	49.23	40.72	70.4	29.6	
Winner/Loser Avg. 1960–1996*	W: 52.01	L: 46.27	W: 76.1	L: 22.3	
2000	48.38	47.87	49.4	50.4	
2004	48.26	50.73	46.7	53.2	
2008	52.86	45.60	67.8	32.2	
2012	51.01	47.15	61.7	38.3	
2016	48.02	45.93	42.2	56.5	1.3
2020	51.27	46.82	56.9	43.1	
Winner/Loser Avg. 2000–2020*	W: 49.95	L: 48.23	W: 57.75	L: 42.0	

Source: Table constructed by author from data drawn from *Dave Leip's Atlas of U.S. Presidential Elections*, https://uselectionatlas.org/.
*Represents average percent for winning candidates versus losing candidates over the time period, regardless of party.

four elections. Only Iowa has split evenly between the parties since 2000. Throughout the period, the battleground states in each election have usually included fewer than 10 states, as some drift into or out of competitiveness.

In this environment, with almost all states locked in to their partisan preference, the swing states typically produce extremely close results. Consider the controversial Florida tally of 2000, decided by less than 600 votes of almost six million, when the U.S. Supreme Court ordered an end to recounting of votes. George W. Bush's victory pushed him just one vote above the minimum required by the constitutional formula. John Kerry lost Ohio to Bush four years later by a comparatively massive 1.5 percent margin, an outcome that cost Kerry an Electoral College majority. While Barack Obama won his two terms with relatively wide Electoral Vote outcomes, Donald Trump's clear Electoral Vote margin was attained in three usually reliable Democratic states (Michigan, Pennsylvania, and Wisconsin), which he won by a combined 77,000 votes of the nearly 14 million votes cast.

The firm lines of demarcation between Democrats and Republicans were in stark relief in 2020, as only five states moved from their 2016 results. All five voted for Biden, with Pennsylvania, Michigan, and Wisconsin returning to the Democratic fold by a combined total of 250,000, while Arizona and Georgia broke from their Republican loyalty by tiny margins. With delays in counting caused by massive numbers of absentee mail ballots and laws prohibiting some states from counting absentee votes before Election Day, it took four days before media outlets declared that Biden had won the election, despite the fact that ultimately he won by the same margin in the Electoral College as Trump had in 2016, and Biden emerged with a national popular vote edge of 7 million out of the record-shattering 159 million votes.

THE TRUMP AND ANTI-TRUMP CONSTITUENCIES

The division into two stable camps seen in the state results is reflective of the realigned partisan electorates, now more consistently dividing voters in ways that tend to reinforce comfort with fellow partisans and distance from members of the opposition party. White evangelical Christians have considerable overlap with rural residents with lower education levels. A growing segment of voters are secular, refraining from religious identification. They are often joined by non-Christian religious adherents who feel marginalized in a predominantly Christian nation. Metropolitan area residents once split into competing factions of urban and suburban voters, but now reflect commonality of interests. Add to these alignments the growing diversity of the population and the declining share of the electorate comprised of white voters, and elections are increasingly seen as a "zero sum" game.

The drift of rural voters to the GOP, the growth of Democratic support in suburbs, and the increasing racial diversity of the electorate moved Democrats into a commanding position following 20 years of GOP electoral dominance. From the election of Ronald Reagan to the end of the Bill Clinton presidency, Democrats never won a majority of the popular vote, twice taking pluralities in races involving the significant third-party candidacy of Ross Perot. In the six most recent elections, Democrats have won majorities or pluralities of the popular vote five times, and the Republicans have won a majority only once, when George W. Bush won reelection in 2004. Twice the GOP won the presidency while losing the popular vote—in 2000 by approximately 500,000 votes and in 2016 by 2.9 million votes.

The Democratic Party appears to be moving toward an advantage in competing for the White House, if somewhat incrementally. As Democrats cut the GOP margin in Texas in half between 2016 and 2020 and sliced the Republicans' edge in North Carolina from 3.6 to 1.3 percent, the urban North states saw a Democratic swing. Trump's three critical 2016 wins, in Michigan, Pennsylvania, and Wisconsin, were reversed and his near miss in Minnesota was not replicated in 2020. The shifts from state to state proved to be marginal, while within states, clearer evidence of realignment in both directions was detected. Significantly, the question that arises from the election is whether the changing levels of support represent a fundamental partisan reorientation or are reflective of particular support for, or opposition to, Donald Trump.

DEVIATING OR REALIGNING IN 2020?

The elections of the Trump era produced notable outcomes. Republican success in attracting white working-class voters, especially in smaller cities and rural areas reduced Democratic performance in these communities to noncompetitive levels. The trend in such communities had been evident for most of the millennial period, but Al Gore and John Kerry both managed to retain enough support to win a significant share of counties with smaller populations. Each subsequent election has seen the number of counties carried by the Democratic nominee decline over the previous contest (Caldera 2020).

Counties, of course, do not matter as units in presidential elections. The trade-off for Democrats was a growing share of the vote in larger counties in metro areas throughout the country, places where the population continues to increase, and which contain a massive share of the nation's population. At this stage, the trajectory of the electorate appears to favor the Democrats, but does provide some worrying tendencies for the party. The role of education has long been understood to relate to vote choice. Over the past 20 years, however, that relationship has reversed, with Republicans losing the college educated and gaining support among whites without a bachelor's degree.

WHAT HAPPENED IN THE STATES?

The presidential election turned on five states that switched from Red to Blue. These five results were of two types. Michigan, Pennsylvania, and Wisconsin followed one path, while Arizona and Georgia results were derived from a similar but not identical path.

As discussed above, the shifts in voting patterns are not all alike. Realigning elections produce lasting change in the preferences of notable groups of voters. In a realignment, it is not uncommon to find countervailing movements. Shifts of one group may be offset by transitions of another group. The durability of these changes alters the composition and prospects for success of political parties. On the other hand, in some elections, shifts in voter attachments tend to be more ephemeral.

The growth of the American population continues an uninterrupted march from a rural majority to an urban nation. In earlier decades, conflict between cities and their surrounding suburbs helped create a partisan divide, but in recent years, increasingly Democratic cities have found common interest with culturally liberal and increasingly diverse suburban voters. High levels of education among metropolitan electorates have led to rejection of the social conservatism that has characterized the GOP since the George W. Bush presidency.

Expansion of the electorate with 18–20-year-olds, rising numbers of non-white voters, and a more politically engaged electorate have also influenced the outcomes of federal elections. Democratic candidates have gained considerably from the increasing participation of racial and ethnic minorities, as the Hispanic vote nationally seems likely to soon surpass Black voters as the largest minority voting bloc. The disparate elements of the broad Latino electorate mean that even as their overall participation increases, the votes are strongly but not overwhelmingly Democratic. Asian and Pacific Islander populations have been growing at the fastest pace, but are still a smaller portion of the overall vote and even more differentiated than Latin voters.

The share of the national electorate that identifies as white continues to decline, even as their Republican advantage remains. Finally, the evangelical vote continues to constitute a major portion of the Republican constituency, assuring that cultural and social conservatism are likely to define the party into the future. These general trends have been evident for at least the past two decades, in some cases extending from decades earlier. In other cases, the party alignments have driven deeper divisions based on these characteristics.

But what has been the impact of Trump as reflected in his performance in the 2016 and 2020 elections? How has Trump impacted the electorate? Has he accelerated or slowed trends already in place? Has he brought to the GOP voters who were not already inclined to the party or mobilized opposition to a greater degree?

The evidence suggests that Trump has certainly had an effect on participation. Turnout in 2020 increased dramatically, producing an outcome that made Trump the second highest vote-getter in American presidential elections, with 74 million votes, but ranking him behind his Democratic competitor. Biden finished with more than 81 million votes, fully 7 million ahead, as part of a turnout exceeding 159 million, two-thirds of the eligible electorate. Biden shattered fundraising records as well, fueled by many "small dollar donors" who contributed through online platforms, primarily ActBlue. Turnout in the election increased without exception in every state and the District of Columbia (Wasserman et al. 2020). The Trump era was also notable for driving higher than normal voter participation in the midterm Congressional elections and off-year state and local elections.

However, it is also true that the elections of the twenty-first century have generally shown higher levels of participation, with a sharp jump in turnout in 2004 and 2008. Though voting dropped off in 2012 (to a still higher level than elections in the late twentieth century), it rebounded in 2016, and surged once again in the 2020 contest. The five years between Donald Trump's entry into the Republican nominating contest and the end of his presidential term infused politics into every aspect of American life.

Yet in terms of the electoral arena, these years seemed like a game of inches. Whether monitoring approval ratings for Trump's presidential performance (prior to the January 6 insurrection), comparing election outcomes in 2016 and 2020, watching a handful of states shift from Republican to Democratic, the order of likelihood was nearly perfect, the outcomes were narrow, and the prospects for future shifts are evident. Consider the states that moved from Trump to Biden. They included three previously Democratic Northern states, Michigan, Pennsylvania, and Wisconsin.

These three states delivered their Electoral Votes to Trump by the narrowest of margins: all three states finished with a margin of less than 1 percent between Trump and Clinton. The three returned to their Democratic tendencies in 2020, with Biden swinging Michigan from a 10,000 vote deficit to a 150,000 vote win. Pennsylvania gave Trump a 40,000 vote edge over Clinton, but Biden was able to convert that result to an 80,000 win. Wisconsin made the slightest move, swinging from a 20,000 vote Trump advantage to an edge of 20,000 votes for Biden.

URBAN, SUBURBAN, AND RURAL VOTERS

In each of these states, Democrats found their path to victory was achieved with stable support from urban Democratic strongholds like Milwaukee, Detroit, and Philadelphia, but more decisively by surging turnout and highly improved performances in suburbs. In Wisconsin, the formerly deep Red WOW (Waukesha, Ozaukee, and Washington) counties became paler, allowing the Madison and Milwaukee metropolitan areas the ability to shift the state to Biden. In Pennsylvania and Michigan, the Democratic surge in suburbs delivered additional margins to overcome reduced rural and small city GOP advantage. The city/suburb analysis was widely aired in the weeks following the election, as Trump improved slightly on his overwhelming big city losses of 2016 (Otterbein 2020).

With turnout flat in many big cities, Biden still won massive margins, but they would not reverse the outcomes in swing states without the increases of turnout and Democratic votes in suburbs (Frey 2020). Given that these areas continue to grow as a proportion of the national population and electorate, the debate on what they mean for the future of partisan competition grows more important. Some see the suburbanites as the new swing voters, not attached to the Democratic Party but repelled by Donald Trump. This analysis has some clear merit, but it is countered by those who note that suburbs are no longer the havens for white voters seeking to escape the racially diverse central cities. In fact, many suburbs have seen their minority populations surge into multiracial, multiethnic communities, where the affluent, college-educated white voters are increasingly distanced not just from Trump but from a GOP that has embraced the president and what they see as his socially reactionary, intolerant, and antiscientific platform.

Public opinion on a range of issues showed suburban voters favored more liberal positions on policies from climate change, to economic inequality, health care to racial justice. So while Democrats certainly cannot count on retaining office without being attentive to both urban and suburban trends, Republicans saw Trump's vote in metropolitan areas reflects an intensification of a prior trend (Jones 2020).

Rural voters retained their strong GOP caste, though in some areas Biden was able to slightly reverse the deep slide away from his party. GOP positions found strongest support among those in these sparsely populated areas (Parker 2018).

RACE AND ETHNICITY

Hispanic voters gathered a great deal of attention both before and after the election, as some polling suggested that Trump was significantly outperforming his 2016 showing, especially among men. The explanations varied, with some expression that Trump was benefiting from the sense, especially among Latin males, that his economic policies were largely successful. In Florida, efforts to paint Biden as sympathetic to socialist regimes in Cuba, Nicaragua, and Venezuela gained traction among voters already open to Republican appeals. Some allegations of disinformation campaigns run on Spanish language social and broadcast media against Biden raised the concern of Democratic leaders in Latino areas. In other parts of the country, there were reports that anti-Latino advertising was targeted to Black voters, while anti-Black messages were being transmitted to Hispanics. Extensive analysis by the *New York Times* found evidence of Trump's improved performance among minority voters at the precinct level in a number of cities (Cai and Fessenden 2020).

Of course, Biden still won the overwhelming majority of these voters, but as we have seen, small movements at the margins could have an outsized impact in such a polarized electorate. In fact, among both Black and Hispanic men, the levels of support for Democrats have usually fallen a few points below that of women of the same race or ethnicity. That is consistent with gender differences overall. Additionally, we know that education plays a significant role in voting, and among Black and Hispanic populations, a larger proportion have not completed college. Donald Trump famously recognized this trend when he said, "I love the poorly educated." Thus, it seems as if race continues to blunt the GOP appeal to voters without a college education.

The populist message of Donald Trump stands as the opportunity and challenge for Republicans who want to succeed him as the Republican Party standard bearer. These potential candidates are currently jockeying to emerge as the logical heir to this bloc of voters who respond to Trump's finger-in-the-eye-of-the-establishment posturing while maintaining a voting record more in line with conventional corporate support. This maneuvering took on a violent and insurrectionist cast as Senators Ted Cruz and Josh Hawley tried to leap to the head of those promoting the president's false claim that the election was stolen from him. The January 6 assault on the U.S. Capitol as Cruz and Hawley attempted to delay the declaration of Biden as president created a crisis which will undoubtedly have implications for the future, including whether or not Donald Trump himself attempts to reassemble his 2016 electorate in 2024.

Democrats anxiously ponder how they can reclaim the mantle of "defender of the downtrodden," searching for a way to convince skeptical whites that this can benefit all races, while reassuring minority voters that their centuries of mistreatment will be addressed. Religion proved to separate the parties once again, particularly socially conservative white Evangelicals from non-Christian adherents and those without religious affiliation. Ideology is a strong predictor of vote, with conservatives uniformly favoring Republicans, a smaller group of liberals favoring Democrats, and a significant pool of self-described moderates splitting roughly 2–1 for Democratic nominees.

THE ROAD AHEAD: HOW STATES WILL DRIVE THE POLITICAL FUTURE

The 2020 election produced a monumental shift in power and policy, accomplished with the movement of five states that flipped from Trump to Biden by a combined margin of fewer than 280,000 votes. With a total of nearly 160 million votes cast, this margin left no room for error. The outcome also showed that Donald Trump was unable to increase the Republican share of the national vote, that he fell 7 million votes short of Biden's total, and that his ability to expand his national constituency faced severe limitations. Though he did show some marginal gains among minority voters in urban areas, his performance in big cities came nowhere near making him competitive. Indeed, his modest gains in cities which often saw no real increase in participation were overwhelmed by suburban votes for Biden.

Biden's win was greeted less by euphoria among Democrats than by relief. Public opinion polls had shown him outperforming Trump by twice the 4.5 percent popular vote margin, and Democrats failed to capture the competitive Senate races on November 3. The loss of Democratic seats in the House, primarily in Trump districts, disappointed Democrats. The narrow margins made Democrats fret about the possibility that the party's success could be undone in the midterm Congressional elections and the 2024 National contest. Dreams of turning Texas Blue years earlier than most had predicted seemed to crash into surprising Trump support among Hispanic voters in areas near the Texas/Mexico border. The decline in Democratic support among Hispanic voters in Florida and in working-class areas in a number of states led to concerns that the Sunshine State might be off the list of swing states, and that Nevada might swing back toward the GOP.

Biden's national victory produced a majority (51.3%) of a national vote which increased by 15.9 percent over the 2016 election. The overall margin of 4.5 percent represented a 2.4 percent increase over the Clinton share of the vote. For the former vice president, the increase was widespread, as only one battleground state (Florida) shifted toward Trump compared to his 2016 vote, along with five noncompetitive states (Arkansas, California, Hawaii, Illinois, and Utah). All five of these states, two for Trump and three for Biden, were still solidly in the same camp as in 2016. In three, the change in margin was less than 1 percent.

The stability of the presidential electorate was reflected in the fact that only 16 states were decided by a margin of less than 10 percent (Maine at 9.1% had the lowest margin among "nonbattleground" states). It remains likely that several states will recur on the "swing" or "battleground" list. The tiny margins by which Biden won Arizona, Georgia, and Wisconsin, as well as Trump's narrow edge in North Carolina and Florida, suggest that these will again be fierce contests. Close wins for Biden in Pennsylvania and Nevada and the Democratic advances in Texas are sure to make both parties test the waters. On the other hand, Colorado and Virginia appear to have moved beyond the reach of the GOP.

A POSTSCRIPT: GEORGIA PROVIDES A CLUE

One of the most consequential outcomes of the 2020 election was Biden's victory in Georgia. Polling that showed the Peach State to be closely divided between the presidential candidates caused both parties to invest late dollars and to send their candidates and surrogates to campaign. When the vote tally was completed, days after the election, Biden had a lead of about 12,000 votes, requiring a recount by machine, which confirmed the results. After pressure from the Trump campaign, the state undertook a complete hand count of the ballots, which again demonstrated Biden's win.

Trump and his supporters refused to accept the results, even though the count was overseen by the state's elected Republican secretary of state and the state's Republican governor validated the win. Efforts to reverse the result included legal challenges, audits of signatures, and presidential intervention, including an hour-long phone call from Trump to the secretary of state asking him to "find" enough additional Trump votes to win the state. The release of the phone call, recorded by the secretary of state, became one of the arguments advanced for impeaching Trump for the second time after the January 6 assault on the Capitol, seeking to block the count of the Electoral College Vote.

But significantly, Georgia was holding a U.S. Senate election for a regular six-year term and another to fill a vacancy. Georgia, unlike most states, requires that candidates receive a majority of the vote to be elected, and failing that, the top two candidates compete in a runoff election several weeks later. As neither race produced a majority winner on November 3, both moved on to runoffs scheduled for January 5, 2021. Democrats nationally realized that if they could win both seats, they would force a partisan tie in the Senate, which could be broken in their favor by Vice President Kamala Harris, once she took office on January 20. But the history of runoffs did not provide much hope for the Democrats, who had not won a statewide runoff in decades. But Raphael Warnock, African American pastor of Ebenezer Baptist Church in Atlanta, had finished first in the special election for a two-year term, finishing substantially ahead of appointed Republican senator Kelly Loeffler. Meanwhile, 33-year-old documentary film producer Jon Ossoff finished close behind incumbent Senator David Perdue, who fell just below 50 percent. Democrats saw opportunity in these two candidates, especially after Biden's win demonstrated growing Democratic support.

This election provided a window into at least the short-term future of both parties. For the Republicans, President Trump displayed little interest in control of the Senate while obsessing over his attempts to overturn the election results for president. His allegations of mail ballot fraud and criticism of the failure of GOP officials to give him the win in Georgia despite the results sent conflicting messages to the Georgia Republican electorate.

Meanwhile, Democrats were inspired by Biden's remarkable victory in the state, with much credit being given to Stacey Abrams. Abrams, the Democratic nominee for governor in 2018, had lost a tight race, alleging voter suppression. She immediately began to organize Black voters in the rapidly growing and diversifying metro Atlanta area as well as rural areas with substantial Black populations. Democrats across the country flooded their two candidates with more than $100 million each for the runoff campaign. Turnout in the runoff came close to 90 percent of the presidential election turnout, a precedent-shattering level.

In the end, both Democrats won, snatching control of the Senate from the Republicans and giving President Biden a much improved Congressional environment, with control of both Houses in Democratic hands, if by tiny margins.

The outcome in Georgia tells us that for Republicans, the specter of Donald Trump will still loom large: Can they generate the base turnout that Trump generated, and can they overcome the ability of Trump to consume all the party's oxygen?

For Democrats, the plan for victory appears to be written in the Georgia wins: commitment to a deep dive into community organizing and connection to find, energize, and mobilize low-propensity voters. The challenge will be found in whether they can convince these voters that their votes matter and can produce policy outcomes that these voters recognize as a direct result of their participation.

REFERENCES

Abramowitz, Alan I. 2018. *The Great Alignment: Race, Party Transformation, and the Rise of Donald Trump.* New Haven: Yale University Press.

———. *Ballotpedia.* "Pivot Counties: The Counties That Voted Obama-Obama-Trump From 2008–2016." Accessed February 12, 2021. https://ballotpedia.org /Pivot_Counties:_The_counties_that_voted_Obama-Obama-Trump_from_2008-2016

Bradner, Eric, Gregory Krieg and Dan Merica. 2020. "5 Takeaways As Joe Biden Scores Stunning Wins On Super Tuesday." *CNN.* March 4.

Cai, Weiyi, and Ford Fessenden. 2020. "Immigrant Neighborhoods Shifted Red and the Country Chose Blue." *The New York Times.* December 20. https://www.nyt imes.com/interactive/2020/12/20/us/politics/election-hispanics-asians-voting.html ?action=click&module=Top%20Stories&pgtype=Homepage

Caldera, Camille. 2020. "Fact Check: Biden Won The Most Total Votes—And The Fewest Total Counties—Of Any President-Elect." *USA Today.* December 10. https:// www.usatoday.com/story/news/factcheck/2020/12/09/fact-check-joe-biden-won -most-votes-ever-and-fewest-counties/3865097001/

Campbell, Angus, Philip Converse, Warren Miller and Donald Stokes. 1960. *The American Voter.* New York: John Wiley & Sons.

Cole, Devan. 2020. "Wisconsin Judge Elected Amid Coronavirus Pandemic Calls Victory 'Bittersweet' Following An 'Uptick' In State's Cases." *CNN.* April 27. https://www.cnn.com/2020/04/27/politics/wisconsin-judge-jill-karofsky-election -bittersweet/index.html

Collins, Michael, Christal Hayes, Savannah Behrmann and David Jackson. 2020. "'You Brought Me Back': Joe Biden Rallies Supporters After Convincing South Carolina Primary Win." *USA Today.* February 29.

Costa, Robert and Philip Rucker. 2020. "Woodward Book: Trump Says He Knew Coronavirus Was 'Deadly' And Worse Than The Flu While Intentionally Misleading Americans." *Washington Post.* September 9. https://www.washingt onpost.com/politics/bob-woodward-rage-book-trump/2020/09/09/0368fe3c-efd2-1 1ea-b4bc-3a2098fc73d4_story.html

Deane, Claudia, and John Gramlich. 2020. "2020 Election Reveals Two Broad Voting Coalitions Fundamentally At Odds." *Pew Research Center.* November 6. https:// www.pewresearch.org/fact-tank/2020/11/06/2020-election-reveals-two-broad-voti ng-coalitions-fundamentally-at-odds/

Dozier, Kimberly and Vera Bergengruen. 2021. "Incited by the President, Pro-Trump Rioters Violently Storm the Capitol." *Time.* January 6. https://time.com/5926883/ trump-supporters-storm-capitol/.

Durkee, Alison. 2020. "Sorting Equipment Removed, Postal Police Duties Scaled Back: Here Are All The Postal Service Changes Raising Alarms." *Forbes.* August 17. https://www.forbes.com/sites/alisondurkee/2020/08/17/sorting-equipment-removed-changes-to-election-mail-all-the-postal-service-usps-changes-raising-al arm-louis-dejoy/?sh=2dac2c75106f

Fandos, Nicholas. 2021. "Can Congress Overturn the Electoral College Results? Probably Not." *The New York Times*. January 6. https://www.nytimes.com/2020/1 2/14/us/politics/congress-election-role.html

Frey, William. 2020. "Biden's Victory Came from the Suburbs." *Brookings Institute*. November 13. https://www.brookings.edu/research/bidens-victory-came-from-the -suburbs/

Greenberg, Stanley, James Carville and Nancy Zdunkewicz. 2015. "Evolving Strategy For Progressives: RAE." https://democracycorps.com/wp-content/up loads/2015/02/Dcorps_WVWV_Combined-Report_Long-Memo_for-web_2.12. 2015.pdf, February 12.

Hecht, Stacey Hunter and David Schultz, eds. 2015. *Presidential Swing States: Why Only Ten Matter*. Lanham, MD: Lexington Books.

Hershey, Marjorie Randon. 2017. *Party Politics in America (17th Edition)*. New York: Routledge.

Hetherington, Marc and Bruce Larson. 2010. *Parties, Politics and Public Policy in America, 11th ed.* Washington, DC: CQ Press.

Isenstadt, Alex. 2019. "Republicans To Scrap Primaries And Caucuses As Trump Challengers Cry Foul." *Politico*. September 6.

Jones, Sarah. 2018. "The Suburbs May Not Be As Progressive As Democrats Would Like—But They Could Be." *New York*. November 27. https://nymag.com/intelli gencer/2018/11/suburban-voters-progressive.html

Key, V. O. 1955. "A Theory of Critical Elections." *The Journal of Politics*. February. 17 (1). 3–18.

Montgomery, David. 2020. "The Abnormal Presidency." *Washington Post*. November 10. https://www.washingtonpost.com/graphics/2020/lifestyle/magazine/trump-presidential-norm-breaking-list/

Muro, Mark, Ely Byerly-Duke, Yang You and Robert Maxim. 2020. "Biden-Voting Counties Equal 70% Of America's Economy. What Does This Mean For The Nation's Political-Economic Divide?" *Brookings Institution*. December 8. https:// www.brookings.edu/blog/the-avenue/2020/11/09/biden-voting-counties-equal-70-of -americas-economy-what-does-this-mean-for-the-nations-political-economic-divide/

Otterbein, Holly. 2020. "Why Biden Didn't Do Better In Big Cities." *Politico*. November 15. https://www.politico.com/news/2020/11/15/big-cities-biden-electio n-436529

Parker, Kim, Jiliana Menasce Horowitz, Anna Brown, Richard Fry, D'Vera Cohn and Ruth Igielnik. 2018. "Urban, Suburban And Rural Residents' Views On Key Social And Political Issues." *Pew Research Center Social & Demographic Trends*. May 22. https://www.pewsocialtrends.org/2018/05/22/urban-suburban-and-rural -residents-views-on-key-social-and-political-issues/

Pew Research Center. 2020. "In Changing U.S. Electorate, Race and Education Remain Stark Dividing Lines." June 2. https://www.pewresearch.org/politics/2020 /06/02/in-changing-u-s-electorate-race-and-education-remain-stark-dividing-lines/

Pfannenstiel, Brianne. 2020. "Iowa Caucus 2020: Inside The Iowa Democratic Party's 'Boiler Room,' Where 'Hell' Preceded The Results Catastrophe." *Des Moines Register*. February 8.

Reynolds, Sarah. 2011. "N.H. Secretary of State Threatens to Move Primary to 2011." *WNYC.org*. October 12.

Skelley, Geoffrey. 2021. "Even Though Biden Won, Republicans Enjoyed The Largest Electoral College Edge in 70 Years. Will It Last?" *FiveThirtyEight*. January 19. https://fivethirtyeight.com/features/even-though-biden-won-republicans-enjoyed-the-largest-electoral-college-edge-in-70-years-will-that-last/

Sprunt, Barbara. 2020. "Supreme Court Rejects GOP Bid to Reverse Pennsylvania Election Results." *NPR*. December 8. https://www.npr.org/2020/12/08/944230517/supreme-court-rejects-gop-bid-to-reverse-pennsylvania-election-results

Wasserman, David, Sophie Andrews, Leo Saenger, Lev Cohen, Ally Flinn and Griff Tatarsky. "2020 National Popular Vote Tracker." *Cook Political Report*. Accessed Feb 12, 2021. https://cookpolitical.com/2020-national-popular-vote-tracker

Whitesides, John and Jarrett Renshaw. 2020. "Confusion, Long Lines At Some Poll Sites As Eight U.S. States Vote During Coronavirus Pandemic." *Reuters*. June 2. https://www.reuters.com/article/us-usa-election/confusion-long-lines-at-some-poll-sites-as-eight-u-s-states-vote-during-coronavirus-pandemic-idUSKBN2391B5

Chapter 6

Women and the 2020 Election

Breaking Down Barriers

Susan A. MacManus and Amy N. Benner

It was fitting that the 2020 election fell on the 100th anniversary of women winning the right to vote. As in 1920, women were in the election forefront. From start to finish they were breaking down barriers at every level (national, state, local) and in every capacity (candidates, campaign strategists, debate moderators, and donors). "The year of the woman really, finally did arrive in 2020. . . . As voters, as candidates and as campaign leaders, women were—and now are—in the driver's seat as never before" (Seib 2020).

Record numbers of women of color successfully ran for office, determined to reverse years of underrepresentation in governing arenas. Kamala Harris broke down the biggest national barrier when she was elected vice president—the first woman and the first Black and first South Asian person to win that post.

Certainly the context in which the election occurred was unique—a pandemic, a faltering economy, high unemployment, small business failures, a child care shortage, and racial justice strife. Campaigns faced challenges in how to microtarget women from younger and older generations with their cultural, racial and ethnic, socioeconomic, and gender identity differences. Considerably higher levels of attention were given to ramping up participation of women of color, particularly Gen Z'ers and Millennials.

While many things changed, some remained the same. Women turned out at a higher rate than men (the gender gap), as they have in every presidential election dating back to 1984. They did not vote as a bloc—nor have they ever. (Even the Women's Suffrage movement faced female opponents.) Within each party, a woman's vote was driven by different factors such as age, race/ethnicity, gender identity, religion, educational level, and/or ideology. As in past elections, the most effective ways of mobilizing low-propensity women

Table 6.1   Ten Firsts for Women in 2020 Election

1. Record number of women running for Democratic Party nomination for president: 6.
2. First woman, first Black and South Asian American to be elected vice president: Kamala Harris (D)
3. First president's spouse to continue working at regular job while in the White House—First Lady Dr. Jill Biden, college professor.
4. First time a political party mandated that every party primary debate would have a woman moderator (Democrats—presidential primary—12 debates); 5th Democratic Party debate in Georgia had a record four women co-moderators; Andrea Mitchell (NBC and MSNBC), Rachel Maddow (MSNBC), Kristen Welker (NBC), and Ashley Parker (*Washington Post*).
5. Birth of news outlets targeted to women and the LGBTQ community—*The 19th*˙ (after the Nineteenth Amendment guaranteeing women's right to vote), *Prism*.
6. Record number of women elected to U.S. House of Representatives—119 (89D, 30R)
7. Record number of women of color elected to Congress—51 (46D, 5R)
8. Record number of Republican women elected to Congress (38)
9. Record number of women elected to state legislatures (2,277)
10. Virtual national political party conventions and presidential debates; more women spoke at each party convention than in past.

Source: Data compiled from Center for American Women and Politics (CAWP); news media.

to register and vote were through personal contacts and community networks (see table 6.1).

WOMEN CANDIDATES RUSH TO RUN

The 2020 election cycle came on the heels of record numbers of women running and winning elective office in the 2018 midterms, as well as the historic nomination of Hilary Clinton for president four years earlier.

Although it was no longer surprising to find a woman listed on a presidential primary ballot, it was incredible to witness *six* women announce their candidacy for the 2020 Democratic nomination. In the Republican Party, the Trump nomination was a done deal, the traditional practice with an incumbent president, although three men (no women) mounted an early tentative primary challenge.

Democratic Primary—Six Women Candidates

The 6 women among over 20 contenders for the Democratic nomination displayed the range of ideological, generational, geographical, as well as racial and ethnic makeup of the party. The first woman to enter the race was Tulsi Gabbard, a four-term congresswoman from Hawaii. She was followed by Senator Kamala Harris (CA), a former California attorney general. She launched her presidential bid in front of a crowd of more than 20,000 in Oakland, California.

Next to enter the race was Marianne Williamson, a political novice and spiritual advisor to celebrities like Oprah Winfrey. Elizabeth Warren, the senior U.S. senator from Massachusetts, entered the primary in February of 2019 with detailed plans to fight corruption and make "big, structural change" in Washington, all of which energized the progressive base of the Democratic Party. Senator Amy Klobuchar (MN) followed a day later. She came with an outstanding reputation in key Midwestern states, appealed to moderate voters, and enjoyed an impressive bipartisan record in the Senate. And finally, U.S. Senator Kirsten Gillibrand (NY) formally announced her bid in March of 2019.

In the 12 Democratic primary debates, the six women displayed their individual personalities and wit. Marianne Williamson, when discussing policy, proclaimed, "If you think we're going to beat Donald Trump by just having all these plans, you've got another thing coming" (Blake 2019). Senator Gillibrand promised that one of her first acts as president would be to "Clorox the oval office" (Manchester 2019). Representative Gabbard, an Iraq war veteran, came on strong with her military experience, but her adversarial approach to the Democratic establishment did not help her in the polls.

Senator Harris distinguished herself early by taking pointed jabs at Donald Trump, as well as criticizing the Republican tax plan and immigration policy. Most notably, however, she confronted Joe Biden for touting his ability to work with segregationist senators and his stance in the 1970s on school busing.

Senator Klobuchar scoffed at Washington governor Jay Inslee's comment about his record on reproductive rights, by observing: "I just want to say that there's three women up here that have fought pretty hard for a woman's right to choose" (Flegenheimer 2019).

At the start of the primary season, Senator Warren was considered a candidate to beat. Her catch phrase, "I've got a plan for that," stuck with her throughout the campaign. Her best fundraising haul came after a strong debate performance in which she relentlessly berated rival former New York City mayor Michael Bloomberg for his treatment of women.

Low fundraising and poor polling eventually led all six women to drop out of the race, although Senators Warren and Klobuchar made it through all the primary debates but one, the final showdown between Joe Biden and Senator Bernie Sanders.

Veep-Stakes

In that last debate, Biden committed to choosing a woman as his running mate. Almost immediately, speculation began about who that woman would be. The list drew from his former primary rivals—namely, Senators Klobuchar, Harris, and Warren—as well as other standouts: former gubernatorial candidate Stacey Abrams (GA), Governor Michelle Lujan Grisham (NM), former National Security Advisor Susan Rice, Governor Gretchen Whitmer (MI), and Congresswoman Val Demings (FL).

Biden's selection of Senator Harris was especially significant for Black women (and women of color generally). Aimee Allison, founder of *She the People*, stated, "for millions of women of color, who had for generations fought to make this country better, for decades have been the backbone vote for Democrats, and the organizations on the ground, this is quite a moment for us" (PBS 2020). Black women had been the party's most loyal voting bloc, so their support was essential for Democrats.

National Party Conventions

Both national party conventions in 2020 highlighted women, particularly with respect to the centennial of the Nineteenth Amendment. Because of safety concerns in the COVID-19 pandemic, both parties held their conventions virtually, demonstrating a creativity unseen in prior election years.

The Democratic convention kicked off with a tribute to women's suffrage, but with special attention to women of color who were excluded from voting rights a century ago. The virtual platform featured prominent women in the party: Senator Warren, Stacey Abrams, Congresswoman Alexandria Ocasio-Cortez (D/NY), former State Representative Gabriel Giffords (D/AZ), and Michelle Obama. Dr. Jill Biden, who would become the *first* Lady to keep her regular job while in the White House, spoke from a classroom setting as a teacher and mother. House Speaker Nancy Pelosi and Hillary Clinton both wore suffragette white in their appearances.

Convention delegates and viewers saw a montage of the suffragettes in 1920, Supreme Court Justice Ruth Bader Ginsberg appearing before the Senate, and the Women's March that followed Trump's election. When Hillary Clinton addressed the convention, she emphasized the importance of getting out to vote, saying, "This can't be another 'woulda-coulda-shoulda' election." Each night of the convention was hosted by a well-known actress/producer: Eva Longoria, Kerry Washington, Tracee Ellis Ross, and Julia Louis-Dreyfus.

On the third night, Senator Harris officially accepted her nomination, paying special tribute to Black women who had come before her: "Without fanfare or recognition, they organized and testified and rallied and marched and fought not just for their vote but for a seat at the table. These women and the generations that followed worked to make democracy and opportunity real in the lives of all of us who followed" (Ruiz 2020).

Harris joined Biden the next night for his acceptance speech in a drive-in-movie style watch party, which ended with a gigantic fireworks display.

The GOP, after vowing to hold an in-person convention, relented and went for a mix of prerecorded videos and live speeches. Not to be outdone by the Democrats, the Republican convention highlighted the centennial of women's right to vote with a montage of key women in that struggle: Elizabeth Cady Stanton and Susan B. Anthony. New York congress-woman Elise Stefanik, a young leader within the party, gave a nod to the suffragettes, saying, "I would not have the honor and opportunity to serve my community in Congress were it not for their incredible leadership" (WCAX 2020).

Like the Democrats, the GOP featured many renowned women in the party: presidential advisor Kellyanne Conway, former attorney general Pam Bondi (FL), Republican National Committee Chair Ronna McDaniel, and White House press secretary Kayleigh McEnany. Republican women governors—Kim Reynolds (R/IA), Kristi Noem (R/SD), and Nikki Haley (R/SC)—took their turns in the spotlight as did members of the Trump family, including daughters Ivanka and Tiffany, and First Lady Melania Trump. The president's daughter-in-law Lara Trump stressed the president's commitment to women's success in his own organization.

Candidates for Congress and State Legislatures

In the rush to run, women entered electoral contests at every level across the country. According to the Center for American Women and Politics (CAWP), more women filed to run for Congress than at any time in U.S. history (Dittmar 2020). A record-breaking 583 women candidates ran for the House of Representatives in 2020, a 22.5 percent increase since the historic 2018 midterm elections. In 2020, the record numbers were largely driven by Republican women (227 women, a 74.6% increase from previous record). A record number of women sought seats in the U.S. Senate as well—60 total, but here more Democrats (37) than Republicans (23).

In the mix of Congressional candidacies were record numbers of Black, Latina, Asian, Middle-Eastern or North African, Native, and multiracial women. This included 248 women of color that ran for the U.S. House of Representatives and 19 for U.S. Senate. Similar to the overall trend for women's candidacies, women of color were better represented on the Democratic side of the aisle.

At the state level, 11 women (4D, 7R) ran for a governorship, and 50 women (30D, 18R, 2 No Party Affiliation) ran for statewide executive positions like labor commissioner and secretary of state. In addition, 3,346 women filed to run for state legislative positions. This number was largely driven by Democratic women (2,315), but also featured 1,105 Republicans, 18 nonpartisans, and 8 from other third parties (CAWP 2020a).

Beyond the record numbers of women candidates, what motivated them to run? On the Democratic side, the reason undoubtedly lies with Trump's behavior and policies, notably his stances on reproductive rights, access to affordable health care, immigration reform, and racial justice. On the GOP side, the reasons may have been the gains made by Democratic women in 2018, and the opportunity to advocate for policies like gun rights, the border wall, religious freedom, and opposition to Obamacare.

Groups That Supported Women's Candidacies

Women candidates received support from women's groups, political action committees (PACs), and social movement organizations. Nonpartisan groups, like IGNITE and She Should Run, focused on women's candidacies, regardless of party. On the Democratic side, EMERGE America along with prominent organizations like EMILY's List trained and funded Democratic, pro-choice women candidates across the country. Matriarch, Rise to Run, Run for Something, and Get Her Elected assisted in helping elect young progressive women. On the Republican side, groups included VIEW PAC and Republican Women for Progress, as well as the newly formed Winning for Women and Elevate PAC, which focused funding on GOP women in primaries.

A number of organizations supported women of color. Chief among them were Black sororities, such as Alpha Kappa Alpha (of which Kamala Harris was a member), Delta Sigma Theta, Phi Beta Sigma, and Sigma Gamma Rho. She the People, an organization designed to bring together a multiracial coalition, hosted the first-ever presidential forum for women of color, which featured some of the Democratic primary candidates. Higher Heights, cofounded in 2011 by Glynda Carr and Kimberly Peeler-Allen, focused on electing Black women to mayoral offices as well as state and federal positions. Latinas Represent, Latinas Lead, and Latino Victory Fund helped elect Latina women to political offices across the country. LGBTQ candidates received help from organizations like The Victory Institute and LGBTQ Victory Fund.

Help also came in the form of endorsements from social movement organizations. Black Lives Matter created its own PAC in 2020 (King 2020). BLM cofounder Patrice Cullors said, "Black Lives Matter is launching our PAC so we can talk directly to voters about who we think that they should be voting for and what we think they should be voting on." Every Town for Gun Safety endorsed candidates, including many women, across the country that committed to its "gun sense" agenda.

Electoral Victories

As in the 2018 midterm elections, the historic numbers of women running for office in 2020 translated to more electoral victories (CAWP 2020b). A record number of women (143) were elected to the 117th Congress (105D, 38R). The previous record, set in the 116th Congress (after the 2018 midterm elections), featured 127 women. Significantly, this included a record high 51 women of color (46D, 5R) and 28 nonincumbents (9D, 19R).

This new record high for women's victories was driven by gains in the House of Representatives, which reached a total of 119 women (89D, 30R). The Senate has a total of 24 women serving (16D, 8R), including one nonincumbent, Senator Cynthia Lummis (R-WY).

Despite these notable electoral wins, women still remain vastly underrepresented in the nation's institutions. And women have yet to shatter the ultimate glass ceiling: president of the United States.

REGISTRATION AND VOTING: WOMEN HEAVILY TARGET WOMEN

Voter interest in the 2020 presidential election was intense. Heading into the election, surveys showed a big share of registered voters (83%) saying it "really matter[ed]" who won (DeSilver 2021). A record number voted, casting more than 158 million ballots. Turnout rates were higher than in 2016 in *every* state.

Women were heavily targeted by both parties and advocacy groups representing nearly every slice of America. Each was well aware of the long-standing pattern of women registering and voting at higher rates than men.

Registration

From the start, the two youngest and most diverse generations (Gen Z'ers and Millennials) were identified as a large pool of potential registrants. Youth organizers from both parties recognized these generations were "ripe for heightened civic awareness, as Americans whose formative years were shaped by national trauma [social and economic]" (Lee, 2020).

Their growing levels of activism via the #MeToo, #BlackLivesMatter, gun violence, and environmental movements elevated awareness of the disconnect between younger Americans and their government—higher levels of distrust and alienation. It was not just liberal-leaning young persons who engaged in activism. The Right-to-Life March on Washington drew many young participants, as did rallies protesting the COVID-19-induced lockdown of businesses that employed many of them.

Women were involved in every registration-focused organization, ranging from the League of Women Voters and Rock the Vote, to NextGen America, Voto Latino, Black Votes Matter, and When We All Vote. Some women's names became synonymous with voter registration in individual states, like Black women (e.g., Stacey Abrams and LaTosha Brown), Latina Maria Teresa Kumar, and Native American Allie Young.

It was not just political and civic groups that strove to register and engage women but also sports leagues and stars (Megan Rapinoe, U.S. Women's National Soccer Team; Naomi Osaka, ranked No. 1 by the Women's Tennis Association; and Maya Moore, Women's National Basketball Association). Musicians (Taylor Swift, Billie Eilish, Lady Gaga) and celebrities (Gabrielle Union, Cynthia Nixon, filmmaker Ava DuVernay) joined the action. So did businesses.

AdAge encouraged young customers and employees to register and vote as "good business"—a way to promote their brand (Liffreing 2020):

> Brands across sectors, including technology, retail, entertainment, are *eager to get young citizens registered to vote and get their ballots in early this year.* Voting merchandise has quickly become a trend, some brands are paying employees to work the polls or building voter registration microsites and, for many, messaging is being developed with inclusivity and diversity in mind.

Some businesses showcased women in their advertising outreach—Gap (Stand United), the Ad Council (Vote For Your Life), and Foot Locker (www .footlocker.com/vote), to name a few. Almost all pushed links to registration portals and how-to-vote information. Most were nonpartisan in their approach, not wanting to alienate their "constituencies."

Registration was going full steam ahead in early 2020. When the pandemic hit, new registrations plummeted. Restrictions on in-person contacts put up registration roadblocks, but they also elevated the urgency of figuring out ways to do it.

For many groups, social media became the prime vehicle for reaching potential registrants, representing a radical change from traditional on-campus rallies, concerts, and sporting events, for example. Door-to-door efforts also came to a halt (although Republicans returned to it much earlier than

Democrats). It was young voters who broke through this barrier by talking to young Black and Latino Americans on platforms like TikTok and Instagram, "with culturally resonant content" (Halper 2020). They turned to imaginative videos linking potential registrants to how-to links:

> One video has a stylish Black woman swiping through a dating app and checking out the playful profile of another user, only to balk when it reveals he's a nonvoter. Viewers of the video can then tap a link that goes to a page where they can register easily. It is supported by pioneering technology that simplifies the process and enables organizers to track the registration status and engage with the new voter through Election Day.

Apps made registering and voting easier and simpler to track and help those having difficulties with these processes. Registration outreach within targeted communities was made simpler via apps using Google Maps and identifying the location of every unregistered voter in an area.

Creativity bloomed everywhere. In the midst of the pandemic, one women's group in Kansas City, Kansas, figured out a way to conduct a registration drive in their community without voters having to get out of their cars. Each weekend, they set up tables at different locations with easy access and vacant space for parking, then took blank registration forms to individual cars (Bergan 2020). "We are everyday people. We're not activists," but they were driven to take action by the turbulent times. They wanted everyday people to have a chance to weigh in on who would lead the country for the next four years.

Voting

Why did record numbers of Americans vote in 2020? Apart from the stark choice between Trump and Joe Biden, one reason was the pandemic-induced differences in *how* and *when* citizens could vote. More voted by mail than ever, seeking to avoid contact with potential COVID-19 carriers at a polling place. A number of states made it easier to vote by mail (VBM), extended times one could vote early in person, and created sites where voters could drop off their ballot or put it in a drop box. A higher share of those voting early in person in states permitting it, often voted in large arenas (civic centers, sports arenas) that permitted more social distancing.

Development of a national voting plan by the National Vote at Home Institute, a nonprofit organization led by CEO Amber McReynolds, became the go-to handbook for state and local officials across the country on how to successfully put VBM in place (Abrams, 2020). In addition, more states made it easier to VBM (absentee) without having to have an excuse to do so, but not without some controversy. Postelection legal challenges by the Trump campaign were raised in some battleground states over extended deadlines, ballots sent to *all* registrants (not just those requesting one), and methods of verifying a voter's signature. VBM was heavily promoted by Democrats, while the Trump campaign pushed voters to cast their ballots in person.

An analysis of voting in several battleground states found that women were much more likely to vote early (by mail or in person) than men. The woman director of political strategy at the Way to Win organization was stunned at the increase over 2016: "The numbers are insane. I've been working in politics in Texas, Nevada, Florida, nationally and nobody has ever seen numbers like these . . . I think this election is a referendum and people are not willing to not speak up" (Padilla 2020). Florida had clear generational differences—Gen Z through Gen X were much more likely to vote early in person (unsure about how to request VBM ballots and leery of the postal service). Majorities of Baby Boomers and older chose to VBM.

In line with historical voting patterns, clear generational differences in who voted showed up before Election Day. Older women, and men, chose the VBM voting method more than younger voters, although younger voters did increase their use of VBM—a change from the past. Early on, Democrats decided to push younger voters to VBM, fearing that many, notably college students, had scattered in the midst of the pandemic.

The strategy of promoting VBM encountered obstacles, largely related to younger voters' inexperience with VBM, their propensity to make mistakes that invalidate a mail ballot (Peeples 2020), and the pandemic. A poll conducted in May–June 2020 by the Center for Information and Research on Civic Learning & Engagement alerted proponents they needed to better educate young voters if they wanted them to VBM. With the election being held in a "national health crisis . . . *young voters aren't getting clear and accurate information about online registration and mail-in voting*" (Golden 2020; author's emphasis).

Many organizations put a lot of time and resources into the educational effort. It paid off. Exit poll data from the Associated Press's VoteCast reported that 70 percent of young people (18–29) ended up voting early or by mail; rates were higher among those with more education. Data from a key battleground state, Florida, found that VBM was most popular, followed by early in-person voting. Considerably fewer voted on Election Day—some of that pattern was clearly driven by COVID-19, but also by many Floridians just wanting to put the election behind them.

Turnout rate (percent) patterns turned out to be similar to previous election cycles. But in nearly every group the *number* who voted in 2020 was considerably higher than in 2016. Nationally, white and Black women turned out at higher rates than other women of color; older women (especially Baby Boomers) more than younger women, and women with higher levels of education at a higher rate than those with less formal education. While *turnout patterns differed by state*, women candidates and advocacy groups—Democratic and Republican—played key roles in increasing women's interest in and motivations for voting.

ISSUES AND MESSAGING: TOUGH TIMES MAKE MICROTARGETING MORE DIFFICULT

The 2020 election presented challenges on how to best target specific populations with messages that would get voters to the polls. Concerns about the economy and health care were exacerbated by the COVID-19 pandemic. Yet, the politically polarizing issues of immigration and reproductive rights still sat at the forefront of many people's minds. Racial justice also became a top priority to voters, particularly after the murders of George Floyd and other members of the Black community. For more conservative women, safety and security became an important issue as violence hit suburban areas like Kenosha, Wisconsin.

The *economy* has always been a top priority for voters in presidential elections. But alongside the pandemic and the economic strife that resulted from job losses, stay-at-home orders, closing of small businesses and schools, as well as market uncertainty presented new challenges for both parties. Undoubtedly, women were significantly more affected by the fallout from the coronavirus, largely a result of existing barriers like pay inequity and access to affordable child care.

Mothers, in particular, were three times more likely to have lost their employment than fathers. Furthermore, women are more often the primary caregivers in the home. With school closings and child care uncertainties, women were more likely to leave their jobs. Women, and especially women of color, were disproportionately represented as frontline workers. For example, women made up almost 80 percent of health care workers, including nurses and aides (Times Up Foundation 2021). They were also more likely to be employed in child care facilities, schools, grocery stores, retail, and restaurants. Thus, the "female recession" that occurred due to the pandemic was a considerable issue on the ballot for women in November.

For women of color, the situation was even more dire. Black women are hired and promoted less often than white men (Carrazana 2020a) and thus are less likely to fill positions that provide greater pay and benefits. Latinas suffered greatly, as they had the highest unemployment rate throughout the year (Carrazana 2020b). In fact, one out of every five Latinas was jobless. It was critical, therefore, for each presidential candidate to effectively message how they were going to support women, and in particular, women of color, in the economy.

Health care. Prior to the pandemic, Republicans had campaigned to replace the Affordable Care Act (Obamacare), whereas Democrats attempted to expand medical care. The parties failed to agree on policies related to insurance premiums, drug pricing, and reproductive health, as well as anti-discrimination protections for specific populations, like transgender people.

Without a doubt, the pandemic magnified the issue. Job losses meant that many Americans lost their employer-sponsored insurance coverage. Medical supplies and equipment (including ventilators and personal protective equipment), particularly for acute care facilities, were lacking. Many women, who are disproportionately represented in the health care field, were on the front lines in hospitals and health care facilities that had direct contact with patients.

The pandemic further aggravated racial and ethnic disparities within the health care system. Racial minorities disproportionately suffered coronavirus infections and deaths. Prior to the pandemic, they were more likely to lack health care coverage. Consequently, existing chronic conditions made their treatment and recovery far more difficult. Furthermore, despite the introduction of vaccines in late 2020, lower rates of vaccination occurred in these populations due to a combination of lack of information and access as well as mistrust.

Among major health care concerns, particularly for women, was reproductive rights. According to a May 2020 Gallup poll, 47 percent of Americans deemed abortion a major issue when they vote (although not the most important) (Brenan 2020). The issue was considered especially critical with the additions on the U.S. Supreme Court, including Trump-nominated justices Neil Gorsuch, Brett Kavanaugh, and Amy Coney Barrett.

Democratic voters, especially women who had previously fought for reproductive rights, were largely concerned about access to affordable reproductive health care. This includes everything from wellness visits, sexually transmitted disease testing and treatment, family planning, birth control, cancer screenings, as well as access to abortion. Republicans, on the other hand, vowed to overturn *Roe v. Wade* and subsequently mounted legal challenges in states across the country in hopes it will one day go to the Supreme Court.

Immigration. In the 2016 election, Trump campaigned on extending a wall along the Mexican border and advocated for limits on legal immigration. Because national security is a top GOP concern, restricting the flow of people across the nation's borders was seen as a necessity. Women voters were especially concerned about the safety of their children and homes. Tana Goertz, a Trump campaign advisor, believed immigration was a winning issue: "When I lay my head down at night, I want to know that my children are safe, that a terrorist is not going to come into our country" (Colvin and Jaffe 2019).

One of the most controversial *immigration* policies of the Trump administration was the separation of children from their families at the border. Supporters of the policy claimed that the action curbed human and child trafficking. During the election, child trafficking was taken up by QAnon conspiracy theorists. The far-right extremist group, which traces back to 2017, gained notoriety by claiming that a secret cabal of Satan worshippers and pedophiles—mostly elite Democrats, journalists, and Hollywood celebrities—was not only running a child sex-trafficking ring but looking to steal the election from Trump (Forrest 2021, Roose 2021).

Yet Democrats, particularly women, were outraged at images of children being left in cages and torn apart from their loved ones. At the end of the Trump presidency, hundreds of migrant children had yet to be united with their families. Consequently, Democrats insisted on immigration reform, as well as more protection for DREAMers.

Racial justice. The Black Lives Matter protests and marches in the summer of 2020 pushed racial justice issues, specifically police and criminal justice reform, to the forefront of the political agenda. Criminal justice reform had always been a critical issue for Black women, not just in the 2020 election. According to Adrianne Shropshire of BlackPAC, "Black women are on the front line, both because it is an issue affecting Black women directly and they care about their communities in general" (Haines 2020). Some from the left advocated for policies like defunding the police and reinvesting in community-based services, as well as more accountability for the actions of individual police officers and departments.

Trump responded to riots, destruction of property, and lootings that occurred alongside the tens of thousands of peaceful protests by demanding that law and order be restored to American cities. Republicans reiterated their support for law enforcement officers and Blue Lives Matter (a countermovement). This included painting protestors as violent thugs and "left-wing radicals" looking to upend the conservative way of life. Others went as far as to say that they didn't believe that systemic racism was pervasive in American society.

The 2020 election was also a critical election for the LGBTQ+ population. The Trump administration consistently supported policies that permitted discrimination in health care, housing, employment, and public accommodations and rolled back protections for transgender students and banned transgender persons from serving in the military. Moreover, the murders of transwomen of color, especially Black transwomen, which was largely unaddressed prior to the election, came to the fore.

Targeting

Both presidential campaigns needed the support of women. Joe Biden and the Democrats faced a significant hurdle in appealing to the progressive end of the party, who failed to show up for Hillary Clinton in 2016. But more so, Democrats needed to figure out how to best reach and turn out their diverse base, which included Black women who have consistently been the party's most loyal voting bloc.

Undoubtedly, Trump and the GOP recognized the "woman" problem in their party. His inflammatory rhetoric and tweets during his presidency, alongside continued accusations of sexual assault, left many women, especially suburban white women, on the fence about voting for him for a second term. Actually, many suburban women had drifted to the Democratic Party during the 2018 midterm elections.

To address women's diminishing support, several key Republican women hit the road to address them directly in the Women for Trump Bus Tour. The campaign highlighted how Trump's economy had helped women thrive. To that end, presidential advisor Kellyanne Conway told audiences that the economy is "more important than approval in the polls" (Cotorno 2019). At a stop in Tampa, one woman said, "I care about my paycheck, my children's future and that my retirement keeps growing. Everything else just falls where it may. The way he talks doesn't bother me at all" (Cotorno 2019).

In addition to the economic message, Trump touted his law-and-order stance, pro-life position, promise of tax cuts, school choice, and opposition to the left's "socialist" policies. Strategists believed that if the president could push traditional Republican issues and talking points, he would bring women back to the fold. But in the chaotic months leading up to 2020 election, women voters were looking for a return to normalcy. Celinda Lake, a Democratic pollster, suggested that "they want someone who will lead them through this, not someone who will make it more chaotic" (Scherer and Dawsey 2020).

Joe Biden, throughout his presidential run, proclaimed he would be the president for all Americans, not just Democrats. His messages centered on *unity*, which directly contrasted with Trump's divisive rhetoric. His campaign targeted not only moderates, but also disaffected Republicans voters. This included the coveted suburban women's vote, which was up for grabs.

One of the Biden campaign's strategies was to show how Trump administration policies had failed women. This strategy entailed promoting numerous Democratic women to advise on his campaign, but also Republican women like Cindy McCain and former New Jersey governor Christine Todd Whitman. Additionally, Biden pitched a proposed White House Council on Gender Equity and highlighted how Trump's promise to dismantle

Obamacare would have negative consequences for women with preexisting conditions (like pregnancy).

Biden tended to support more moderate Democratic positions, including the expansion of Obamacare. Access to affordable health care was an important issue for women of all racial and ethnic backgrounds, as well as the LGBTQ+ population. But Democrats needed to be able to talk about how the lack of access to affordable health care and inequities within the health care system affected different populations. For example, Black women have 2–3 times higher maternal mortality rates than white women. Thus, to mobilize these diverse populations, the Democrats up and down the ballot had to be cognizant of how these issues affected groups differently. And most important, they needed to be able to communicate how they intended to advocate for policies that would uplift these communities.

In addition, the Biden campaign insisted on greater federal involvement to fight the pandemic, which had detrimental effects on women across the country. This included policies like mandatory mask mandates, as well as additional stimulus money to boost the economy and provide relief to citizens and small businesses. To address criminal justice reform, he promised that his Justice Department would hold cities accountable for the actions of their police officers and advocated for increased funding for programs like community policing.

Money—More of It

Women not only ran for office in record numbers during 2020 but women candidates also raised more money than in previous election years and women donors contributed more to political campaigns. According to the Center for Responsive Politics, women candidates raised more money in Congressional contests than their male counterparts. Although donations to both political parties had risen, Democratic women received the most.

Women that ran for president also received more of their campaign contributions from women than men (Ye He Lee and Narayanswamy 2020). As of January 2020, almost 60 percent of the donations received by Senators Warren, Klobuchar, and Harris came from women. But these women candidates did not have a lock on all women contributors—Joe Biden received most of his monetary support from women donors.

Nor was the increase in women's donations limited to the Democratic Party. Trump received more donations from women than in 2016 (Kurtzleben 2019). Republican National Committee Chairwoman Ronna McDaniel tweeted that Trump's 2020 campaign received more donations from women than any of the Democratic contenders, as his first quarter consisted of 10,329 women donors (Orr 2019).

MEDIA: WOMEN TAKE CHARGE

The perennial complaints about the media's gender bias surfaced at the beginning of the presidential campaign—less, and more negative, coverage of women; stereotypical labeling; fewer women journalists at top levels; too few women given major roles in devising which type of media to use in messaging voters; and a dearth of women with major input into ad content. Once viewed as deterrents to running for office, these barriers were seen as a real impetus to breaking them down.

The #MeToo movement brought gender inequities in the media industry to the forefront: "[F]emale reporters not only earn less than their male colleagues, they also are a smaller percentage in the newsroom. Even though women outnumber men in journalism programs and colleges, they become the minority voice soon after entering the workforce" (Roy 2020). Even disparities in news photographs came under attack. An analysis of news photos posted publicly on Facebook by 17 prominent national news outlets found gross underrepresentation of women made more significant by the fact that social media as a whole was more often sought for news than print newspapers.

Women's increased media involvement in the presidential campaign took many forms. For the first time ever, all three major broadcast networks (ABC, NBC, CBS) put female executive producers in charge of their morning shows—designed to appeal to women viewers. For example, "The View," a daytime talk show with its large, diverse female audience, became "the most important political TV show in America—an essential campaign stop for Democrats and Republicans alike" (FitzSimons 2019).

Major studies detailed a high level of underrepresentation of women in key news positions, pushing newspapers, TV networks, into hiring and promoting more women executives, reporters, anchors, and political analysts (Women's Media Center 2019; Roy 2020). Diversity—racial and ethnic, gender—is vital to making news credible. "Inclusiveness in the newsroom means inclusiveness in the news. Racism and sexism puts blinders on everyone," Gloria Steinem, cofounder of Women's Media Center reported (Poynter 2018). News outlets scrambled to have more women in prominent positions covering politics. Abby Phillip, a young (31), Black political correspondent at CNN, rose to becoming one of three analysts on the CNN election desk for five days. This "NextGen CNN" star (Rosman 2020) got kudos from Bernice King, the Reverend Martin Luther King Jr.'s daughter, for her coverage of the role of Black women and built a big presence on social media (Instagram). To add more partisan balance to its coverage, CNN hired a prominent Republican spokeswoman, Sarah Isgur, to be one of its political editors for on-air and online content, with occasional appearances on air.

A high-profile project supported and executed by Nicole Carroll, editor-in-chief of *USA Today*, detailed the fight for the right to vote and highlighted 150 women involved in the fight—past and present. The *USA Today* network (multiple newspapers across the United States) in partnership with Univision also created "Womankind" videos featuring women doing critical work in their own communities.

From 1996 to 2016, almost half of all primary debates had no women moderators; three-fourths had no people of color (Lee 2019). With so many women running for president, the Democratic National Committee mandated that every Democratic presidential debate (12 sanctioned) have at least one female moderator and at least one person of color. The new rule was to "help ensure that a variety of perspectives and issues, such as child care costs, paid family leave, and maternal mortality" were included in debate discussions (Gontcharova 2019). Women of color serving as moderators or comoderators included Gayle King (CBS), Kristen Welker (NBC), Linsey Davis (ABC), and Vanessa Hauc (Telemundo).

The senior vice president for specials on NBC News and MSNBC, Rashida Jones, handpicked "four of the best journalists ever" (all women) to moderate the fifth Democratic presidential debate in Atlanta (Rachel Maddow, Andrea Mitchell, Kristen Welker—all NBC and Ashley Parker of the *Washington Post*). Significantly, it was the first debate to ask Democratic candidates about paid family leave (Ellefson, 2019).

For the sixth debate, two women of color—Amna Nawaz and Yamiche Alcindor, PBS NewsHour correspondents—served as moderators. Both women were praised for their direct and unrelenting questioning of candidates. For example, when Bernie Sanders sidestepped a question on race, Nawaz insisted he answer: "Senator, with all respect, this question is about race. Can you answer the question as it was asked?" (Angyal 2019).

The nonpartisan Commission on Presidential Debates tapped Kirsten Welker to moderate the second of two debates between Trump and Biden, and Susan Page, *USA Today*'s Washington Bureau Chief, to moderate the vice presidential debate between Mike Pence and Kamala Harris. Because the second presidential debate was canceled due to COVID-19, each candidate did a town hall but on different networks—Biden on ABC, Trump on NBC.

Savannah Guthrie (NBC Today Show coanchor) moderated a fiery town hall featuring President Trump. She was credited by other journalists with tough questioning of the president, showing others "how to interrogate" him (Stewart 2020) but criticized by Trump supporters for "hostile and biased behavior" toward him (Saavedra 2020).

New news outlets were created by and for women. "Prism," a nonprofit site founded in 2018, was designed to give voice to marginalized people. "We're committed to producing the kind of journalism that treats Black,

Indigenous, and people of color, women, the LGBTQ+ community, and other invisibilized groups as the experts on our own lived experiences, our resilience, and our fights for justice" (Prism 2020). In August 2020, *The 19th**, a nonpartisan news platform was launched "to empower women—particularly those historically underserved by American media—with the information, community and tools they need to be equal participants in our democracy" (*The 19th** 2020). The asterisk stands for the "unfinished business of the 19th Amendment, recognizing those still omitted from democracy." Senator Kamala Harris gave her first interview as the Democratic nominee for vice president to *The 19th**.

Women got involved in expanding social media. For example, Sofia Gross, Snap Inc.'s public policy manager, took charge of the company's social media platform (Snapchat) that helped more than a million young people register to vote. Vijaya Gadde, top lawyer for Twitter, convinced the CEO to ban political ads from Twitter—a monumental, and controversial, decision in the world of social media, having a big negative impact on the ability of candidates to microtarget voters.

To get around some social media advertising roadblocks, the Biden and Trump campaigns often paid "social media influencers," typically those with fewer than 10,000 captive followers. These "digital door knockers," often women, were seen as "more authentic and trustworthy by their followers and better positioned to change their behavior" (Goodwin, Joseff, and Woolley 2020). By campaign's end, some of these influencer sites were accused of being major sources of misinformation and conspiracy claims, usually by a group with an opposing ideological perspective.

Others turned to social media when unable to get their messages out on traditional media. Social media enabled Candace Owens, a Millennial and conservative Black political commentator, to appear on Fox News and Newsmax as a strong Trump supporter. She founded "Blexit," patterned after Brexit, "to encourage Black Americans to ditch their historic ties with the Democratic Party" (Panetta and Collman, 2020).

Liberal Black women launched social media-based campaigns to elevate awareness of high-priority issues. A well-known example was the #SayHerName campaign begun by the African American Policy Forum to call attention to Black women killed by police. The "ShareTheMicNow" campaign to "magnify Black women's lives and stories" gained a national audience of approximately 300 million on Instagram (Feminist Majority, 2020).

With COVID-19 minimizing face-to-face campaigning, television and online political ads were more critical than ever. Advertising Analytics gauged spending on national TV advertising in 2019 and 2020 at nearly $250 million, up from $85 million in 2016 (Steinberg 2020). The presidential campaigns ran more TV ads in 2020 for two reasons: the campaigns had more money and more people were home because of lockdowns for COVID-19. Women were heavily featured in the TV ads visually, by voice, and content. Two of the women-focused ads getting the most attention featured older women (McManus 2020). Each reflected a major theme of that candidate's campaign:

"Donna" was a TV ad paid for by Biden campaign, with a COVID-19 theme: "Roger and I decided that we wanted to move to The Villages," a woman identi- fied only as Donna says in the ad. "We were ready to retire, we were both 60." She added, "[w]hile I don't blame Donald Trump for the virus, I blame him for his lack of action. And because of that, we're sitting here Zooming or FaceTiming with our grandchildren instead of hugging and kissing them. And that's hard."

"Joe Biden knows that every moment is precious," she says. "I trust Joe Biden to get this virus under control."

"Break In" was a TV ad paid for by the Trump campaign, with a law and order theme (Dale 2020):

An elderly woman is at home watching a news broadcast that is talking about a proposal to reduce Seattle's police budget by 50 percent and transfer manage- ment of its 911 call center to an entity other than the police department.

The woman then notices that an intruder is scurrying around outside her door and she begins to dial 911. In the background, Fox News host Sean Hannity says, "Joe Biden said he's absolutely on board with defunding the police. Listen closely." Biden's voice says, "Yes, absolutely." The ad shows a darkened, empty office with unmanned phones.

As the intruder breaks in, an automated message says, "Hello, you've reached 911. I'm sorry that there is no one here to answer your emergency call. But leave a message, and we'll get back to you as soon as we can."

The words "you won't be safe in Joe Biden's America" come on screen as the intruder confronts the woman. The phone falls to the ground.

Most of the money spent for campaigns' online advertising "involved a call to action, such as give money, sign a petition, answer a poll, sign up to get emails or watch the latest video" (Stromer-Galley 2020). Social media professor Karen North cited the advantages of microtargeting women via social media ads:

The real, huge change with social media versus traditional media is that it makes us feel like we have a personal connection with somebody. You can say you want to send this message to soccer moms and a different message to swim team moms. It feels like they are whispering in my ear. It feels like they are speaking to me directly.

The two presidential campaigns spent more than $36 million on Facebook and Instagram between June and September 2020 targeting women—Biden, $20 million, Trump, $16 million (Statista 2021). Between late September and mid-October, Biden social media ads on Facebook alone targeted more women (59%) than men and voters 44 and younger (56%) more than older voters (Manthey 2020). Trump's ads were more evenly targeted by gender (men 49.8%; women 49.4%) and more focused on those 45 and older (67%).

In general, Facebook and Google were used more to target older women, and Snapchat younger women (Gen Z, Millennials). Snapchat more easily permitted "geotargeting" ads to ZIP codes and specific states. For example, the Biden campaign targeted Snapchat users within 1–3 miles of four histori- cally Black colleges and universities (HBCU) in South Carolina prior to the Democratic primary with this message: "Joe Biden is ready to invest $70 billion in HBCUs and minority-serving institutions—an investment in your future; HBCU Students for Biden" (Dean 2020). Black women predominated in these institutions' student bodies.

In a sharp reversal from his 2016 campaign, 52 percent of Trump's 2020 top-level campaign staff were women—senior advisors, national press secretary, director of coalitions, and the head of operations. The reason was simple: "[O]ptimize the campaign's outreach to suburban women—an enormously important voting bloc—by *having women oversee the outreach themselves*" (Orr 2019; authors' emphasis).

Women made up 58 percent of the Biden campaign's senior officials— department heads, senior advisors, deputy campaign managers, and senior consultants who spent the majority of their time on the campaign. Biden touted the diversity of his campaign staff both in terms of race (38% people of color) and gender. He also valued the experience and insights of Anita Dunn, senior advisor to the campaign charged with "keeping track of who crosses Biden—staff, reporters, politicians"—watching, listening, remembering, and "completely comfortable with giving a firm no" (Dovere 2020). With Biden's election, she became the first person in years to be in the inner circle of two winning candidates—Obama, then Biden.

BIDEN WINS WOMEN'S VOTE, BUT NOT BY MARGIN EXPECTED

The race between Joe Biden and Donald Trump was often described as "a battle between male and female voters—with more men supporting the president and more women backing his challenger" (Zhang and Fox 2020). Women turned out to vote at high levels, reflective of successful registration and get-out-the-vote efforts by both campaigns, and the turbulent times that made voters more likely to believe their vote would make a difference. No one doubted that more women than men would vote. The big questions were whether a considerably larger number of women would vote for Joe Biden than for Hillary Clinton in 2016 and whether the gender gap would be wider.

Virtually every poll and news account leading up to Election Day predicted there would be an historic gender gap—with a much larger share of women than men voting for Joe Biden. This projection was hardly surprising based on the nation's changing demographics (the growth of the racially/ethnically diverse and more liberal Gen Z and Millennial generations), record numbers of women candidates seeking the Democratic nomination for president, the death of Justice Ruth Bader Ginsburg, and Trump's unfavorable job performance ratings among women. Expectations were that Biden would make inroads with white college- and non-college-educated women, older women upset with Trump's handling of COVID-19 and his "less-than-presidential" demeanor, and suburban moms offended by his bullying style and suffering from the economic downturn. Hopes were that Biden would turn out younger women at higher rates than in 2016 when many favored Bernie Sanders over Clinton and did not vote.

Shocking to many, the gender gap turned out to be *narrower* than in 2016! A headline in the *Washington Post* said it all: *"The gender gap was expected to be historic. Instead, women voted much as they always have"* (Schmidt 2020; authors' emphasis). In 2020, 56 percent of women voted for Biden, 48 percent of men—a gender gap of 8 percent. In 2016, 54 percent of women but only 41 percent of men cast their ballot for Hillary Clinton—a gap of 13 percent. Not surprisingly, the gender gap was widest among Black (11%) and Latino (9%) voters, and narrowest among white voters (3%). Ironically, it was white men more than white women who increased their support for Biden. Moreover, the results differed across states, driven by demographic and partisan composition (see figure 6.1).

Ahead of Election Day, the big storyline in the news media was that female voters were souring on Trump and a mass migration of women would flow into the Democratic Party. That did not happen, leading some to conclude that "one pattern continues to be clear year after year: Party is usually a stronger force in presidential politics than gender" (Schmidt 2020).

Large numbers of suburban women who voted for Trump in 2016 did not shift toward Biden as anticipated by Democrats, although he made some gains. The lower-than-expected gains were attributed by some to failures in tailored messaging—and ad placement—to individual media markets that differ significantly in the composition of women who live in suburbs. Others

Biden (D)   □ Other   ■ Trump (R)

GENDER
Men (48%)   45   53
Women (52%)   57   42

GENDER AND RACE AND ETHNICITY
White men (35%)   38   61
White women (32%)   44   55
Black men (4%)   79   19
Black women (8%)   90   9
Hispanic men (5%)   59   36
Hispanic women (8%)   69   30
All other races and ethnicities (8%) 58   38

GENDER AND EDUCATION
White college grad women (14%)   54   45
White non-college women (17%)   36   63
White college grad men (17%)   48   51
White non-college men (18%)   28   70
Voters of color (33%)   71   26

GENDER AND MARITAL STATUS
Married men (30%)   44   55
Married women (26%)   47   51
Unmarried men (20%)   52   45
Unmarried women (23%)   63   36

GENDER AND PARENTAL STATUS
Men with children (17%)   48   49
Women with children (17%)   56   43
Men without children (34%)   47   51
Women without children (33%)   55   44

0   20   40   60   80   100

Support in Percent (%)

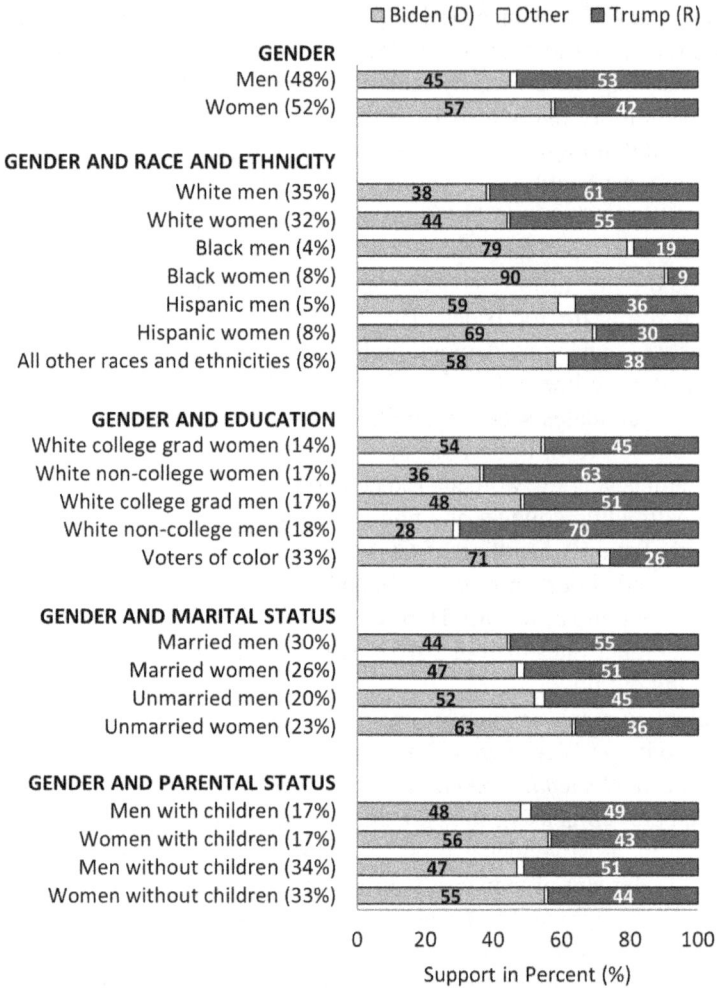

Figure 6.1   National Gender Gap Varied across Demographic Groups. Note: Numbers in parentheses for each group of voters reflect that group's share of the total votes cast nationally. "Other" is share of votes to other minor party candidates. Data for voters of color by educational attainment not shown due to small sample sizes. Source: National Election Pool exit poll conducted nationally by Edison Research, as reported by CNN.

said suburban women drifted back to the GOP by issues such as security and jobs. By far, the most cohesive racial/ethnic group was black women. "Black women's activism, Black women's organizing" was a much bigger story than white suburban women (Schmidt 2020). While less cohesive than Black women, Latinas and Asian American women also voted more heavily for Biden than their male counterparts.

While neither the heavily anticipated mass migration of women into the Democratic Party nor the historic gender gap materialized, there is no denying that women proved their power in politics in 2020. They broke down one barrier after another in the male-dominated arena. Women ran for office and were elected at record-breaking levels; they moderated debates, led campaigns, took part in activist movements, and dug deep into their pocketbooks to contribute to candidates. They registered and turned out to vote, playing a major role in electing Joe Biden as the nation's 46th president and Kamala Harris as a trailblazing vice president.

REFERENCES

Allison, Aimee. 2020. "Women of Color: The Fastest Growing Voting Group." *Democracy Journal*. Summer No. 57. https://democracyjournal.org/magazine/57/women-of-color-the-fastest-growing-voting-group

Angyal, Chloe. 2019. "Women of Color Ruled Last Night's Debate." *Marie Claire*. December 20. https://www.marieclaire.com/politics/a30297301/sixth-democratic-primary-debate-amna-nawaz-yamiche-alcindor/

Blake, Aaron. 2019. "Winners and Losers from the Democratic Presidential Debate's Second Night." *Washington Post*. June 27.

Brenan, Megan. 2020. "One in Four Americans Consider Abortion A Key Voting Issue." *Gallup*. July 7. https://news.gallup.com/poll/313316/one-four-americans-consider-abortion-key-voting-issue.aspx

Carrazana, Chabeli. 2020a. "Black Women are Promoted at Far Lower Rates Than White Men, Report Finds." *The 19th*. August 13. https://19thnews.org/2020/08/black-women-equal-pay-day-2020-report-gender-race/

———. 2020b. "Latinas Had The Highest Unemployment Rate This Year – And It's Driving Them to Vote." *The 19th*. October 9. https://19thnews.org/2020/10/latinas-unemployment-voting/

Center for American Women and Politics (CAWP). 2020a. "2020 Summary of Potential Women Candidates." *Center for American Women and Politics*. December 22. https://cawp.rutgers.edu/potential-candidate-summary-2020#governor

———. 2020b. "Results: Women Candidates in the 2020 Elections." *Center for American Women and Politics*. November 4. https://cawp.rutgers.edu/election-analysis/results-women-candidates-2020-elections

Center for Responsive Politics. 2020. "In 2020 Women Ran, Won and Donated in Record Numbers." *OpenSecrets.org*. December 21. https://www.opensecrets.org/news/2020/12/women-ran-won-donate-record-numbers-2020-nimp/

Colvin, Jill and Alexandra Jaffe. 2019. "Making a Case to Women: Trump Female Defenders Go on Offense." *AP News*. August 2019. https://apnews.com/article/2f5a348dca974cb79526fd2a7edf5894

Contorno, Steve. 2019. "Donald Trump's Strategy for Women: It's the Economy. Is that Enough?" *Tampa Bay Times*. August 24. https://www.tampabay.com/flori

da-politics/buzz/2019/08/24/donald-trumps-strategy-for-women-its-the-economy
-is-that-enough/

Dale, Daniel. 2020. "Fact Check: Trump's Dishonest '911' Ad Fear-Mongers About Biden." *CNN*. July 21. https://www.cnn.com/2020/07/21/politics/fact-check-trump
-ad-biden-police-911/index.html

Dean, Spencer. 2020. "Presidential Advertising by Candidates Reveals Microtargeting Tactics on Snapchat." DELTA Lab, Wesleyan Media Project. October 28. https://deltalab.research.wesleyan.edu/2020/10/28/presidential-advertising-on-snapchat/

DeSilver, Drew. 2021. "Turnout Soared in 2020 as Nearly Two-Thirds of Eligible U.S. Voters Cast Ballots for President." *Pew Research Center*. January 28. https://www.pewresearch.org/fact-tank/2021/01/28/turnout-soared-in-2020-as-nearly-two
-thirds-of-eligible-u-s-voters-cast-ballots-for-president/

Dittmar, Kelly. 2020. "What You Need to Know About the Record Numbers of Women Candidates in 2020." *Center for American Women and Politics*. August 10. https://cawp.rutgers.edu/election-analysis/record-numbers-women-candidates-2020

Dovere, Edward-Isaac. 2020. "The Mastermind Behind Biden's No-Drama Approach to Trump." *The Atlantic*. November 30.

Ellefson, Lindsey. 2019. "MSNBC Praised for All-Female Debate Moderating Team." *The Wrap*. November 21. thewrap.com/msnbc-praised-for-all-female-debate-moderating-team/

Feminist Majority. 2020. "#ShareTheMicNow Campaign Amplifies Black Women's Voices on Social Media." June 12. https://feminist.org/news/sharethemicnow
-campaign-amplifies-Black-womens-voices-on-social-media/

FitzSimons, Amanda. 2019. "How 'The View' Became the Most Important TV Show in America." *New York Times*, May 22.

Flegenheimer, Matt. 2019. "There Were 3 Women Onstage, And A Man Had a Lot to Say About His Work on Abortion." *New York Times*. June 26.

Forrest, Brett. 2021. "What Is QAnon? What We Know About the Conspiracy-Theory Group." *The Wall Street Journal*. February 4. https://www.wsj.com/articles
/what-is-qanon-what-we-know-about-the-conspiracy-theory-11597694801

Golden, Amanda. 2020. "Younger Americans Embrace Mail-In Voting If They Can Figure Out How." *NBC News*. July 5. https://www.nbcnews.com/politics/2020-election/younger-americans-embrace-mail-voting-if-they-can-figure-out-n1232929

Gontcharova, Natalie. 2019. "Exclusive: DNC Requires Female Moderators At Every 2020 Debate." *Refinery29*. May 30. https://www.refinery29.com/en-us/2019/05
/234148/democratic-presidential-debate-info-2020-dnc-female-moderator

Goodwin, Anastasia, Katie Joseff, and Samuel C. Woolley. 2020. "Social Media Influencers and the 2020 Election: Paying 'Regular People' for Digital Campaign Communication." Center for Media Engagement, University of Texas. October. https://mediaengagement.org/research/social-media-influencers-and-the-2020-election/

Haines, Errin. 2020. "For Black Women, 'Race and Violence in Our Cities' Isn't About Protests." *The 19th**. September 29. https://19thnews.org/2020/09/race-and
-violence-in-our-cities-black-women-voter/

Halper, Evan. 2020. "As Voting Rolls Plunge Amid Pandemic, Progressives Try to Reinvent the Registration Drive." *Los Angeles Times*. July 8.

King, Maya. 2020. "Black Lives Matter Launches a Political Action Committee." *Politico*. October 9. https://www.politico.com/news/2020/10/09/black-lives-matter-pac-428403

Kurtzleben, Danielle. 2019. "Here Are the Presidential Candidates Women Have Been Donating To." *NPR*. November 26. https://www.npr.org/2019/11/26/764179752/heres-which-presidential-candidates-women-have-been-donating-to

Lee, Barbara. 2019. "The Women in the Democratic Primary Debates Will Make History. Here's How Moderators Can Do the Same." *NBCNews.com*. June 23. https://www.nbcnews.com/think/opinion/women-democratic-primary-debates-will-make-history-here-s-how-ncna1020381

Liffreing, Ilyse. 2020. "How Brands Are Getting Voters to the Polls (and Mailboxes) in 2020." *AdAge*. September 17. https://adage.com/article/cmo-strategy/how-brands-are-getting-voters-polls-and-mailboxes-2020/2281291

Manchester, Julia. 2019. "Gillibrand: First Thing I'll Do If Elected Is 'Clorox the Oval Office'." *The Hill*. July 31. https://thehill.com/homenews/campaign/455663-gillibrand-first-thing-ill-do-if-elected-is-clorox-the-oval-office

Manthey, Grace. 2020. "Presidential Campaigns Set New Records for Social Media Ad Spending." ABC7 (KDOC-TV). October 29. Data from Bully Pulpit Interactive's 2020 Campaign Tracker. https://abc7.com/presidential-race-campaign-spending-trump-political-ads-biden/7452228/

McManus, Doyle. 2020. "Column: This Year's Political Ads: The Good, the Bad, and the Deceptive." *Los Angeles Times*. October 25.

Orr, Gabby. 2019. "The Women Behind Trump's 2020 Election Bid." *Politico*. November 1. https://www.politico.eu/article/women-behind-trump-2020-election-bid/

———. 2019. "Trump is Finally Catching Fire With Female Donors." *Politico*. May 14. https://www.politico.com/story/2019/05/14/trump-campaign-women-donations-1319877

Padilla, Mariel. 2020. "More Women Than Men Are Voting Early in Key Battleground States." *19thnews*. November 2. https://www.elle.com/culture/career-politics/a34549594/women-driving-2020-election/

Panetta, Grace and Ashley Collman. 2020. "The Life and Career of Candace Owens, The Black Conservative Activist Who Attacked Black Lives Matter and Said George Floyd Was 'Not a Good Person.'" *Business Insider*. June 13. https://www.businessinsider.com/candace-owens-Black-conservative-activist-life-career-attacks-2020-6

PBS News Hour. 2020. "What Kamala Harris Offers the Biden Campaign as VP Nominee." *PBS*. August 11. https://www.pbs.org/newshour/show/what-kamala-harris-offers-the-biden-campaign-as-vp-nominee

Poynter Staff. 2018. "New Report Shows Lack of Progress for Women of Color in the Media." Poynter Institute. March 6. https://www.poynter.org/business-work/2018/new-report-shows-lack-of-progress-for-women-of-color-in-the-media/

Prism. 2021. "Mission." Accessed February 2, 2021. https://www.prismreports.org/mission/

Roose, Kevin. 2021. "What Is QAnon, the Viral Pro-Trump Conspiracy Theory?" *New York Times.* February 4.

Rosman, Katherine. 2020. "Abby Phillip Is Next-Gen CNN." *New York Times.* November 13.

Roy, Katica, 2019. "There's a Gender Crisis in Media, and It's Threatening Our Democracy." *FastCompany.* September 10. https://www.fastcompany.com/90401548/theres-a-gender-crisis-in-media-and-its-threatening-our-democracy

Ruiz, Rebecca. 2020. "On One Woman's Big Night at the Democratic Convention, Many Women Celebrated." *New York Times.* August 20.

Saavedra, Ryan. 2020. "Savannah Guthrie Blasted For Hostile Behavior Toward Trump During Town Hall." *Washington Post.* October 15.

Scherer, Michael and Josh Dawsey. 2020. "As Trump Slumps, His Campaign Fixes On a Target: Women." *Washington Post.* June 22.

Schmidt, Samantha. 2020. "The Gender Gap Was Expected to be Historic. Instead, Women Voted Much as They Always Have." *Washington Post.* November 6.

Seib, Gerald F. 2020. "The Year Of The Woman Really, Finally Did Arrive In 2020." *Wall Street Journal.* November 16.

Steinberg, Brian. 2020. "Trump Biden Presidential Campaigns Gave the TV Ad Business a Much Needed Influx of Cash." *Variety.* November 4. https://variety.com/2020/biz/news/trump-biden-presidential-campaigns-ads-1234822556/

Stewart, Emily. 2020. "Savannah Guthrie Delivered the Trump Interview We've Been Wanting For Years." *Vox.* October 15. https://www.vox.com/policy-and-politics/2020/10/15/21518763/savannah-guthrie-trump-town-hall-nbc-miami

Stromer-Galley, Jennifer. 2020. "Trump and Biden Ads on Facebook and Instagram Focus on Rallying the Base." *The Conversation.* October 29. https://theconversation.com/trump-and-biden-ads-on-facebook-and-instagram-focus-on-rallying-the-base-146904

Time's Up. 2021. "Women on the Front Lines." *TimesUpFoundation.org* Accessed February 2, 2021. https://timesupfoundation.org/work/women-on-the-front-lines/

WCAX. 2020. "Stefanik Featured in Republican National Convention Video On Women's Suffrage." August 25. https://www.wcax.com/2020/08/25/stefanik-featured-in-republican-national-convention-video-on-womens-suffrage/

Women's Media Center. 2019. "Divided 2019: The Media Gender Gap." January 31. https://www.genderavenger.com/blog/gareads-divided-2019-the-media-gender-gap

Ye Hee Lee, Michelle and Anu Narayanswamy. 2020. "Women Running for President are Raising More Money From Women Than Are Their Male Opponents." *The Washington Post.* January 15.

Zhang, Christine and Brooke Fox. 2020. "How a Coalition of Women Won It For Joe Biden." *Financial Times.* November 23. https://www.ft.com/content/2b0eba6f-ba33-42e6-b49a-f7e53d67341f

Chapter 7

Democracy, When?

The Democratic Vision of Dr. Martin Luther King Jr. and the Political Moment of Race in American Politics and the Political Science Discipline

Shayla C. Nunnally

INTRODUCTION

On January 18, 2021, we commemorated the 35th anniversary of observing the national holiday in honor of the Rev. Dr. Martin Luther King.[1] This commemoration happened during a moment in American history that was rife with political strife related to the contestation over the 2020 presidential election and the racial injustice in the wake of the senseless deaths of George Floyd and Breonna Taylor, two African Americans among several, who either lost their lives or were assaulted in police-related violence. Summer 2020, Black Lives Matter became a movement embraced around the world, when a video showed a police officer kneeling on the neck of George Floyd for more than 9 minutes. Many Americans and people around the world seemed forever changed, in recognizing the cruelty that Black people face in their everyday lives (Herndon and Searcey 2020).

Within two weeks of one of the most infamous moments in American history, when on January 6, 2021, a crowd of thousands, waving Trump flags, and avowed white nationalists marched to the U.S. Capitol and declared that the 2020 presidential election was illegitimate and that President Donald J. Trump was reelected and, instead, presidential candidate, former U.S. Vice President Joseph Biden, had lost the election (*Associated Press* 2021). In the professed view and understanding of many who supported President Trump's claim, the election had been "stolen" by unfair election counting of ballots.

As we commemorate Dr. King's legacy, we are reminded that we cannot view his life and vision of democracy in a vacuum. That is, we must not extract Dr. King as a sole, monumental figure, who did not live in an environment that was hostile to him and the people, who looked like him, and who supported him and his cause. Even the passage of the national King Holiday was contested and took over 32 years to become a national holiday observed by all 50 states (King National Holiday 1986; Constitution Daily 2020). Even in states like Alabama and Mississippi, the observance occurs on the same day as the one honoring Confederate General Robert E. Lee—a racialized counterbalancing that detracts from the civil rights activism that King professed to dismantle the legacies of slavery represented in the institutionalization of Jim Crow across the South (Lam and Bote 2020).

Rather, it is important for us to understand the context in which Dr. King's leadership and activism occurred, and it is also important for us to contextualize Dr. King's life and journey in activism within the larger framework of American society and its theory of democracy. King's "The Other America" speech, delivered to Stanford University in 1967, calls us to look at the "other side" of America, which is not ideal and not comfortable in the face of democracy. In this frame, the reality of America is not exceptional and is questionable, at best. It is also in this Kingsian view that we are able to inquire about the true meaning of democracy to the point of societal reflection and aspirations for racial change. Thus, almost six decades later, race is at the cornerstone of democracy and its manifestation, even as it arguably always has been (Mills 1997), and we as political scientists must understand this, in order for even what we do in our research to be truthful to our public opinion models and theories about the functioning of democracy. Race and politics scholars have long professed the significance of race in American politics, and the blatant and heightened elite cueing and mass exchanges with racial communication should center our understanding of American politics within this framing. Race and politics studies can no longer be marginalized: They are part and parcel of American democracy and American politics—in American political institutions, public opinion, and political consciousness.

As I argue, hereafter, through the symbolism of the contested 2020 presidential election, the contestation of the knowledge about the founding of the nation, the racialization of the American party system, the constitutional protection of slavery to define national expansion and states' interests, and racialized acknowledgments of citizenship and political interests, the political landscape of American politics has shaped over time to evoke the democracy that Dr. Martin Luther King questioned in 1967. It is the "other America" that has manifested as "the America" that we cannot deny and can only press toward democratic perfection, exclusive of white supremacy and a blind, critical eye of these imperfections in our political science discipline's analyses of American politics.

RACE, TRUTH, AND THE "BIRTH OF A NATION"

In light of all that has been troubling us since January 6, 2021, when the U.S. Capitol was compromised by mostly white American, insurrectionists, especially, it is important for us to reflect upon who we are as a nation. We witnessed members of Congress (8 U.S. senators and 139 members of the U.S. House of Representatives, all Republicans) who voted to challenge, whether through rhetoric or formal debate, the 2020 presidential election results of the states of Arizona and Pennsylvania (Yourish, Buchanan, and Lu 2021). Months prior to the November 2020 presidential election, the Electoral Votes of Georgia and Michigan, all states which have large concentrations of nonwhite voters, we also find President Donald Trump and some Republicans outside these states rallying around the objection of Electoral Votes from these states (Faussett, Corasaniti, and Haberman 2021; Ruger 2021).

With the compromised security of our U.S. Capitol, with insurrectionists claiming what they felt was the "steal" of the 2020 U.S. presidential election by Electoral Votes that had been certified by the various states, we saw white nationalists march down the streets of Washington, DC, some using force to overcome law enforcement and besiege the offices and main floor of the Capitol, where Congress conducts its business for the people. It is the voice of the people about which I think we should take a moment to reflect upon what we saw happen. These actions were not the ramblings of a new-age "1776" American Revolution. Rather, we witnessed the declaration of "taking the nation back," "making America great"—to the end of whiteness and white supremacy. These actions also find some intellectual support in the controversies over the campaign to contest the *NY Times*' 1619 Project, through the mobilization of the "1776 Project" to denounce how we understand the effect of slavery on U.S. society (Friedersdorf 2020; Hays 2020).

These contestations over truth, democracy, and redress are not new (Mills 1997). However, the evincing of force was unprecedented in its magnitude to overtake the U.S. Capitol, disrupt Congress and the formal acceptance of the presidential Electoral Votes, and most importantly, attempt to reestablish the American presidency based upon prevarication about electoral fraud. Such political exactings have played out surreally for us in what also has been depicted in the 1915 film, "Birth of a Nation," by D. W. Griffith, who developed the film based upon the book, *The Clansman*, by Thomas Dixon. Depicting what has now become the reference to the "Lost Cause," when the American South lost its "way of life"—hence, slavery and plantation economy and opulence—to the fault of the Union Army. Society was sup-posedly ravaged by Reconstruction and a population of newly freed Black Americans, who were empowered by the franchise, a concept that they were depicted not to be able to understand, but were employed to use by Northern whites who wanted to reap their politics on white Southerners, in order to overtake their Southern society.

In the process, "Birth of a Nation" depicts Blacks overtaking the results of the Southern election in the favor of the North by stuffing ballots and cheating in elections. From this, they were portrayed as being able to elect Black politicians, and these politicians ran amok, like newly freed Blacks, who changed Southern etiquette such that whites were forced to assume the command of Blacks, and ultimately, through political power, Black men were able to make interracial marriages (and hence, interracial sex) legal, when it had not been. Thus, white women were vulnerable to what was depicted as the innate, diabolical nature of Black men, who were rapacious and greedy for white women. Slavery was depicted as necessary to "tame" the nature of Black people, including even assertive Black women who were depicted as best serving in the roles of domestics. In a new world of Reconstruction, whites were beholden to the power of Blacks, and there was no end to the power that Blacks would be willing to yield, other than one—the white-hooded cavalry that swoops in to save the day, terrorizing Blacks out of town, leaving whites to enjoy the peace of the Southern way that they felt best comforted them. In film, the depiction of the negative racial stereotypes of Black Americans occurred in blackface performance by white actors with blackened faces to portray Blacks and Black actors, themselves.

This fiction film was believed to have been touted as being truthful by a son of the South himself and a noted scholar and past U.S. president and past, president of the American Political Science Association (APSA), Woodrow Wilson (Nunnally 2016). Despite requests by the then nascent civil rights organization, the National Association for the Advancement of Colored People (NAACP), founded in 1909, and civil rights activist William Monroe Trotter (Greenidge 2019), to denounce the film, even other protests by the NAACP for the film not to be released in theaters, it was. And, as fearful as the NAACP was about the consequences of the film, it proved fateful. What was fictional became grasped as public knowledge about the "Lost Cause" of the American South and white Southerners. As Brody (2017) asserts, the film helped recruit a larger number of members into the Ku Klux Klan dur-ing the early 1900s. The film's believed calamitous effects led to it being banned in several states. Yet, another amazing response in American history was the introduction of "race films" in the 1920s by Black filmmaker, Oscar Micheaux, in an effort to produce and illustrate positive images of Black Americans on film (Bowser, Gaines, and Musser 2001).

This historic "fake news" and racist propaganda depicted Blacks as "happy slaves," inept without white leadership and enslavement, deceitful, innately criminal and rapacious, and most notably, ready to use their vote and new access to public office to assume leadership so that they could punish whites and wield their Black power to whites' detriment. The film used imagery to concretize the image of Black power (at the behest of white Northern, outside, aggression) ravaging white Southerners' quality of life. The South had no other choice but to redeem itself to its previous grandeur in slavery—when white plantation owners possessed land, Black people were property, and white landed interests exerted control over poor and nonlanded whites to the benefit of an economy that supported white supremacy—the intersection of race and political economy.

There are historic references to state-related violence against Black Americans. For example, in 1898, the mostly Black-run government of Wilmington, North Carolina, was overthrown by a terroristic mob of white insurrectionists, who installed themselves into power, after overtaking the mostly, Black-elected public officials. In 1921, now, 100 years ago this year, on May 30, 1921, a race massacre in Tulsa, Oklahoma (one of the Black Wall Streets), unfolded when a white woman was reportedly (through a rumor mill among white residents) raped by a Black man in an elevator. Planes bombed over 30 blocks of properties owned by Black Americans (1921 Tulsa Race Massacre). It is important for us to understand the making of falsehoods, distorted facts, negative racial stereotypes, racialized challenges to elections and electoral power, and racialized violence onslaught against people of color—whether symbolically or actually—in the name of white supremacy and the notion of dominance in the name of purported popular sovereignty and American democracy.

PARTISAN VITRIOL AND THE RACIAL DIVIDE

This disfiguring thought and conception of democracy, however, undergirded the redemption of the American South through the American political party system at the conclusion of the American Civil War and the beginning and end of Reconstruction. American society had to figure out how it would be able to reunite, after fissures over the question of states' rights to sustain slavery divided even white families. Fissures between the North and the South, or what was called sectional politics, governed American politics well into latter twentieth century. Because

Black Americans (men, in particular) acquired the right to vote via the Fifteenth Amendment (in 1870) and mostly supported President Abraham Lincoln's Republican Party, the Anti-Slavery Party, their votes became deciding votes in many Southern elections, as white Southerners were often divided along the two parties. Black men voters thus held a balance of power to determine elections. This is why it became important for Southern states to draft new state constitutions, beginning with the State of Mississippi, in 1890, to introduce measures to disfranchise Black voters, so that they could no longer determine representatives, who had Blacks' interests in mind (Woodward 1964). As it was at that time, Black interests often were conceived as anathema to whites' interests because white supremacy translated into the subjugation of Blacks by whites.

A Republican Party that welcomed Black votes, however, soon turned into a party that was willing to relinquish the safety of Black Americans to win the votes of an electoral commission appointed by Congress to determine the breaking of a tie between Republican candidate, Rutherford B. Hayes, and Democratic candidate, Samuel B. Tilden, in 1876. Republican Rutherford B. Hayes agreed to a deal with the Southern commissioners to remove federal troops from the American South, and in what is now referred to as the Compromise of 1877, established the political and social context for the end of Reconstruction and the lack of security protections to protect Blacks as citizens, who could, through the ratification of the Thirteenth Amendment to end slavery and the Fourteenth Amendment to provide for natural-born citizenship, prescribed for Blacks to govern their own persons, and outside of a slavery-oriented ideology, actually legally make claims about their bodies as free persons with citizenship rights. The making of space with no law enforcement to enforce these rights left Black Americans in the South, especially vulnerable to the whims of whites, who clung to white supremacy and denunciation of Black equality on the same level as whites' (Logan 1965).

Jim Crow was born of an environment wherein lawlessness left unchecked and unsanctioned the behavior of whites, which collectively across Southern states emboldened white supremacy by "looking the other way," when it came to democratic principles for Blacks. These behaviors, enforced by the rule of law that placed whites supreme above nonwhites (and Blacks in particular), making custom de facto practices, as well—Blacks not being able to bear witness against whites, who committed offenses against them, all white juries upholding their "Southern duty" to hold whites not guilty of crimes committed against Blacks, and allowing extrajudicial violence to occur against Blacks, without law enforcement making arrests, with law enforcement standing by or actually participating in egregious violence committed against Blacks (as we have seen footage from the Civil Rights Movement), and the court of law ignoring and/or dismissing charges against whites who assailed Black victims.

Raw with impunity, the justice system, just like the signs affixed to restaurants, bus stations, and salons and the exclusion of Blacks from pools and even cemeteries, said "whites-only," with the U.S. Constitution still governing our larger democracy. Democracy is not only what is conceived. It is also what is done, and not until even racial discrimination was banned in housing in 1968 with the Fair Housing Act did the gap between democratic theory and practice come closer to abridgment, when neighborhoods today still remain segregated, although, now, with a declining trend (Williams and Emamdjomeh 2018; Frey 2018).

Even in the late twentieth century, as even U.S. presidential candidates tried to figure out how they could attract Southern white voters, who had become long vested into the Republican Party, after the fissure of the Democratic Party 100 years after the Civil War, the civil rights movement, nationalized with Dr. King's leadership, influenced President Lyndon B. Johnson to advocate for both a Civil Rights Act of 1964 and Voting Rights Act of 1965. The once Democratic Party Solid South, could no longer see itself with a national Democratic Party that now advocated for Black civil rights, making it even a new party of as many as 90 percent of Black Americans (Carmines and Stimson 1989; McClain and Carew 2018).

In my previous writing about race and party politics (Nunnally 2013), I predicted that the Republican Party would best serve its interests to court the electoral support of Latinx voters to shore up its support mostly observed among (older generations of) Cuban American voters, in order to win future national elections. With the increasing Latinx population, projected by 2050 to assume as much as 30 percent of the American population (Passel and Cohn 2008), the Republican Party stood to develop a base of voters that could potentially become as strongly supportive as the Black voters, who are the base of the Democratic Party. However, what has become clear is that the party decided against this mobilization and political courting effort, turning instead, to a mobilization of mostly white voters. White voters also have become increasingly more Republican, since the Obama presidency (Pew Research Center 2012).

Rather, through the divisive and racially offensive candidate announcement of Donald J. Trump, who declared his candidacy in 2015 to the pronouncement of "Mexicans being murderers and rapists and some of them being good people," the Republican Party charted a different course in the vein of anti-immigration policies that consolidated support of anti-immigrationists. Moreover, with the eventual win of candidate Trump over Secretary of State Hillary Clinton in the 2016 presidential election, the Trump administration advanced "family-separation" policies in immigration and travel bans against predominately Muslim-faith nations that effectuated a less-than-embracing, anti-immigrant, and racist policy framing. Further defined by President Trump in declaring neo-Nazi and white supremacists and antifascist protesters at the Unite the Right rally in Charlottesville (August 11–12, 2017) as "very fine people on both sides" and by an affirmation during a 2020 preside debate that the Proud Boys (an arguably white nationalist) organization should "stand back and stand by" (Ronayne and Kunzelman 2020) the signaling of acceptance and praise emboldened the public mention and presence of these white nationalist groups.

CENTURIES OF RACIAL CONSTRUCTION: EVERY "BODY" DEFINED

Many of us, who were born in the 1990s and 2000s, may think that our nation is far removed from the politics that Dr. King, his colleagues, and fellow civil rights activists challenged American democracy to match its theory with its practices. But as I am a Black woman born in the American South and under the age of 50, with parents also born in the American South, I am a mere conversation away from the memories of parents, who in different cities of Virginia, grew up in Jim Crow and lived their formative years within the cultural practices, beliefs, knowledge, and laws of this institution, which limited their access to full citizenship, with unencumbered voting rights, liberty, and justice. Jim Crow, however, is not decades removed from our contemporary society. It is in the breath of Black and white Southerners (and people across the country), whose lives were defined by yet another institution—race—that has evolved over time to define every human "body" within its context—the idea, the concept, the psychology, the experience, the laws of *race* (Crenshaw 1991; Gossett 1997).

Race in America is the truth that we must allow ourselves to understand how much it affects our lives and has done so for several centuries. And, evolving over literal centuries, race has defined who is beautiful, knowledgeable, intellectual, work-worthy, and horridly, expendable. It has defined the making of the entire Western Hemisphere, and it has defined how the color of our skins affects the way that our bodies are treated and the quality of life that our bodies experience in society. Namely, by way of the institution of slavery, which started among Indigenous Peoples in the New World and transitioned into the Trans-Atlantic slave trade of Africans, during the sixteenth through nineteenth centuries, there was the making of an economy based upon race, gender, and class, which involved economic production, the political economy of reproduction to produce African enslaved laborers, with a system that defined the bodies of African people based upon their likelihood to produce the most labor over a lifetime.

Through the institutionalization of both slavery and race, in tandem, Africans in colonial America and what was to become the United States of America, occurred within a 40-year period. Although Africans had a presence in the Americas prior to 1619, 1619 is the 402-year history that marks the imbalanced experiences of Africans' labor compared to European debtors' behavior in the Colonial American economy. We have learned more recently that Africans in 1619 were not "20 and some odd" Negroes, who were indentured servants. Rather, as they were a part of a Portuguese ship's cargo to the Caribbean, the Africans aboard the White Tiger ship were kidnapped, yet again, and taken to the present-day Point Comfort, Virginia (Waxman 2019).

By the 1640s, Africans were recognized as enslaved persons, to the extent of the label being synonymous with their bodies, and while at one point, the assumption of Christianity could lead one toward freedom, within this same decade the status of one as enslaved or free depended on the free or enslaved status of her African mother (Painter 2006; Franklin and Moss 2007). Moreover, eventually, by law, those who were deemed enslaved (and African) were deemed so for a lifetime as an inheritance at birth, and thus, were more easily traceable than following the patrilineage of fathers, who also included European enslavers, who reproduced their wealth through duress and rape of African and African descendant women, who were considered property (Threadcraft 2016).

This is important to note that the making of who was enslaved and the attachment of "who was also considered 'Black,'" also entailed the making of a binary that also defined people of European descent as "white." These binaries were most stringent and lasting over time, as Indigenous people's populations differed by geographic concentration. Class and gender defined access to rights of European descendants, and European descendants without land and who were women had limited political power—voice and franchise—in Colonial America.

Through what became the empowerment of the aggrieved to distinguish themselves and reform government to break free from the reign of King George III of England to ignite the Revolutionary War in 1776, already a century and a few decades defined how Europeans, Africans, and Indigenous people interacted with one another, and yet, the first casualty of this Revolution was a patriot fighting for the cause of freedom, Crispus Attucks, who also was a person of African descent. While the nation defined and ratified part of our contemporary U.S. Constitution in 1787, it is important to note that it does not mention race nor does it mention slavery. However, we find that there were several instances within the U.S. Constitution, prior to the

Civil War, that addressed what would be the operations and implicit legaliza-
tion of slavery as an institution:

1. The Three-Fifths Compromise (affecting the apportionment of Representatives and Presidential electors in the Electoral College—Article I,
   Section 2);
2. The inhibition to decide on servitude prior to 1808—Article I, Section 9;
3. The inhibition to change the year 1808 in the decision of law about
   slavery—Article V; and
4. The Fugitive Slave Clause—Article IV, Section 2 (returning by legal
   observance persons who were in "service" or "labor").

These legal prescriptions for enslaved persons did not define race, but
through practice, the enslaved person became synonymous with people of
"African descent." Moreover, it inhibited the liberties of persons of African
descent who were free, as they had to prove by legal documentation on
their person whether they were, indeed, manumitted or enslaved persons.
In whiteness being constructed as the negation of blackness, the oppressive
subjugation of African enslaved persons also constructed the foundational
freedoms, liberty, and wherewithal of white supremacy (Roediger 2007;
Roediger 2019).

The Naturalization Act of 1790 defined free citizenship based on "white
persons," and over the next 150 years, the citizenship of nonwhite persons
was defined by the distinctive racial experiences of each nonwhite group over
time. For example, only through the American Civil War would people of
African descent acquire access to natural-born citizenship. Indigenous people
would have access until 1924, and despite some ethnic groups among Asian
Americans and Latinx Americans (principally, Mexican Americans) had been
in the United States for several generations before having their fullest access
to citizenship via legislation like the Naturalization and Immigration Act
of 1965. Meanwhile, laws like the Chinese Exclusion Act of 1892 and the
Immigration Quota Act of 1924 converge in their barring access to citizenship for Asian Americans. Blood quanta (or, drops of blood) eventually also
defined who was "black" and who was "Indian" (Davis 1991; Wilkins and
Stark 2018).

As for Blacks, the states used different fractions (1/4, 1/8, 1/32, one-drop
of African blood) to define who was "black" (Davis 1991). The language of
the day captured the expressions of race and categorization—"quadroon" (1/4
Black) and "octoroon" (1/8 Black). For government agencies, Indigenous
peoples have had to use fractions of blood to have government recognition
and sovereignty status. For Blacks living in the American South, when these
fractions by law also interpreted how one would follow Jim Crow laws,

moving across state lines could redefine one's lack of citizenship and quality of life similar to moving across free and slave states, like decades before in the case of Dred Scott, the enslaved Black man who sought his freedom in the U.S. Supreme Court because he had moved to a free state.

In denying his humanity, the U.S. Supreme Court Chief Justice Roger Taney, himself a slave owner, told Dred Scott in the famous *Dred Scott v. Sanford* (1857) case that at the time of the Declaration of Independence, Blacks "as slaves nor their descendants, whether they had become free or not, were then acknowledged as a part of the people nor intended to be included in the general works used in that memorable instrument." And, as Taney said further, "Negroes," as they were called, were "of an inferior order and altogether unfit to associate with the white race, either in social or political relations, and so far inferior that they had no rights for which the white man was bound to respect."

The pseudoscience of race and inheritable traits being connected contributed to our medical knowledge about racial difference, and through the white supremacist lens of defining social order and human evolution, Black Americans and other nonwhite racial groups were detached from their intellect, comportment, and humanity. This is why legal originalism of the U.S. Constitution as it was understood in the context of its writing also can become problematic. For if we were to turn to this principle, we would be considering the interpretation of people (nonwhite, women, nonbinary) whose "personhood" had not yet been acknowledged or even attributed as having the possibility of citizenship or rights, and all nonwhites have this track record of exclusion from this rule of law, until court cases or laws prescribed either their humanity, citizenship, or equality.

These aspects of academic enterprise and inquiry stemmed from the eighteenth-century Enlightenment Period and lasted through the latter part of the nineteenth century—a two-century, pseudo-informed knowledge base about human development. Carrying over into the twentieth century, this pseudoscience informed the basis of eugenics that used the links among race, blood, and heredity to inform public policies to control human reproduction through sterilization, population and demographic limitations, and attributions of criminality to the existence of nonwhite populations. This pseudoscience informed our intellectual understandings about human behavior and its capacities and limitations, especially in nonwhite populations. It also defined a science and body of knowledge of "others," which made "whiteness" defined as the negation of all that was explained and known to be attributed to people of color.

Our public policies and laws divided the American public along racial lines, and our purported pseudo-knowledge informed the psychology of racism—negative racial stereotypes and racial animus—that rests with and divides us along the colorline, today. The media have been contrite in advertising runaway slave ads, publishing alarming reports of racial stereotypic behavior of nonwhites, harping on criminality, and excluding positive media about nonwhite groups, all to the initial equivalent of what was real, "fake news" for centuries. The contributions of nonwhite groups have been largely omitted from public knowledge and left to the lore and ethnic consciousness of these groups (and scholars) to challenge what they knew happened to them and what they knew they contributed to American society. Meanwhile, our textbooks have eloquently omitted the contributions of nonwhite peoples to the "making of America's greatness," in effect contributing to the mythology that white people, alone, have built America.

Enslaved African people only within the past 15 years have been recognized for actually erecting the U.S. Capitol, and the multiple cogwheels of streets that people follow in Washington, DC, today, were designed by Benjamin Banneker, a Black American genius scientist and inventor, who even marveled Thomas Jefferson, as he wrote to him to speak about the need for enslaved Africans' rights. Indigenous people have lived for centuries with a democratic government informed by a Constitution. Mexican Americans in the Southwest region of the United States have had the U.S. border placed on them and citizenship denied, despite provisions in the Treaty of Guadalupe Hidalgo (1848), and generations of Asian Americans (Chinese Americans, notably) being brought to the nation for labor to mine gold and to build railroad transportation to connect the East and West railroads.

That, as Black Americans were incorporated into the American polity as rights-bearing citizens, the war that led to this moment of U.S. Reconstruction occurred after the states were at war about whether they could sustain slavery. Slavery even affected how our nation would grow in land mass and new states, as states entered the Union as either "Slaveholding" or "Free" states. Slavery was as much about the enslavement of African peoples as it was about the evolution of the Western Hemisphere's economies, laws in the formation of the United States before and after the Civil War, news and media enforcements and re-enforcements of racial frenzies, while limiting the free speech of people of color, who had to devise their own news outlets to counter negative, false, hyperbolic, and terroristic coverage of their behavior and the announcements of Jim Crow era lynchings, as if they were everyday. The United States Postal Service delivered post cards of actual lynchings, with smiling white bystanders—men, women, and children ("Without Sanctuary" Exhibit).

Each group of nonwhites deemed as a social problem in the nineteenth century—the Negro problem (the question of social and political equality with whites), the Asian problem (how much should Asian people [and other immigrants] have access to citizenship), and the Indigenous problem (how much should there be coexistence with Indigenous people, when their land is attractive and valuable). The projects of empire and imperialism spanned the world to acquire U.S. territories (often occupied by people of color), deeming the people unfit to govern themselves, with democracy being the beacon of hope for their supposed "civilization" and "civility."

CITIZENSHIP AND RACE: WHITE PRIVILEGE IN THE FACE OF JUSTICE

I share this information for us to think about how we understand the history of democracy in the United States—a representative democracy based on the will of the people, most notably, what we call "popular sovereignty." Who are citizens? How are the voices of citizens most notably heard? They are heard through casting a vote at the ballot box, and depending upon the office in which we are electing a representative, our votes are mostly counted as a plurality of those cast to determine a representative, unless otherwise noted, as in the Electoral College, wherein votes are cast by voters and based on the count of plural votes, states determine how electors' ballots will be counted in determining the electors allocated for U.S. presidential candidates running for office. Yet, access to the ballot has not been one that has been accessible to all of what I describe is a test over time to move our democracy toward "a more perfect Union."

Might I also note that both my parents' parents were born in the early 1900s in the South, and their parents, of only one set of grandparents did I have the fortune to have met and known, were born in the later 1800s. They all were born into Jim Crow, and as Black Americans, what had been defined as citizenship for them and our ancestors in the Fourteenth Amendment of the U.S. Constitution was elusive until 1965 with the U.S. Congress' passage of the Voting Rights Act, which ensured the right of Black Americans, especially, and all persons to vote without the infringement of disfranchisement via poll taxes and other tactics used to discourage Black Americans from voting. Prior to 1965, for all who were above the age of 21 (before ratification of the Twenty-sixth Amendment in 1971, which lowered the eligible voting age to 18), as Black Americans they were met with poll taxes (before ratification in 1964 of the Twenty-fourth Amendment, which prohibited them in federal elections) and possible other impediments to their vote.

Being in Virginia, my forebears' experiences with voting were not sanctioned and opposed as violently by white Southerners as much as they would have been for Black Americans, who lived in Deep South states like South Carolina, Georgia, and Mississippi, for example. But, nevertheless, the power of the vote could make a difference in voting on representatives who were less supportive of de jure and de facto discrimination practices, and the racial etiquette of Jim Crow meant that my family members, as did others of African ancestry, should observe racialized customary practices whereby Blacks were supposed to show deference to whites by, for example, stepping off the sidewalk, so that whites could pass; not looking whites directly into their eyes, buying clothes in downtown stores and not being able to try them on, placing money on the counter and not in the hand of a white person to make a purchase, entering the back door of public places, using "colored-only" shabby water fountains, and burying loved-ones in Black-only cemeteries (Chafe et al. 2001).

And, over decades of direct experiences for some Black Americans and white Americans, the vestiges of slavery either were pronounced or sidestepped by the covers of businesses. For example, in Fredericksburg, Virginia, just only a year ago, the city resolved whether to remove from public view and display in its downtown a stump that had been used to sell enslaved Africans in its public square. Even I have the memory of going to teen dances in the 1990s in the Farmers Market of my Petersburg, Virginia, town without having known that the land on which I danced had been a market of formal slave selling.

Practically lost as well is the documentation of the state's oldest Black public high school, Peabody High School, which is also believed to be the oldest public high school for Blacks in the American South. With an 1870 establishment year, it rivals the year of establishment of the famous M Street School/Paul Laurence Dunbar High School of Washington, DC. And, mind you, the movement for public schools period for education was a major accomplishment of formerly enslaved Africans, who, themselves, had been barred from education by law via the Slave Codes (Williams 2006). Through their initiative in the Reconstruction era, poor whites, who were unable to afford private education also acquired access to public education. Formerly enslaved Africans equated education with their liberation, and in some cases, like Virginia, made public education a condition of the states' readmission to the Union, post-Civil War (Dailey 2000).

We must be mindful of the tumultuous times that defined the era of the Civil Rights Movement, beginning, now, almost 68 years ago with the bus boycott that began in Baton Rouge, Los Angeles, in 1953 (Morris 1984). We must situate ourselves in the context of a U.S. Supreme Court case, *Brown v. Board of Education* in 1954, when the Court overruled and found unconstitutional the "separate but equal" doctrine found in the 1896 *Plessy v. Ferguson* case and by 1955 ruled that desegregation in public schools (and beyond) should occur "with all deliberate speed." Infamously, in 1955, two white men (and reported other marauders) in Money, Mississippi, kidnapped a 14-year-old boy, Emmett Till, from his uncle's home.

The boy had been visiting from Chicago, and in what was purported as a fateful gesture to a white woman, defied the supposed "ways" of the South by implying interracial intimacy. Till was lynched, and his assailants escaped conviction by an all-white jury that found them not guilty within an hour's time. Months after the trial, the assailants admitted their guilt and their need to lynch Till, because he needed to pay for what was done. Within a year's time, Southern white members of Congress rallied behind the leadership of a congressman from Virginia and declared the "Southern Manifesto," whereby they challenged the U.S. Supreme Court's authority to overturn the laws of states that possessed "Tenth Amendment" rights, and through rallying across the South, set the terms of "massive resistance," setting forth almost two decades of resistance from desegregation (Day 2015). Let us keep in mind even the extensive battle to desegregate even in northern areas, like Boston, Massachusetts, that were challenging the bussing of children of color into white schools in the 1970s, in order to desegregate.

From the 1960s, we think about the emergence of various protest movements to challenge the nation to be inclusive and rights bearing for all persons born in the United States. In 2021, we face the challenge of defining ourselves. Democracy was and is "radical" itself. The esprit de corps of liberty undergirded the opposition to a despotic King George III in our Declaration of Independence in 1776, and our search of a "more perfect union" prefaces our U.S. Constitution of 1787. It is what we bring to democracy that makes it what it is and can "radically" be in providing rights and voice to people equally. Although built in conjunction with a dehumanizing institution—slavery—and the practice of human genocide toward both African and Indigenous peoples—our truthful understanding of this can only make us better people, if we accept the continuing inclusion of people, a new and more diverse electorate than America has ever seen because public policies and a "radical" vision to think beyond the founding of our nation to see our mistakes and improve upon them towards the eye of perfection have strengthened our resolve to be a great nation.

This leads us to an important epoch in American history—the Trump era. In addition to anti-immigration policies, proclamations of Black Lives Matter as a "domestic terror organization" by former mayor Rudolph Giuliani and President Trump (Creitz 2020; Villarreal 2020), and challenges against the Electoral College outcomes in states like Georgia, Pennsylvania, Michigan, and Arizona, where there were large concentrations of voters of color, who voted in plurality for Joe Biden's candidacy, we can not overlook the political maneuvering by the Republican Party leadership to contest holding an impeachment trial during President Trump's occupation of the office, for this claim about constitutionality of impeaching a nonsitting U.S. president reappeared as a rationale for the Republican voting not to convict in Trump's second impeachment trial (Gardner et al. 2021). We are left wondering how in the face of injustice Black lives can be murdered on film without justicial sanctioning and a president can be acquitted with blatant film and evidence supporting his conviction, and yet, many Republicans who were themselves victims of the Capitol breach failed to convict due to a reported "technicality" of President Trump not being an incumbent president. What are the wages of whiteness? What are the taxes of blackness (and people of color)?

CONCLUSION: DEMOCRACY, WHEN?

Diverse is who we as a Nation are and actually who we have been over time. However, we must counter our resistance to account for the diverse American perspectives that contribute to the American politics that we are attempting to examine and predict. Intellectually inclusive is what we can become and what we must be. Supremacist and disparate is what can be diminished, undone, and unforgotten, so that we can plan for a future with the best minds, who have access to the most opportunities, because they were not systemically excluded by a concept—white supremacy—which defines a way of life for ALL people across every social identity imaginable, and yet, deprives us of the innovation, thought, talent, and labor that is constructed as being invaluably conceived as "whites-only." It is through understanding that the exclusion of white supremacy can lead us further towards equality, towards democracy, towards inclusive knowledge, towards inclusive understanding.

Barring bias trainings in federal employment and denoting critical race theory as conducive of racial and gender stereotypes, through executive order, as President Trump did (see Executive Order No. 13950 2020), only further antagonizes the employment spaces of people of color (who had been historically barred from them), when trainings do not highlight racial and gender biases. As President Trump purported by the executive order, his power invested in him as president supported this measure "in order to promote economy and efficiency in Federal contracting, to promote unite in the Federal workforce, and to combat offensive and anti-American race and sex stereotyping and scapegoating." The text of the executive order further elucidates the point of an ideology to contest America's history:

> Today, however, many people are pushing a different vision of America that is grounded in hierarchies based on collective social and political identities rather than in the inherent and equal dignity of every person as an individual. This ideology is rooted in the pernicious and false belief that America is an irredeemably racist and sexist country; that some people, simply on account of their race

or sex, are oppressors; and that racial and sexual identities are more important than our common status as human beings and Americans.

The order's indirect attack on intersectionality studies (Crenshaw 1991) and its direct and explicit critique of critical race theory "uncomplicates" our understanding of the founding of America as a nation and reduces our analyses to the omissions of race and American political development that leave our knowledge incomplete and half-true (Lowndes, Novkov, and Warren 2008). Furthermore, without critical race theory, our knowledge of public policies being implemented for the sake of de jure discrimination becomes lost. Referencing Dr. Martin Luther King and his vision for his children not to be judged based on their color but rather based on the content of their character, the executive order also suggests that America has made much progress since the 57 years of King's "I Have a Dream" speech.

While the United States has made progress, racial and economic disparities remain (McClain and Carew 2017). Moreover, part of King's appreciation and optimism for democratic principles matching democratic practices in American politics changed. His disenchantment with the politics of the South and the politics of the North and their effects on the livelihoods of Black people in these regions and across the country led him to question democratic and economic inequality more deeply (Dawson 2001; Joseph 2020). The quality of Black (and other people of color and poor people's) lives appeared impaired by systemic factors related to the nation's history of racial construction.

Although President Biden has revoked this executive order (among numerous others of the Trump presidency) (Crews 2021), through issuing on January 20, 2021, the "Executive Order On Advancing Racial Equity and Support for Underserved Communities Through the Federal Government" (Biden Administration Revocation of Executive Order 13950), the executive order, in addition to Trump's attacks on the 1619 Project (including verbal denouncements and the pronouncement of a counter-logic via his appointment of a 1776 Commission; see "What Trump Is Saying About 1619 Project, Teaching U.S. History" 2020), help perpetuate the implicit and explicit mythologies of "whiteness" and "white grandeur" that, otherwise, a lens that accounts for the projects of white supremacy would offer (Omi and Winant 1994).

To this end, I ask for us as political scientists and as a larger nation to consider, "Democracy, when?" Is it now? Is it the return to an undemocratic, miserable, violent, and romanticized past that forgets the ravagement of culture, thought, neighborhoods, educations, lands, and lives of nonwhite peoples? Or, is it a future, that we can collectively and diversely conceive to make a more perfect union for us all, and not just some? Think: "Democracy, when?" and Think: "Democracy for humankind." Think about how we must reeducate ourselves to unlearn the half-truths and un-truths that have distorted our understandings of "what is America." At what point, will we make this view, this living, this understanding "E pluribus Unum," without white supremacy at its helm?

So, I think it best to leave you with the words of Dr. King, who, through increasing dissatisfaction and disdain with white Southerners' resistance to Blacks' civil rights, had become, as Dawson (2001) describes, "disillusioned" with democracy in its roughest state. Dr. King's the "Other America" speech (1967) at Stanford University:

> Now the other thing that we've gotta come to see now that many of us didn't see too well during the last ten years—that is that racism is still alive in American society. And much more wide-spread than we realized. And we must see racism for what it is. It is a myth of the superior and the inferior race. It is the false and tragic notion that one particular group, one particular race is responsible for all of the progress, all of the insights in the total flow of history. And the theory that another group or another race is totally depraved, innately impure, and innately inferior . . . .

> And all of this, and all of these things tell us that America has been backlashing on the whole question of basic constitutional and God-given rights for Negroes and other disadvantaged groups for more than 300 years . . . .

> And as long as America postpones justice, we stand in the position of having these recurrences of violence and riots over and over again. Social justice and progress are the absolute guarantors of riot prevention.

In light of the two-time acquittal of impeachment charges against President Donald J. Trump, questions of (racial) justice for everyday citizens test the principles of democracy. We have not yet attained the best of democracy. So, when will there be the fullest realm of democracy? Democracy will prevail, when:

• We acknowledge and educate about slavery and Jim Crow and their vestiges and their effects on every aspect of American society—the admission and readmission of states, education, politics, political parties, housing, banking, criminal justice, law enforcement, music, art, culture, labor, and the economy.
• We acknowledge and educate about intersectionality in the experiences of all people in the United States and what effects it has on people's quality of life. This also means that within American politics and its study, our

methodologies and approaches must be sensitive to the cross-sections of life that social groupings, including race, present.

- We acknowledge years of data that report racial disparities and disproportionate effects and move forward with the will to move beyond race-based, inherent-based explanations of human behavior, to acknowledge centuries of institutions, policies, pseudo-knowledge and learning, and attitudes that undergird inequalities.
- We acknowledge years of data that report racial disparities and disproportionate effects and redress them with institutions and public policies, in committed ways similar to what Reconstruction offered the Black population, upon its acknowledgment of humanity and citizenship.
- We acknowledge that our criminal justice has and continues to be flawed by racial influences in every aspect of perceptions about the innate criminality of nonwhite people, especially Black people, affecting decisions made in the processing of justice at every level and when we acknowledge, principally, that white Americans (including former president Donald J. Trump) experience criminal justice and justice extremely different from people of color in the United States.
- We acknowledge that democracy is incomplete without the accessibility of all eligible voters to participate. Election Day should be a day when all eligible voters can register to vote and cast ballots in whatever safe form.
- We acknowledge that we have to "unlearn ourselves," because race has influenced every aspect of society, including the Academy and how we approach the study of people and their contributions.
- We recognize that undoing white supremacy assumes a unique responsibility of white Americans, who can not only be allies but also activists in sanctioning other white Americans who cling to white supremacy—in places of decision-making and everyday life in public and private spaces.
- We are willing to see that citizenship, voting, participation, and humanity are accessible to all people without white supremacy, because white supremacy damages us ALL from being the great humans that we can be by assuming that the best and all talent comes from one race only.

The exclusions about who we as a nation are and have been only damages us. It is up to us to speak up and challenge what we have been gaslighted about in our understanding of the United States: we are great as the United States—US, together, and not without "them." It is only with an overhaul of understanding what we "were" and currently manifest that we can lay bare and be the best of our tomorrows and our future generations. As former APSA president Dianne Pinderhughes appointed a task force to determine the future of diversity in political science (Political Science in the 21st Century 2011), the politics of the past 12 years since the Obama presidency illustrate that our discipline of political science must be foremost in this effort, first, by teaching American government, politics, and public opinion truthfully with respect to race, politics, and context for various groups within the American polity (Shaw et al. 2015; McClain and Tauber 2016; McClain and Carew 2018).

NOTE

1. Much of the text from this chapter is based upon a keynote address that I delivered to Wofford College on January 18, 2021, in commemoration of its 2021 Dr. Martin Luther King Jr. Day.

REFERENCES

"1921 Tulsa Race Massacre." https://www.tulsahistory.org/exhibit/1921-tulsa-race-massacre/.

Associated Press. 2021. "Capitol Insurrection Displayed Many of the Symbols of American Racism." *Los Angeles Times*. January 14. Accessed February 15, 2021. https://www.latimes.com/world-nation/story/2021-01-14/years-of-white-supremacy-threats-culminated-in-capitol-riots

Biden Administration Revocation of Executive Order 13950 Eliminates Workforce Training Restrictions for Federal Contractors and Grant Recipients. 2021. January 25. Accessed February 15, 2021. https://www.natlawreview.com/article/biden-administration-revocation-executive-order-13950-eliminates-workforce-training

Bowser, Gaines, and Musser. 2001. *Oscar Micheaux and His Circle: African-American Filmmaking and Race Cinema of the Silent Era*. Bloomington, IN: Indiana University Press.

Brody, Richard. 2017. "Against D.W. Griffith's 'Birth of a Nation.'" *The New Yorker*. February 6. Accessed February 13, 2021. https://www.newyorker.com/culture/richard-brody/the-black-activist-who-fought-against-d-w-griffiths-the-birth-of-a-nation

Carmines, Edward G. and James A. Stimson. 1989. *Issue Evolution: Race and the Transformation of American politics*. Princeton, NJ: Princeton University Press.

Chafe, William H., Raymond Gavins, Robert Korstad, Paul Ortiz, Robert Parrish, Jennifer Ritterhouse, Keisha Roberts, Nicole Waligora-Davis, eds. 2001. *Remembering Jim Crow: African Americans Tell About Life in the Segregated South*. New York: New Press.

Constitution Daily. 2021. "How the Martin Luther King, Jr. Day Became a Holiday." January 18. Accessed February 14, 2021. https://constitutioncenter.org/blog/how-martin-luther-king-jr-s-birthday-became-a-holiday-3

Creitz, Charles. 2020. "Giuliani Calls on Trump to Declare Black Lives Matter a Domestic Terror Organization." *Fox News*. August 17. Accessed February 14, 2021. https://www.foxnews.com/us/giuliani-trump-black-lives-matter-domestic-terrorism

Crenshaw, Kimberlé. 1991. "Mapping the Margins: Intersectionality, Identity Politics, and Violence against Women of Color." *Stanford Law Review* 43(6): 1241–1299.

Crews, Clyde Wayne, Jr. 2021. "Biden Repudiates Trump Era with Revocation of Certain Executive Orders Concerning Federal Regulation." *Forbes.com.* January 26. Accessed February 14, 2021. https://www.forbes.com/sites/waynecrews/2021/01/26/biden-repudiates-trump-era-with-revocation-of-certain-executive-orders-concerning-federal-regulation/?sh=768d495312b4

Dailey, Jane. 2000. *Before Jim Crow: The Politics of Race in Poste-Emancipation Virginia.* Chapel Hill: University of North Carolina Press.

Davis, F. James. 1991. *Who Is Black?: One Nation's Definition.* University Park, PA: Pennsylvania State University Press.

Day, John Kyle. 2015. *Southern Manifesto: Massive Resistance and the Fight to Preserve Segregation.* Oxford, MS: University Press of Mississippi.

Executive Order No. 13950. 2020. "Combating Race and Sex Stereotyping." Accessed February 15, 2021. https://www.federalregister.gov/documents/2020/09/28/2020-21534/combating-race-and-sex-stereotyping

Faussett, Richard, Nick Corasaniti, and Maggie Haberman. 2021. "Georgia and Michigan Deliver Blows to Trump's Efforts to Undo the Election." *NY Times.* November 20. Accessed February 13, 2021. https://www.nytimes.com/2020/11/20/us/politics/georgia-trump-michigan-election.html

Franklin, John Hope, and Alfred A. Moss, Jr. 2007. *From Slavery to Freedom: A History of African Americans.* 8th ed. New York: Knopf.

Frey, William H. 2018. "Black-White Segregation Edges Downward Since 2000, Census Shows." Brookings Institute. December 17. Accessed February 13, 2021. https://www.brookings.edu/blog/the-avenue/2018/12/17/black-white-segregation-edges-downward-since-2000-census-shows/

Friedersdorf, Conor. 2020. "1776 Honors America's Diversity in a Way 1619 Does Not." *The Atlantic.* January 6. Accessed February 13, 2021. https://www.theatlantic.com/ideas/archive/2020/01/inclusive-case-1776-not-1619/604435/

Gardner, Amy, Mike DeBonis, Seung Min Kim, and Karoun Demirjian. 2021. "Trump Acquitted on Impeachment Charge of Inciting Deadly Attack on the Capitol." *Washington Post.* February 13. Accessed February 15, 2021. https://www.washingtonpost.com/politics/trump-acquitted-impeachment-riot/2021/02/13/dbf6b172-6e12-11eb-ba56-d7e2c8defa31_story.html

Gossett, Thomas F. 1997. *Race: The History of an Idea in America.* New York: Oxford University Press.

Greenidge, Kerri J. 2019. *Black Radical: The Life and Times of William Monroe Trotter.* Penguin: Random House Canada.

Griffith, D.W. 1915. "Birth of a Nation." https://www.youtube.com/watch?v=N_yU8rRQKoA.

Hays, Charlotte. 2020. "1776 Project vs. 1619 Project: Black Historians Correct New York Times." *Independent Women's Forum.* February 19. https://www.iwf.org/2020/02/19/1776-project-vs-1619-project-black-historians-correct-new-york-times/.

Herndon, Astead W. and Dionne Searcey. 2020. "How Trump and the Black Lives Matter Movement Changed White Voters' Minds." *NY Times.* June 27. Accessed February 14, 2021. https://www.nytimes.com/2020/06/27/us/politics/trump-biden -protests-polling.html

Joseph, Peniel. 2020. *The Sword and the Shield: The Revolutionary Lives of Malcolm X and Martin Luther King, Jr.* New York: Basic Books.

King National Holiday. 1986. The Martin Luther King, Jr. Research and Education Institute. Stanford University. January 20. Accessed February 14, 2021. https://ki nginstitute.stanford.edu/encyclopedia/king-national-holiday

King, Rev. Dr. Martin Luther. 1967. "The Other America Speech." Accessed January 18, 2021.

https://www.youtube.com/watch?v=dOWDtDUKz-U

Lam, Kristin and Joshua Bote. 2020. "How Did Martin Luther King, Jr. Day Become a Federal Holiday? Here is the History." January 21. February 14, 2021. https://ww w.usatoday.com/story/news/nation/2020/01/16/mlk-day-martin-luther-king-jr-holi day-monday/2838025001/

Logan, Rayford W. 1965. *The Betrayal of the Negro, from Rutherford B. Hayes to Woodrow Wilson.* New York: Collier Books.

Lowndes, Joseph, Julie Novkov, and Dorian Warren, eds. 2008. "Race and American Political Development." In *Race and American Political Development.* New York: Routledge. 1–30.

McClain, Paula D. and Steven C. Tauber. 2016. *American Government in Black and White.* New York: Oxford University Press.

———— and Jessica D. Johnson Carew. 2018. *"Can We All Get Along?" Racial and Ethnic Minorities in American Politics.* Boulder, CO: Westview Press.

Mills, Charles W. 1997. *The Racial Contract.* Ithaca, NY: Cornell University Press.

Morris, Aldon D. 1984. *Origins of the Civil Rights Movement: Black Communities Organizing for Change.* New York: Free Press.

Nunnally, Shayla C. 2013. "Race and the 2012 Presidential Election: The Declining Significance of the White Majority and the Future of American Party Politics." In William J. Crotty, ed. *Winning the Presidency 2012.* Boulder: Paradigm. 126–144.

————. 2016. "How We Remember (and Forget) in Our Public History." *Perspectives on Politics* (September), featured in the Reflections Symposium on President Woodrow Wilson. 14(3): 764–765.

Omi, Michael and Howard Winant. 1994. *Racial Formation in the United States: From the 1960s to the 1980s.* New York: Routledge.

Painter, Nell Irvin. 2006. *Creating Black Americans: African-American History and Its Meanings, 1619 to the Present.* Oxford: Oxford University Press.

Passel, Jeffrey S. and D'Vera Cohn. 2008. U.S. Population Projections: 2005–2050. Pew Research Center Report. February 11. https://www.pewresearch.org/hispanic /2008/02/11/us-population-projections-2005-2050/.

Pew Research Center Report. 2012. "A Closer Look at the Parties in 2012: GOP Makes Big Gains among Working-Class Voters." 23 August. Accessed October 7, 2015. http://www.people-press.org/2012/08/23/a-closer-look-at-the-parties-in-2012/

Political Science in the 21st Century. 2011. Report of the Task Force on Political Science in the 21st Century. https://www.apsanet.org/portals/54/Files/Task%20Fo rce%20Reports/TF_21st%20Century_AllPgs_webres90.pdf.

Roediger, David R. 2007. *The Wages of Whiteness: Race and the Making of the American Working Class.* New York: Penguin Random House.

———. 2019. *How Race Survived U.S. History From Settlement and Slavery to the Eclipse of Post-Racialism.* New York: Penguin Random House.

Ronayne, Kathleen and Michael Kunzelman. 2020. "Trump to Far-Right Extremists: 'Stand Back and Stand By." *Associated Press.* September 30. Accessed February 14, 2021. https://apnews.com/article/election-2020-joe-biden-race-and-ethnicity-donald-trump-chris-wallace-0b32339da25fbc9e8b7c7c7066a1db0f

Ruger, Todd. 2021. "Election Vote Divides Republicans as Party Wrestles with Post-Trump Identity. *Roll Call.* January 7. Accessed February 13, 2021. https://www .rollcall.com/2021/01/07/election-vote-divides-republicans-as-party-wrestles-with -post-trump-identity/

Shaw, Todd, Louis DeSipio, Dianne Pinderhughes, Toni-Michelle C. Travis. 2015. *Uneven Roads: An Introduction to U.S. Racial and Ethnic Politics.* Thousand Oaks, CA: CQ Press.

Villarreal, Daniel. 2020. "Trump Says the Black Lives Matter Movement is 'Destroying Many Black Lives." *Newsweek.* September 25. Accessed February 14, 2021. https://www.newsweek.com/trump-says-black-lives-matter-movement-d estroying-many-black-lives-1534411

Threadcraft, Shatema. (2016). *Intimate Justice: The Black Female Body and the Body Politic.* New York: Oxford University Press.

Waxman, Olivia B. 2019. "First Africans in Virginia Landed in 1619: It Was a Turning Point for Slavery in American History But Not the Beginning." *Time.* August 20. Accessed February 15, 2021. https://time.com/5653369/august-1619 -jamestown-history/

"What Trump Is Saying about 1619 Project, Teaching U.S. History." 2020. *PBS News Hour.* September 17. Accessed February 15, 2021. https://www.pbs.org/newshour/ show/what-trump-is-saying-about-1619-project-teaching-u-s-history

Wilkins, David E. and Heidi Kiiwetinepinesiik Stark. 2018. *American Indian Politics and the American Political System.* Lanham, MD: Rowman & Littlefield.

Williams, Aaron and Armand Emamdjomeh. 2018. "America Is More Diverse Than Ever—But Still Segregated." *Washington Post.* May 10. Accessed February 13, 2021. https://www.washingtonpost.com/graphics/2018/national/segregation-us-cities/

Williams, Heather Andrea. 2006. *Self-Taught: African American Education in Slavery and Freedom.* Chapel Hill, NC: University of North Carolina at Chapel Hill Press.

"Without Sanctuary: Lynching Photography in America." Accessed February 13, 2021. https://withoutsanctuary.org/

Woodward, C. Vann. 1964. *Origins of the New South, 1877–1913.* Baton Rouge, LA: Louisiana State University Press.

Yourish, Karen, Larry Buchanan, and Denise Lu. 2021. "The 147 Republicans Who Voted to Overturn Election Results." *NY Times.* January 7. Accessed February 13, 2021. https://www.nytimes.com/interactive/2021/01/07/us/elections/electoral-college-biden-objectors.html

Chapter 8

Environmental Issues in
the 2020 Campaign

John C. Berg

The votes in the Congressional election of 2018 had been scarcely tallied when environmental issues were injected strongly into the 2020 campaign. A youth climate strike, the dramatic appearance of Swedish teenage activist Greta Thunberg at the United Nations, and the introduction of the Green New Deal resolution, with a brand new representative and a Washington veteran as lead sponsors, seemed to promise major attention to climate (if not to other environmental problems) during the presidential campaign. But the path forward was not easy. The Democratic National Committee (DNC) rightly or wrongly saw climate as a no-win issue for Democrats, reasoning that a strong climate program would attract no new Democratic voters but would be seen by moderates as a threat to jobs and the economy. The DNC worked mightily to keep climate out of the primary debates, with considerable success. But nature, public pressure, and President Donald Trump served to bring it back into the mix during the general election. Ultimately, President Biden took office committed to a strong environmental program, including a significant climate component in two of his signature legislative proposals, the $1.9 trillion stimulus package and the pandemic recovery bill to follow. This chapter will trace the many steps in this winding path.

GRETA THUNBERG AND YOUTH CLIMATE ACTIVISM

In mid-August 2018, Greta Thunberg, a 15-year-old Swedish climate activist, began to spend Fridays sitting outside the Swedish Parliament building with a sign that read "SKOLSTREJK FÖR KLIMATET," or "School Strike for Climate." Thunberg had been concerned about climate change since she was nine, had won an essay contest on the issue, and had decided that a student strike from school would be a good way to inspire change. When she initially failed to convince other students to strike with her, she decided to do it by herself. Following Swedish media coverage of her protest, other students began to join her; by the next spring the youth climate strike movement had spread across Europe, Australia, and the United States, with 1.6 million young people in 125 countries joining a global climate strike in March (Thunberg 2018; Schreuer, Peltier and Schuetze 2019; Albeck-Ripka 2018; Thunberg and Goodman 2018; Sangupta 2019; National Geographic).

Thunberg became an international force; she was invited to address a United Nations plenary on climate in Poland in December 2018, and the World Economic Forum in Davos, Switzerland, in January 2019 (Ramzy 2019). Thunberg traveled to New York in a sailboat with solar auxiliary power, where she addressed a crowd of 250,000 as part of the global climate strike; millions of people in more than 160 countries, primarily youth, took part in the strike that day (Lewis and Almasy 2019; Kaplan, Lumpkin and Dennis 2019). Three days later Thunberg addressed the United Nations Climate Action Summit, a conference at which China made no new commitments and the U.S. representatives made no statements at all. Thunberg cried "How dare you!" in reaction to statements that the world looked to young people for hope, explaining that there was not enough time to wait for young people to get power (Sengupta and Friedman 2019). Thunberg's initiative had inspired young people everywhere to take initiative and demand immediate action on climate. While many of these activists were as yet too young to vote, they had nevertheless placed the need for climate action squarely on the political agenda. Meanwhile, a more tightly focused campaign was emerging around the concept of a Green New Deal.

THE GREEN NEW DEAL

The Democratic Party regained its House majority in the election of 2018. A few days later 150 environmental activists held a sit-in at the Washington office of Representative Nancy Pelosi (D-CA), due to become speaker of the House in the new Congress. The demonstrators demanded that the Democrats propose legislation to create jobs and achieve zero carbon use, as well as refusing to accept campaign contributions from the fossil fuel industry. The sit-in was joined by one of the newly elected Democrats, Representative Alexandria Ocasio-Cortez (D/NY), who had defeated a member of the Democratic leadership team in the primary. Once she had taken office in January, Ocasio-Cortez joined with Senator Ed Markey (D/MA) to propose House (H Res 109) and Senate (S Res 59) Resolutions prescribing a similar program under the name of "The Green New Deal." The resolution called for spending $13 trillion over 10 years to create high-paying jobs and eliminate greenhouse gas emissions.

The name "Green New Deal" was meant to evoke Franklin Roosevelt's New Deal, with its emphasis on job creation and economic well-being. In doing so, its sponsors sought to overturn the common charge that environmental protection is bad for the economy. It asserted, to the contrary, that eliminating greenhouse gas emissions and cleaning up the air and water would require massive federal spending that would create jobs, rather than destroying them.

History of the Concept

The Green New Deal concept dates back to at least 2006, when it was proposed by the European Greens: "In addition to a call for both climate action and a bill of economic rights, the approach by the European Greens sought to democratize the world's financial system" (Green Party of the United States). The next year, the same phrase was used by the journalist Thomas L. Friedman, who wrote, "We will only green the world when we change the very nature of the electricity grid—moving it away from dirty coal or oil to clean coal and renewables. And that is a huge industrial project—much bigger than anyone has told you. Finally, like the New Deal, if we undertake the green version, it has the potential to create a whole new clean power industry to spur our economy into the 21st century" (Friedman 2007). In Britain, the Green New Deal Group, which included two members of Parliament (one Green and one Labour) had met since 2008; in March 2019, those two MPs cosponsored the Decarbonisation and Economic Strategy Bill (Green New Deal Group). The phrase had also been used by Achim Steiner, director of the United Nations Environmental Program, when he called for a "Global Green New Deal" in 2008 (Eccleston 2008). Applying a related concept, President Obama had appointed the activist Van Jones to be the White House "Green Jobs Coordinator." Although Jones was hounded out of office by the right when the Marxist manifestos of his youth came to light, the concept lived on (Berg 2019, 110). It was developed further by the Green Party of the United States and, separately, the Sunrise Movement, which described it as "a 10-year plan to mobilize every aspect of American society to 100 percent clean and renewable energy by 2030, a guaranteed living-wage job for anyone who needs one, and a just transition for both workers and frontline communities" (Sunrise Movement). Working with the Sunrise Movement and another group, Justice Democrats, Rep. Ocasio-Cortez drafted a 13-page House Resolution to be introduced in the new Congress (Adler-Bell 2019). For a Senate sponsor she enlisted Senator Ed Markey (D/MA), who had cosponsored the last climate legislation to be considered seriously by

Congress, the Waxman-Markey Act in 2009, when he was still in the House. The resolutions set out five goals, spelled out in considerable detail: net-zero greenhouse gas emissions through a "fair and just transition"; creation of millions of good, high-wage jobs; investment in infrastructure and industry "to sustainably meet the challenges of the 21st century"; securing a clean environment with healthy food to the people of the United States; and justice and equity for "frontline and vulnerable communities," beginning with Indigenous peoples. The goals were to be achieved by a 10-year mobilization, at a projected cost of $13 trillion.

Political Response to the Green New Deal

Democratic leaders in Congress were not enthusiastic about the Green New Deal proposal. Asked about it on February 6, 2019, the day before the resolution was introduced, Speaker Pelosi said, "It will be one of several or maybe many suggestions that we receive . . . the green dream or whatever they call it, nobody knows what it is, but they're for it right?" She was somewhat more supportive in her morning press conference the next day:

> Quite frankly I haven't seen it, but I do know that it's enthusiastic, and we welcome all the enthusiasms that are out there. . . . The green new deal points out that the public is much more aware of the challenge that we face, and that is a good thing, because the public sentiment will help us pass the most bold— common-denominator bold—initiatives, with an interest in, again, saving the planet while we create jobs, protect the health of our children and pass the planet on in a very serious way. (Daugherty 2019)

Eleven Democratic senators joined Markey in cosponsoring the resolution, including all six of those who were then seeking the Democratic presidential nomination. Seeing an opportunity to embarrass the Democrats, then-Majority Leader Mitch McConnell scheduled a quick floor vote, with no hearings or committee markup, which Senate Democrats denounced as a "sham." For complex procedural reasons, the vote was not on the Ocasio-Cortez/Markey resolution, but on a different, binding resolution that McConnell introduced himself to make the Green New Deal the policy of the United States. The resolution was defeated, 0–57. Most Democrats voted "present," although Democrats Manchin (WV), Sinema (AZ), and Jones (AL), along with Maine independent Angus King, joined the Republicans to vote no (Carney and Green 2019; Lavelle 2019). However, the idea of the Green New Deal had found a home in the public mind; like "Medicare for All," it was to become convenient shorthand by which candidates could position themselves, as could be seen as the Democratic primary season got underway.

THE DEMOCRATIC PRIMARIES

As the campaign for the Democratic nomination moved forward, it was clear that one issue dwarfed all others in importance to voters: which candidate had the best chance of defeating Donald Trump? This question could be reduced to a choice between two contrasting strategies. One was to seek to win over independent and Democratic voters who had opted for Trump in 2016. The way to do so, it was thought, was by decrying the bitter partisanship that Trump had provoked, while relying on the median-voter theory by taking positions near the center on the left-right ideological spectrum (Downs 1957). The other strategy was to win by mobilizing those who had not voted before: young people, voters of color, and recently naturalized immigrants. This would have to be done by a combination of intensive grassroots organizing and adopting more radical positions on taxation, job creation, financial inequity, union rights, reproductive rights, antiracism, and climate. It quickly became clear that the DNC held to the first theory; in regard to climate, in particular, as commentator Justin Gillis put it, "The party has always made that most basic of political calculations—which voters does this issue get us that we don't already have?—and come up with the answer: none." The DNC feared that the winning candidate would make a climate statement in the primaries that could later be portrayed by Trump as antijobs, and felt that the best way to avoid such an eventuality was to keep climate out of the campaign debates (2019). They had some success with this approach at first, but climate considerations eventually forced their way in, first through pro-environment candidates, and ultimately through popular pressure aided by natural events.

Jay Inslee, Climate Candidate

The Green New Deal was not the only climate initiative in the Democratic primary campaign. Jay Inslee, the governor of Washington, focused his campaign for the Democratic nomination on climate. Inslee announced his candidacy on March 1, 2019, declaring that he would make controlling climate change his top priority, unlike any other candidate, and that a focus on 100 percent clean energy would also create millions of jobs. "We're the first generation to feel the sting of climate change, and we're the last that can do something about it," he declared (Johnson, K. 2019).

Inslee issued detailed proposals on climate and other issues. He called for new electric power plants, new motor vehicles, and new buildings to be carbon neutral by 2030, and for the closing of all coal-fired power plants by 2035, positioning himself in direct opposition to Trump's promise to save the coal industry. Those three sectors are responsible for 70 percent of greenhouse gas emissions in the United States; Inslee promised that similar proposals for other sectors would come soon (Friedman and Stevens 2019).

Inslee solicited contributions to his campaign fund on Facebook and elsewhere with the argument that if he raised enough money from enough donors to qualify for the primary debates he would concentrate his statements on climate, which otherwise was likely to be absent from the issues debated. Inslee did receive the 65,000 contributions needed to qualify for the first debate, but the DNC refused his request of April 22, 2019, that there be a separate debate on climate. In order to gradually narrow the candidate field, the DNC raised the requirements for inclusion in official debates as time went by. Inslee's support in the polls never reached the 2 percent needed to qualify for the September debates; he withdrew his candidacy on August 21, 2019 (Burns and Stevens 2019). The next spring Inslee endorsed Biden, "after extensive private conversations in which Mr. Biden signaled he would make fighting climate change a central cause of his administration" (Burns 2020). The drive to include more environmental discussion in the debates continued, however, not only because of the public support for doing so, but also because the need to reverse so many of Trump's environmental policy actions was a major grievance for many voters.

Trump's Attacks on Obama's Environmental Policies

President Obama had had filibuster-proof Democratic support in Congress for only the first year of his first term. He worked with these Congressional Democrats to pass two major bills: the American Recovery and Reinvestment Act of 2009, or "stimulus bill," and the Affordable Care Act, or "Obamacare." His third priority, the Waxman-Markey bill to reduce the emission of greenhouse gases, passed the House but could not advance in the Senate once the election of Republican Scott Brown in Massachusetts meant Senate Democrats could no longer win a cloture vote. From that date forward, Obama's environmental achievements, which were considerable, had to be attained without Congressional approval. Four of these were particularly important. Three of them were EPA regulations: The Waters of the United States (WOTUS) rule greatly expanded the areas that were defined as "navigable waters" and their tributaries, and were therefore subject to federal regulation. In particular, the rule placed stricter controls on development in wetlands. Two other major EPA regulations dealt with climate change: a significant increase in auto mileage requirements, and the Obama Clean Power Plan, which placed strict limits on greenhouse gas emissions from electric power plants, and would have probably led to the elimination of coal-fired plants. Finally, Obama negotiated the Paris Agreement under the United Nations Framework Convention on Climate Change, which committed the signatories to making sufficient reductions in their own greenhouse gas emissions to limit the increase in mean global temperature since the beginning of the industrial age to 2 degrees Celsius, and to make every effort to limit it further to 1.5 degrees. The Agreement was structured to be an executive agreement, rather than a treaty, so that Senate ratification would not be required (Berg 2019, 103–20).

President Trump had sought to reverse each of these Obama accomplishments, although none of the reversals had been made permanent by the time of the election, given the lengthy procedures required. Trump had notified the Paris Agreement of the U.S. intention to withdraw, but under the terms of the agreement the withdrawal could not be made until November 4, 2020, one day after the election. EPA administrator Scott Pruitt, and his successor Andrew Wheeler, had initiated the withdrawal and replacement of the three regulations just mentioned (along with many others), but had to overcome challenges in court. It was clear that the 2020 election would be very consequential for the environment. A Trump second term would give him time to complete the legal process of weakening the regulations, while any Democrat would seek at a minimum to restore what Obama had done. Both environmental advocates and the coal industry were well aware of these realities (Berg 2019, 121–39). However, environmentalists sought to solidify Democratic support for these issues by making them part of the primary debates.

Pressures on the DNC to Debate Climate

The DNC had refused Inslee's April request for a climate debate, but the issue did not end there. The demand for a climate debate was supported by at least seven other candidates, and by over 50 of the DNC's members (about 10% of the voting members) (Frazin 2019). Meanwhile, in early April the U.S. branch of the Youth Climate Strike had launched an Internet petition for a debate on the ecological crisis. The petition declared a need to "ensure environmental issues from climate change, access to clean water, environmental racism, and everything in between that are disproportionately impacting people of color and working class folks are given the serious attention they deserve," and asserted that "With the magnitude of the oncoming climate crisis it's no longer sufficient to have a single token environmental question that 2020 candidates get to brush off with a soundbite. We need an entire debate on environmental policies." The petition drew over 30,000 signatures in its first 48 hours (Johnson, J. 2019).

With the DNC continuing to refuse a climate debate, the Sunrise Movement joined with local climate groups in Detroit as "Frontline Detroit" to organize a demonstration of thousands a few hours before the first debate in that city on July 30, 2019. The *New York Times* reported that organizers were not specifically seeking a debate, but rather "to see more top-tier Democratic candidates put climate change at the forefront of their policy agendas. They also wanted to pressure the candidates to visit some of Detroit's most marginalized communities, many of which have seen devastating effects from water contamination and air pollution." Meanwhile, both MSNBC and CNN announced that they would hold their own forums for the candidates to discuss their climate proposals (Herndon 2019).

The CNN Climate Forum was held September 4, 2019. At the time the Forum was planned, the DNC had promulgated a rule that any candidate who took part in a debate sponsored by anyone else would be barred from future DNC debates. "Debate" was defined as appearance on stage with another candidate to discuss issues; CNN had therefore planned a 7-hour town hall, where candidates would appear individually, in different locations, one after another. The DNC had withdrawn its rule in August (at the same meeting where they formally refused Inslee's request for a climate debate), but CNN went ahead as planned. Ten of the twenty remaining candidates had qualified for the DNC debate the next week, and all ten participated in the forum. The expanded format gave candidates time to make detailed presentations of their climate plans, but it did not allow for back-and-forth debate. The overall length of the program kept down the number of viewers who sat through the whole thing, but the candidates' statements were on record for anyone, including any opponents, to look up, debate, and criticize.

Significantly, candidates proposed climate programs—both in the forum and during the preceding week—that in many cases were stronger than they had committed to previously. Announced price tags ranged from a minimum $2 (Buttigieg) to $3 (Booker) trillion to Sanders's $16 trillion version of the Green New Deal. And everyone but Sanders proposed some sort of carbon tax as a way to bring down greenhouse gas emissions. It should be noted here that while carbon pricing is "the one policy that most environmental economists agree is the most effective way to cut emissions," it is opposed by many progressive activists as a tax on working people (Davenport and Gabriel 2019). Even those who favored a carbon tax also pointed out that "the people hit hardest by extreme weather are those with the fewest resources to cope with it"; several used the term "environmental justice" (Stevens and Astor 2019).

By the end of the year, climate issues had worked their way into the debate mainstream. Emily Pontecorvo of *Grist* put it this way:

After five Democratic debates where candidates were often asked superficial questions about climate change, or no questions at all, the burning planet finally got its 15 minutes of fame on Thursday night. Well, 13 minutes, if we're being precise. But those 13 minutes contained one of the strongest climate discussions in the primary so far. (Pontecorvo 2019)

With the exception of a dig at Buttigieg by Tom Steyer, there was little dispute over the seriousness of the problem or what to do about it. Everyone asked agreed that curbing greenhouse gas emissions took priority over jobs in the oil and coal industries. By the seventh debate, in mid-January, climate issues took up the last half-hour of the formal schedule, and erupted into the debate at several earlier points (Teirstein 2020). The next three debates, held in New Hampshire, Nevada, and South Carolina shortly before the respective primaries in each of those states, paid less attention to climate than to electability, democratic socialism, and the cost of Medicare for All. With the field narrowing rapidly, the surviving candidates were looking for clear ways to demarcate themselves from others, and climate, with only minor disagreements, did not serve that purpose. This applied even more to the eleventh debates, with only Biden and Sanders still running, which descended into the minutiae of each candidate's voting record over the decades. Sanders suspended his campaign three weeks later, on April 8, and endorsed Biden on April 13.

Although it featured less prominently in the last few debates, the point had been won. Climate, and environmental issues more broadly, had joined the handling of the pandemic, racial justice, economic revival, women's rights, and Trump's incompetence in the core of what the Democratic Party stood for. This was partly due to grassroots pressure. But another reason was surely the strong warning from Mother Nature that we had better pay more attention to her.

NATURE STEPS IN

Whatever the DNC may have thought about climate as an issue in 2019, the events of 2020 made it impossible to evade. The COVID-19 pandemic shut down much of the U.S. economy and triggered a worldwide economic downturn. The summer hurricane season set a new record for the number of named storms, exhausting the official list of names and running through the Greek alphabet as far as Iota. Meanwhile dry, hot weather in California led to a record-breaking season of wildfires. Each of these natural phenomena had an important bearing on the environmental debate.

The COVID-19 Pandemic

The pandemic was caused by the novel coronavirus, which probably spread to humans from bats. There have been pandemics throughout history, although some have argued that the destruction of natural habitats has increased the contact between humans and wild animals, so that incidents of disease transfer from animals to humans have become more frequent (Tobias and d'Angelo 2020). However, the pandemic's greatest relevance to environmental issues is the debate it inspired over the role of science. Trump and some Republican politicians refused to wear masks, decried the closing of businesses for safety, and insisted that the pandemic was always about to go away. Dr. Anthony Fauci of the National Institutes of Health became a national hero, and "trust the scientists" became a Democratic mantra. The parallel between COVID-19 denial and climate denial became clear, producing a strong desire on the part of Democratic partisans to be seen as the party that took science seriously in both health and environment. Climate issues were brought into the campaign more forcefully by the storms and fires of the summer of 2020.

Hurricanes

The 2020 hurricane season featured more named storms—30—than had ever been recorded. Thirteen of these storms became hurricanes, and six of those major hurricanes with winds over 111 miles per hour. Twelve of the named storms made landfall in the United States, bringing substantial human suffering and economic damage. Hurricanes were constantly in the news, with the increase in number and severity of storms widely attributed to climate change. Although it is very difficult to attribute any single weather event to the climate, rather than to local circumstances, the political effect of having so many storms was to raise the salience of climate issues (National Oceanic and Atmospheric Administration 2020).

California Wildfires

According to the California Department of Forests and Fire Protection (CAL FIRE), some 10,000 fires burned 4.2 million acres, about 4 percent of the state, during the 2020 fire season (CAL FIRE 2021). Although the federal government was supportive of the state in providing emergency aid as requested, President Trump repeatedly denied the assertions of Governor Newsom and other California officials that the intensity and frequency of fires was a result of climate change. Trump famously asserted that the real cause of the fires was the failure of state officials to rake the forest floors to remove fallen leaves and sticks.

Newsom and Trump held a joint press briefing when Trump visited the state. After thanking him for providing aid, the following exchange was reported by *USA Today*:

During a briefing with Trump, California Gov. Gavin Newsom, a Democrat, told him forest management is an issue, but "climate change is real, and that is exacerbating this."

"Please respect, and I know you do, the difference of opinion out here as it relates to this fundamental issue . . . of climate change," Newsom said.

When Wade Crowfoot, California secretary for natural resources—identified climate change as the primary cause of the wildfires, Trump interrupted: "It'll start getting cooler—you just watch."

"I wish science agreed with you," Crowfoot told the president.

Trump responded, "I don't think science knows, actually." (Jackson 2020)

The widespread coverage of the devastating fires coupled with the president's proclaimed disdain for science served to further heighten the importance of environmental issues in the campaign.

Of course climate matters were not the only topic in the news; in fact, they were far outpaced by two immediate crises, the COVID-19 pandemic and the graphic demonstration of police racism through the callous murders of George Floyd, Breonna Taylor, and other African Americans by police officers. These killings touched off nationwide protests, leading both to a growing awareness of the problem of racism within the white population, and to Trump's attempt to mobilize racist support through talk of law and order, criminals taking over the suburbs, and the use of massive force to suppress the protests. These crises are beyond the scope of this particular chapter. The point to be made here is that they did not lead to a sense that climate was less important, but rather to a sense that all these issues were manifestations of the same problem, namely, that the social system of the United States was unable to protect and meet the needs of its people. This became clear as the Biden general election campaign developed.

BIDEN'S NOMINATION

Public health concerns compelled both the Democratic and Republican conventions to be largely virtual events. The Democratic national Convention was formally held in Milwaukee from August 17 to 20, 2020. However, the hosts for each night were working from Los Angeles, and convention events were a combination of prerecorded segments and live speeches from locations around the country. Each state cast its roll call votes from a location in that state, and Joe Biden accepted the nomination from an auditorium in Delaware.

After accepting the nomination, Biden emphasized national unity, implicitly contrasting himself with Trump:

But while I will be a Democratic candidate, I will be an American president. I will work as hard for those who didn't support me as I will for those who did. That's the job of a president. To represent all of us, not just our base or our party. This is not a partisan moment. This must be an American moment . . . . America isn't just a collection of clashing interests of red states or blue states. We're so much bigger than that. We're so much better than that.

His very next paragraph called up the spirit of Franklin D. Roosevelt, and went on to articulate a contemporary version of Roosevelt's progressive values:

This campaign isn't just about winning votes. It's about winning the heart, and yes, the soul of America. Winning it for the generous among us, not the selfish. Winning it for the workers who keep this country going, not just the privileged few at the top. Winning it for those communities who have known the injustice of the "knee on the neck." For all the young people who have known only an America of rising inequity and shrinking opportunity. They deserve to experience America's promise in full.

He went on to say that the nation faces:

Four historic crises. All at the same time. A perfect storm. The worst pandemic in over 100 years. The worst economic crisis since the Great Depression. The most compelling call for racial justice since the '60s. And the undeniable realities and accelerating threats of climate change. (Biden 2020)

With these few paragraphs Biden summed up the spirit of the campaign to come. He sought national unity, but unity of a particular kind—a government that would take on the problems of all the people, and would do so competently and responsibly. It would not be a unity that asked African Americans to compromise on their rights, or that deferred action on climate or the pandemic until those who opposed such action had been won over. Moreover, the four great crises he pointed to were seen as four sides of one problem. Tackling climate change would be part of economic recovery, ending racial disparities in health care would be part of controlling the pandemic, no one of the crises could be solved unless the other three were solved at the same time. Political attention now turned to the Republican National Convention and the nomination of Donald Trump for a second term.

TRUMP'S ACCEPTANCE SPEECH

After a convention that was even more pro forma than the Democrats'— several states did not hold Republican primaries but simply pledged their delegates to Trump, while the Convention itself simply reiterated the 2016 platform, rather than adopting positions on the issues of the day—Trump accepted the party's nomination on August 28 in a speech from the White House lawn. The general theme of the speech was that Trump had made America great before China unleashed the coronavirus on us, and would make it great again after his reelection. A Biden victory, on the other hand, would turn the country over to radical socialism, uncontrollable violence and crime, and the export of American jobs to China.

Trump summed up his environmental program in a few sentences. For context the entire paragraph is quoted here:

> Days after taking office, we shocked the Washington Establishment and withdrew from the last Administration's job-killing Trans Pacific Partnership. I then approved the Keystone XL and Dakota Access Pipelines, ended the unfair and costly Paris Climate Accord, and secured, for the first time, American Energy Independence. We passed record-setting tax and regulation cuts, at a rate nobody had ever seen before. Within three short years, we built the strongest economy in the history of the world.

This is contrasted with what Trump portrays inaccurately as the Democratic program:

> Biden has promised to abolish the production of American oil, coal, shale, and natural gas—laying waste to the economies of Pennsylvania, Ohio, Texas, North Dakota, Oklahoma, Colorado, and New Mexico. Millions of jobs will be lost, and energy prices will soar. These same policies led to crippling power outages in California just last week. How can Joe Biden claim to be an "ally of the Light" when his own party can't even keep the lights on? (Trump 2020)

As usual, Trump relied on emotional connotations rather than arguments, in this case evoking the trope that environmentalists are rich elitists who do not care about ordinary people, and are happy to support measures that destroy working-class jobs, whether through trade or clean air regulations. While Biden and the Democrats were presenting climate change, racism, economic collapse, and the pandemic as different faces of the same problem, Trump was creating a similar image of how to "Make America Great Again," but in his case with emphasis on the goal, and very little discussion of the means whereby that could be achieved. This was to set the tenor for the general election campaign.

THE ENVIRONMENT IN THE GENERAL ELECTION

With the COVID-19 pandemic once again surging, the general election campaign was unusual. President Trump continued to hold public rallies, mostly well attended; approximately 59 between his acceptance speech and the general election, with four or five rallies on each of the last three days. Biden's strategy contrasted markedly with Trump's; he made video speeches from his basement office, appearing occasionally in sparsely populated local venues, and issuing a steady stream of policy positions. Both parties devoted major resources to turning out the vote, and there were many disputes about the rules for mail-in ballots and early voting. Biden's policy proposals defined his environmental plans. In addition, 15 minutes of the second of the two debates were devoted to climate, and let the candidates offer a sharp contrast.

BIDEN'S ENVIRONMENTAL POLICY PROPOSALS

While Trump was flying from airport to airport for campaign rallies, the Democratic nominee devoted time and energy to developing and releasing policy proposals. At least three of these were relevant to the environment: "The Biden Plan for a Clean Energy Revolution and Environmental Justice," "The Biden Plan to Build a Modern, Sustainable Infrastructure and an Equitable Clean Energy Future," and "The Biden Plan to Secure Environmental Justice and Equitable Economic Opportunity." The interrelationships of these three plans can be seen in the titles. The first and the second refer to clean energy, the first and the third to environmental justice, and the second and the third to equitability. Taken together, they lay out the general outline of Biden's overall plan. On climate, the future president pledged to achieve "100 percent clean energy economy and zero net emissions by 2050" through a combination of executive orders "on day one" and Congressional legislation. He also promised to "build a stronger, more resilient nation" by smart infrastructure investments, to "rally the rest of the world to meet the threat of climate change," to stand up to the abuse of polluters who harm communities of color and low-income communities, and to "fulfill our obligation to workers and communities" that built the industrial revolution: "we're not going to leave any workers or communities behind" (Biden 2000).

The infrastructure plan goes into greater detail. The major points include pledges to "build a modern infrastructure, position the U.S. auto industry to win the 21st century with technology invented in America, achieve a carbon pollution-free power sector by 2035, make dramatic investments in energy efficiency in buildings, including completing 4 million retrofits and building 1.5 million new affordable homes, pursue a historic investment in clean energy innovation, advance sustainable agriculture and conservation, [and] secure environmental justice and equitable economy opportunity" (Biden 2000).

Finally, Biden's environmental justice plan pledged the candidate to "Use an inclusive and empowering All-of-Government approach; make decisions that are driven by data and science; target resources in a way that is consistent with prioritization of environmental and climate justice; and assess and address risks to communities from the next public health emergency" (Biden 2000).

In each plan, the bullet points quoted here are spelled out in greater detail. Overall, Biden had adopted the strategy, if not the name or the magnitude, of the Green New Deal. Climate change would be brought under control by spending money and creating jobs, and any workers in fossil fuel industries would be taken care of through compensation and retraining, as appropriate. Environmental justice would be a theme throughout. The presidential debates offered a chance for the two candidates' programs to confront each other.

THE DEBATES OF THE 2020 CAMPAIGN

The presidential debates of 2000 were unusual. Three were scheduled. The first, on September 29, descended into near chaos as Trump resorted to the tactics of bullying and intimidation that had served him well against Hillary Clinton four years before. He regularly interrupted Biden, and refused to stop talking at the end of his own allotted time, leading Biden to exclaim, "Will you shut up, man!" at one point. There was little discussion of climate. The second debate, scheduled for October 9, was canceled, as Trump was recovering from a serious case of COVID-19, and refused to debate virtually. The third scheduled debate was held October 22 at Belmont University in Nashville. In order to prevent its becoming another brawl, it had been agreed that each candidate's microphone would be turned off by the technical staff during his opponent's scheduled time; both microphones would be on for the back-and-forth discussion after the scheduled presentations on each issue. Fifteen minutes were to be devoted to climate policy, the only head-to-head debate on this topic during the campaign (Grullón Paz 2020; Goldmacher 2020).

The climate section of the debate featured competing factual claims and back-and-forth charges. Trump said that the Paris Agreement would have cost "tens of millions of jobs, thousands and thousands of companies," because it was "so unfair." Biden replied that climate change was "an existential threat to humanity," and added that "we don't have much time. We're going to pass the point of no return within the next eight to 10 years. Four years of this man eliminating all the regulations that were put in by us to clean up the climate, to clean up—to limit the—limit of emissions will put us in a position where we're going to be in real trouble." He gave some examples of his plan, which he said was supported by both labor unions and environmental groups, to invest in clean energy, and asserted that "My plan will, in fact, create 18.6 million jobs, seven million more than his. This from Wall Street and I'll create $1 trillion more in economic growth than his proposal does, not on climate just on the economy." Finally, in response to a question from Trump, he affirmed that "I would transition from the oil industry. Yes." He added "it has to be replaced by renewable energy over time. Over time. And I'd stop giving to the oil industry—I'd stop giving them federal subsidies. You won't give federal subsidies to the gas and, excuse me, to solar and wind. Why are we giving it to the oil industry?" The debate also touched on environmental justice for people of color living close to polluting plants. Trump asserted that those people were getting jobs with good pay; Biden responded that Trump obviously did not understand the issue, and that a Biden administration would force the companies involved to stop polluting (Trump, Biden and Welker 2020).

By this point in the campaign, there was no room for doubt about where the candidates stood on the environment, and there was little further discussion of the issue. Attention focused instead on the election itself: would it be fair, would voters be allowed to protect themselves from the pandemic by casting mail ballots, would the millions of mail and early ballots already cast be handled securely and honestly? The last days of the campaign featured grassroots mobilizations to get out the vote and legal clashes over balloting rules, as Biden and his supporters put together the largest vote ever obtained by a presidential candidate. Ultimately, Biden was elected president, with many bumps and conflicts along the way. The details of those conflicts are recounted elsewhere in this volume; the rest of this chapter will examine environmental issues in the transition and the opening days of the Biden presidency.

BIDEN'S VICTORY AND THE TROUBLED TRANSITION

With the environmental issues clearly defined, both campaigns spent the last few weeks focused on getting out the vote for their candidate and, on the Republican side, on casting doubt on the validity of the expected result. Almost all claims of fraud were rejected by the courts, if they even got that far, and Republican election authorities in such states as Georgia, Arizona, and Michigan confirmed that Biden had won their states. Electors were picked, met to cast their votes, and those votes were forwarded to Congress to be counted formally on January 6, as the Constitution required. Biden received 306 votes, and Trump 232 (National Archives 2021).

The time from Election Day to the Inauguration was spent in recounts, lawsuits, unfounded denunciations of fraud from Trump, all leading up to the attack and temporary occupation of the Capitol on January 6, which interrupted the Congressional counting of the vote for a few hours before Biden and Harris were certified as President- and Vice President-Elect. Meanwhile, Biden moved ahead with arrangements to take office. The formal transition was delayed until November 23, due to the refusal of Emily Murphy, head of the General Services Administration, to "ascertain" that Biden was the "apparent winner" of the election until that date. The ascertainment made $7.3 million available for transition expenses, as well as office space in federal buildings, and facilitated access of the transition team to agencies (Naylor and Wise 2020).

Biden had not waited for the ascertainment before beginning to plan. He announced a 13-member virus task force on November 10, and began to describe his plans to the public (Stevens 2020). The next day he announced his choices as appointees for most key national security positions, and named his chief of staff, Ron Klain, the day after that. Most of his Cabinet was in place well before he took office, although their confirmation was delayed by an interparty dispute in the Senate about committee assignments.

Biden's key environmental appointments included Michael Regan, head of the Department of Environmental Quality in North Carolina, as EPA administrator; Representative Deb Haaland (D-NM), a member of the Laguna Pueblo, as secretary of the interior; Jennifer Granholm, former governor of Michigan and a strong advocate of renewable energy, as secretary of energy; and not one but two special high-ranking climate aides: former secretary of state John Kerry as Special Presidential Envoy for Climate with a seat on the National Security Council, and former EPA administrator Gina McCarthy as White House Climate Coordinator. Tom Vilsack, a former governor of Iowa who had been secretary of agriculture in the Obama administration, was named to that position again (Montague 2021).

For the most part, these appointees are seen as embodying a strong environmental agenda, with particular emphasis on stopping climate change. Vilsack is an exception; his appointment was heavily criticized by environmentalists, progressive farm policy advocates, and small farmers, all of whom see him as too friendly to corporate agriculture, the big chemical companies, and genetically modified plants. His appointment was seen as a concession, perhaps a necessary one, to conventional agriculture interests (Rappeport and Corkery 2020). McCarthy, on the other hand, had guided the development of Obama's Clean Power Plan, and was seen as a very strong advocate for action on climate.

The Biden team's transition included policy initiatives, as well as personnel; the President-elect unveiled plans for major pieces of legislation on an economic stimulus, infrastructure, and immigration.

Many of Biden's early environmental initiatives did not require legislation: rejoining the Paris Agreement (and seeking more global action through diplomacy), and restoring or improving Obama-era regulations on the WOTUS, emissions from power plants, and motor vehicle mileage, each of which had been undermined or repealed by Trump. These regulatory changes will take time due to procedural requirements, but Biden has made his intentions clear.

On January 27, 2021, Biden announced a number of executive orders on climate, declaring that "Today is climate day in the White House, which means today is jobs day in the White House." Among other things, the orders established environmental justice as a whole-of-government imperative, made limiting climate change part of national security, and committed his administration to getting more electric cars on the road and helping coal miners transition to good new jobs. In language reminiscent of the Green New Deal—a concept he did not mention—he continually presented action against climate change as a major source of good, high-paying new jobs (Friedman, Davenport and Flavelle 2021).

In addition to his executive orders, the President-elect proposed a major two-part legislative package. The first part, described as a coronavirus relief bill, would provide $1.89 trillion for direct payments to individuals and to state, local, and tribal governments to compensate for loss of income due to pandemic shutdowns and the resulting recession. In addition, it would provide for expanded and extended unemployment compensation, aid to communities and small businesses, and funds specifically for vaccine distribution and for making schools safe to reopen. A second major bill, to be introduced in the spring of 2021, would provide funds for economic recovery, and was specifically intended to include support for renewable energy and other climate-related efforts as part of a larger program of job creation (Lerman and Lesniewski 2021). While details have not yet been released, limiting climate change was to be a major part of the bill.

Both of these major bills must go through the legislative process, where unexpected changes may occur; and executive and regulatory actions may be challenged in the courts. However, it is clear that the new president is strongly committed to action to protect the environment in general, and to save the earth from climate disruption in particular.

CONCLUSION

This chapter began with the dramatic events of the youth climate strike and Greta Thunberg's forceful bursting upon the scene. Although the DNC tried to keep environmental issues out of the primaries, strong action on the environment, and especially on climate, had somehow become part of the core principles of grassroots Democratic voters. Biden adopted a strong climate program in his campaign, and seems determined to make that program into policy. His proposals will not be enough—nor will the programs adopted by any other country—but we can hope that they will generate hope and faith that will allow the nations of the world to accept feedback and strengthen policies when such strengthening is needed. That may be our best hope for the future.

REFERENCES

Adler-Bell, Sam. 2019. "The Story Behind the Green New Deal's Meteoric Rise." *New Republic*. February 6. https://newrepublic.com/article/153037/story-behind -green-new-deals-meteoric-rise.

Albeck-Ripka, Livia. 2018. "Climate Change Protest Draws Thousands of Australian Students." *New York Times*. November 30.

Berg, John C. 2019. *Leave It in the Ground: The Politics of Coal and Climate*. Santa Barbara: Praeger.

Biden, Joseph R. 2019. "The Biden Plan For A Clean Energy Revolution And Environmental Justice." January 15. https://joebiden.com/climate-plan/

———. 2020. "The Biden Plan to Build A Modern, Sustainable Infrastructure And An Equitable Clean Energy Future." July 20. https://joebiden.com/clean-energy/

———. 2020. "The Biden Plan to Secure Environmental Justice And Equitable Economic Opportunity." July. https://joebiden.com/environmental-justice-plan/

———. 2020. "Joe Biden Accepts Presidential Nomination: Full Transcript." With an introduction by Matt Stevens. *New York Times*. August 20.

Burns, Alexander. 2020. "Jay Inslee Endorses Biden, Citing Private Conversations on Climate Policy." *New York Times*. April 22.

——— and Matt Stevens. 2019. "Jay Inslee, Dropping Out of 2020 Race, Will Run for Governor Again." *New York Times*. August 21.

CAL FIRE. 2021. "2020 Fire Season." https://www.fire.ca.gov/incidents/2020/

Carney, Jordain and Miranda Green. 2019. "Senate Blocks Green New Deal." *The Hill*. March 26.

Daugherty, Owen. 2019. "Pelosi Praises Enthusiasm Behind 'Green New Deal' After Seeming to Brush It Off." *The Hill*. February 7.

Davenport, Coral and Trip Gabriel. 2019. "Climate Town Hall: Several Democratic Candidates Embrace a Carbon Tax." *New York Times*. September 6.

Downs, Anthony. *An Economic Theory of Democracy*. New York: Harper, 1957.

Eccleston, Paul. 2008. "UN Announces Green 'New Deal' Plan to Rescue World Economy." *The Telegraph*, October 22. https://web.archive.org/web/2012092 2050440/http://www.telegraph.co.uk/earth/earthnews/3353698/UN-announces-gre en-New-Deal-plan-to-rescue-world-economies.html

Frazin, Rachel. 2019. "Members Petition DNC Chairman to Hold Presidential Debate on Climate Change." *The Hill*. June 7.

Friedman, Lisa, Coral Davenport, and Christopher Flavelle. 2021. "Biden, Emphasizing Job Creation, Signs Sweeping Climate Actions." *New York Times*. January 27.

————— and Matt Stevens. 2019. "Jay Inslee, Running as a Climate Candidate, Wants Coal Gone in 10 Years." *New York Times*. May 3.

Friedman, Thomas L. 2007. "A Warning from the Garden." *New York Times*. January 19.

Gillis, Justin. 2019. "The Democratic Party Is Trying to Downplay Climate Change. Don't Let It." *New York Times*. June 7.

Goldmacher, Shane. 2020. "Six Takeaways From the First Presidential Debate." *New York Times*. November 7.

Green New Deal Group. 2021. *The Green New Deal*. https://greennewdealgroup.org/

Green Party of the United States. 2021. "Green New Deal." https://www.gp.org/green_new_deal

Grullón Paz, Isabella. 2020. "2020 Election Presidential Debate Calendar: Key Dates." *New York Times*. October 16.

Herndon, Astead W. 2019. "Why Climate Activists Packed the Streets Outside the Democratic Debate." *New York Times*. July 30.

Jackson, David. 2020. "Scientists and Officials Say Climate Change Causes Wildfires; Trump Says 'Forest Management' Is To Blame." *USA Today*. September 14. https://www.usatoday.com/story/news/politics/2020/09/14/trump-california-oregon-wildfires-result-forest-management/5791302002/

Johnson, Jake. 2019. "Youth-Led Petition Urges 2020 Democratic Candidates to Hold Climate Debate." *EcoWatch*. April 17. https://www.ecowatch.com/2020-democratic-candidates-climate-debate-petition-2634869782.html?rebelltitem=1#rebelltitem1

Johnson, Kirk. 2019. "Jay Inslee, Washington Governor and Environmentalist, Enters 2020 Race." *New York Times*. March 1.

Kaplan, Sarah, Lauren Lumpkin and Brady Dennis. 2019. "'We Will Make Them Hear Us': Millions of Youths Around the World Strike for Action." *Washington Post*. September 20.

Lavelle, Marianne. 2019. "Senate's Green New Deal Vote: 4 Things You Need to Know." *Inside Climate News*. March 26. https://insideclimatenews.org/news/26032019/green-new-deal-senate-vote-mcconnell-climate-change-policy/

Lerman, David, and Niels Lesniewski. 2021. "Biden Pushes for $1.9 Trillion Coronavirus Relief Package." *Congressional Quarterly News*. January 14.

Lewis, Aimee, and Steve Almasy. 2019. "Teen Activist Tells Protesters Demanding Action on Climate Change: 'We Need to Do This Now.'" *CNN*. September 20. https://www.cnn.com/2019/09/20/world/global-climate-strike-september-intl

Montague, Zach. 2021. "Biden's Cabinet and Senior Advisers." *New York Times*. 16 February 16.

National Archives. 2021. "2020 Electoral College Results." https://www.archives.gov/electoral-college/2020

National Geographic. 2021. "Greta Thunberg." *National Geographic Kids*. https://www.natgeokids.com/uk/kids-club/cool-kids/general-kids-club/greta-thunberg-facts/

National Oceanic and Atmospheric Administration. 2020. "Record-Breaking Atlantic Hurricane Season Draws to an End." November 14. https://www.noaa.gov/media -release/record-breaking-atlantic-hurricane-season-draws-to-end

Naylor, Brian, and Alana Wise. 2020. "President-Elect Biden To Begin Formal Transition Process After Agency OK." *NPR*. November 23. https://www.npr.org/ sections/biden-transition-updates/2020/11/23/937956178/trump-administration-to -begin-biden-transition-protocols

Pontecorvo, Emily. 2019. "Climate Gets a Prime Spot in the Sixth Democratic Debate." *Grist*. December 20. https://grist.org/politics/climate-gets-a-prime-spot -in-the-sixth-democratic-debate/

Ramzy, Austin. 2019. "Students Across the World Are Protesting on Friday. Why?" *New York Times*. March 14.

Rappeport, Alan and Michael Corkery. 2021. "Biden's Choice of Vilsack for U.S.D.A. Raises Fears for Small Farmers." *New York Times*. January 19. https:// www.nytimes.com/2020/12/21/us/politics/vilsack-usda-small-farmers.html

Sangupta, Somini. 2019. "Becoming Greta: 'Invisible Girl' to Global Climate Activist, With Bumps Along the Way." *New York Times*. February 18.

Schreuer, Milan, Elian Peltier, and Christopher F. Schuetze. 2019. "Teenagers Emerge as a Force in Climate Protests Across Europe." *New York Times*. January 31.

Sengupta, Somini, and Lisa Friedman. 2019. "At U.N. Climate Summit, Few Commitments and U.S. Silence." *New York Times*. September 23.

Stevens, Matt. 2020. "As the Transition Begins, the Stark Contrast Between Biden and Trump Persists." *New York Times*. November 10.

——— and Maggie Astor. 2019. "Climate Change Takes Center Stage: This Week in the 2020 Race." *New York Times*. September 7.

Sunrise Movement. "Green New Deal." https://www.sunrisemovement.org/green-ne w-deal

Teirstein, Zoya. 2020. "At the 7th Democratic Debate, Candidates Took Every Opportunity to Talk Climate." *Grist*. January15. https://grist.org/politics/at-the-7th -democratic-debate-candidates-took-every-opportunity-to-talk-climate/

Thunberg, Greta. 2018. "I'm Striking from School to Protest Inaction on Climate Change – You Should Too." *Guardian*. November 26. https://www.theguardian .com/commentisfree/2018/nov/26/im-striking-from-school-for-climate-change-too -save-the-world-australians-students-should-too

——— and Amy Goodman. 2018. "School Strike for Climate: Meet 15-Year-Old Activist Greta Thunberg, Who Inspired a Global Movement." In *Democracy Now!* 2018. Interview. https://www.democracynow.org/2018/12/11/meet_the_15_yea r_old_swedish

Tobias, Jimmy, and Chris d'Angelo. 2020. "Environmental Destruction Brought Us COVID-19. What It Brings Next Could Be Far Worse." *HuffPost*. April 21. https:/ /www.huffpost.com/entry/emerging-disease-environmental-destruction_n_5e9db5 8fc5b63c5b58723afd

Trump, Donald J. 2020. "Full Text: President Trump's 2020 RNC Acceptance Speech." *NBC News*. August 28. https://www.nbcnews.com/politics/2020-election/read-full-text-president-donald-trump-s-acceptance-speech-rnc-n1238636

———, Joseph R. Biden, and Kristen Welker. 2020. "Debate Transcript: Trump, Biden Final Presidential Debate Moderated by Kristen Welker." *USA Today*. October 23. https://www.usatoday.com/story/news/politics/elections/2020/10/23/debate-transcript-trump-biden-final-presidential-debate-nashville/3740152001/

Chapter 9

Health Care and the 2020 Elections

Three Competing Visions Plus a Pandemic

Thomas R. Marshall

Health care is now regularly a major issue in American elections. The 2020 presidential election offered Americans a choice among three competing visions for delivering health care. The first vision, commonly called a single-payer plan or Medicare for All, envisions a health care system almost wholly managed and financed by the federal government. The second vision, as embodied in President Barack Obama's landmark Affordable Care Act (ACA), envisions a partly public, partly private health care system with heavily regulated private employer plans and with nearly all the remaining Americans covered through a variety of government-managed plans. The third vision, backed by President Donald Trump, envisions a far smaller role for the federal government and very likely a large number of uninsured Americans. Unforeseeably, the coronavirus pandemic added an extra twist to the 2020 election.

None of these three competing visions is new to the 2020 election. Americans have long been divided on how best to deliver health care (Morone and Fauquert 2015; Starr 2017). Nor does a consensus now exist on this question. Yet elections have consequences. President Joe Biden's presidential win signaled that the second vision will likely dominate policy-making for the next several years.

Critics often describe the American health care system as fragmented and expensive, but one with only mediocre health outcomes. A few figures may suffice. American health care costs in 2019 equaled 18 percent of gross domestic product (GDP)—a figure higher than in any other prosperous country and roughly double the average costs for all OECD countries.[1] Annual health care spending now averages over ten thousand dollars per capita. That figure is much higher than in France, Britain, Germany, or Canada, all of which countries offer predominantly government-run health systems. Health care costs tally roughly a quarter of the federal budget. Health care spending typically rise at least two times the general inflation rate. In large part, the high levels of American health care spending result from advanced medical techniques, a partly privately managed health insurance system, extremely high pharmaceutical prices, and high salaries across the medical industry (Papanicolas, Woskie, and Jha 2018). The short-term future is bleak. By current estimates, the Medicare's Hospital Insurance Trust Fund will become insolvent by 2024, two years sooner than projected, in large part due to the coronavirus pandemic.

Heavy spending notwithstanding, the American health care system yields uneven and often unimpressive results. Among 35 OECD countries, the United States ranks only 28th in life expectancy, only 33rd in infant mortality, and at best average on most basic measures such as child immunizations. Compared to prosperous countries the United States has high rates of avoidable hospitalization for diabetes and asthma, high rates of overweight and obese adults, high rates of avoiding care because of costs, and low satisfaction with the health system (Papanicolas, Woskie, and Jha 2018). The ACA's generous subsidies notwithstanding, 14 states in 2020 still offered very limited Medicaid coverage for low-income Americans. According to 2018 Census estimates, about 28 million Americans lacked any health insurance plan, a figure that compares to 48 million Americans in 2012. Nearly half of Americans hold health insurance plans through a private employer. As a result, health coverage is sensitive to the unemployment rate. The percentage of Americans who lack a health insurance plan is higher than in any comparable prosperous democracies. The coronavirus pandemic not only led to in excess of 230,000 deaths by November 2020; the resulting job losses also cost several million Americans their health care coverage.

These health care realities long predate Donald Trump's presidency, the coronavirus pandemic, or the 2020 election. U.S. health care spending began rapidly to outpace that of other prosperous countries during the early 1980s (Escarce 2019), as income inequality in the United States rapidly rose. The U.S. poverty rate (at 18% in 2019) is now the highest among prosperous countries. Disparities in health care outcomes remain large and at times are growing, particularly so by education, income, and race (Case and Deaton 2017). The incomplete Medicaid expansion during the past decade limited health care gains that might otherwise have resulted (Alker, Kenney, and Rosenbaum 2020; Cawley, Soni, and Simon 2018; Miller et al. 2018).

Not surprisingly, health-related issues become important issues in American elections. During his 2016 campaign, Donald Trump repeatedly promised to repeal and replace President Obama's signature policy, the ACA. A November 2016 Gallup survey put the split among Americans nationwide at 42 percent "generally approve" of the Trump proposal but with

53 percent disapproving. Trump's promise to repeal and replace the ACA was at least popular among Republicans among whom only 7 percent "generally approve(d)" of the ACA—compared to 76 percent of Democrats who "generally approve(d)." Queried a bit further, only 14 percent of Americans favored keeping the ACA in place "as is" but 37 percent favored "repeal and replace" and 43 percent said to "keep but significantly change." Many of the ACA's provisions were popular. Yet high levels of partisanship and a few distinctly unpopular provisions, particularly the so-called individual mandate provision that required individuals to purchase a health insurance plan or pay a tax penalty, limited the ACA's overall popularity. Opposition to a highly bundled health care package also reflects Americans' widespread distrust of government regulation, widespread perceptions of wasteful government spending, and unfavorable views of the federal government, per se (Newport 2012).

Many different health issues won attention during 2019 and 2020. Some issues are long-standing, including reducing the harm of cigarette smoking, vaping, obesity, and opioid addiction. Politicians returned to the issues of the uninsured, drug pricing, drug reimportation, so-called surprise medical bills, Medicaid expansion, and allowing Medicare coverage at ages younger than 65. In mid-November 2020, the U.S. Supreme Court held a hearing on *California v. Texas*, an appeal of a lower federal court ruling striking down the entire ACA (Morone 2020). Proposals for a single-payer plan, commonly called Medicare for All, emerged as a key issue during the Democratic Party nominations race.

Short-term, unforeseeable health issues also affected the 2020 campaign. By mid-March 2020, the coronavirus pandemic sent the economy into an election-year downturn, shut down most large-scale campaign rallies, and later briefly hospitalized President Trump. By Election Day, over nine million Americans had contracted coronavirus and well over 200,000 Americans had died.

Public concerns on health care issues do not arise in a vacuum. The Trump administration did not focus on expanding government health care programs or spending, but rather the reverse, as described below. Nonetheless, poll support in favor of more government involvement on health care rose. In a July/August 2020 Pew survey, 63 percent of adult Americans said that the government has a responsibility to provide health care coverage for all—up slightly from 59 percent a year earlier and up sharply from 42 percent in a 2013 Gallup survey. Only a third (37%) of Americans said that providing health care coverage for all is not the federal government's responsibility. Support for greater involvement by the federal government rose in both political parties notwithstanding a large partisan divide. Among self-described Republicans, support for a greater federal role rose from 30 percent in 2019 to 34 percent in 2020. Among Democrats, support rose from 83 percent in 2019 to 88 percent in 2020.

American attitudes on the coronavirus follow this pattern of rising expectations. Pew Research Center's April and May 2020 polling asked whether the federal government or the states are responsible for adequate COVID-19 testing. A 61-to-37 percent nationwide majority picked the federal government. The gap between Democrats and Republicans was again large. Democrats picked the federal government by a 78-to-21 percent margin, but among Republicans only 42 percent picked the federal government and 57 percent picked the states.

Not surprisingly, health care issues were top concerns throughout 2019 and 2020. Pollsters query public concerns in many different ways. In a January 2019 Pew nationwide survey, reducing health care costs ranked second in importance only to the economy (at 69% and 70%, respectively) as a top national concern. Prescription drug prices and the overall costs of health care topped the list of specific health care concerns (Blendon, Benson, and McMurtry 2019). A December 2019 Gallup survey asked voters to evaluate the importance of 16 issues. Health care scored first with 35 percent of respondents describing it as "extremely important." Terrorism and international security (at 34%), gun policy (at 34%), education policy (at 33%), and the economy (at 30%) closely followed.

Health concerns continued as top concerns during 2020. By Gallup figures, coronavirus surged from under 1 percent as a "most important problem" in February 2020 to 13 percent in March and to 45 percent in April 2020. By early September 2020, the two top concerns on Gallup's open-ended question as the "most important problem" facing the country were coronavirus and the government, tied at 25 percent apiece. Other top concerns included racism and race relations (at 13%), crime and violence (at 8%), and unifying the country (at 6%). A July/August 2020 Pew survey reported similar results. Health care ranked second only to the economy (at 68% and 79%, respectively) as "very important" issues among 12 issues presented to registered voters.

As the election neared, several health issues were top public concerns. In an October 7–12, 2020, Kaiser Health Tracking Poll, the economy was ranked as the single most important problem by 29 percent of registered voters, but with the coronavirus outbreak (at 18%) and health care (at 12%), combined, were as often cited. On specific health issues, an overwhelming majority (92%) of registered voters rated "lowering the cost of health care for individuals" as very or somewhat important in deciding their choice for president. The figures for "maintaining protections for people with pre-existing health conditions" or "determining the future of the Medicare program" were 94 and 92 percent, respectively. The figures for "lowering prescription drug costs," "dealing with the many health aspects of coronavirus," "expanding health insurance coverage for the uninsured," or "determining the future of the Affordable Care Act" were 89, 85, 81, and 74 percent, respectively.

THE RISE AND FALL OF MEDICARE FOR ALL WITHIN THE DEMOCRATIC PARTY

Support for a single, nationwide universal health insurance plan featured heavily in the 2020 Democratic presidential nominations contest. Proposals for government-run or government-managed health insurance that enroll nearly all adults are not new. After World War II the British National Health Service, a comprehensive if not all-inclusive "single payer plan," was implemented in 1948. Other plans followed in Canada, Italy, France, and the Netherlands, all using a mix of national or regional providers and sometimes with competing insurers (Tuohy 2018b). During the 1930s and early 1940s, President Franklin Roosevelt considered several versions of a comprehensive government-run health coverage plan. However, FDR never sent a plan to Congress. President Harry Truman proposed a comprehensive and compulsory government-run plan during his come-from-behind presidential win in 1948. Yet once elected, Truman shelved the controversial and costly plan due to the many other pressing issues and an apparent lack of poll or Congressional support. Nor did Presidents Dwight Eisenhower, John Kennedy, Lyndon Johnson, Richard Nixon, Gerald Ford, Jimmy Carter, Ronald Reagan, or George H. W. Bush seriously try to pass all-inclusive health coverage.

In 1965, President Johnson and Congress passed the Medicaid and Medicare programs that covered many, but not all services for low income and for most senior citizens, respectively. Medicaid and Medicare left undisturbed the tax-exempt employer-based health care plans that became popular during the 1940s and 1950s. As a result, most working-age Americans and their families receive health care through tax-exempt employer plans. Medicare, Medicaid, and private employer plans are not the only government-run health care plans that cover several million people. Other plans cover veterans, children in lower-income families, American Indians, and prisoners. The fragmentation of American health care is unique among prosperous democracies (Starr 2011). That most Americans already have health care coverage, coupled with strong vested interests in maintaining the system, creates a "policy trap" that makes enacting universal health care exceedingly difficult (Starr 2017, 470).

Over the years, a few politicians proposed a universal health care plan. Most notably, Massachusetts senator Edward Kennedy proposed a Health Security Program, a plan akin to Medicaid for All. Yet no such plan ever passed in Congress (Oberlander and Marmor 2015, 63–65). Comprehensive and compulsory health care proposals reemerged during President Bill Clinton's 1992 presidential campaign. Once elected, Clinton proposed the Health Security Act (HSA), not a nationwide single-payer plan, but one that would require employers to cover all employees, expand bare-bones plans, and cover most of the remaining uninsured under mandatory state government plans. The HSA plan died in Congressional committee without ever reaching a House or Senate floor vote. Divisions among Democrats on whether to back the Clinton plan versus a single-payer plan, widespread opposition from small and mid-size businesses and insurers, and a lack of strong grassroots support or any Congressional Republican support doomed the plan. After heavy Democratic Party losses in the 1994 midterm election, the Clinton Plan never reemerged.

Although the Clinton plan died, it set off a persisting pattern of sharp partisan divisions over health care. Before the 1990s, the percentage difference between grassroots Republicans and Democrats (the "partisanship gap") on health care was often small (Marshall 2015). In Gallup's polling on President Truman's proposal, between 37 and 43 percent of Democrats favored the plan while between 13 and 20 percent of Republicans did—an average partisanship gap of 24 percent. On President Johnson's Medicare plan, Gallup reported that 73 percent of Democrats but only 36 percent of Republicans favored the plan—a partisanship gap of 37 percent. In Gallup's polling on President Clinton's plan, the partisanship gap grew larger, averaging 46 percent.

President Obama's landmark ACA, as passed in 2010, did not include a nationwide single-payer provision, but retained employer-based plans, and virtually mandated states to expand their Medicaid programs to cover Americans earning up to 138 percent of the federal poverty level. As passed, among its many provisions, the ACA required employers to provide broader health care coverage, imposed both individual and employer mandates, and offered health care plans for the uninsured on an exchange (Lantz and Rosenbaum 2020; McDonough 2020). Gallup polling during 2009 and 2010 put the average partisanship gap at 64 percent (Marshall 2015). A large partisanship gap on the ACA continued after 2014 when most of the plan went into effect. A February 2020 Gallup survey put public support at a virtual tie with 52 percent approval and 47 percent disapproval. The partisanship gap (at 83%) remained large and growing slightly since 2013. Among Democrats 94 percent approved but among Republicans only 11 percent approved.

The 2010 ACA expanded health care coverage but failed to cover all Americans. The number of uninsured Americans did drop from 46 million in 2010 to 26 million in 2016. Since Medicare covers nearly all Americans over 65, surveys on the uninsured often report estimates for working-age adults. Census Bureau surveys put the uninsured rate among adults aged 19–64 at

20.4 percent in 2013, at 16.3 percent in 2014, at 13.2 percent in 2015, at 12.2 percent in 2016 and 2017, and at 12.4 percent in 2018. By another Census estimate, the percentage of working-age Americans who avoided health care because of costs dropped from 18.5 percent in 2013 to 15.1 percent in 2018. By 2018, however, the downward trends flattened, and the number of uninsured Americans thereafter grew by about two million.

Health care policy-making often occurs through litigation. The U.S. Supreme Court's five-to-four ruling in *NFIB v. Sibelius* (2012) upheld most ACA provisions, but by five-to-four struck down a virtual requirement that states expand Medicaid to cover nearly all adults up to 138 percent of the federal poverty level. By October 2020, 12 states, mostly Southern states, had not adopted the Medicaid expansion, with two more states yet to implement an expansion. The results are striking. By 2017, states that expanded Medicaid coverage averaged an 8.7 percent uninsured rate versus an average 18.2 percent rate in states that did not expand Medicaid (Keith 2018a). *King v. Burwell* (2015), a later Supreme Court decision, enabled federally run exchanges to continue to provide subsidies for low-income enrollees, thereby keeping uninsured rates low in states that relied on federally rather than state-run exchanges.

Although the ACA expanded health insurance and coverage, it did not cover all health care services. Notably, the ACA exchanges did not cover most long-term care, a growing and costly expense for many American families (Feder 2015). Nor did the ACA mandate that employer plans provide long-term care. Nor did the ACA prevent so-called surprise out-of-network medical bills. Nor did the ACA preclude many copays and deductibles that many employer plans use to limit employer costs. Since its enactment, states and the federal government have continuously modified the ACA (Keith 2018a, 2020).

Neither did the ACA effectively reduce total health care spending. Controlling total costs is a chronic issue in American health care (Starr 2011, Altman and Shactman 2011). Expanding health care to the uninsured and including mandates for services previously not covered by health insurance plans often raise total costs. Cutting total costs is politically difficult and likely entails unpopular options such as sharply cutting medical reimbursements to doctors, pharmaceutical companies, hospitals, and other health care providers; eliminating private health insurers; raising copays and deductibles; penalizing high-cost insurance plans; or instituting health rationing (Patashnik 2020, White 2020). In practice, determining which policy measures will actually reduce total health care costs is itself very difficult (Baicker and Chandra 2017).

The ACA expanded health care coverage but never achieved a consensus level in public support (McIntyre et al. 2020). Over the decade since its enactment, public approval for the ACA hovered around the 50:50 mark, reaching a low of 37 percent in 2014 and a high of 55 percent in 2017, according to Gallup polling. By February 2020, 52 percent of Americans approved of the ACA but 47 percent disapproved. Kaiser Family Foundation (KFF) polling put the ACA's favorable ratings at 45 percent or lower until 2016, thereafter rising slightly to 55 percent. Pew surveys show similar results, with a slight uptick in support, yet with most Americans saying that the ACA did not directly affect them. These divided results sharply contrast to the "politics of consensus" achieved by the Medicare and Medicaid programs (Campbell 2015; Oberlander 2003). In part, these sharply divided attitudes reflect a polarized and highly partisan media environment and competing political narratives (Gollust, Fowler, and Niederdeppe 2020; Tuohy 2018a).

One should interpret polling on health care preferences cautiously. A careful survey in 2019 asked respondents to choose between the ACA, a Medicare for All approach, or a state-based approach (McIntyre et al. 2020). Respondents split almost evenly. Twenty-eight percent favored keeping and improving the ACA, a third (32%) supported a Medicare for All approach, and 29 percent supported a state-based option. Predictably, respondents' partisan loyalties and personal experiences with health care closely relate to their choices. So do opinions on whether health care is a basic right, views on the proper scope of government, views on employer-provided health care, and willingness to pay higher taxes for comprehensive health care.

Large partisanship gaps between Republicans and Democrats occur across many health care issues. A January 2019 Pew survey asked respondents whether government or private health insurance companies would better control health care costs. Overall, preferences nearly evenly divided with 47 percent saying government and 38 percent saying private companies would better control costs. The partisan divide was again large—65 percent of Democrats said the federal government but 61 percent of Republicans said private companies (Blendon, Benson and McMurtry 2019). Simply put, grassroots Democrats and Republicans hold very different visions of what is a well-run health care system. So too do top Democrats take very different approaches than do top Republicans.

As all this shows, support for comprehensive and inclusive health care coverage at the grass roots and among elected officeholders has long centered within the Democratic Party (Oberlander and Marmor 2015). The 20-plus Democratic contenders in 2020 took two different positions on how best to expand health care coverage. Several candidates supported comprehensive single-payer plans, while others supported expanding the ACA. In the first camp, Vermont senator Bernie Sanders had cosponsored the best-known Congressional single-payer plan, now commonly called Medicare for All. This wide-ranging plan had several key features. It would replace all public and private health insurance plans with the existing age- and disability-restricted Medicare program; would feature comprehensive benefits for life; would be almost entirely tax financed; and would virtually ban premiums, copays, and cost-sharing. The plan would include mental health care, long-term care, and dental care; would feature lifetime enrollment; and would allow all state-licensed health care providers to apply to the network. While taxes would rise, employer- and employee-shared costs, deductibles, and copays would disappear. Presumably, marketing and administrative costs would drop sharply. Very likely, so would payments to hospitals, pharmaceuticals, and health care providers. Massachusetts senator Elizabeth Warren signed on as a Senate cosponsor, as did 16 Democratic senators including Kamala Harris of California, Cory Booker of New Jersey, and Kirsten Gillibrand of New York.

The 2020 Democratic nominations contest showed the limits of Medicare for All as a campaign issue. Three top contenders endorsed a Medicare for All plan during the nominations campaign. Vermont senator Bernie Sanders faced repeated questions about his plan's costs, which by widely differing estimates ranged from 17 trillion up to 60 trillion dollars over a decade. Sanders mostly deflected the question, answering that no one could know the true dollar totals. Sander's poll numbers among Democrats ranged from 17 percent in January 2019 to 19 percent by January 1, 2020, sometimes rising as high as 24 percent or falling as low as 15 percent, and seemingly little affected by the cost issue. California senator and eventual vice presidential designee Kamala Harris appeared to endorse a Medicare for All plan at a Democratic Party-sponsored debate, but soon modified it to include a heavily regulated role for private insurers with a 10-year phase-in to a government-run plan. Harris's vacillations drew much criticism and her poll numbers among Democrats fell from 15 percent in July 2019 to 4 percent by December 2019 when she dropped out of the race. Harris later reemerged as the party's vice presidential nominee.

Massachusetts senator Elizabeth Warren also found Medicare for All a problematic campaign issue. Warren steadily rose in polls among Democrats from 4 percent in January 2019 to 27 percent by early October 2019. Yet Warren's inability to quell doubts about her plan's total costs, whether taxes on the middle class would rise, whether her plan would abrogate existing union contracts, or how to finance the plan led to fierce criticism from the media and fellow Democrats. Warren's national polling averages among Democrats fell from 27 percent in mid-October 2019 to 16 percent by January 1, 2020, according to RealClearPolitics. By mid-December 2019, Warren recast her plan to include a three-year transition window with a choice between existing plans and Medicare with an opt-out for union-negotiated contracts. Warren's campaign survived until the March 2020 Super Tuesday primaries but increasingly shifted its focus to economic inequality.

THE ACA APPROACH

Several Democratic contenders—most importantly former vice president, eventual nominee, and President-elect Joe Biden—eschewed Medicare for All. Instead, Biden supported building on the existing ACA with a wide range of added benefits and regulations. Taken together, these proposals are ambitious. Biden proposed expanding health coverage in those states that did not expand Medicaid under the ACA, thereby allowing up to five million low-income people to enroll without paying premiums if they would have qualified for coverage had their states expanded the Medicaid program. For those buying exchange plans under the ACA, Biden's proposals included eliminating the income caps for receiving subsidies. Eliminating the existing income caps (at the time set at roughly $49,000 for an individual and $100,000 for a family of four) would make exchange plans more affordable for middle-income individuals and families. Further, individuals and families buying health coverage on the individual marketplace would need to spend no more than 8.5 percent of their income. Some Biden proposals reached further, including resuming U.S. funding for the World Health Organization, sharply reducing pharmaceutical costs, using antitrust actions against market concentration in the medical industry, and ending so-called surprise medical bills.

A major Biden proposal would allow people at age 60 to buy into the federal Medicare program which now mostly only covers individuals who are age 65 and older. Premiums for people who buy into the Medicare plan would be lower than premiums paid for private plans sold on the individual market. The proposal is ambitious, possibly adding up to 20 million people to the Medicare rolls. Biden also argued that Medicare should negotiate lower hospital, health provider, and pharmaceutical prices. A proposed tax penalty would fall on pharmaceutical companies that increase some drug prices over the inflation rate. During the campaign, Biden's health care promises grew more generous. At one point, Biden supported expanding health care coverage to undocumented immigrants, although later limited that to include immigrants when they are sick. The Biden proposals would mandate a wide array of coverage, including contraceptives; would eliminate plans with lower premiums but limited coverage; and would reinstate the so-called individual mandate requiring that individuals purchase a health insurance plan.

Even so, the Biden campaign proposed keeping the existing array of employer and government plans but with an important addition: the public option plan. Under that plan, the uninsured, the self-insured, or even people with employer-provided health coverage could enroll in a tax-supported government plan, presumably one that charged lower premiums than did competing private plans. Given generous tax subsidies and a tax-free status, a public option plan might eventually drive out most competing private plans, or so critics charge. A public option plan, although widely discussed in 2009 and 2010, never became part of the ACA.

A public option plan would have significant consequences on federal spending and on tax rates. As proposed, a public option has two key assumptions. First, premiums would be actuarially fair, subject to community rating requirements, and would grow only at the rate of general inflation. Second, reduced payments to hospitals and health care providers would approximate Medicare reimbursement rates. These optimistic assumptions do not reflect historical experience in the Medicare program, interest group and enrollee demands for expanded services, adverse selection in enrollments, Congressional behavior, or the political influence of health care providers. Assuming that a public option plan follows historical patterns for Medicare, large deficits would inevitably ensue, by some estimates equaling about 800 billion dollars a decade. If, hypothetically, no other tax increases occur, the program could cover these added costs in several different ways. By raising taxes only on higher incomes, marginal federal tax rates would reach or exceed 47 percent (Chen, Church, and Heil 2020, as recomputed). Alternatively, using broader-based tax increases, all personal income tax rates, except those on the lowest fifth of taxpayers, would increase, raising median taxes on middle-income families by about $1,000 annually, and raising median taxes on the highest fifth of income earners by about $8,000 annually. Alternatively, payroll taxes for Medicare would rise from 2.9 to 4.4 percent in 2050. Still alternatively, the corporate tax rate would rise to 56 percent by 2050. The public option plan would become the third-largest federal government program by 2050, smaller only than Social Security and Medicare. Growing federal subsidies would likely lead to large-scale switching to a tax-subsidized public option plan, with a (hypothetical) 174 million enrollees by 2050.

These projected enrollments, spending, and taxes arise in the face of daunting fiscal trends over the next three decades. Given the impact of the coronavirus pandemic, the ratio of federal debt to GDP exceeded 100 percent by fall 2020, a decade sooner than expected. The Congressional Budget Office (CBO) predicts flat economic growth until 2022 and unemployment rates at 6 percent or above until 2025. CBO estimates that federal debt relative to GDP will rise to 189 percent for 2049. The annual federal budget deficit, estimated at nearly 9 percent of GDP in 2019, would rise to 12.6 percent for 2049. In short, a public option plan would face stiff competition for additional spending.

Divisions over health care plans among the top Democratic contenders mirror the split among grassroots Democrats. On a July 2019 Pew question, three-quarters (78%) of Democrats said that it is the federal government's responsibility to make sure that all Americans have health care coverage.

When asked how so, a plurality (44%) of Democrats favored a single nation-wide government program, while 34 percent favored a mix of government and private programs. Fewer Democrats (only 16%) said that the federal government is not so responsible but still favored continuing the Medicare and Medicaid program. Only 1 percent opposed any government role at all. Support for a single nationwide government program was highest among Democrats under age 50 and among self-described liberal Democrats. Only 35 percent of Democrats age 50 and older and only 33 percent of conservative and moderate Democrats supported a single national government program. A consensus clearly exists among grassroots Democrats for a larger federal role in providing health care, but not so a consensus on the specifics.

Further, many Americans are unclear on or misunderstand the specif-ics of sweeping health care proposals such as Medicare for All. This helps to explain why Medicare for All was a problematic issue during the 2020 Democratic nominations contest. A January 2019 KFF Health Tracking Poll queried those aged 18–64 with employer-sponsored insurance about a pos-sible Medicare for All plan. A large majority (77%) of respondents, presum-ably correctly, said that they would "have to pay more in taxes to cover the cost of health insurance" under Medicare for All. However, a majority (55%) incorrectly said that they "would be able to keep their current health insur-ance." As Oberlander (2003) and Marmor and Oberlander (2011), among others, argue, many Americans lack detailed information on or misunderstand the specifics of health care plans.

Predictably, many Americans change their views on health care cover-age, once informed of potential positives or negatives. A January 2019 KFF Health Tracking Poll reported that 56 percent favored and 42 percent opposed "having a national health plan, sometimes called Medicare for All." The 56 percent figure rose to 67 percent when told that the plan would "eliminate all health insurance premiums and reduce out-of-pocket health care costs for most Americans." Support rose to 71 percent when also told that the plan would "guarantee health insurance as a right for all Americans." Yet support fell to 37 percent when a follow-up question told respondents that the plan would "eliminate private health insurance companies" or told respondents that the plan would "require more Americans to pay more in taxes." Support fell to 32 percent when told the plan would "threaten the current Medicare program." Support fell to 26 percent when told the plan would "lead to delays in people getting some medical tests and treatments." A November 2019 KFF survey among Americans nationwide put initial support for "a national health plan, sometimes called Medicare for All, in which all Americans would get their insurance from a single government plan" at 53 percent favorable versus 43 percent negative. After asking several questions about the plan's likely effects, the survey asked respondents how Medicare for All would affect them personally. Only 22 percent of respondents said they would be better off, but 34 percent said they would be worse off and 39 percent said it would not have much impact.

High rates of opinion change on health care-related issues are not new. Since the 1930s, when modern surveys began, polling shows that many Americans drop their support for comprehensive health care when reminded of the possible downsides such as additional costs, delays, limits on seeing their own physician, or limits on receiving medical treatment (Starr 2017: 278–89). In surveys conducted in 2004 and 2006, for example, between 56 and 62 percent of Americans favored a universal tax-funded, government-managed, Medicare for All-like program. If told that a universal plan might limit their choice of doctors, support fell to between 28 and 35 percent (Bernstein 2009).

Nor was there any consensus on the likely results of a Medicare for All plan. In the 2019 KFF survey, a third (31%) of respondents said that "people like you" would be better off "if a national Medicare for All plan was put into place." However, slightly more respondents (39%) said such a plan would not have much impact on them, and 26 percent said they would be worse off.

These poll results are not surprising since Americans hold very mixed views on government-run health care. Polling in February and May 2020 by the Associated Press and NORC Center provide examples. By large margins, respondents trusted private entities over government to drive innovations in health care (70% to 28%), to improve quality (62% to 36%), and to provide insurance coverage (53% to 44%). By contrast, respondents saw government as better able to reduce costs than the private sector (54% to 44%). Perhaps surprisingly, given the high levels of U.S. spending compared to other prosperous countries, most (56%) Americans said that the government spends too little on "improving and protecting the nation's health." Only 7 percent said that the government spends too much.

The debate between Medicare for All and an expanded ACA influenced the 2020 Democratic Party nominations race. Yet the evidence is mixed. Early caucus and primary contests in Iowa, New Hampshire, and Nevada featured multiple candidates and produced no clear frontrunner. Former vice president Biden's showings in the early contests were unimpressive: a weak third-place finish in Iowa, an even weaker fifth-place finish in New Hampshire, and a weak second-place finish in Nevada. Biden emerged as the nominee apparent only in the February 29 South Carolina primary where his first-place win with 48 percent of the vote far outpaced any of his remaining rivals. The collapse of several competitors' campaigns and Biden's wins in 10 of 14 March 3 Super Tuesday states effectively won Biden the Democratic nominations. Even so, Biden's nomination win was not sweeping. In the 10 Super Tuesday contests that he won, Biden averaged only 42 percent of the vote, while in the four contests he lost, Biden averaged only 23 percent of the vote. With Biden's nomination, any chance collapsed that the Democratic Party platform would endorse a Medicare for All plan.

In exit and entrance polls through Super Tuesday, given a choice of four issues (in most contests: health care, climate change, race relations, and income inequality), health care was always Democratic voters' top issue in deciding which candidate to vote for. When asked, "How do you feel about replacing all private health insurance with a single government plan for everyone?" majorities of Democrats in all the contests (except South Carolina) favored a single government plan. Candidate support tracked health care preferences. In the Super Tuesday polls, Sanders led Biden 40-to-26 percent among those who supported a single government plan for everyone. Among those who opposed the idea, Biden led Sanders 51-to-11 percent. As a comparison, Biden's support equaled 51 percent only among those 65 or older, and was higher only among Black voters (at 58%). Arguably, a fair reading is that most Democratic Party primary voters and caucus goers favor a single-payer plan, but that in a crowded field Biden won the nomination regardless.

THE TRUMP HEALTH CARE VISION

The third vision for health care is quite different from the first two described above and aims to reduce the federal role. President Trump is the only recent president not to propose a major expansion of health care. Trump won the presidency in 2016 albeit running nearly three million votes behind his Democratic opponent, Hillary Clinton. During his 2016 campaign, Trump repeatedly pledged to repeal the ACA. This Congress did not do (Hacker and Pierson 2018). Even so, by 2019 Congress and the White House weakened the ACA by eliminating the tax penalty for failing to enroll in a health care plan and by ending cost-sharing subsidies for insurance plans within the exchanges. The Trump administration also sharply limited outreach efforts during open enrollment periods, shortened the enrollment period for the exchanges, repealed taxes on medical devices, and created limited-coverage health insurance markets (Keith 2018a, 2018b). All this led to an uptick in the percentage of Americans without insurance coverage in mid-2017 and 2018, particularly so in non-Medicaid expansion states and among those ineligible for subsidies in exchange programs (Griffith et al. 2020). In 2018, the Trump administration also implemented the so-called public charge rule, whereby using government benefits such as Medicaid might adversely affect immigrants' prospects of permanent residence or future citizenship (Barofsky et al. 2020).

Congress' refusal to repeal the ACA led to another tact. In June 2020, the Trump administration filed a legal brief supporting the lawsuit filed by a coalition of Republican-led states to overturn the entire ACA. The lawsuit argued that Congress' 2017 action to set at zero the tax penalty for failing to carry health insurance undermined the legal basis of the 2012 Supreme Court ruling in *NFIB v. Sibelius decision* upholding most of the ACA as a tax measure. Taking that view might not only eliminate coverage for the 11.4 million people who enrolled who signed up for the exchanges in 2020, but might also end the Medicaid expansion that covers another 12 million people. If wholly successful, the lawsuit would allow health care insurers to deny coverage or to charge higher premiums for preexisting conditions, and would eliminate a host of other ACA provisions.

The Trump administration did set out some health care plans, although many proposed actions remained only proposals. Mr. Trump often promised to release details on a new, better health plan, presumably one that would give states and consumers more options, but never did so. Nor did the Trump administration provide specifics on ending surprise medical bills or ensuring continued insurance protection for those with preexisting conditions. In September 2020, the president signed an executive order that might eventually reduce Medicare Parts B and D drug prices to levels found in other prosperous countries, but the rule-making process ensured that no action would occur prior to the election. The Trump administration did not reopen the ACA annual enrollment period during the 2020 coronavirus pandemic. In early October 2020, the president announced that 33 million Medicare beneficiaries would receive a gift card worth up to two hundred dollars to help pay for up for prescription drugs. As did many presidents in prior years, President Trump's budget proposals called for slower growth in the Medicare budget. The president did enact a faster-track process for approving new generic drugs to reduce drug prices.

Taken individually, a few of the Trump administration's health care policies were popular, but most were not. The so-called individual mandate, effectively repealed in 2018 when the tax penalty was set at zero, was never popular. In a March 2012 Kaiser Health Tracking Poll, half (51%) of American adults said "the Supreme Court should rule that it is unconstitutional for the federal government to require all Americans to have health insurance" with only 28 percent saying that the Supreme Court should rule it constitutional. In a December 2013 CBS/*New York Times* survey, a 68-to-31 percent majority opposed the provision "requiring nearly all Americans to have health insurance coverage by 2014 or pay a penalty." KFF surveys reported that three-fifths or more of Americans opposed the so-called Cadillac tax on high-spending health insurance plans with less than a third favored keeping it. The Cadillac tax, originally a provision of the ACA, never went into effect.

More often, the Trump administration's health policies were unpopular. A 57-to-38 percent majority of Americans opposed "allow(ing) employers to be exempt from providing prescription birth control" in their health plans if the employer objected to birth control for religious or moral reasons, according to a November 2018 KFF survey. In an April 2019 KFF survey, only 26 percent favored, but 67 percent opposed, insurance companies selling short-term health plans that are cheaper but that provide far fewer benefits. In an October 2020 CNN survey, a 61-to-32 percent majority opposed a lawsuit backed by the Trump administration asking the Supreme Court to overturn the 2010 ACA. On nearly all the Trump administration's initiatives, the polls split sharply along partisan grounds.

As the election neared, polls showed that voters preferred Biden rather than Trump by wide margins across a variety of health issues. In an October 2020 Kaiser Health Tracking Poll, registered voters preferred Biden rather than Trump by 55-to-35 percent on "maintaining protections for people with pre-existing health conditions" and by 50-to-41 percent on "overseeing development and distribution of a coronavirus vaccine." The split was 54-to-38 percent in favor of Biden on "dealing with the coronavirus outbreak," 52-to-35 percent for Biden on "protecting people from surprise medical bills from out-of-network care," 50-to-42 percent for Biden on "lowering prescription drug costs," and 56-to-37 percent for Biden on "determining the future of the Affordable Care Act, sometimes called Obamacare."

As a comparison, the Trump administration's health care policies were about equally unpopular as were many other major Trump administration policies. Averaging across poll questions in the iPOLL archive on building the border wall along the U.S.–Mexico border, public opinion was negative toward the border wall by a 39-to-60 percent majority. On the travel ban from several Islamic countries, poll questions in 2017 and 2018 averaged 42 percent in favor but 48 percent opposed. On the 2017 tax cuts, Gallup put average support at 39 percent in favor but 48 percent opposed. Roughly, four-fifths of Americans favored implementing the Deferred Action for Childhood Arrivals program, despite the Trump administration's on-and-off-again attempts to end the program. Substantial support existed for a Trump campaign promise with 88 percent calling "increasing spending for roads, bridges and other infrastructure" a top or important priority in a December 2018 Pew survey, yet no major legislation ensued. Gallup's May 2020 polling put approval of "allowing openly transgender men and women to serve in the military" at 71 percent despite a Trump administration ban. In a June 2017 SSRS poll, only 30 percent approved but 70 percent disapproved of the United States withdrawing from the Paris climate change agreement. On adding Amy Coney Barrett to the Supreme Court, public opinion averaged 42 percent in favor and 43 percent opposed. In short, no major Trump proposals won majority poll support. The administration's health care was no exception to this pattern.

As the coronavirus pandemic peaked, the Trump administration continued its approach of reducing the federal role in health care. In January 2020, the president established a task force to manage the federal government's response to the coronavirus pandemic. Yet the administration left most issues to the states including contact tracing; shutdowns of businesses, schools, universities, gyms, bars, churches, and restaurants; and obtaining adequate medical supplies. Across all such poll questions in the iPOLL archive during 2020, public opinion averaged 41 percent positive but 56 percent negative. Gallup polls reported a downward trend in approval on handling the coronavirus dropping from 60 percent in March to 44 percent in September. This overtime drop in approval is akin to that found during long and inconclusive wars with mounting casualty counts. President Trump's own brief hospitalization from coronavirus made a short-term dent in President Trump's reelection prospects. Just before his hospitalization, Trump trailed Biden by 6 percent in the RealClearPolitics polling averages; 10 days later Trump trailed Biden by 10 percent.[2]

In retrospect, the Trump presidency was always beleaguered. Despite a strong economy throughout most of his term in office, President Trump continually suffered from weak approval ratings. By RealClearPolitics polling averages, throughout his presidency Trump's approval ratings were always more negative than positive. His worst approval ratings were 37 percent positive but 58 percent negative in December 2017, while his best approval ratings were 50 percent negative but 47 percent positive in March 2020. Health care was no exception to these patterns of low public opinion support.

HEALTH CARE IN THE POST-TRUMP ERA

Health care played an important role in the 2020 elections. From three very different visions, continuing to expand the ACA emerged as the winning vision. This was by no means a foregone conclusion. Arguably, less than half of grassroots Democrats favor this approach and virtually no Republicans do. Further, President-elect Biden was widely seen as too old, too dull, too undistinguished, and seemingly unlikely to win the White House. Yet win the nomination and the general election he did. In Biden's seemingly unlikely win, health care issues played a major, if not always foreseeable path.

Elections have consequences. The 2020 elections will likely lead to significant expansions in publicly financed and regulated health care coverage. Historically, such changes have occurred only when Democrats control the White House and both the U.S. House and the U.S. Senate. Enacting Medicaid and Medicare in 1965 and enacting the ACA in 2010 are two historical examples. The 2020 elections provided unified government, although by very thin margins in both houses of Congress. Conceded, even unified government is not certain to result in expanded health care coverage. The failed efforts of Presidents Truman, Kennedy, and Clinton stand as counterexamples.

The Biden presidency faces a wide array of pressing challenges. The federal budget deficit and the national debt grow explosively. When a full economic recovery will occur is uncertain. Foreign crises, ill health, and scandals can arise suddenly. The federal courts are unpredictable. The 2022 Congressional elections loom. Delivering health care is clearly an important priority for the Biden administration, but major changes will not come easily or at low cost. The Medicare trust fund rapidly approaches insolvency. Tax and fee hikes, cuts in reimbursement rates to health care providers, individual mandates, and health care rationing are unpopular. The health care sector has many well-organized stakeholders. The coronavirus pandemic remains.

The 2020 elections effectively ended the debate over whether American voters favor rolling back the federal government's role in health care. What will emerge remains unclear. Some health care reforms would be popular. A Medicaid expansion is among the most likely outcomes. A public option plan that reaches widely enough to compete with private health care plans will require considerable political will from the White House. A better coordinated and more nationalized response to the coronavirus pandemic would be widely popular (Frenier, Nikpay, and Golberstein 2020) Among the many other foreseeable measures are repealing the public charge rule, increasing funding for outreach and navigator funding, and providing more generous enrollment periods for the ACA. Other options include reducing the numerous glitches in ACA, including lowering or eliminating the surcharges for tobacco users that do little to reduce nicotine addiction (Friedman et al. 2016; Manz, Waters, and Kaplan 2020), or reducing the high charges for older Americans under the exchanges. Few if any of these options will likely reduce spending on health care and many of these changes will do quite the reverse.

As a final question, how greatly will expanding publicly financed health insurance actually improve health outcomes? Increasing the number of Americans with a health insurance plan and increasing the range of services covered will improve many health outcomes (Hadley 2003; Sommers, Gawande, and Baicker 2017). Yet health outcomes also have many other determinants (Braveman and Gottlieb 2014). Some determinants are provider-, patient-, or plan-related, such as hurried services, a lack of language translation services, mistrust, distant locations, copays, long delays, biased diagnostic algorithms, a limited array of specialists, a lack of evidence-based treatment plans, or provider payments that fail to account for hard-to-treat patients. Other determinants are socially determined such as living in polluted, crime-ridden, impoverished, and stressful neighborhoods lacking adequate groceries, transportation, schools, or exercise facilities (House 2015; Acevedo-Garcia et al. 2020). Others include workplace conditions such as a lack of paid sick leave. Others include programs, practices, and regulations that offer individuals little incentive to healthier outcomes (Cohen, Fernandez-Lynch, and Robertson 2016). Still others include the many widely available unhealthy products such as so-called junk foods and beverages, tobacco products, opioids, alcohol, or addictive drugs. With the benefit of hindsight, one might add pandemics to this long list.

Organizing better health care is neither a new nor a simple challenge. Nor is there a ready or inexpensive answer. The 2020 elections reset this debate in favor of a more expansive federal role, yet likely short of enacting universal health care. What directions the delivery of health care should take will remain a pressing and complex debate long after the Trump era fades into American history.

NOTES

1. For recent comparisons, see the Organisation for Economic Co-operation and Development report at https://stats.oecd.org/
2. No recent evidence exists by which to measure a pandemic's impact on American elections. During the so-called Spanish Flu pandemic, Woodrow Wilson, a Democrat, held the presidency but Democrats suffered sweeping losses in the 1918 and 1920 Congressional elections and lost the White House in 1920. The analogy is inexact since this period also marks the end of World War I, the failed ratification of the League of Nations, and Wilson's own physical collapse.

REFERENCES

Acevedo-Garcia, Dolores, Clemens Noelke, Nancy McArdle, Nomi Sofer, Erin F. Hardy, Michelle Weiner, Mikyung Baek, Nick Huntington, Rebecca Huber, and Jason Reece. 2020. "Racial And Ethnic Inequities In Children's Neighborhoods: Evidence From The New Child Opportunity Index 2.0." *Health Affairs* 39: 1693–1701.

Alker, Joan C., Genevieve M. Kenney, and Sara Rosenbaum. 2020. "Children's Health Insurance Coverage: Progress, Problems, And Priorities For 2021 And Beyond." *Health Affairs* 39: 1743–51.

Altman, Stuart and David Shactman. 2011. *Power, Politics, and Universal Health Care: The Inside Story of a Century-Long Battle.* New York: Prometheus Books.

Baicker, Katherine and Chandra, Amitabh. 2017. "Evidence-Based Health Policy." *New England Journal of Medicine* 377: 2413–15.

Barofsky, Jeremy, Ariadna Vargas, Dinardo Rodriguez, and Anthony Barrows. 2020. "Spreading Fear: The Announcement Of The Public Charge Rule Reduced Enrollment In Child Safety-Net Programs." *Health Affairs* 39: 1752–61.

Bernstein, Jill. 2009. "Public Perspectives on Health Delivery System Reforms." Robert Wood Johnson Foundation, June 1. www.rwjf.org/en/library/research/2009/01/public-perspectives-on-health-delivery-system-reforms.html.

Blendon, Robert J., John M. Benson, and Caitlin L. McMurtry. 2019. "Perspective: The Upcoming U.S. Health Care Cost Debate — The Public's Views." *New England Journal of Medicine* 380: 2487–92.

Braveman, Paula and Laura Gottlieb. 2014. "The Social Determinants of Health: It's Time to Consider the Causes of the Causes." *Public Health Reports* 129: 19–31.

Campbell, Andrea. 2015. "Independence and Freedom: Public Opinion and the Politics of Medicare and Medicaid." In Cohen, Alan B., David C. Colby, Keith A. Wailoo, and Julian E. Zelizer, eds. *Medicare and Medicaid at 50.* New York: Oxford University Press. 213–229.

Case, Anne and Angus Deaton. 2017. "Mortality and Morbidity in the 21st Century." Brookings Papers on Economic Activity (Spring): 397–476.

Cawley, John, Aparna Soni, and Kosali Simon. 2018. "Third Year of Survey Data Shows Continuing Benefits of Medicaid Expansions for Low-Income Childless Adults in the U.S." *Journal of General Internal Medicine* 33:1495–97.

Chen, Lanhee J., Tom Church, and Daniel L. Heil. 2020. "The Budget and Tax Effects of a Federal Public Option After COVID-19." October 20. Palo Alto, CA: The Hoover Institute.

Cohen, Glen I., Holly Fernandez-Lynch, and Christopher T. Robertson. 2016. *Nudging Health: Health Law and Behavioral Economics.* Baltimore, MD: John Hopkins University Press.

Escarce, José J. 2019. "Health Inequity in the United States." Working Papers, Leonard Davis Institute of Health Economics. Philadelphia, PA: University of Pennsylvania.

Feder, Judith. 2015. "The Missing Piece: Medicare, Medicaid, and Long-Term Care." In Cohen, Alan B., David C. Colby, Keith A. Wailoo, and Julian E. Zelizer, eds. *Medicare and Medicaid at 50.* New York: Oxford University Press. 253–272.

Friedman Abigail S., William L. Schpero, and Susan H. Busch. 2016. "Evidence Suggests that the ACA's Tobacco Surcharges Reduced Insurance Take-Up and Did Not Increase Smoking Cessation." *Health Affairs* 35: 1176–83.

Frenier, Chris, Sayeh S. Nikpay, and Ezra Golberstein. 2020. "COVID-19 Has Increased Medicaid Enrollment, But Short-Term Enrollment Changes Are Unrelated To Job Losses." *Health Affairs* 39: 1822–31.

Gollust, Sarah E., Erika Franklin Fowler, and Jeff Niederdeppe. 2020. "Ten Years of Messaging about the Affordable Care Act in Advertising and News Media: Lessons for Policy and Politics." *Journal of Health Politics, Policy and Law* 45: 711–27.

Griffith, Kevin N., David K. Jones, Jacob H. Bor, and Benjamin D. Sommers. 2020. "Changes in Health Insurance Coverage, Access to Care, and Income-Based Disparities among US Adults, 2011–17." *Health Affairs* 39: 319–26.

Hacker, Jacob S. and Paul Pierson. 2018. "The Dog That Almost Barked: What the ACA Repeal Fight Says about the Resilience of the American Welfare State." *Journal of Health Politics, Policy and Law* 43: 551–77.

Hadley, Jack. 2003. "Sicker and Poorer—The Consequences of Being Uninsured: A Review of the Research on the Relationship between Health Insurance, Medical Care Use, Health, Work, and Income." *Medical Care Research and Review* 60: 3S–75S.

House, James S. 2015. *Beyond Obamacare: Life, Death, and Social Policy*. New York: Russell Sage Foundation.

Keith, Katie. 2018a. "A Hot Health Policy Summer." *Health Affairs* 37: 1544–45.

———. 2018b. "Two New Federal Surveys Show Stable Uninsured Rate." *Health Affairs*, September 3. www.healthaffairs.org/do/10.1377/hblog20180913.896261 /full/.

———. 2020. "A Hot Summer Brings More ACA Litigation." *Health Affairs*, September 14. https://www.healthaffairs.org/doi/10.1377/hlthaff.2020.01716

Lantz, Paula M. and Sara Rosenbaum. 2020. "The Potential and Realized Impact of the Affordable Care Act on Health Equity." *Journal of Health Politics, Policy and Law* 45: 831–45.

Manz, Karina C., Teresa M. Waters, and Cameron M. Kaplan. 2020. "Marketplace Premiums Rise Faster For Tobacco Users Because Of Subsidy Design." *Health Affairs* 39: 1540–5.

Marmor, Theodore R. and Jonathan Oberlander. 2011. "The Patchwork: Health Reform, American Style." *Social Science & Medicine* 72: 125–28.

Marshall, Thomas R. 2015. "The Debate Over Health Care." In William Crotty, ed. *Polarized Politics: The Impact of Divisiveness in the US Political System*. Boulder, CO: Lynne Rienner. 309–26.

McDonough, John E. 2020. "Lost in the ACA: Bit Parts in a Landmark Law." *Journal of Health Politics, Policy and Law* 45: 533–45.

McIntyre, Adrianna, Robert J. Blendon, John M. Benson, Mary G. Findling, and Eric C. Schneider. 2020. "The Affordable Care Act's Missing Consensus: Values, Attitudes, and Experiences Associated with Competing Health Reform Preferences." *Journal of Health Politics, Policy and Law* 45: 729–55.

Miller, S., S. Altekruse, N. Johnson and L. R. Wherry. 2019. "Medicaid and Mortality: New Evidence from Linked Survey and Administrative Data." National Bureau of Economic Research Working Paper 26081.

Morone, James. 2020. "Diminishing Democracy in Health Policy: Partisanship, the Courts, and the End of Health Politics as We Knew It." *Journal of Health Politics, Policy and Law* 45: 757–69.

——— and Elisabeth Fauquert. 2015. "Medicare in American Political History: The Rise and Fall of Social Insurance." In Cohen, Alan B., David C. Colby, Keith A. Wailoo, and Julian E. Zelizer, eds. *Medicare and Medicaid at 50*. New York: Oxford University Press. 297–317.

Newport, Frank. MARCH 28, 2012. "The Paradox of the Affordable Care Act and Public Opinion." https://news.gallup.com/opinion/polling-matters/170048/paradox -affordable-care-act-public-opinion.aspx

Oberlander, Jonathan. 2003. *The Political Life of Medicare*. Chicago: University of Chicago Press.

———— and Theodore R. Marmor. 2015. "The Road Not Taken: What Happened to Medicare For All?" In Cohen, Alan B., David C. Colby, Keith A. Wailoo, and Julian E. Zelizer, eds. *Medicare and Medicaid at 50*. New York: Oxford University Press. 55–74.

Patashnik, Erik M. 2020. "Comparatively Ineffective? PCORI and the Uphill Battle to Make Evidence Count in US Medicine." *Journal of Health Politics, Policy and Law* 45: 787–800.

Papanicolas Irene, Liana R. Woskie, and Ashish K. Jha. 2018. "Health Care Spending in the United States and Other High-Income Countries." *JAMA* 319 (10):1024–39. doi: 10.1001/jama.2018.1150. Erratum in: JAMA. 2018 May 1; 319(17):1824.

Sommers, Benjamin D., Atul A. Gawande, and Katherine Baicker. 2017. "Health Insurance Coverage and Health—What the Recent Evidence Tells Us." *New England Journal of Medicine* 377: 586–93.

Starr, Paul. 2011. *Remedy and Reaction: The Peculiar American Struggle over Health Care Reform*. New Haven CN: Yale University Press.

————. 2017. *The Social Transformation of American Medicine*. Second Edition. New York: Basic Books.

Tuohy, Carolyn. 2018a. "Welfare State Eras, Policy Narratives, and the Role of Expertise: The Case of the Affordable Care Act in Historical and Comparative Perspective." *Journal of Health Politics, Policy and Law* 43: 427–53.

————. 2018b. *Remaking Policy: Scale, Pace and Political Strategy in Health Care Reform*. Toronto: University of Toronto Press.

White, Joseph. 2020. "Costs versus Coverage: Then and Now." *Journal of Health Politics, Policy and Law* 45: 817–30.

Chapter 10

A Nation in Crisis

John Kenneth White

Amid a hard-fought political campaign during a bloody Civil War, Abraham Lincoln received the poet and essayist Ralph Waldo Emerson at the White House. Emerson came bearing good news, telling Lincoln, "The great West is with you." But the commander-in-chief, upon hearing this welcome report about his reelection prospects, was grim: "Yes—but I am sometimes reminded of Old Mother Partington on the sea beach. A big wave came up and waves began to rise till the water came in under her cabin door. She got a broom and went to sweeping it out. But the water rose higher and higher, to her knees, to her waist, at last to her chin. But she kept on sweeping and exclaiming, 'I'll keep on sweeping as long as the broom lasts, and we'll see whether the storm or the broom lasts the longest'" (Sandburg, 1969, 659). With that, Lincoln clenched his jaw, and the visit was over.

Like 1864, the 2020 contest came at a moment when the nation faced several existential crises—each striking at the core of the American experiment: (1) a pandemic that killed as many Americans by Inauguration Day as those who died during *all* of World War II; (2) an economic crisis that saw millions laid off and thousands businesses shuttered; (3) racial protests sparked by the deaths of unarmed African Americans—especially the executions of Ahmaud Arbery, George Floyd, Breonna Taylor, Rayshard Brooks, and the near death of Jacob Blake—all slain either by police or armed white citizens; (4) a climate crisis that saw wildfires rage through the West, while in the East and Gulf Coast there were so many hurricanes and tropical storms that meteorologists had to resort to the Greek alphabet to name them; (5) a federal government that did not effectively respond to these challenges; and (6) a president whose unprecedented efforts to invalidate the election led to riots on Capitol Hill and his second impeachment.

Each of these traumas set the nation on edge; together they metastasized into an election contest that became "the most important" of our lifetimes. Lara Trump, the president's daughter-in-law, put it this way: "This is not just a choice between Republican and Democrat or left and right. This is an election that will decide if we keep America America—or if we head down an unchartered, frightening path towards socialism" (Trump 2020). Barack Obama likewise saw the contest as a political Armageddon: "You can give our democracy new meaning . . . . But any chance of success depends entirely on the outcome of this election. This administration has shown it will tear our democracy down if that's what it takes to win" (Obama 2020). Voters saw things the same way: 77 percent said the outcome mattered more than in prior years, a view shared by 85 percent of Democrats and 79 percent of Republicans (Brenan 2020).

This rare point of partisan agreement was reflected in the 66.6 percent of eligible Americans who voted, the highest figure since 1908 (Schaul, Rabinowitz, and Mellnik 2020). All were baptized into a rancid partisanship. Party animosity is nothing new. George Washington warned of its "baneful effects" (Washington 1796). During the 1830s, Alexis de Tocqueville described a virulent partisanship that gripped the country: "As the election draws near, intrigues grow more active, agitation is more lively and wider spread. The citizens divide up into several camps, each of which takes its name from its candidate. The whole nation gets into a feverish state; the election is the daily theme of comment in the newspapers and private conversations, the object of every action and the subject of all thought, the sole interest for the moment" (Lane 2020a). In 2020, this feverish state reached a boiling point. Democrats and Republicans disagreed on basic facts, including the necessity of mask-wearing precautions advocated by government scientists and the legitimacy of the election outcome. Unlike George W. Bush and Barack Obama, two presidents who promised to restore national unity but failed, Donald Trump thrived on stoking division. And Trump would not let the postelection acrimony subside, despite Joe Biden's plea that his fellow citizens give him "a chance" (Biden 2020a). According to one postelection poll, just 21 percent of Republicans said Biden was the legitimate winner, and only 19 percent of Trump voters promised to give Biden the chance he so desired (Todd, Murray Dann, and Holzberg 2021; Pramuk 2020).

Yet for all the *sturm und drang* in the postelection aftermath, the results had something for everyone. Joe Biden won more popular votes than any presidential contender in U.S. history, and his share of the popular vote was larger than any other challenger to an incumbent president since Franklin D. Roosevelt beat Herbert Hoover in 1932. But Donald Trump won the second-largest vote share. Democrats won the popular vote for the seventh time in the past eight presidential elections. But Republicans added to their depleted ranks in the House of Representatives while the Senate was evenly divided. Biden won large majorities in white-collar, college-educated metropolitan suburbs, once a lynchpin of Republican support. But "Middle-Class Joe" could not dislodge the newfound Republican loyalties of non-college-educated white blue-collar voters, once the bedrock of the New Deal coalition. Colorado and Virginia became solid Democratic states, but Iowa and Ohio solidified their Republican support. Georgia and Arizona fell into the Democratic column. But Florida was slipping more firmly into the Republicans' grasp. And Texas, long predicted to become a swing state, remained as elusive from the Democrats' reach as ever.

For every argument that 2020 was a realigning election, there was a counter "what-about-ism" to rebut it. This does not mean that 2020 was unimportant—it was. A close look at history finds other presidential contests (none considered realigning) that were crucial to the nation's continued existence. Four stand out: the 1864 reelection of Abraham Lincoln, the 1940 and 1944 reinstatements of Franklin D. Roosevelt, and the 1964 affirmation of Lyndon B. Johnson. All were held amid a serious national emergency, and in each there were echoes of what happened in 2020. Before further examining the Biden–Trump contest, it is important to look back.

1864: NO PARTY NOW, BUT ALL FOR OUR COUNTRY

In 1864, Abraham Lincoln declared that he would "finish this job of putting down the rebellion and restoring peace and prosperity to the country." For Lincoln, the normal partisan rivalry was upended because the future of the Republic was at stake: Should the Union Party win, Lincoln believed the people would have acted "for the best interests of their country and the world, not only for the present, but for all future ages." But a loss, he warned, meant that voters "should deliberately resolve to have immediate peace even at the loss of their country, and their liberty." In that event, Lincoln said, "I know not the power or the right to resist them" (Donald 1996, 540).

Lincoln's 1864 slogan reflected the stakes, "No Party Now but All for Our Country" (Donald 1996, 537), the catchphrase adopted by the hybrid (Lincoln–Johnson) Union Party ticket. At dawn on Election Day, the *New York Times* editorialized that "before this morning's sun sets, the destinies of this Republic, so far as depends on human agency, are to be settled for weal or for woe." Electing Lincoln, the *Times* declared, was to choose "war, tremendous and terrible, yet ushering in at the end every national security and glory." But to mark a ballot for the Democrats was to choose "the mocking shadow of a peace . . . sure to rob us of our birthright, and to entail upon our children a dissevered Union and ceaseless strife" (Goodwin 2005, 664).

In the immediate aftermath of victory, Lincoln declared that the result was "to the lasting advantage, if not to the very salvation of the country" (Sandburg 1969, 688). Ralph Waldo Emerson was equally elated, writing to a friend: "I give you the joy of the election. Seldom in history was so much staked on a popular vote" (Sandburg 1969, 688). More bloodshed and sacrifice lay ahead, and the nation would face yet another crisis with Lincoln's assassination just weeks into his new term. But in Lincoln's words, 1864 showed that our democracy faced a "severe test" (Lorant 1951, 266) and passed it with the Union flag held high: "Until now it had not been known to the world that this was a possibility" (Sandburg 1969, 690). Six months after that fateful Election Day the war was won, and the nation's democratic experiment continued.

1940 AND 1944: A SUMMONS TO DUTY

By 1940, World War II was underway in Europe, and Adolf Hitler's Nazis were on the march. Germany seized Czechoslovakia and Poland, France fell, and the Battle of Britain was underway. Meanwhile, an aggressive Japan captured French Indochina and emerged as a Pacific power. Americans did not want to fight another war but worried about the nation's security. The Greatest Generation was drafted into the armed forces, as the military desperately needed new recruits. Voters wanted a steady hand, and Franklin D. Roosevelt set aside his desire to return to his tranquil Hyde Park estate to offer his continued public service, telling the 1940 Democratic Convention:

> Today all private plans, all private lives, have been in a sense repealed by an overriding public danger. In the face of that public danger all those who can be of service to the Republic have no choice but to offer themselves for service in those capacities for which they may be fitted. . . . If our Government should pass to other hands next January—untried hands—we can merely hope and pray that they will not substitute appeasement and compromise with those who seek to destroy all democracies everywhere, including here. (Roosevelt 1940)

Four years later, with the United States firmly engaged in the war, Roosevelt addressed another Democratic conclave, saying: "The people of the United States will decide this Fall whether they wish to turn over this 1944 job—this worldwide job—to inexperienced and immature hands . . . or whether they wish to leave it to those who saw the danger from abroad, who met it head on, and who now have seized the offensive and carried the war to its present stages of success" (Roosevelt 1944). A few months later, Roosevelt took the oath of office for the fourth time in a scaled-down 20-minute inauguration before 7,000 people on the South Lawn of the White House—a ceremony absent the usual inaugural parade and evening balls.

In 1940 and 1944, Americans saw danger and duty, and they deputized Roosevelt to become Dr. Win the War. Promising to be "a good soldier" (Burns 1970, 503), in 1945 FDR quoted Lincoln's Second Inaugural Address saying, "Let us strive on to finish the work we are in" (Burns 1970, 507). A few months later the war was won and the threat to our democratic institutions ceased. But the exigencies World War II created altered the nation's governing and societal arrangements for decades to come.

1964: "LET US CONTINUE"

Days after John F. Kennedy's burial in 1963, Lyndon B. Johnson addressed Congress and declared, "Let us continue" (Johnson 1963). The country was grievously shaken by the assassination of the youngest elected president in American history, scarred in the words of Theodore H. White by "death and unreason" (White 1965, 3–31). Kennedy's passing created a national emergency that attacked not only democracy itself, but the nation's psyche. Johnson promised to complete Kennedy's unfinished work by securing a new civil rights law, tax cut, and immigration reform. Addressing the Democratic National Committee in 1964, Johnson said, "We are going to finish the work that Jack Kennedy left us, but we have a mandate to begin a new program of our own—The Great Society" (Johnson 1971, 104). Winning the popular vote by the greatest percentage in history, Johnson claimed "a mandate for action, and I meant to use it that way" (Johnson 1971, 110). The late president's brother, Robert, gave Johnson credit: "In 1964, [President Johnson] won the greatest popular victory in modern times . . . . He has gained huge popularity, but he has never failed to spend it in the pursuit of his beliefs or in the interests of his country. He has led us to build schools and clinics and homes and hospitals, to clean the water and clear the air, to rebuild the city and to recapture the beauty of the countryside, to educate children and to heal the sick and comfort the oppressed on a scale unmatched in our history" (Johnson 1971, 110).

Amid a national crisis whose hangover was palpable, the Republican Party underwent its own cataclysm. Accepting the Republican nomination, Barry Goldwater declared: "I would remind you that extremism in the defense of liberty is no vice. And let me remind you also that moderation in the pursuit of justice is no virtue" (Goldwater 1964). Suddenly, the ideological distance between the two parties, a distance once considerably shortened by Dwight D. Eisenhower, widened to give voters, in Goldwater's words, "A Choice, Not an Echo." Johnson happily seized the contrast: "If

Goldwater wants to give the voters a choice, I concluded, then we'll give them a *real* choice—a choice not between conservatism and 'stand-patism' but between programs of social retreat and programs of social progress" (Johnson 1971, 103).

While Johnson welcomed his mandate for a Great Society, he also saw benefits in the magnitude of the GOP's trouncing: "I think an overwhelming defeat for them will be the best thing that could happen to the Republican Party in this country in the eyes of all the people. Because then you would restore moderation to that once great party of Abraham Lincoln and the leadership then could unite and present a solid front to the world" (Johnson 1971, 103). While moderation would quickly return in the person of Richard M. Nixon, the Republican Party persisted on its rightward course for decades to come.

2020: ECHOES OF ELECTIONS PAST

Novelist William Dean Howells once observed that Americans like "a tragedy with a happy ending" (quoted in Will 2020). In many ways, the contests of 1864, 1940, 1944, and 1964 had happy endings. The Civil War and World War II were won, landmark legislation was passed, the Republican Party moderated its stance, and the nation's democratic experiment continued unabated. In many ways, these happy endings had echoes in 2020. In 1864, the nation refused to postpone the election, while in 2020, Donald Trump threatened to cancel the election because of the pandemic (Trump 2020b). In both instances, the constitutional date with destiny was met. Echoing Franklin Roosevelt in 1940, 78-year-old Joe Biden (now the nation's oldest president) followed Roosevelt's summons to "offer themselves for service in those capacities for which they may be fitted" (Roosevelt 1940). And, like Roosevelt, Biden sacrificed a tranquil retirement. Just as in 1940 and 1944, voters saw Biden's decades of public service as meeting the moment. Finally, like Lyndon Johnson, Joe Biden viewed his presidency as an opportunity not just to heal the country but transform it—to "Build Back Better" as he repeatedly promised. And like 1964, there was hope (however small) that the Republican Party would return, once more, to its conservative principles— with debates no longer dominated by Donald Trump's name-calling tweets but centered around real policy differences. All these happy endings, if they occurred, would let the ardor of the 2020 election subside. Joe Biden echoed Abraham Lincoln and pleaded for such a happy ending: "I know this won't be easy. I know how deep and hard our opposing views are in our country on so many things. But I also know this as well. To make progress, we have to stop treating our opponents as enemies. We are not enemies. What brings us together as Americans is so much stronger than anything that can tear us apart" (quoted in Rucker and Costa 2020).

However, in 2021, old Mother Partington was still sweeping, and her broomstick was barely intact. The crises of the year before not only persisted but intensified. More than a year before his election, Joe Biden said of Donald Trump, "I don't think anybody thought he would be as bad as he is" (quoted in Steinberger 2019). George F. Will saw Trump leave "the American project . . . more battered than at any time in 160 years" (Will 2020). The American project took a further beating on January 6, 2021, another date that will live in infamy, when Donald Trump incited a crowd to march to the Capitol and invalidate the election. Incited by Trump, his son, Donald Jr., and former New York City mayor Rudy Giuliani who promised a "trial by combat" Trump told his adoring fans: "You will never take back our country with weakness. You have to show strength and you have to be strong. We have come to demand that Congress do the right thing. . . . We fight. We fight like hell, and if you don't fight like hell, you're not going to have a country anymore" (Danner 2021, 4). With that, the crowd marched down Pennsylvania Avenue, invaded the Capitol, paraded a Confederate flag inside its hallowed halls (something that never occurred during the Civil War), threatened to assassinate Vice President Mike Pence and Speaker Nancy Pelosi, and postponed the certification of the electoral count for several hours. As President Biden reminded Americans in his inaugural address our democracy remains "precious" yet "fragile" (Biden 2021).

Although Joe Biden promised to restore "the soul of America," it was unclear whether the nation's soul had been saved. Maryland Republican governor Larry Hogan noted that Trump made America look like a "banana republic" (Hogan 2020). Expressing his own doubts about a forthcoming happy ending, Barack Obama said: "America as an experiment is genuinely important to the world not because of the accidents of history that made us the most powerful nation on Earth, but because America is the first real experiment in building a large, multiethnic, multicultural democracy. And we don't know yet if that can hold. There haven't been enough of them around for long enough to say for certain that it's going to work" (quoted in Goldberg 2020).

On January 20, 2021, surrounded by thousands of National Guard troops, Joseph Robinette Biden Jr. was sworn in as the nation's 46th president. It was a scaled-down ceremony, absent the usual parades and inaugural balls. And like Roosevelt's 1945 inauguration, the 2021 event was a ritual riven with solemnity, given the 400,000 Americans (and counting) who died from the coronavirus. But it was also a rite of passage marred by unprecedented acts and uncertain outcomes. For the first time since Andrew Johnson stood up Ulysses S. Grant in 1869, the outgoing president refused to attend the swearing-in of his successor. Donald Trump's overt attempts to subvert the election result—including calls to Republican officials in Arizona, Georgia, Wisconsin, and Pennsylvania to void the results—upended every norm of presidential transitions that followed the bitter John Adams–Thomas Jefferson contest of 1800. From issuing a *cri de coeur* to stop counting ballots, to losing one frivolous lawsuit after another, to threatening to name rival slates of electors in Republican-controlled state legislatures, to delaying the Biden transition for several weeks, and later asking federal and state courts to void the election, Donald Trump undermined not just the legitimacy of the incoming administration but democracy itself. The Attorney General of Pennsylvania called Trump's attempt to overturn the election results a "seditious abuse of the judicial process" (quoted in Barnes 2020). The Supreme Court, Trump's last hope, unanimously refused to grant him the relief he sought. Once the court rendered its verdict and the Electoral Votes were counted, Joe Biden addressed the nation, noting, "In America, politicians don't take power, people grant power to them" (Biden 2020b).

Donald Trump's postelection shenanigans were foreshadowed by threats he issued in 2016, when even he thought he would lose. Back then, Trump claimed the system was "rigged," and he threatened to put his rival, Hillary Clinton, in jail (Blake 2016). Four years later—now wielding the powers of the presidency to pardon his friends, punish his enemies, and stoke government agencies and the courts with his appointees—Trump sought to undermine a democratic process that had withstood every test since 1789. That he failed was welcome. That he tried set a dangerous precedent. Defeated presidents despising their successors is nothing new. Back in 1801, John Adams loathed Thomas Jefferson and their once-friendly relationship was torn asunder. The victorious Jefferson—who saw Adams's presidency as a threat to democracy when opposition journalists were jailed and criticizing the Chief Executive was made a crime—believed he had won a democratic triumph. One Jefferson supporter captured the prevailing sentiment: "To reign by fear and not by affection was ever bad policy. I am confident that the people of America are too fond of freedom to surrender it passively; and that whenever any body of men disclose views inimical to their interests, they will hurl them into insignificance" (quoted in Larson 2007, 106). Adams's acceptance of the election result—one that hurled him into a temporary insignificance and his Federalist Party into a permanent one—created what James MacGregor Burns called an extra-constitutional right: the peaceful transition from a party-in-power to its opposition. Burns noted that this customary transfer of power—one that eludes many other nations—showcased America at its best:

> A crucial liberty, one that had not been tested during the twelve-year hegemony of Federalist government, was established in the election of 1800—the freedom of the opposition not only to oppose, but to prevail peacefully. Not only did this

constitute evidence to the world that the American polity was far more stable than it may have appeared, it was a notice to future American political leaders that they need not contemplate coups or venture violence in order to succeed. Much to the contrary, the path to political power in the United States was shown to lead directly to and through the ballot box, ensuring for generations to come the freedom of meaningful political opposition and the regular, orderly, peaceful transfer of political power. (Burns 1990, 29)

The inauguration of Joe Biden sought to echo past rituals that were peaceful, harmonious transitions from one president to the next. The theme for the inaugural ceremony set a hopeful tone: "Our Determined Democracy: Forging a More Perfect Union." The slogan was designed to illustrate "our continued and unbroken commitment to continuity, stability, perseverance, and democracy" (Davies and Jouvenal 2020). Past crises that gripped the contests of 1864, 1940, 1944, and 1964 and their successful resolutions gave inaugural planners hope that the American experiment was more durable than present-day doubters thought. Alexis de Tocqueville observed that once an election ends "the ardor is dissipated, everything calms down, and the river which momentarily overflows its banks falls back into its bed" (quoted in Lane 2020a). But unlike prior contests, the swirling rivers of antagonism continued to flood the body politic.

An ex-president who refused to accept defeat—a refutation too long indulged by many members of his party—calls to mind the stern warning issued by the American Political Science Association in 1950. In a report titled *Toward a More Responsible Two-Party System*, the nation's leading political scientists warned that a too-powerful president could trample the underlying precepts of democracy:

When the President's program actually is the sole program . . . , either his party becomes a flock of sheep or the party falls apart. In effect, this concept of the presidency disperses the party system by making the President reach directly for the support of a majority of the voters. It favors a President who exploits skillfully the arts of demagoguery, who sees the whole country as his political backyard, and who does not mind turning into the embodiment of personal government.

A generation ago one might have dismissed this prospect as fantastic. At the midway mark of the twentieth century the American people have reason to know better, from recent and current examples abroad, what it does not want. Because Americans are so sure on that score, they cannot afford to be casual about overextending the presidency to the point where it might very well ring in the wrong ending. (Committee on Political Parties 1950, 94)

The warning issued by those political scientists in 1950 came to pass during the Trump presidency. The upsetting of the delicate constitutional balance damaged the authority wielded by *all* institutions of government and increased the chances of a "wrong ending." The absence of authority was reflected in a lack of trust, particularly when it came to the coronavirus: 61 percent had either little or no confidence that the federal government provided accurate information about the pandemic (Ipsos 2020). This lack of confidence meant that Americans were left to their own devices to cope and they were exhausted. Parents had to combine working at home with being classroom teachers for their homeschooled children. Masks were haphazardly worn, with each state and business making its own rules. Economic dislocations left many in food or unemployment lines or both. Racial crises saw street protests, as individuals pressured governments to act while white supremacists and ad hoc militia groups were encouraged by President Trump to "stand back and stand by" (Trump-Biden 2020). Climate change became a top tier issue, yet the clash between clean technologies and an oil-based economy created its own tension.

Alexis de Tocqueville once noted that in the absence of authority there is a "perpetual agitation" (quoted in Just 2020). Such was the case in 2020. An exhausted and depleted country was ready for relief. In some ways, 2020 had echoes of another change election—that of 1920. That year, Republican Warren Harding declared: "America's present need is not heroics, but healing; not nostrums, but normalcy; not revolution, but restoration; not agitation, but adjustment; not surgery, but serenity; not the dramatic, but the dispassionate; not experiment, but equipoise" (Harding 1920). In many ways, Joe Biden offered the country a similar prescription. His temperament, empathy, and personal story of tragedy and triumph set a moral example. On the campaign trail, Jill Biden spoke of an America where parents did not have to switch off the television at night but could see a president busy at work guided by his religious faith. For his part, Joe Biden offered a richness of governing experience that could meet the exigencies of the moment. For the first time since 1988, when George H. W. Bush promised to be "Ready on Day One," government experience became a campaign asset. And like Lyndon Johnson before him, Joe Biden promised he could cut legislative deals that would propel the country forward. But the weakening of America's political parties—once lauded as the "extra-constitutional organs so indispensable for representative government" (Charles 1955)—meant that Biden's task would be difficult at best, impossible at worst.

DIVIDED DEMOCRATS

On November 7, 2020, when the cable networks called the election for Joe Biden, Democrats had much to celebrate. Their nemesis, Donald Trump, received an eviction notice and would join the ranks of ignominious one-term presidents that included James Buchanan, Andrew Johnson, Warren Harding, and Herbert Hoover. Biden's win was substantial: more than 81 million votes, 11 million more than Barack Obama received in 2008.[1] Crucially, Biden reconstructed the Blue Wall winning back Pennsylvania, Wisconsin, and Michigan, and his combined margin of victory in those states was more than three times that of Trump's in 2016.[2] And, in an ironic twist, Biden's 306 to 232 Electoral Vote tally was the exact reverse of 2016, a result Donald Trump referred to back then as a "massive landslide victory" (Seipel 2016).

Equally impressive, Georgia and Arizona fell into the Democratic column. Georgia had not voted Democratic since 1992; Arizona, not since 1996. A shifting demography pushed each into competitive territory. In Arizona, Biden's win was fueled by his overwhelming margins among Hispanics. Exit polls showed Biden winning 61 percent of their votes as their vote share grew to 19 percent (Edison Research 2020). Even more impressively, Biden won Maricopa County (which includes Phoenix and its suburbs) by 45,109 votes, the first time a Democrat had won the county since Harry Truman. Undoubtedly, Biden benefited from disgruntled McCain Republicans led by McCain's wife, Cindy, who remembered Donald Trump's 2015 mockery of her late husband: "I like people who weren't captured" (Schreckinger 2015). The Democratic Party's success in Arizona was mirrored throughout the entire Southwest. For the first time since 1941, Democrats held all eight Senate seats from Arizona, Colorado, Nevada, and New Mexico (Brownstein, Twitter 2020). Together, these states are moving at different paces but all in the same direction into the Democratic column.

Joe Biden's Georgia victory was even more impressive. While Bill Clinton carried the state in 1992, third-party candidate Ross Perot received 13 percent of the vote. Before that, native son Jimmy Carter twice won the state in 1976 and 1980. But by 1984, Georgia had become reliably Republican. One reason was the overwhelming proportion of white voters. But a shifting demography meant that there were fewer white voters Republicans could harvest to win. In 2020, whites comprised just 61 percent of the Georgia electorate, and Biden received a mere 30 percent of their votes. However, a growing minority population gave Biden the victory, as he won 88 percent backing from African Americans, and 62 percent support from Hispanics (Edison Research 2020). Most important, Biden had undeniable strengths in the state's suburban counties. In Fulton County, which includes Atlanta and its suburbs, Biden received 377,000 votes—80,000 more than Hillary Clinton. Likewise, in Cobb and Gwinnett counties, Biden topped Clinton's 2016 totals by 100,000 votes (Brownstein 2020b).

Biden's suburban strength was evident in Austin, Charlotte, and Raleigh in the South, and Madison, Detroit, Philadelphia, and Columbus, in the North.

Across the United States, the suburban counties Biden carried accounted for 70 percent of the nation's total economic output; Trump counties, just 29 percent (Brownstein 2020b). As Americans climb into moving vans searching for better opportunities, the political and economic clout wielded by these dynamic metropolises will only continue to grow.

But there was disappointing news, too. For years, Democrats relied on identity politics to carry them to victory, paying little attention to the issues that motivate people of color. Nowhere was this more apparent than in Miami Dade County, Florida. Heavily Hispanic, with large Cuban and Venezuelan populations, Biden's winning margin was just 7 points, far below Hillary Clinton's 30-point win. Donald Trump's accusation that Biden would capitulate to the democratic socialism of Bernie Sanders and Alexandria Ocasio-Cortez carried weight with refugees from Fidel Castro's Cuba and Hugo Chavez's Venezuela. To deliver this message, Republicans relied on a strong organization that continuously communicated with these voters, not just once every four years. In this, was a powerful example for Democrats. After losing her gubernatorial race in 2018, Stacey Abrams formed Fair Fight and registered 800,000 new Georgians. The results were dramatic: in 2016, 22 percent of eligible voters in the state were not registered; by 2020, it was *2 percent*. Moreover, turnout rose from 63 percent in 2008 (the previous record) to 67 percent in 2020 (Schaul, Stevens, and Keating 2020, A-2). The lesson for Democrats is clear: organize, organize, organize. To win swing counties and keep them, Democrats must not simply tell voters they are on their side; they must listen and deliver results.

In 2008, Democrats were elated at the election of the first African American president. But in 2020, Democrats replaced joy with relief—an emotional rollercoaster for an already exhausted party. Relief that Trump soon depart was overshadowed by Republican strength in down ballot races. Nowhere was this more apparent in Omaha. Nebraska divides its electoral college votes by Congressional district, and Biden easily carried Nebraska's Second District (which includes Omaha) with 52 percent of the vote. Donald Trump did not help his cause there after leaving hundreds stranded in the cold (several suffering from hypothermia) following a rally. But the district's Republican Congressman, Don Bacon, comfortably won reelection with 51 percent of the vote.

Similar results occurred elsewhere. Instead of gaining an expected 5-to-10 House seats, the Democratic majority was reduced to the low single digits. Speaker Nancy Pelosi tried to reassure her distressed colleagues, saying, "We did not win every battle, but we won the war" (quoted in Bade and Warner 2020, A-26). But a stunned Cheri Bustos, chair of the Democratic Congressional Campaign Committee, who survived her own close contest countered: "I'm furious. Something went wrong here across the entire political world. Our polls, Senate polls, gubernatorial polls, presidential polls, Republican polls, public polls, turnout modeling and prognosticators all pointed to one political environment—that environment never materialized" (quoted in Bade and Warner, A-26).

Democrats also lost marquee Senate races in North Carolina, Maine, Iowa, Montana, Kentucky, and South Carolina, even as they won the barest of Senate majorities. These failures were especially painful given the flood of campaign cash from an army of motivated partisans. All told, Democrats outspent their GOP opposition by *$280 million*. In South Carolina, Jaime Harrison raised a whopping $104 million; in nearby North Carolina, Cal Cunningham raised $45.9 million. Other Democrats posted eye-popping totals: Amy McGrath (Kentucky), $73 million; Sara Gideon (Maine), $47.9 million; Steve Bullock (Montana), $38.6 million. Putting these numbers through a different lens, Kentucky's McGrath spent $92 per vote and lost by 20 points to Mitch McConnell who spent $34 per vote. In South Carolina, Jaime Harrison spent $95 per vote and lost by 10 points to Lindsey Graham who spent $44 per vote (Lane 2020b). As the Beatles famously opined, "Money can't buy you love."

State legislative results were yet one more Democratic disappointment. Republicans retained or won control of 30 state legislatures—including Pennsylvania, Michigan, Wisconsin, New Hampshire, Florida, Arizona, Georgia, Texas, and North Carolina (Ballotpedia 2020). Such dominance is especially important in years ending in zero, with reapportionment looming on the horizon in 2021. In 2010, Republicans did a masterful job of drawing legislative districts, creating artistic masterpieces that secured their Congressional majorities for nearly a decade. Given the unexpected Democratic losses, Republicans rejoiced at their party's good fortune and salivated over winning a House majority in the 2022 midterms which, if history repeats itself, the incumbent president's party loses seats.

These dashed expectations led to internal squabbling that made governing even more challenging than usual. Rural and suburban Democrats were furious with their liberal counterparts. Abigail Spanberger, a Virginia Democrat who won a Republican district in 2018, and was reelected by an unexpectedly close margin, admonished her fellow Democrats: "We need to not ever use the word 'socialist' or 'socialism' ever again . . . . We lost good members because of that . . . . If we are classifying Tuesday as a success . . . we will get f----ing torn apart in 2022" (quoted in Bade and Warner 2020, A-26). Conor Lamb, a Pennsylvania Democrat who likewise won a surprisingly close contest, agreed: "We pay the price for these unprofessional and unrealistic comments about a number of issues, whether it is about the police or shale gas. These issues are too serious for the people we represent to tolerate them being talked about so casually" (quoted in Bade and Warner 2020, A-26).

Socialism, Medicare for All, and Defund the Police were sledgehammers Republicans used to beat their Democratic opponents into submission. Delaware senator Chris Coons summarized the problem: "The results in the House and Senate elections make it clear that while a majority of Americans are sick of Trump and Trumpism in the White House and voted for more normalcy and measured leadership with Joe Biden, they are not yet fully sold on the agenda that the Democratic Party is presenting. We need to find better ways to demonstrate . . . that we will actually deliver results that will make people's lives better" (Balz 2020, A-2). Joe Biden agreed, saying Republicans "beat the living hell out of us" on issues like defunding the police (Memoli 2020).

But Progressives and so-called Justice Democrats saw things very differently. Congresswoman Alexandria Ocasio-Cortez blamed moderates for their close calls and losses, asserting that "not a single one of these [moderate] campaigns were firing on all cylinders" (Dionne 2020, B-1). Ocasio-Cortez then went even further, denouncing Biden's appeals to white non-college-educated voters: "That's my frustration with politics today, that they're willing to give up every single person in America just for that dude in a diner. Just so you can get this very specific slice of Trump voters? If you pick the perfect candidate like Joe Biden to win that guy in the diner, the cost will make you lose because you depress turnout as well" (quoted in Dougherty 2019). Pramila Jayapal, cochair of the Congressional Progressive Caucus, agreed: "I don't know how, the day after the election, people can start pointing fingers at progressives for somehow ruining things when in fact we never would have won the presidential election if we hadn't turned out people" (quoted in Sullivan and Bade 2020, A-6). Rashida Tlaib likewise denounced those who criticized the emphasis on defunding the police, socialism, and Medicare for All: "To be real it sounds like you are saying stop pushing for what black folks want" (quoted in Bade and Warner 2020, A-26).

Justice Democrats, like Tlaib, Ocasio-Cortez, Cori Bush, Ayanna Pressley, and Jamaal Bowman, came to power because they won primaries in heavily Democratic districts. But none defeated a Republican in a contested district. As one House Democrat put it: "There has to be a reckoning within our ranks about this because a lot of Justice Democrats don't give a damn about the Democratic Party . . . . They're all about purity and orthodoxy, and it is damaging our opportunities" (quoted in Bade and Warner 2020, A-26). Obama campaign manager David Plouffe agrees: "In just about every battleground state, there are more conservative voters than liberal voters. So a Republican nominee starts out closer to the goal line than a Democrat does" (quoted in Steinberger 2020). The challenge, says Plouffe, is to find candidates who can excite the base and bring blue-collar voters back into the fold: "We need a candidate . . . who has the ability to get a 45-year-old welder in Racine,

Wisconsin, back in the Democratic column" (quoted in Bade and Warner 2020, A-26). Kurt Schrader, a member of the Blue Dog Coalition, agrees: "Democrats' messaging is terrible; it doesn't resonate. When voters see the far left that gets all the news media attention, they get scared. They're very afraid that this will become a supernanny state, and their ability to do things on their own is going to be taken away" (quoted in Bade and Warner 2020, A-26).

On the eve of the Biden presidency, House Majority Whip James Clyburn acknowledged the intraparty divisions and the challenges they present: "We've got a caucus that's blue dogs, yellow dogs, moderates, conservatives, liberals. We've got them all. [Biden] may have a harder job keeping us united than getting bipartisanship going" (Viser 2021, A-1). The task of securing party unity raises an important question: Will Democrats embark on a course of addition or subtraction? Addition makes for winning majorities but necessitates unhappy compromises, thereby threatening party unity. But subtraction provides the comfort of uniform thinking but risks the discomfort of minority status.

A PERSONALITY CULT ENDANGERS THE REPUBLIC

When a presidential nominee loses, that person is referred to as the "titular head" of their party. Historically, the title meant nothing, as the losing party is enveloped by a cacophony of voices, each calling upon the faithful to follow a different path to victory. But in the case of Donald Trump, there is nothing "titular" in the title he holds as head of the Republican Party. Utah senator Mitt Romney sadly observes that "without question" Trump is "the 900-pound gorilla when it comes to the Republican party" (quoted in Costa, Rucker, and Downey 2020, A-8). A 2020 NBC News/*Wall Street Journal* poll found 54 percent of Republican identifiers consider themselves supporters of Donald Trump; only 38 percent say their primary allegiance is to the Republican Party (NBC News/*Wall Street Journal*, poll, 2020).

One reason Trump became such a dominant force was a paucity of conservative ideas. Back in 1980, New York Democratic senator Daniel Patrick Moynihan wrote, "Of a sudden, the GOP has become a party of ideas" (quoted in White 2016, 88). Moynihan's prescient observation was based on a surge of conservative intellectual ferment. The Republican National Committee published *Commonsense* which included contributions from intellectuals of all partisan persuasions (including the editor of this book). Republican intelligentsia prowled the halls of the American Enterprise Institute, Heritage Foundation, and Cato Institute. Two billionaire brothers, Charles and David Koch, used their vast fortune to fund 350 programs at more than 250 organizations to promote their libertarian ideas (Koch Foundation 2021). And the Federalist Society, with its list of law school alumni, began to plot how to move the judiciary in a conservative direction.

Forty years after this conservative juggernaut animated the Reagan presidency, many of their ideas are well past their expiration dates. Donald Trump happily filled the void with policies that were apostate to Reagan's New Right beliefs, including his free trade and anti-immigration policies, and, most especially, Reagan's denunciation of Russia as an "evil empire" (Reagan 1983). In 1987, Trump spent nearly $100,000 to purchase advertisements in the *New York Times*, *Washington Post*, and *Boston Globe* chastising Reagan's governance: "End our huge deficits, reduce our taxes, and let America's economy grow unencumbered by the cost of defending those who can easily afford to pay for the defense of their freedom. Let's not let our great country be laughed at anymore" (Ben-Meir, 2015). Pollster Frank Luntz noted that Trumpism is built around a persona, not a philosophy. According to Luntz, being *for* things is much more potent than being *against* things: "Ronald Reagan was for freedom. Donald Trump was against the swamp. That's why Reaganism lasted from 1976 through 2016" (Costa, Rucker and Downey 2020, A-8).

Donald Trump became a vessel for grievances first exploited by the Tea Party in 2010. A changing demography (most graphically represented by the nation's first African American president), a transforming Information Age economy that saw manufacturing decline and stagnant wages provided Trump with a ready market for his "Make America Great Again" pitch. But for Trump's followers making America great wasn't about the future; instead, the slogan romanticized a bygone era. When Henry Luce, founder of the *Time-Life* empire, coined the term "The American Century" in 1941, he lionized the United States as "the dynamic center of the skillful servants of mankind, America as the Good Samaritan, really believing again it was more blessed to give than to receive, and America as the powerhouse of the ideals of Freedom and Justice" (quoted in White 1997, 22). These words were applauded by a white Anglo-Saxon Protestant establishment that Richard Rovere argued "maintains effective control over the Executive and Judicial branches of government; . . . dominates most of American education and intellectual life; . . . [and] has very nearly unchallenged power in deciding what is and what is not respectable opinion in this country" (Rovere 1962, 3, 9).

Today, the WASP establishment is in tatters, as the United States has morphed into a multiracial, multiethnic, religiously diverse, and nontraditional familial country. With each passing year, whites approach minority status; church attendance declines; and the "nuclear family" of a Mom, Dad, and kids is relegated to a Cold War relic. Democrats welcome these changes, and their party has been transformed into a "Coalition of Transformation" led by these emerging groups. Republicans look askance at the changing demography and are a "Coalition of Restoration," one dominated by Evangelicals and the white working class (Brownstein 2020c). As Michael Madrid, a cofounder of the Lincoln Project, writes: Trump has solidified the GOP's transformation into a "white-identity party . . . a nationalist party, not unlike parties you see in Europe . . . [while] the Democratic Party [is] becoming the party of literally everyone else." Over time, Madrid concludes, "The Republican party is going to continue to shrink and become more monolithic and more regionalized. They believe they are the last stand for America and [that] America is a white Christian nation. They believe they are what America is. And that kind of identity gets stronger as it loses—it becomes more self-righteous as it loses" (Brownstein 2020c).

Voter backlash against demographic change is nothing new. After waves of Irish emigration during the 1840s, the Know Nothing Party's 1856 platform sounded like something out of the Trump playbook: "*Americans must rule America;* and to this end *native-born* citizens should be selected for all state, federal, or municipal offices of government employment, in preference to naturalized citizens" (Porter and Johnson 1970, 22, emphasis in the original). Trump's politics of resentment led to his elevation as a kind of savior, someone who understands older white non-college-educated voters and dares to speak truths they quietly believe. Steve Schmidt, an ex-Republican and founder of the Lincoln Project, observes that Trump's rise had "fascistic markers" that led to a "cult of personality" (Costa, Rucker and Downey, A-8). Back in 1964, Richard Hofstadter forecast an emerging "paranoid style" whose followers were willing to abide by a "militant leader": "Since what is at stake is always a conflict between absolute good and absolute evil, what is necessary is not compromise but the will to fight things out to a finish. Since the enemy is thought of as being totally evil and totally unappeasable, he must be totally eliminated" (quoted in White 2016, 90). Donald Trump's willingness to be that militant leader who demonized his opponents and defied conventional norms endeared him to his followers who believed a political Armageddon, if not a real one, was imminent.

Another reason for Trump's dominance lies in the deference Republicans gave to their presidents starting with Dwight Eisenhower in 1952. After trying every conceivable path to achieve victory against Franklin D. Roosevelt and Harry Truman—from nominating a true conservative in Alf Landon, to a former Democrat in Wendell Willkie—and failing, Republicans endured a 20-year White House exile. Former Army general and World War II hero Eisenhower provided a path to victory. But restoration came at a price. Eisenhower deliberately distanced himself from the Republican Party, creating a personalized campaign organization led by businessmen, ex-generals, apostate Democrats, and independents. Thus, one could be for Eisenhower without ever becoming a Republican. Other GOP presidents (and later Democratic ones) emulated Ike and created their own apparatuses while renting space at the top of the ticket. For Republicans, Eisenhower's success marked an era of Republican presidential dominance but nothing more. Between 1952 and 1988, Republicans won 7 of the 10 presidential contests, but captured both houses of Congress just once. The party gave considerable deference to its "plebiscitary presidents," and it celebrated the expansion of presidential power, since, after all, controlling Congress was beyond its reach. Adding insult to injury these Republican presidents often elevated those with broad executive experience to administrative positions, but most never sought elective office. By hallowing out the party base and relying on presidents to give them a taste of power, Republicans expressed nothing but gratitude toward their party's leaders and were reluctant to abandon them, even in the most dire of circumstances. Watergate and the resignation of Richard Nixon was a notable exception (see White 1997, 86–89, 144–50).

With the party establishment weakened, Donald Trump's hostile takeover met with little resistance. Because Trump so captivated an aggrieved base that despised its coming minority status, fear became an animating force in binding Republican officeholders to Trump. Former Arizona senator Jeff Flake, whose opposition caused him to abandon his reelection bid, says his fellow Republicans "fear Trump and his base and know he can take about any one of them out. . . . . There's a lot of fear, but no love" (quoted in Costa, Rucker, and Downey 2020, A-8). That fear beat most Republican officeholders into a state of quiescence. Pennsylvania senator Patrick Toomey typified the response: "I don't spend a lot of time focusing on the president's tweets and things the president says" (Montgomery 2021, 17). Vice President Pence agreed: "Everyone has their own style. And frankly, people on both sides of the aisle use strong language about our political differences. But I just don't think you can connect it to threats or acts of violence" (Montgomery 2021, 17). Mitch McConnell defended Trump while attacking the establishment: "No matter what some Washington Democrats may try to claim, you're not crazy or a conspiracy theorist if you see a pattern of institutional unfairness toward this president" (Montgomery 2021, 19).

Trump's political clout has made him the Boss Tweed of his day. Having caused a riot on Capitol Hill that threatened our democracy, and whose participants sought to assassinate Vice President Mike Pence and Speaker Nancy Pelosi, the House promptly passed an article of impeachment. The article charged that Trump "threatened the integrity of the democratic system, interfered with the peaceful transition of power, and imperiled a coequal branch of government" (House Resolution, 117th Congress). Ten Republicans joined all Democrats in support, including GOP Whip Liz Cheney, who scathingly wrote, "There has never been a greater betrayal by a President of the United States of his office and his oath to the Constitution" (Cheney 2021). But Trump's vise-like grip on his party caused many Republicans to return to their default position of defending Trump, even though they privately believed his claim that he "won this election, and we won it by a landslide" was false (House Resolution, 117th Congress 2021). Minority Leader Kevin McCarthy's defense was typical: "President Trump won this election. So everyone who's listening: Do not be quiet. Do not be silent about this. We cannot allow this to happen before our very eyes" (Montgomery 2021, 22). Senate Republicans likewise stood by Trump, with just five members supporting the continuance of an impeachment trial.[3]

Donald Trump's political power is entirely personal, not confined to an ideology or a cadre of partisan stalwarts. Far from being a "titular leader," the former president remains a powerful force within the Republican Party and can stymie (at least for the moment) whatever plans others may have for taking a different path. The result is a likely fracturing of the traditional two-party system, with the possibility that third parties could gain traction. Donald Trump has threatened that if the Republican Party abandons him, he could join a new "Patriot Party," thereby insuring Democratic victories. More likely, however, is that Trump will insert himself into GOP primaries, supporting those candidates who stand by him to the last and, in return, delivering them their party's nomination—much like the party bosses of old who dictated their choices to voters.

A POLITICS OF DISAPPOINTMENT 2.0?

Writing the first draft of history for every presidential election from 1980 to 1996, the late Wilson Carey McWilliams summed up his work in a book aptly titled *Beyond the Politics of Disappointment?* In it, McWilliams cited Alexis de Tocqueville's prescient observation about the United States during the pre-Civil War 1850s: "After having believed ourselves capable of transforming ourselves, we now believe ourselves incapable of improving ourselves; after having had an excessive pride, we have fallen into a humility that is just as excessive; we thought that we could do everything, and now we think we can do nothing . . . . This, to put it simply, is the great malaise of our age" (McWilliams 2000, 1). When McWilliams quoted these words, he noted that "most Americans, looking backward, find it hard not to see a long, slow slide: real wages declining, society deteriorating, gaps widening between old and young and rich and poor, the hopeful integration of the civil rights movement turned into a bitter politics of race. Even victory in the Cold War has resulted in international disorder, new threats, and few visible dividends. Briefly, [Jimmy] Carter, [George H. W.] Bush, and [Bill] Clinton roused hopes, and Ronald Reagan had a longer, more disastrous run, but all fell short of America's probably unrealizable expectations" (McWilliams 2000, 1). As it turned out, these disappointments led to a populist uprising that enhanced what was to become a decades long polarization between Red and Blue States.

Yet the question mark in McWilliams's title raised hopes that an exhausted country might embark on a more hopeful era that would reconstruct the nation's civic life: "After a generation and more of disappointment, restoring or rebuilding the foundations of democratic politics will require us to translate that ideal into a language and practice adequate for the new century. Risks, obstacles, and all, that venture, like the Yellow Brick Road, is our only way home" (McWilliams 2000, 119). More than two decades later those risks and obstacles are even more daunting. Yuval Levin, a conservative scholar at the American Enterprise Institute, echoes McWilliams's call for restoration. However, in *A Time to Build*, Levin writes that a politics of continued disappointment makes such a rebuilding more difficult than ever before: "Younger Americans have grown up bombarded with examples of institutional failure that tend to reinforce such [populist anger]. A country repeatedly disappointing itself is the only America they have known, and so they take it as a norm, not an exception. And now they see it culminating in a national politics that feels like a debauched rampage of alienation and dysfunction—depraved and degrading, corrupting everyone who goes near it, always finding surprising new ways to reach lower" (Levin 2020, 5). The pandemic has only accentuated their disappointment. For the first time since the Great Depression, a majority of the nation's young adults spent 2020 living with their parents (Gramlich 2020).

This politics of disappointment has eroded public confidence not only in the presidency, Congress, and the judiciary, but in all civic institutions: religious, media, universities, medicine, and large corporations. It has also led to a lack of trust in what Tocqueville once called the genius of America, that is, the ability to think of the nation as a place where the American Dream can be realized, a place where one can think anew and become someone who is truly self-made. Today, more Americans not only question the capacity of our institutions to deal with the crises facing the nation, they are losing confidence in their ability to remake themselves. Joe Biden likes to describe America in one word: "Possibilities" (Biden 2020). But the fragility of the American Dream, coupled with the anger and incivility Americans have toward their fellow citizens, casts doubt on what Barack Obama described as the Founders greatest gift: "the freedom to chase our individual dreams through our sweat and toil and imagination, and the imperative to strive together, as well, to achieve a common good, a greater good" (Obama 2017).

The toxic combination of populism with polarization has created its own groupthink that limits freedom of thought. Thanks to the rise of social media, Americans are "free" to choose what information they receive; yet they frequent websites that ratify their preexisting political viewpoints. This groupthink often dismisses opposing views (when it deigns to consider them).[4] During the 2020 campaign, overwhelming majorities of Trump and Biden supporters said they disagreed not merely on policies but on *core American* values (Gramlich 2020). Specifically, 81 percent of Republicans believe that the Democratic Party has been taken over by socialists; 78 percent of Democrats say the Republican Party has been taken over by racists (Cook 2020). Complaints from partisans now extend to all aspects of civic life. Conservatives protest that they cannot find space to express themselves at most universities and on most major social media platforms. Liberals gripe that they are excluded from conservative networks and websites. Thus, those who live in Blue States find solace in neighbors who ratify their views, while those in Red States maintain their own comfort level with like-minded neighbors. In 2020, 85 percent of counties with a Whole Foods Market voted for Joe Biden, while 74 percent of counties with a Cracker Barrel restaurant voted for Donald Trump (Cook Political 2020). Even the personal has become political, as those whose lifestyles do not conform to the conventional families of the 1950s often choose to live in more welcoming regions of the country. In 2017, when another presidential transition was underway, Vice President-Elect Mike Pence rented a home in Chevy Chase, Maryland. Neighbors, outraged by Pence's antigay comments, displayed colorful gay rights flags on their front porches, a political statement designed to express their displeasure at the change of government and cause the Pences to feel unwelcome.

This politics of comfort seemingly gives voters the freedom to express themselves, but only in limited ways. Few seek to challenge their preexisting views or entertain opposing ideas. In 2010, Barack Obama advised graduates at the University of Michigan to "actively seek out information that challenges our assumptions and our beliefs," warning that if Americans "choose only to expose ourselves to opinions and viewpoints that are in line with our own, studies suggest that we become more polarized, more set in our ways. That will only reinforce and even deepen the political divides in this country" (Obama 2010). In the decade since, the bubbles in which Americans find comfort have been fortified and our politics even more polarized. When Public Opinion Strategies asked hidden Trump voters (19% of the total) why they refused to state their preference, the answers were revelatory:

- "I have a lot of liberal friends. They get angry. They have anger issues when it comes to politics. Oh my God, I can't believe you're voting for him, what's wrong with you, oh he committed fraud. He's a racist. Homophobic."

- "Prior to Trump you could talk to people about politics without them flipping out."
- "If I voice my opinions, my friends stop talking to me."
- "I have had three people unfriend me on Facebook."
- "Why would I engage with people who don't read the facts?"
- "I got called a white supremacist and a racist so I kept it to myself so I wouldn't hear those words."
- "I don't want to get beat up."
- "I had neighbors say they would like to kill all Trump supporters. These were people with whom I really got along with well" (Public Opinion Strategies 2020).

The result is a cold civil war that makes rebuilding our institutions and civic life extremely difficult. Whenever the country has been polarized, presidents have sought healing. In 1801, Thomas Jefferson told a divided nation: "Let us restore to social intercourse that harmony and affection without which liberty and even life itself are but dreary things" (quoted in Will 2020). Sixty-four years later, nearing an end to a bloody Civil War, Abraham Lincoln hoped to recreate "a Union of hearts and minds as well as states" (quoted in Will 2020). In a new century, George W. Bush promised to be "a uniter, not a divider," and Barack Obama set forth the powerful imagery of "not a liberal America and a conservative America—there's the United States of America" (Obama 2004). Now, after four extraordinary years of division, argument, and disillusionment, with the long-standing problems McWilliams cited still intact, Joe Biden, like George W. Bush and Barack Obama before him, pleaded for unity, saying: "Without unity, there is no peace, only bitterness and fury" (Biden 2021). For his part, Biden promised he would do what he could to provide a season of unity and healing:

> I pledge to be a President who seeks not to divide, but to unify. Who doesn't see Red and Blue States, but a United States. And who will work with all my heart to win the confidence of the whole people. I sought this office to restore the soul of America. To rebuild the backbone of the nation—the middle class. To make America respected around the world again and to unite us here at home.
>
> The Bible tells us that to everything there is a season—a time to build, a time to reap, a time to sow. And a time to heal. This is that time for America. A time to heal. (Biden 2020)

As Joe Biden takes the presidential oath, the hinge of history's door swings open once more. What will be revealed is yet to be determined. In his inaugural address, Joe Biden correctly noted that history's judgment of how he meets "the cascading crises of our era" is not merely about him, but us: "Will we rise to the occasion? Will we master this rare and difficult hour? Will we meet our obligations and pass along a new and better world for our children?" (Biden 2021). As the inaugural poet laureate, Amanda Gorman, so brilliantly noted: "For there is always light, if only we're brave enough to see it. If only we are brave enough to be it" (Gorman 2021).

One can hope that the question mark McWilliams deliberately placed in *Beyond the Politics of Disappointment?* can be replaced with a new, more optimistic title that marks the third decade of the twenty-first century. Hope in the face of adversity, the belief that better days are ahead, that America is a land of possibilities, these are things that propel American Exceptionalism, the idea that we are an extraordinary nation distinct from all others. During the dark days of November 1940, as Europe was consumed by another world war and the United States stood on the precipice of danger, Franklin D. Roosevelt delivered this prayer: "Bless our land with honorable industry, sound learning, and pure manners. Save us from violence, discord, and confusion, from pride and arrogance, and from every evil way. Defend our liberties and fashion into one united people the multitudes brought hither out of many kindreds and tongues" (Lorant 644). In his time, Roosevelt's prayer was answered. Let's hope that this prayer, one that bears repeating now, will find a favorable response from the Almighty.

NOTES

1. Obama received 69,499,428 votes.

2. Biden's lead in Pennsylvania was 82,147; Wisconsin, 20,510; and Michigan, 154,188 for a total of 256,845 votes. In 2016, Trump's lead in Pennsylvania was 44,284; Wisconsin, 22,748; and Michigan, 10,704 for a total of 77,736 votes. It should be noted that the much-ballyhooed Blue Wall was always fragile, particularly in Pennsylvania, Wisconsin, and Michigan.

3. They were Susan Collins (Maine), Lisa Murkowski (Alaska), Ben Sasse (Nebraska), Mitt Romney (Utah), and Patrick Toomey (Pennsylvania).

4. I am grateful to Dr. Samuel C. Sprunk for his insights here.

REFERENCES

Bade, Rachael and Erica Warner. 2020. "Centrist House Democrats Pin Blame on Far-Left Rhetoric." *Washington Post.* November 6.

Ballotpedia. 2020. "Election Results, 2020: State Legislative Chambers that Changed Party Control." December 4.

Balz, Dan. 2020. "Big Problems Leave Biden No Room for Early Missteps." *Washington Post.* November 29.

Barnes, Robert. 2020. "Justices Reject Bid to Reverse Election." *Washington Post*. December 12.

Ben-Meir, Ilan. 2015. "That Time Trump Spent Nearly $100,000 on an Ad Criticizing U.S. Foreign Policy in 1987." *BuzzFeed.News*. July 10.

Biden, Joe. 2020a. "Victory Speech." Wilmington, Delaware. November 7.

———. 2020b. "Address to the Nation." Wilmington, Delaware. December 14.

———. 2021. Inaugural Address. Washington, D.C. January 20.

Blake, Aaron. 2016. "The Final Clinton-Trump Debate Transcript, Annotated." *Washington Post*, October 19.

Brenan, Megan. 2020. "More Voters Than in Prior Years Say Election Outcome Matters." Gallup Poll. October 19.

Brownstein, Ronald. 2020a. Twitter. November 13.

———. 2020b. "Democrats 2024 Problem Is Already Clear." *Atlantic*. November 12.

———. 2020c. "Why the 2020s Could Be as Dangerous as the 1850s." *Atlantic*, October 30.

Burns, James MacGregor. 1970. *Roosevelt: Soldier of Freedom, 1940–1945*. New York: Harcourt Brace and Jovanovich.

———. 1990. *Cobblestone Leadership: Majority Rule, Minority Power*. Norman: University of Oklahoma Press.

Charles, Joseph. 1955. "Adams and Jefferson: The Origins of the American Party System." *The William and Mary Quarterly*, Volume 12, Number 3: 410–46.

Charles Koch Foundation. 2021. List of Supported Colleges. January.

Cheney, Liz. 2021. "Statement in Support of Trump's Impeachment." *Politico*. January 12.

Committee on Political Parties. 1950. *Toward a More Responsible Two-Party System*. New York: Rinehart and Company.

Cook, Charlie. 2020. "'Forgive and Forget' Has Turned to Just 'Forget.'" *Cook Political Report*. December 18.

Cook Political. 2020. "36 Facts about the 2020 Elections." *Cook Political Report*. December 22.

Costa, Robert, Philip Rucker, and Josh Downey. 2020. "Even in Defeat, The Embers Of Trumpism Still Burn In The Republican Party." *Washington Post*. November 9.

Danner, Mark. 2021. "'Be Ready to Fight.'" *New York Review of Books*. February 11.

Davies, Emily and Justin Jouvenal. 2020. "What Will Inauguration Day Look Like Amid a Pandemic?" *Washington Post*. November 19.

Dawsey, John, Michael Scherer, and Matt Viser. 2021. "Senate Losses, Trump's Incitement Open Rifts in a Party Once in Thrall." *Washington Post*. January 8.

Dionne, E. J., Jr. 2020. "Why They Fight." *Washington Post*. November 29.

Donald, David Herbert. 1996. *Lincoln*. New York: Touchstone Edition.

Dougherty, Owen. 2019. "Ocasio-Cortez on Biden: 'I think he's not a pragmatic choice.'" *The Hill*. June 26.

Edison Research. 2020. Exit poll. November 3.

Goldberg, Jeffrey. 2020. "Why Obama Fears for Our Democracy." *Atlantic*. November 16.

Goldwater, Barry. 1964. "Acceptance Speech." Republican National Convention. July 16.

Goodwin, Doris Kearns. 2005. *Team of Rivals*. New York: Simon and Schuster.

Gorman, Amanda. 2021. "The Hill We Climb." January 20.

Gramlich, John 2020. "20 Striking Findings from 2020." Pew Research Center, December 11.

Harding, Warren G. 1920. *Speech*. June 29.

Hogan, Larry. 2020. "State of the Union." *CNN*. November 22.

House Resolution, 117th Congress, First Session. 2021. "Impeaching Donald John Trump, President of the United States, for High Crimes and Misdemeanors." January 13. Ipsos. Poll. November 23.

Johnson, Lyndon B. 1963. Address to Congress. Washington, DC, November 27.

———. 1971. *The Vantage Point: Perspectives of the Presidency, 1963–1969*. New York: Holt, Rinehart, and Winston.

Just, Richard. 2020. "God Save America." *Washington Post Magazine*. November 8.

Lane, Charles. 2020a. "We've Been Here Before. Just Ask Tocqueville." *Washington Post*, November 3.

———. 2020b. "Money Didn't Buy Democrats Love at the Polls." *Washington Post*. November 24.

Larson, Edward J. 2007. *A Magnificent Catastrophe: The Tumultuous Election of 1800, America's First Presidential Campaign*. New York: Free Press.

Levin, Yuval. 2020. *A Time to Build: From Family and Community to Congress and the Campus, How Recommitting to Our Institutions Can Revive the American Dream*. New York: Basic Books.

Lorant, Stefan. 1951. *The Presidency: From Washington to Truman*. New York: The Macmillan Company.

McWilliams, Wilson Carey. 2000. *Beyond the Politics of Disappointment? American Elections, 1980–1998*. New York: Seven Bridges Press.

Memoli, Mike. 2020. "In Leaked Recording, Biden Says GOP Used 'Defund the Police' to 'Beat the Living Hell' Out of Democrats." *NBC News*. December 10.

Montgomery, David. 2021. "The Origins of an Insurrection." *Washington Post Magazine*. January 24.

NBC News/*Wall Street Journal*. 2020. Poll. October 29–31.

Obama, Barack. 2004. "Keynote Address to the Democratic National Convention." Boston. July 27.

———. 2010. "Commencement Address: University of Michigan." Ann Arbor, May 1.

———. 2017. "Farewell Address." Chicago. January 10.

———. 2020. "Address to the Democratic National Convention." August 19.

Porter, Kirk and Donald Bruce Johnson. 1970. *National Party Platforms, 1840–1968*. Urbana: University of Illinois Press.

Pramuk, Jacob. 2020. "Almost No Trump Voters Consider Biden the Legitimate 2020 Election Winner." *CNBC*. November 23.

Public Opinion Strategies. 2020. Poll. November 3.

Reagan, Ronald. 1983. "Address to the National Association of Evangelicals." Orlando, Florida. March 8.

Roosevelt, Franklin D. 1940. "Address to the Democratic National Convention." July 19.

———. 1944. "Address to the Democratic National Convention." July 20.

Rovere, Richard. 1962. *The American Establishment and Other Reports, Opinions, and Speculations*. New York: Harcourt, Brace, and World.

Rucker, Philip and Robert Costa. 2020. "America's Deep Divides Won't Vanish on Inauguration Day." *Washington Post*. November 5.

Sandburg, Carl. 1969. *Abraham Lincoln: The War Years (1864–1865)*. New York: Dell Publishing Company.

Schaul, Kevin, Kate Rabinowitz, and Ted Mellnik. 2020. "2020 Turnout Is the Highest in Over a Century." *Washington Post*. November 5.

———, Harry Stevens, and Dan Keating. 2020. "How Georgia Became a Swing State." *Washington Post*. November 9.

Schreckinger, Ben. 2015. "Trump Attacks McCain: 'I like people who weren't captured.'" *Politico*. July 18.

Seipel, Annie. 2016. "Fact Check: Trump Falsely Claims a 'Massive Landslide Victory.'" *NPR*. December 11.

Steinberger, Michael. 2019. "Joe Biden Wants to Take America Back to a Time Before Trump." *New York Times Magazine*. July 23.

Sullivan, Sean and Rachael Bade. 2020. "Left's Breakout Stars Fight to Shape Democratic Agenda." *Washington Post*. November 30.

Todd, Chuck, Mark Murray, Carrie Dann, and Melissa Holzberg. 2021. "In the Trump Era of Public Opinion, It's the GOP vs. Everyone Else." *First Read*. January 18.

Trump-Biden. 2020. Debate. Cleveland, Ohio. September 29.

Trump, Lara. 2020. "Address to the Republican National Convention." August 26.

Trump, Donald. 2020b. *Twitter*. July 30.

Viser, Matt. 2021. "Biden Plans a Burst of Action." *Washington Post*. January 17.

Washington, George. 1796. Farewell Address, September 19.

White, John Kenneth. 1997. *Still Seeing Red: How the Cold War Shapes the New American Politics*. Boulder: Westview Press.

———. 2016. *What Happened to the Republican Party?* New York: Taylor and Francis.

White, Theodore H. 1965. *The Making of the President, 1964*. New York: Atheneum.

Will, George F. 2020. "An Outcome the Nation Needed to Avoid." *Washington Post*. November 5.

Index

Note: Page numbers in "italic" refer to figures and tables; page numbers followed by "n" refer to notes.

About the Contributors

William Crotty is Thomas P. O'Neill Jr. Chair in Public Life and professor emeritus of political science at Northeastern University. He is the founder and former director of the Center for the Study of Democracy. He is a recipient of the Samuel J. Eldersveld Lifetime Achievement Award of the Political Organization and Parties Section of the American Political Science Association and the Hubert H. Humphrey Award of the Policy Studies Association. He served as president of the Policy Studies Association, chair of the Political Organizations and Parties Section of the American Political Science Association, and as president of the Midwest Political Science Association. He is the author, editor, and coauthor of numerous publications including *Winning the Presidency 2016* (2017); *Polarized Politics: The Impact of Divisiveness in the US Political System* (2014); *Winning the Presidency 2012* (2013); *Winning the Presidency 2008* (2009), which along with *A Defining Moment: The Presidential Race of 2004* (2005) received CHOICE awards from the Academic Library Association for Outstanding Academic Titles; *The Obama Presidency: Promise and Performance* (2012); *The Politics of Terror: the U.S. Response to 9/11* (2004), CHOICE: "Outstanding Academic Title . . . This should be required reading for all Americans . . . One of the best chapters is the Editor's . . . Essential for general readers, and upper-division undergraduates and above"; *Handbook of Party Politics*, co-editor and co-author with Richard S. Katz (2006); *Party Reform* (1983); *Decision for the Democrats: Reforming the Party Structure* (1979); and *Presidential Primaries and Nominations*, coauthored with John S. Jackson III and selected by CHOICE as an Outstanding Academic Book of 1985–1986 (1985), CHOICE: "It is unlikely that a better book on this subject will be forthcoming."

Amy N. Benner is receiving her PhD from the Department of Political Science at Rutgers University—New Brunswick. She serves as a research assistant at the Center for American Women and Politics. She has a BA in criminology and political science from the University of South Florida. She was a contributor to the USF Nielsen Sunshine State Survey, an annual policy survey which provides insight on both newly emerging issues and trend-line data for both private and public officials in the state of Florida. Her research interests include women's political participation, barriers to representation, campaign finance, and political psychology. She has coauthored research focusing on the experiences of first-time candidates and political contests featuring women running against women. Recent published work includes, "Women and Campaigns: Generational Change, Growing Activism," featured in the fourth edition of *Campaigns on the Cutting Edge* with coauthor Dr. Susan A. MacManus.

John C. Berg is an emeritus member of the Department of Government, Suffolk University. His research interests include legislative politics, environmental politics, interest groups and lobbying, ethical issues in politics and parties and party systems, especially minority parties in the United States. His most recent publications are *Leave it in the Ground: The Politics of Coal and Climate* (2019) and "Environmental Policy: The Success and Failure of the Obama Presidency" in *The Obama Presidency: Promise and Performance*, W. Crotty, ed. (2012). He is also the author of *Teamsters and Turtles? Progressive U.S. Political Movements in the 21st Century* (2003) and *Unequal Struggle: Class, Gender, Race and Power in the U.S.* (1994). His teaching has included courses in Environmental Studies, Policy and Politics, American Political Thought, Radical and Revolutionary Political Thought, Legislation and Lobbying. He has served as a contributor to Commonwealth Magazine and a commentator for C-SPAN. He served as president of the New England Political Science Association, 2013–2014.

Susan A. MacManus is distinguished university professor emerita in the Department of Government and International Affairs, School of Interdisciplinary Global Studies, University of South Florida. She recently authored *Florida's Minority Trailblazers: The Men and Women Who Changed the Face of Florida Government* (with Barbara A. Langham, Lauren K. Gilmore, and Tyler B. Myers, 2017). MacManus was past director of the annual USF-Nielsen Sunshine State Survey, the state's most extensive annual public policy survey of adult Floridians. She has been the political analyst for Tampa's ABC affiliate since 2016 and is Florida's chief political news analyst. Among her many publications are *Florida's Politics*, 5th ed. (with Aubrey Jewett, David J. Bonanza, and Thomas R. Dye, 2019),

Politics in States and Communities, 15th ed. (with Thomas R. Dye, 2015), and *Florida's Politics: Ten Media Markets, One Powerful State* (with Kevin Hill and Dario Moreno, 2004). She served as chair of the Florida Elections Commission from 1999 to 2003 and helped the Collins Center for Public Policy, Inc. draft Florida's Help America Vote Act state plan. MacManus received the first biennial Diane Blair award for "Outstanding Achievement in Politics and Government" from the Southern Political Science Association in 2001, the Walter Cronkite Award for Excellence in Television Political Journalism from the Annenberg School for Communication, University of Southern California in 2005, and in 2014, the SPSA Manning Dauer Award for Exceptional Service to the Profession.

Thomas R. Marshall is professor of political science at the University of Texas at Arlington. He recently authored *Public Opinion, Public Policy and Smoking* (revised edition, 2018). Other publications include *Presidential Nominations in a Reform Age*, *Public Opinion and the Supreme Court*, and *Public Opinion and the Rehnquist Court*. His upcoming book is *The Supreme Court as a Representative Institution* (2021). He has authored numerous studies of the politics and substance of health care, including "The Debate over Health Care" in *Polarized Politics: The Impact of Divisiveness in the US Political System* (2014). Recent publications for conference proceedings include "The Supreme Court as a Representative Institution: Ranking the Justices" (2019); "Forecasting Issue Elections through Message Testing" (2019); and "Justice Anthony Kennedy in the Court of Public Opinion" (2018). Marshall is an expert on health policy, the Supreme Court, public opinion, interest groups, and campaigns and elections. He is a frequent media commentator on presidential, judicial, and Texas politics.

John J. McGlennon is professor of government at the College of William & Mary since 1974 and served as chair of the Department of Government for 16 years. He specializes in U.S. politics with a special focus on the South and Virginia. He has a number of publications to his credit, including *The Life of the Parties: A Study of Presidential Activists*, with Alan Abramowitz and Ronald Rapoport, coeditors (1986) which analyzed the attitudes of over 17,000 state party convention delegates; and *Party Activists in Virginia*, with Alan Abramowitz and Ronald Rapoport (Institute of Government, University of Virginia, 1981). His research has been published in the *Journal of Politics*, *International Political Science Review*, *American Politics Review*, and *Australian Political Science Review* as well as in multiple edited volumes. Professor McGlennon has been a long-term party activist and practicing politician. He ran in close races for the United States Congress as a Democrat in 1982 and 1984. In 1997, he was elected to the James City County Board of

Supervisors and he continues to serve on the Board and served as chairman of the Board, a rotating position, several times.

Barbara Norrander is a professor in the School of Government and Public Policy at the University of Arizona. Her teaching and research focus is American politics, specializing in elections, public opinion, and political parties. She is the author of *The Imperfect Primary: Oddities, Biases, and Strengths of U.S. Presidential Nomination Politics* (Routledge, 3rd ed., 2020) and coeditor with Clyde Wilcox of *Understanding Public Opinion*, 3rd ed. (CQ Press, 2010). Norrander investigates factors influencing the election of women to public office, with emphasis on explaining the election of women to state legislatures. She also conducts research on public attitudes on a variety of social issues, the link between public opinion and policies in the U.S. states, and the nomination of candidates for the U.S. presidency. Among her numerous articles are "Open Versus Closed Primaries and the Ideological Composition of Presidential Primary Electorates," coauthored with Jay Wendland, *Electoral Studies* (2016) and "Minority Group Opinion in the U.S. States," coauthored with Sylvia Manzano, *State Politics and Policy Quarterly* (2010). She served as president of the Western Political Science Association in 2004–2005 and has been a member of the executive board for the Midwest Political Science Association and the editorial boards of the *American Journal of Political Science, Journal of Politics,* and *State Politics & Policy Quarterly.*

Shayla C. Nunnally is professor of political science and chair of the Africana Studies Program at the University of Tennessee, Knoxville. Her teaching and research interests include African American politics, public opinion and political behavior, Black intraracial trust, Black elite-cuing, racial and political socializations, and political development. She authored *Trust in Black America: Race, Discrimination, and Politics* (2012). Other publications include "(Re)Defining the Black Body in the Era of Black Lives Matter: The Politics of Blackness, Old and New" in *Politics, Groups, and Identities* (2018), "How We Remember (and Forget) in Our Public History" in *Perspectives on Politics* (2016), and "Zero-Sum Politics as a Trust Dilemma? How Race and Gender Affect Blacks', Whites', and Latinos' Trust in Obama's and Clinton's Representation of Group Interests," *Ralph Bunche Journal of Public Affairs* (2014). She has served as a research team member with the National Conference of Black Political Scientists for the Cooperative Congressional Election Study (2008 and 2010, Tyson King-Meadows, principal investigator) and with the research group for the study of Black, White and Latino political attitudes in the New South (Paula D. McClain, principal investigator). Professor Nunnally has appeared on several international, national, and local radio and TV shows (local and national) to discuss American politics and race and politics. She served as the 39th president of the National Conference of Black Political Scientists (2017–2019) and as an appointee on the American Political Science Association's Committee on the Status of Blacks in the Profession (2014–2016). She serves as an editorial board member with the Congressional Black Caucus Foundation's new biennial journal, *Journal of the Center for Policy Analysis and Research.*

Arthur C. Paulson is professor emeritus of political science at Southern Connecticut State University, where he served as chair of the Political Science Department. He is a lifelong student of parties and elections, and his teaching and research interests include American politics, presidential elections, and constitutional law. He has written extensively on electoral politics and democracy. Among his publications are *Donald Trump and the Prospect for American Democracy: An Unprecedented President in an Age of Polarization* (Lexington Books, 2018); "Presidential Nominations in a Polarized Party System: The Republican Primaries of 2012" in *Winning the Presidency 2012*, W. Crotty, ed.; "Coalitional Divisions and Realignment Dynamics in the Obama Era" in *The Obama Presidency: Promise and Performance* (W. Crotty, ed., Lexington Books, 2012); *Electoral Realignment and the Outlook for American Democracy* (2006) and *Realignment and Party Revival: Understanding Electoral Politics at the Turn of the Century* (2000).

John Kenneth White is professor of political science at the Catholic University of America. He has written extensively on religion and politics, the American party system, and the U.S. presidency. White has authored *Party On! Political Parties from Hamilton and Jefferson to Trump* (with Matthew R. Kerbel, 2017), which examines the historical role of the major parties in American political life and the ways in which the parties shape our political landscape; *The American Dream in the Twenty-First Century* (with Sandra Hanson, 2011), *Latino/a American Dream* (with Sandra Hanson, 2016); and *What Happened to the Republican Party? And What It Means for Presidential Politics* (2015). Other recent publications include: *Barack Obama's America: How New Conceptions of Race, Family, and Religion Ended the Reagan Era* (University of Michigan Press, 2009) and *The Values Divide: American Politics and Culture in Transition* (CQ Press, 2003) which examines how values play an important role in motivating people to vote and have contributed to significant changes within the Democratic and Republican Party coalitions. He has appeared on numerous television programs including "This Week with David Brinkley" and on BBC, National Public Radio, Christian Science Monitor Radio, and U.S.I.A. television programs. His analyses of contemporary politics have appeared in the *The Hill, New York Daily News,* on wire services, and in numerous other national newspapers.

www.ingramcontent.com/pod-product-compliance
Lightning Source LLC
Chambersburg PA
CBHW022303280326
41932CB00010B/962